Energy and Buildings: Thermal Storage, Emissions, Transports, Control and Their Effects

Energy and Buildings: Thermal Storage, Emissions, Transports, Control and Their Effects

Guest Editors

Mark Bomberg
Paulo Santos
Anna Romańska-Zapała

MDPI

Basel • Beijing • Wuhan • Barcelona • Belgrade • Novi Sad • Cluj • Manchester

Guest Editors

Mark Bomberg
Department of Mechanical & Aeronautical Engineering
Clarkson University
Potsdam
USA

Paulo Santos
Department of Civil Engineering
University of Coimbra
Coimbra
Portugal

Anna Romańska-Zapała
Faculty of Electrical and Computer Engineering
Cracow University of Technology
Krakow
Poland

Editorial Office
MDPI AG
Grosspeteranlage 5
4052 Basel, Switzerland

This is a reprint of the Special Issue, published open access by the journal *Energies* (ISSN 1996-1073), freely accessible at: https://www.mdpi.com/journal/energies/special_issues/BHF96VL85Q.

For citation purposes, cite each article independently as indicated on the article page online and as indicated below:

Lastname, A.A.; Lastname, B.B. Article Title. *Journal Name* **Year**, *Volume Number*, Page Range.

ISBN 978-3-7258-7937-3 (Hbk)
ISBN 978-3-7258-7938-0 (PDF)
https://doi.org/10.3390/books978-3-7258-7938-0

Contents

About the Editors

Mark Bomberg

Since 2019, has been a research professor at Clarkson U, Potsdam, NY, USA, and since 2017, he has been a visiting professor at Cracow U of Tech, Poland. In the years 2012–2020, he was an adjunct prof. at McMaster University, Hamilton, Ontario, Canada. From 2012 to 2015 he was a visiting prof. at the Mechanical Dept of Tongji, Shangai and Architecture Southeast University in Nanjing, China; in 2014–2017 he was a visiting prof. at TU in Kielce and Olszyn. He worked for 23 years for the National Research Council of Canada, leading the field of thermal insulation. After an early retirement, he taught at Concordia University (Montreal, 3 years) and Syracuse Univ. (New York State, 9 years). From 1984 to 2018, he served as editor-in-chief of the *Journal of Building Physics* (Sage Corp., London, UK) and, upon stepping down, he accepted several positions, including as an associate editor in sustainable construction at the *Frontiers in Build Environment*, academic editor in MDPI journals *Energies* and *Sustainability*, but remains in his position for MDPI's *Buildings* and *Frontiers*. He is an honorable member of the Building Enclosure Technology and Environment Council of the National Inst. of Building Science in Washington DC. His interest in the path from materials to sustainable buildings is possible because of his research background in heat, air and moisture transfer, material science, and evaluation methodology, with a particular interest in the durability of construction materials. He has published over 220 papers and 7 books; he is one of three people who instituted BEST Conferences in the US and received the highest awards in building physics in both the USA and Canada, namely the Ontario Building Envelope Council (BECKIE, 1999) and the Building Enclosure Technology and Environment Committee of the National Institute of Building Science, Washington DC (2012).

Paulo Santos

Paulo Santos is an Associate Professor at the Department of Civil Engineering (DEC) of the Faculty of Sciences and Technology, University of Coimbra (FCTUC), Portugal. He is a research member of the Institute for Sustainability and Innovation in Structural Engineering (ISISE), Functional Performance (FP) research group. His main research topics are thermal behavior, energy efficiency in buildings, and sustainable construction, with a main focus on the Lightweight Steel-Framed (LSF) construction system and sustainable construction materials. As a result of his research work, he is the author of around 225 publications, including 4 books, 2 dissertations, 4 book editions, 17 journal special editions, 5 book chapters, 87 articles published in peer-reviewed scientific journals, and 109 papers published in proceedings of scientific conferences, with 101 publications indexed and listed in the Web of Science Core Collection. He has around 3,950 citations and 96,050 reads on Research Gate (Berlin), with a h-index of 30. He was a supervisor of 57 doctoral and master's theses that have already been completed within his research topics. He participated in around 16 funded European and national research projects within his research areas, and he is the Principal Investigator of the Tyre4BuildIns research project. He was a member of the scientific committee and has been an organizer of several national and international scientific conferences. He has been an editorial board member of 20 international scientific journals, for which he already has 1010 verified Web of Science editor records. He reviewed, at the request of the editors, around 135 articles submitted to international journals. He was also a member of the scientific evaluation committees of several national and international research projects proposed for funding.

Anna Romańska-Zapała

Anna Romańska-Zapała is an Assistant Professor at the Department of Infotronics and Cybersecurity, Faculty of Electrical and Computer Engineering, Kraków University of Technology, Poland. Her main research interests are building and industrial automatics, including renewable energy sources and energy efficiency in buildings.

Preface

The long-term renovation strategy supports the change of the national building stock into a highly efficient and decarbonized building stock by 2050, and this is a cost-effective transformation of existing buildings into nearly zero-energy buildings (nZEB). About 70% of the building stock of 2050 already exists today, which means that most of the energy reductions will have to be achieved by deep energy renovation of existing buildings. To increase the renovation rate, we need industrialization and modular renovation. The difference between the predicted and real energy performance can be significant. To overcome these problems, more information, results, and successful case studies targeted at nZEB renovation are needed.

This Special Issue, published in *Energies*, is dedicated to the analysis of the recent advances on the following topics: (1) optimizing the passive measures before adding renewable energy sources; (2) reduction of carbon emissions with climate change and their monitor and performance evaluation (MAPE); (3) indoor environment and durability in building market value; (4) hydronic systems of heating and cooling, and use of different types of heat pumps, especially water-sourced (geothermal type) heat pumps; (5) integration of solar panels, heat pumps, and thermal mass (short-time storage) with long-term thermal storage; (6) advanced zero-energy (AZER) and emission (AZEM) buildings that use building automatics and control systems to optimize building field performance; and (7) finally, any type of energy co-simulation in buildings is welcomed. In this context, the objective is to compile scientific works within these topics, making use of different possible research approaches, such as theoretical, experimental, numerical, computational, analytical, case studies, and their combinations, in order to collect a set of original research works of an excellent academic standard and of complete scientific soundness.

The guest editors would like to extend their heartfelt gratitude to the contributors, whose expertise and dedication have enriched this compilation, as well as to the reviewers who have significantly contributed to improving the quality of the manuscripts. As editors, it is our sincere hope that this collection inspires dialogue, sparks creativity, and serves as a catalyst for transformative action in the pursuit of highly energy-efficient buildings, including the existing ones, as well as more sustainable construction and renovation practices.

Mark Bomberg, Paulo Santos, and Anna Romańska-Zapała
Guest Editors

energies

MDPI

Article

Importance of Window Installation in Residential Building Envelopes Having Continuous External Insulation in Order to Realize Energy Efficiency

Bipin Shah [1], Mahabir Bhandari [2,*] and Mengjia Tang [2]

1 WinBuild Inc., Fairfax, VA 22030, USA; winbuild.usa@gmail.com
2 Buildings and Transportation Science Division, Oak Ridge National Laboratory, Oak Ridge, TN 37831, USA; tangm@ornl.gov
* Correspondence: bhandarims@ornl.gov; Tel.: +1-865-574-0989

Abstract: Residential buildings are one of the prime candidates in the United States for reducing energy consumption. Continuous exterior insulation (CEI) is being used increasingly often in residential buildings to improve energy efficiency. Windows constitute 15–40% of a building envelope and are the weakest component in energy performance. The installation of windows in walls with CEI has not been well evaluated. We identified four cases of installing windows in walls with CEI of 25–76 mm (1–3 in.) thickness and analyzed the energy loss between the window and wall interface (flanking loss), structural issues, air leakage, and moisture penetration. Thermal analysis showed that the insulation value (RSI) of the 305 mm (12 in.) perimeter wall surrounding a window decreased by 7.6–34.5% in the four cases when compared with the RSI of the wall without the window. A window installation method is proposed to address the issues likely to occur with installation methods currently being used in the field. An out-of-the-box installation system was also designed to achieve a better thermal performance, cost effectiveness, and structural performance in high-performance residential buildings.

Keywords: continuous exterior insulation; flanking loss; window installation; air leakage

1. Introduction

An estimated 1.4 million housing units were completed in the United States in 2022 [1]. In the same year, the residential sector consumed 1.3×10^{19} J (12.3 quadrillion Btu) of total energy [2]. These statistics make residential buildings one of the prime candidates for reducing energy consumption in the US. Energy-related requirements for residential buildings are regulated by the International Energy Conservation Code (IECC) [3] and the International Residential Code (IRC) [4]. The IECC has been updated every 3 years, and the 2021 IECC (the most recent update) seeks to provide residential building energy performance that is approximately 40% more efficient than the energy efficiency defined by the 2006 IECC [5].

To deliver a higher energy efficiency, the requirements for building wall insulation and the fenestration U-value became more stringent from the 2009 IECC to 2021 IECC [6,7]. The insulation value of wood frame walls increased from RSI-2.3 to RSI-5.3 in IECC Climate Zone 4 and from RSI-3.5 to RSI-5.3 in Climate Zone 5. Continuous insulation, which is "insulating material that is continuous across all structural members without thermal bridges other than fasteners and service openings" [3], was mentioned only in Climate Zones 5 and 6 in the 2009 IECC, but it became prominent in the 2021 IECC, being mentioned in every climate zone. Continuous insulation is referred to as continuous exterior insulation or CEI when installed on the exterior of the building envelope. As for fenestration, its maximum U-factor decreased from 2.0 to 1.7 W/(m^2-K) in Climate Zone 4 and above. The fenestration insulation requirements are also set by the ENERGY STAR program administered by the US Environmental Protection Agency. Currently ENERGY STAR version 7 [8] has fenestration U-value requirements ranging from 1.2 to 1.8 W/(m^2-K), depending on the climate zone. A review of these requirements shows that the residential building wall insulation requirement in IECC Climate Zones 4–8 is RSI-3.5 + RSI-0.9 (i.e., a total of RSI-4.4, with RSI-3.5 in the wall cavity and an additional RSI-0.9 in CEI), whereas the window requirements are RSI-0.6 per 2021 IECC and RSI-0.9 in accordance with ENERGY STAR version 7. Therefore, the energy performance of windows needs to be improved to match that of opaque walls.

Augmenting the energy performance of windows in walls will help achieve overall building energy efficiency. Research has been conducted to develop windows with a high insulation value. The US Department of Energy (DOE) is supporting innovations [9] to improve window energy performance by developing higher-performing glazing (thin triple-pane and vacuum glazing), insulating spacers (super spacers), and better insulated frames (fiberglass and composite material). These higher-insulating window products are now being deployed in the market. However, they still do not match wall insulation levels because they have RSI-values of only 1.1–1.8. Such products are currently more expensive and thus have longer returns on investment.

While addressing individual building product performance (i.e., windows and walls), issues related to the interface between building components are often neglected. Windows need to be installed properly to deliver the target energy performance of the entire envelope because they are in contact with the components in walls. Thermal bridging between wall framing components and window frames is a major issue for new high-performance residential buildings if not addressed adequately. Depending on the types of windows, weight and frame widths differ. Conventional triple or quad glass pane products incorporate thicker frames, which make them heavier, therefore requiring more structural analysis, especially when installed in walls with CEI. Newer products with insulated glass units (IGUs) in a configuration of three or quad glass pane products have thinner middle glass panes (0.5–1 mm thick), which reduces the overall weight of the window and provides a better energy performance. Therefore, identifying the appropriate installation method of windows based on their types is important.

Several industry and organizational publication reviews [10–13] explain the window installation in CEI and the results of tests performed on such windows. A review of test results for various types of windows installed in rough openings of walls with foam plastic insulating sheathing showed that none of the configurations tested had water leakage or structural failure at a ~1.58 times design pressure. However, the foam plastic insulating sheathing included in this report had a maximum thickness of 51 mm (2 in.) and a limited range of compressive resistance of 103–172 kPa (15–25 psi) [10]. Peavey and Shah [11] developed generic installation procedures for installing all windows over CEI but noticed operability failures for double-hung windows during structural performance tests; such results were improved by modifying manufacturers' installation instructions on oriented strand board (OSB; i.e., increasing the length of fasteners by 25 mm (1 in.) when compared with the manufacturers' instructions to accommodate the 25 mm (1 in.) thick CEI). The thermal performance of the two different installation methods was not evaluated. Lstiburek and Baker [12] proposed procedures to install windows in the rough opening of walls with CEI that is thicker than 38 mm (1.5 in.), but these procedures require further testing to validate their performance. Ueno [13] discussed the advantages of two window plane locations in thick walls with CEI (i.e., toward the exterior and toward the interior). While these documents explain the guidance for windows with a wide frame, they do not offer guidance on windows in the market with slimmer (narrow thickness) frames that would not anchor properly in a rough opening. Furthermore, the window installation guidance is not clear on matters regarding energy use impact, air leakage, moisture, and structural issues in walls with CEI, which are not well understood by field installers in the industry.

Window installation in walls of high-performance residential buildings with CEI poses a challenge for installers. Window manufacturers usually do not provide installation instructions as part of the shipped products for installation in CEI wall construction. A small number of manufacturers provide installation instructions through their contracted consultants, who in turn provide instructions online [14], but these instructions are seldom viewed by general field installers. Important sizing information or installation steps are usually missing from the instructions on manufacturers' websites [15]. To their credit, large window manufacturers do provide training at their company for registered installers. However, construction companies seldom use registered installers owing to issues of cost, installation time, and other logistics. This barrier should be overcome by providing readily available training materials and certification requirements. Code officials should also have access to window installation requirements in CEI walls, allowing them to check and verify the proper installation has been carried out before approving building permits. This would prevent problems with installing any market-available window in CEI wall construction.

To address barriers associated with window installation in CEI wall construction, we analyzed the effect of window installation on energy loss between the window and wall interface (flanking loss), structural issues, air leakage, and moisture penetration. We also propose alternatives and an innovative system design concept that could address the issues holistically.

2. Window Installation Methods in Walls with CEI

Traditionally, windows are installed in 51 mm by 102 mm (2 in. by 4 in.) or 51 mm by 152 mm (2 in. by 6 in.) wood frame walls in residential buildings, as shown in Figure 1. Windows currently available in the market are designed for installation in these standard building envelope construction window rough openings.

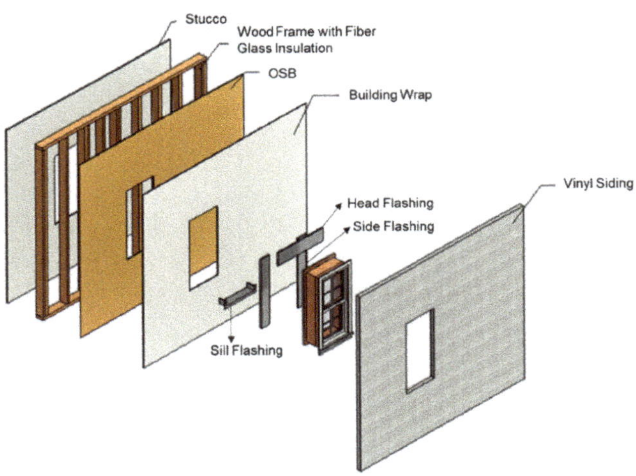

Figure 1. Typical window installation in a wood frame residential home.

When CEI is added to the exterior sheathing (i.e., OSB or plywood) of a standard wood frame wall construction, an additional frame structure may have to be added to accommodate the CEI thickness for installation of the window. This additional framing must be thermally and structurally sound.

Based on a literature review of suggested installation methods [10–13], methods (cases) identified for installing windows in walls with a CEI of 25–76 mm (1–3 in.) thickness are described in the following list and shown in Figure 2.

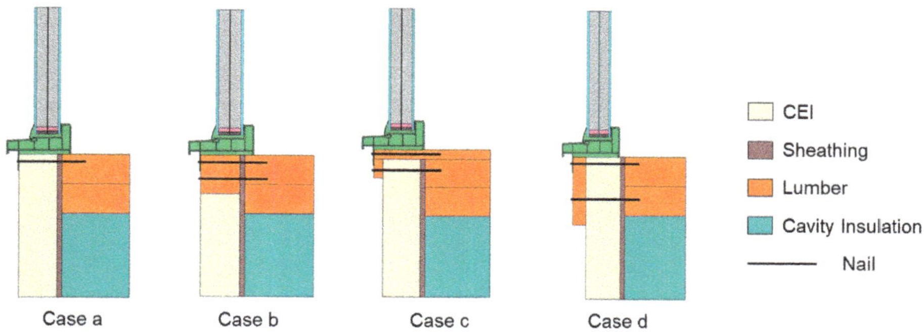

Figure 2. Window installation methods—labeled as Cases a, b, c, and d—in walls with CEI.

- Case a: The most common method of new construction window installation over CEI has the window flanges mounted directly over the CEI. This method of installation is generally used for CEI thicknesses up to 51 mm (2 in.). In this case, the CEI should have a minimum of 103 kPa (15 psi) compressive strength [12] to provide structural support for a window.
- Case b: A wood frame of CEI's overall thickness, made of lumber, is added to the wood frame wall, and then the window flange is mounted to this wood frame. This method is commonly used with a foam thickness equal to common lumber dimensions.
- Case c: A wood frame of up to 13 mm (0.5 in.) thickness is fitted over the rough opening and attached to the face of the CEI on which the window flange is mounted to provide support for the window. Such frames are also made from insulating materials that are rigid to provide structural support for the window and reduce flanking loss. They are most common for wood frame walls with more than 38 mm (1.5 in.) of CEI thickness.
- Case d: Rainscreens (furring strips) are placed vertically above the CEI, typically spaced equal to wood stud spacing to maintain structural strength to hold siding. These strips are used to drain out water or moisture that enters from the siding. The window flange is mounted directly to these furring strips. This method can be used for walls over any thickness of CEI.

3. Thermal Analysis of Window Installation Methods in Walls with CEI

To estimate the impact of the thermal performance of window installation methods, Cases a–d, a standard wood frame wall section (Figure 3) over which 25–76 mm (1–3 in.) CEI can be installed, were used. The wall section used for performing thermal analysis represents the area of the wood frame wall on which a window is installed. The structure has two 51 mm by 102 mm (2 in. by 4 in.) wood studs (actual size 38 mm by 89 mm [1.5 in. by 3.5 in.], pine wood) faced with 13 mm (0.5 in.) thick OSB at the exterior and 13 mm (0.5 in.) thick stucco board at the interior. CEI of 51 mm (2 in.) thickness is added to the OSB exterior.

The following environmental boundary conditions were used for all simulations and calculations: (1) the exterior boundary condition represents 6.7 m/s (15 mph) wind velocity at −18 °C (0 °F) temperature, and (2) the interior boundary condition represents indoor conditions with natural convection at 21 °C (70 °F). The THERM 7.8 software was used for carrying out two-dimensional thermal modeling. THERM is a state-of-the-art computer program developed at the Lawrence Berkeley National Laboratory.

The wood frame wall section, which is 305 mm (12 in.) high, representing the section below the window, was modeled to have a U-value of 0.242 W/m^2-K or RSI-4.10 (Figure 3). The variation in heat loss in the wall region owing to non-homogeneity is evident from the thermal image.

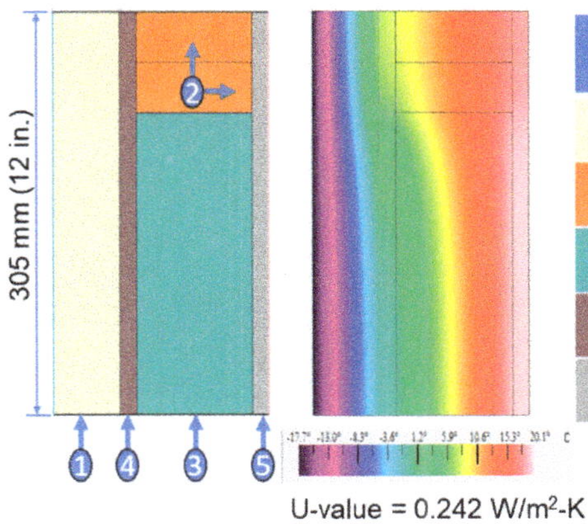

Color	Material	Conductivity (W/m-K)
1	CEI	0.024
2	Pine Wood	0.140
3	Glass Fiber	0.034
4	OSB Board	0.170
5	Stucco Board	0.400

Figure 3. Modeled wood frame wall section with CEI.

3.1. Window Assembly Analysis

The modeled window is a PVC window with a triple-pane glazing system composed of the glazing "thin triple" (i.e., two 3 mm low-E coated glass panes plus a 0.7 mm center pane). The gap between panes is 14 mm and is filled with 95% argon gas. The window has a warm-edge spacer with silicon on the top, butyl rubber at the bottom, and a frame of PVC material with a flange (Figure 4).

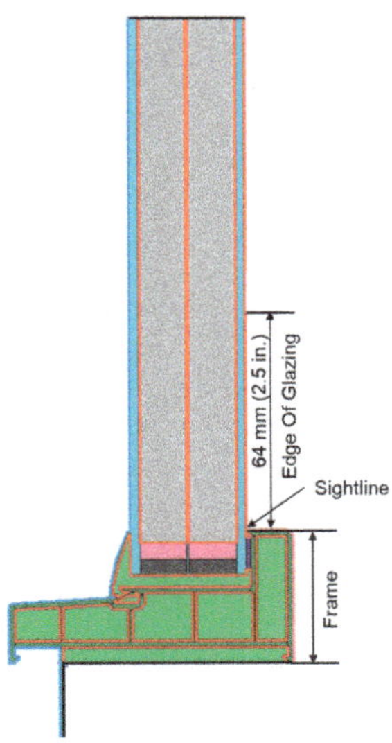

Figure 4. Frame, edge of glazing, and sightline of the modeled window.

WINDOW 7.8 software was used to simulate the thermal performance of the glazing configuration. WINDOW is a publicly available computer program developed at Lawrence Berkeley National Laboratory for calculating total window thermal performance indexes (i.e., U-values, solar heat gain coefficients, shading coefficients, and visible transmittances). The Insulated Glazing Unit (IGU) performance was modeled to have a U-value of 0.652 W/m^2-K or RSI-1.54.

The THERM 7.8 software program was used for carrying out two-dimensional thermal modeling of the window "frame" and "edge of glazing" (EOG) area. The EOG is 64 mm (2.5 in.) from the sightline (Figure 4). Per the National Fenestration Rating Council (NFRC)

600 [16], the edge of glass is defined as the line formed by the highest opaque member of the frame, sash, spacer, divider, or shading system that is interior, exterior, or within the glazing system cavity of the fenestration cross-section and the glazing in a plane perpendicular to the surface of the cross-section. Modeling results showed that the frame had a U-value of 1.325 W/m^2-K or RSI-0.76 and that the EOG had a U-value of 0.920 W/m^2-K or RSI-1.08.

The WINDOW 7.8 program was then used to model the whole window U-value. The modeled window was sized per ANSI/NFRC 100-2023 [17] as a fixed operator type with an overall size of 1.2 m (47 in.) wide by 1.5 m (59 in.) high. The whole window had a U-value of 0.779 W/m^2-K or RSI-1.29. This window would meet the ENERGY STAR requirement and the 2023 most efficient criterion defined by DOE for tax incentives.

3.2. Wall and Window Assembly Analysis

The window/wall installation methods for all four cases in Figure 2 were modeled using THERM 7.8, and results are shown in Table 1. Compared to the RSI of the wall without the window installed, the RSI of the 305 mm (12 in.) perimeter wall surrounding the window was decreased in the four cases by 7.6–34.5%. The decrease in the RSI of the perimeter wall was caused by the flanking loss owing to window installation, and it varied among different window installation methods. Case b had the highest flanking loss because a portion of the CEI next to the window was replaced with lumber; Case d had the lowest flanking loss owing to the additional furring strips on the exterior surface. In all cases, the RSI of the whole window was similar.

Table 1. Overall RSI of window and wall.

	Overall RSI * (m^2-K/W)					
	Wall without Window Installed	**Window**	**Case a**	**Case b**	**Case c**	**Case d**
IGU		1.54	1.54	1.54	1.54	1.54
Frame		0.76	0.85	0.66	0.71	0.78
Edge of glazing		1.08	1.11	1.10	1.11	1.08
Whole window		1.29	1.33	1.26	1.28	1.30
Wall section	4.10		3.52	2.68	3.33	3.79
% change from wall section			14.2	34.5	18.9	7.6

* Overall RSI includes the convective boundary condition resistance.

Figure 5 shows the isotherm plot of the modeled wall section; the area where the isotherms are not parallel indicates flanking loss. In Case b (worst case), the colder outdoor temperature at the frame and wall interface area penetrated closer to the interior, which may form condensation and damage wood or other material. Consequently, the long-term structural stability may be impaired.

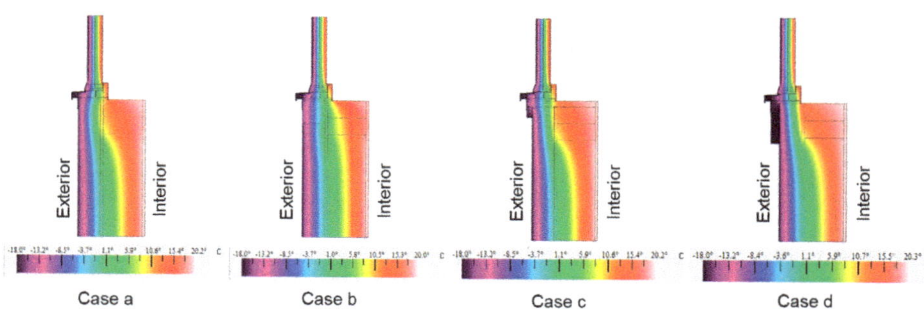

Figure 5. Thermal image and flanking loss in window/wall assembly for each case.

3.3. Building Envelope Energy Analysis with and without Flanking Loss

A building envelope's wood frame wall consists of several components, as shown in Figure 3, of varying thermal properties. Therefore, heat flow through different sections of the wall will depend on each path's thermal resistance. A window, which is also part of the wood frame wall assembly, is a path of the least thermal resistance compared to the wall and can affect energy flow through the immediate wall perimeter area surrounding the window. The difference in heat flow at the interface area of the window frame and wall is different from the heat flow calculated by area-weighting the heat flow separately through the window and the wall. Such a difference is flanking loss, which is currently not accounted for in most building energy calculations. Flanking loss could have a substantial impact on energy use and contribute to other issues such as condensation and rotting, which lead to durability issues. To achieve real energy savings, the energy consumption in residential buildings needs to be analyzed more accurately by considering this flanking loss.

As an example, consider a window-to-wall ratio of 15% for a wood frame wall (Figure 6). For a 9.3 m^2 (100 ft^2) wall section (3.8 m by 2.4 m [12.5 ft by 8 ft]) with a window measuring 1.5 m (5 ft) high by 0.9 m (3 ft) wide, the perimeter area of a 0.3 m (1 ft) wall section surrounding the window is 1.9 m^2 (20 ft^2). The RSI of the perimeter wall was reduced by 7.6–34.5% in Cases a–d, as noted in Table 1.

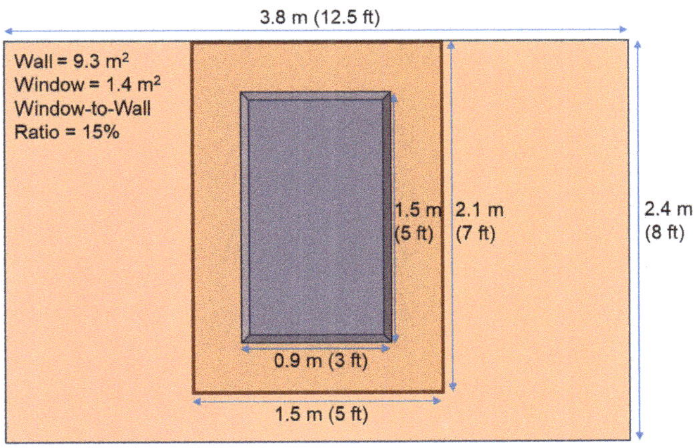

Figure 6. Representative 15% window/wall ratio and perimeter wall affected by flanking loss.

Total energy flows through a building's vertical envelope (i.e., fenestration and opaque walls) via (1) conductive and convective heat transfer caused by the temperature difference between outdoor and indoor air, (2) solar gain, and (3) air leakage. The equation for calculating energy flow through a fenestration or opaque wall can be found in the ASHRAE Handbook of Fundamentals [18]. Because the window is common for all model cases and air leakage is assumed to be the same or nonexistent, the second (solar gain) and third (air leakage) terms can be omitted. Therefore, Equation (1) was used to calculate the heat flow resulting from a temperature difference across the fenestration or opaque wall.

$$Q = U \times A \times (T_{out} - T_{in}) \quad (1)$$

where

Q = instantaneous energy flow, W (Btu/h);
U = overall coefficient of heat transfer (U-factor), W/m^2-K (Btu/h-ft^2-°F);
A = area of the fenestration or opaque wall, m^2 (ft^2);
T_{in} = indoor air temperature, °C (°F);
T_{out} = outdoor air temperature, °C (°F).

The wood frame wall in Figure 6 had a 1.4 m^2 (15 ft^2) window area, a 1.9 m^2 (20 ft^2) perimeter wall area, and a 6.0 m^2 (65 ft^2) other wall area. The indoor and outdoor air temperatures used in the calculation were 21 °C (70 °F) and −18 °C (0 °F), respectively. Table 2 shows the heat flow through the building envelope assembly, measuring 9.3 m^2 (100 ft^2) with a 15% window-to-wall ratio, for Cases a–d.

Table 2. Heat flow through the building envelope wall assembly measuring 9.3 m^2 (100 ft^2) for Cases a–d.

Results	Unit	Baseline without Flanking Loss	Case a	Case b	Case c	Case d
Heat flow of whole window	W	42.2	40.8	42.9	42.2	41.7
Heat flow of perimeter wall	W	17.6	20.5	26.9	21.7	19.1
Heat flow of other wall	W	57.3	57.3	57.3	57.3	57.3
Total heat flow	W	117.1	118.6	127.1	121.2	118.0
Difference in total heat flow	W		1.5	10.0	4.2	1.0
% difference in total heat flow	%		1.3	8.5	3.5	0.8

The method used for framing the window in a CEI wall impacts instantaneous energy flow through the building envelope, which can be as large as 8.5% when compared with the baseline without flanking loss. Note that Case b is the method currently used for installing windows in CEI walls, and it has the highest energy loss. Conventionally, U*A, which is the overall coefficient of heat transfer (U-factor) multiplied by the area (A) of the wall, is used to calculate the energy load in a building [18]. The flanking loss is currently not accounted for even in building energy simulation models. In both cases, energy flow through the building envelope would be underestimated.

4. Other Important Attributes to Be Considered for CEI Walls: Structural Analysis, Air Leakage, and Moisture

The attributes of structural, air leakage, and moisture performance are related to the installation quality of new construction fenestration units on standard wall constructions with CEI. Currently, extruded polystyrene insulation (XPS), expanded polystyrene insulation (EPS), and polyisocyanurate insulation (Polyiso or PI) up to 76 mm (3 in.) thick are commonly used. Insulating foam sheathings are split into two basic categories: (1) thermoplastics, and (2) thermosets. Both EPS and XPS foams are thermoplastic foams, while polyisocyanurate is a thermoset foam [19]. Table 3 lists important properties of different insulation materials currently used in the market [20,21].

Table 3. Properties of typically used CEI.

Property	Unit	Expanded Polystyrene (EPS)	Extruded Polystyrene (XPS)	Polyisocyanurate	Graphite Polystyrene (Neopor)
Cell form	Not applicable	Closed cell	Closed cell	Closed cell	Closed cell
Thermal conductivity	W/m-K	0.033–0.045	0.029–0.031	0.022–0.024	0.031
R-value/inch	h-ft^2-°F/Btu/in.	3.2–4.4	4.6–5.0	6.0–6.5	4.7
Permeance	ng/Pa-s-m^2	114–286	63	1.7–257	143–229
	perm	2.0–5.0	1.1	0.03–4.5	2.5–4.0
Water absorption	% by volume	2.0–4.0	0.3	1.0	1.1
Compressive strength	kPa	34–172	103–414	172	69–172
	psi	5–25	15–60	25	10–25
Density	kg/m^3	12–32	19–35	26–32	14–29

Structural—Windows currently available in the market typically have frame thicknesses varying from 64 mm (2.5 in.) to 114 mm (4.5 in.) The distance from the flange to the outside edge is designed to accommodate the wall finish (i.e., siding, stucco wall, or brick cladding). Choosing a window with a sufficient frame thickness is critical to ensure the frame base from fin to inside edge (Figure 7) will be well-rested and anchored to the wall frame (not only on the CEI) for structural strength. Also, the CEI should have a compressive strength of 103 kPa (15 psi) or greater [12] to provide sufficient structural strength for window units to meet the dynamic wind stresses in the field.

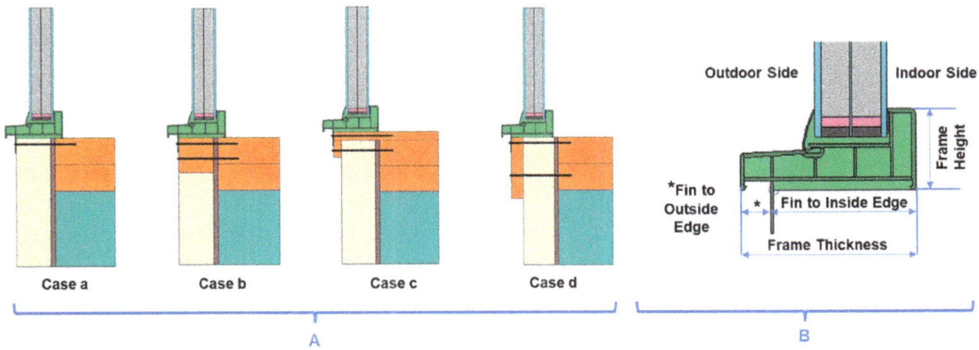

Figure 7. (**A**) Structural assemblies of a window wall in CEI; (**B**) details of a window frame section.

We recommend that the window be installed in the rough opening where the nail on the fin goes into the wall CEI surface; the nails used should have the appropriate grip and requisite length to penetrate the OSB (i.e., going well into the wood stud for structural strength).

Air leakage—Window installations in walls with CEI require additional framing around the rough opening to provide structural support and anchoring. If the workmanship of the framing is not proper or if the installation is not sealed properly, the result may be extraneous air leakage, which is the amount of air entering or leaving a building through unintended gaps, cracks, or holes in the building envelope. This problem can lead to energy loss, increased utility bills, and decreased indoor air quality. Therefore, site supervisors should take particular care to make sure that workers are well informed and trained to properly install windows. Materials used for sealing cracks and openings must be weather resistant and have long-term field exposure durability. Testing the windows and surrounding wall perimeters for air leakage to verify that no extraneous air leakage occurs is recommended before installation of exterior siding and interior wall finish (typically stucco board). When performing the air leakage test, modifications should be made to include a 305 mm (12 in.) perimeter wall in the test.

Moisture—Preventing moisture and water from affecting the building envelope structures, especially CEI, is very important because it decreases the thermal resistance of the insulation (wet insulation is more thermally conductive [22]). It also causes structural damage and mold growth, which is harmful for residents' health. Closed-cell rigid insulation with water-resistant barriers can mitigate moisture problems in building construction. Also, when installing CEI, one should follow the manufacturer's installation guidelines. Poor workmanship and poor-quality sealants have been reported to cause the failure of face-sealed sealant joints for exterior insulation and finish systems (EIFSs) and, subsequently, excessive water penetration and failure of the assembly [23]. Appropriate nails, adhesive tapes, and moisture barriers are warranted for window installation [24]. The water control layer of the window and that of the wall with CEI should be properly connected [25].

Rigid insulation along with rainscreen can act as an integral part of a wall's wind-driven rain screen and vapor and condensation barrier to mitigate the moisture problem [23]. The CEI can be used with or without rainscreen (with 25 mm by 102 mm [1 in. by

4 in.] furring strips attached at intervals over the CEI and on which the exterior sidings are mounted; Figure 8). Rainscreens are strongly recommended with use of CEI and are mainly used to drain water from rain or condensate that enters the area between the siding and the CEI. This helps keep the insulation free from moisture ingress and degradation.

Figure 8. Rainscreen over CEI.

5. Testing Requirements for CEI Walls and Windows

For better long-term performance of windows in CEI walls, builders should request that manufacturer provide test results in accordance with the testing standards listed in Table 4. The applicable window-wall assembly should be tested to these standards and meet the threshold required by local codes or industrial standards. Some of these tests (e.g., ASTM E783 [26] and E331 [27]) will need modifications to evaluate the window perimeter area along with the window in a CEI installation.

Table 4. Testing standards relevant to window installation in walls with CEI.

Reference	Title	Scope	Remark
	ASTM Standards		
ASTM E283-19 (2019) [28]	Standard Test Method for Determining Rate of Air Leakage Through Exterior Windows, Skylights, Curtain Walls, and Doors Under Specified Pressure Differences Across the Specimen	Laboratory air leakage test of windows	Needs to be adapted to measure leakage associated with installation
ASTM E330-14 (2021) [29]	Standard Test Method for Structural Performance of Exterior Windows, Doors, Skylights and Curtain Walls by Uniform Static Air Pressure Difference	Structural performance under uniform static air pressure differences using a test chamber	
ASTM E331-00 (2016) [27]	Standard Test Method for Water Penetration of Exterior Windows, Skylights, Doors, and Curtain Walls by Uniform Static Air Pressure Difference	Resistance to water penetration	Need modifications to evaluate the window perimeter area and the window in CEI installation
ASTM E1886-19 (2019) [30]	Standard Test Method for Performance of Exterior Windows, Curtain Walls, Doors, and Impact Protective Systems Impacted by Missile(s) and Exposed to Cyclic Pressure Differentials	Structural performance subjected to windborne debris and cyclic air pressure differentials representing a windstorm in a test chamber	
ASTM E779-19 (2019) [31]	Standard Test Method for Determining Air Leakage Rate by Fan Pressurization	Air leakage rates through a building envelope under controlled pressurization and depressurization	

Table 4. *Cont.*

Reference	Title	Scope	Remark
ASTM E783-02 (2018) [26]	Standard Test Method for Field Measurement of Air Leakage Through Installed Exterior Windows and Doors	Field air leakage test of installed windows	Needs modifications to evaluate the window perimeter area and the window in CEI installation
American Architectural Manufacturers Association (AAMA) Standard			
FMA/AAMA/WDMA 500-16 (2016) [32]	Standard Practice for the Installation of Mounting Flange Windows into Walls Utilizing Foam Plastic Insulating Sheathing (FPIS) with a Separate Water-Resistive Barrier (WRB)	Standard practice in residential and light commercial buildings of three or fewer stories	Does not include non-flanged and brick mold windows; does not consider structural support for windows

6. Observations and Discussion

As observed, window installations in wood frame walls with CEI may have some drawbacks such as (1) energy loss owing to flanking loss, (2) air leakage and moisture issues owing to poor workmanship, and (c) structural issues owing to poor selection of CEI materials. This is especially the case when field workers do not have adequate knowledge and skillsets to work with CEI, and it can affect the objective of the codes to achieve desired energy efficiency.

To mitigate barriers, a coordinated approach is proposed between the wood frame wall fabrication teams (framers) and the window installers. Framers should be educated about window installation requirements, and conversely, window installers should be educated about framing requirements. The window installation process for wood frame walls with CEI should be as close as possible to the current practice followed for installing windows in standard wood frame wall construction.

One such suggested approach is shown in Figure 9. The window installer first installs the flashing in the rough opening where a window is to be installed, to prevent water and air leakage. Then, the window is installed, plumb and square, in the rough opening by nailing the flange to the wall. Care should be taken to ensure that the nails follow manufacturer's and/or code requirements. These steps are currently followed in the field, and therefore, no additional skills should be required.

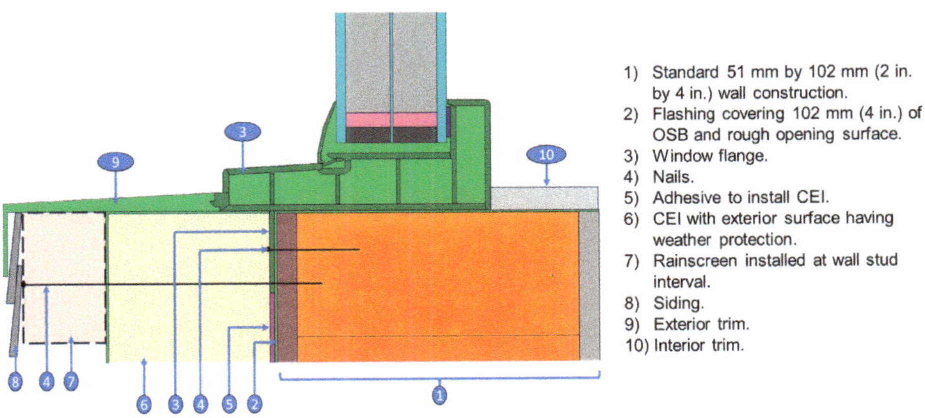

Figure 9. Suggested window installation method and steps in wood frame wall with CEI. The figure shows the details of wall and window parts for illustration only and is not to scale.

This approach ensures that the window base is adequately supported on the wood framework to be structurally sound. Thereafter, the wall framers will apply adhesive to the wall surface and install the CEI with the required thickness. It is important to note that the adhesive should be compatible with the CEI and weather-exposure-proof.

The CEI should be faced with weather barrier material to prevent moisture and air leakage. Also, the compressive strength of the CEI should be at least 103 kPa (15 psi) [12] to provide support to the installed window. The CEI should have a closed-cell structure for reduced permeability.

A rainscreen is then installed over the CEI using nails long enough to penetrate OSB or plywood and to enter about 13 mm (0.5 in.) into the studs, to provide structural strength. Thereafter, the wall sidings are installed over the rainscreen in a way that provides gaps to allow for drying out any moisture entering the gaps.

One additional recommendation is to install exterior trim attached to the window profile on the exterior, sloped to send down any water drained from the window weepholes. The trim also should cover the exposed top surface of the CEI to prevent possible water damage. The window is caulked from the inside, and interior trim is added to provide an aesthetic finish.

These steps need to be coordinated between the wall framers and window installers because window installers must complete their work in two separate stages. First, the window installer installs the window in the rough opening; next, the framer installs the CEI, rainscreen, and sidings; and finally, the window installer returns to install the trims. This is one of the inherent difficulties for window installations in walls with CEI.

7. An Innovative System Concept for Window Installation in CEI Walls

A recommendation in Section 6 is to address the current installation method in the field. However, for better thermal performance, cost effectiveness, and structural performance in high-performance residential buildings, an out-of-the-box installation system needs to be designed. One such design is shown in Figure 10.

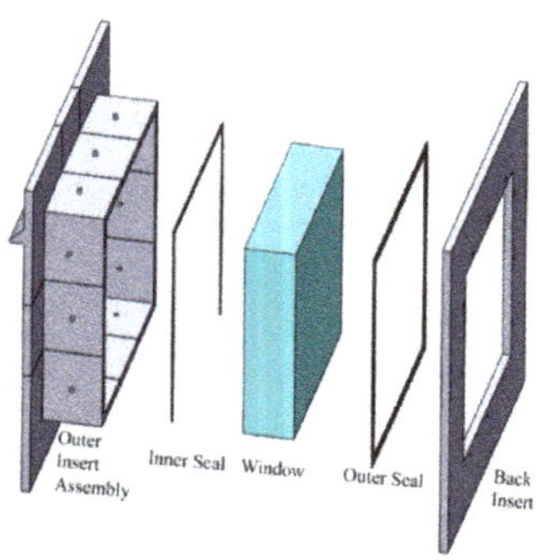

Figure 10. Proposed design of a window installation kit.

The proposed window installation kit will be made of a material with thermal conductivity close to that of the CEI and is structurally sound to withstand structural stresses such as wind or weather exposure. The proposed kit comprises (1) an outer insert assembly, (2) an inner seal, (3) an outer seal, and (4) a back insert. A window is installed in this kit, which can be installed in the wall at a construction site or in panelized construction at a factory.

This design offers several benefits:

1. The system eliminates almost all traditional steps of window installation, such as installing a water barrier, flashings, caulking, and trimming.
2. Future full window replacement is efficient because parts can easily be disassembled, the window can be removed and replaced, and then the kit can be reassembled.

3. The kit material is of low thermal conductivity, thus eliminating flanking loss. Therefore, the system retains energy efficiency and prevents condensation at intermediate wall construction layers.
4. The installation kit can be preinstalled in a modular wall construction, which saves window installation time and reduces the cost.

However, the system may have a few disadvantages:

1. It requires a decision on who holds responsibility for providing the installation kit—the window manufacturers or the wall framers.
2. Meeting code requirements, which may specifically spell out traditional window installation requirements, can be a problem.
3. Inertia of market deployment can slow adoption.
4. Installers may need to develop new skillsets.

8. Conclusions

CEI has been increasingly used in residential buildings to improve energy efficiency, and the installation of windows to walls with CEI can significantly affect the performance of the whole wall. We summarized four cases of installing windows to walls with CEI of 25–76 mm (1–3 in.) thickness. Flanking loss, which is the energy loss between window and wall interface, was quantified in the four cases. The insulation value (RSI) of the 305 mm (12 in.) perimeter wall surrounding a window was decreased in the four cases by 7.6–34.5% when compared with the RSI without the window. Case b, which is the conventional method currently used for installing windows in CEI walls, had the lowest RSI.

Issues of structural performance, air leakage, and moisture penetration owing to installing windows to CEI walls were described, and recommendations were made. For structural strength, the frame thickness of the window should be large enough for the frame base to be anchored to the wall frame and not anchored only on the CEI. Additionally, the CEI should have a compressive strength of 103 kPa (15 psi) or greater. To prevent air leakage, materials used for sealing the cracks and openings must be weather resistant and have long-term field exposure durability. For moisture durability, rainscreens are strongly recommended with the use of CEI. When measuring the performance of the windows installed in CEI walls, the standards ASTM E783 (air leakage test) and E331 (water penetration test) need to be modified to include the 305 mm (12 in.) perimeter area along with the window.

We proposed two approaches to overcome the difficulties in installing windows to CEI walls. The first one provides the window installation method and steps in a wood frame wall with CEI to address the current installation method in the field. The second proposed approach is an out-of-the-box window installation kit with the potential to offer better thermal performance, cost effectiveness, and structural performance in high-performance residential buildings.

The results will inform the improvement of the rating program referenced by the building energy codes by considering the impact of window and wall interfaces, which is currently ignored. It will also advance the development of new installation systems and aid faster market transformation, improving the quality of building constructions and energy efficiency in buildings.

Future research should be focused on developing window frames that are more insulating, to reduce flanking loss at window and wall interfaces. Development of alternative stud materials that are more durable, insulating, and structurally sound to replace wood studs in a wood frame wall will also increase energy efficiency in buildings. Moreover, physical testing of the whole wall assembly will need to be carried out to validate the results.

Author Contributions: Conceptualization, B.S. and M.B.; Methodology, B.S. and M.B.; Validation, M.T.; Formal analysis, B.S.; Investigation, M.T.; Writing—original draft, B.S.; Writing—review & editing, M.B. and M.T.; Project administration, M.B.; Funding acquisition, M.B. All authors have read and agreed to the published version of the manuscript.

Funding: This research was supported by DOE's Office of Energy Efficiency and Renewable Energy, Building Technologies Office, under Contract No. DE-AC05-00OR22725 with UT-Battelle LLC.

Data Availability Statement: The original contributions presented in the study are included in the article, further inquiries can be directed to the corresponding author.

Acknowledgments: The authors specifically thank Marc LaFrance, Windows Technology Manager at DOE, for guiding this research.

Conflicts of Interest: Author Bipin Shah was employed by the company WinBuild Inc. The remaining authors declare that the research was conducted in the absence of any commercial or financial relationships that could be construed as a potential conflict of interest.

Abbreviations

IGU	Insulated Glazing Unit
COG	Center of Glazing
EOG	Edge of Glazing
Low-E	Low Emissivity
U-value [W/(m^2-K)]	Thermal Transmittance (Thermal Conductance)
RSI [(m^2-K)/W]	Thermal Resistance (Inverse of U-Value)
CI	Continuous Insulation
CEI	Continuous Exterior Insulation
OSB	Oriented Strand Board

References

1. United States Census Bureau. New Residential Construction. 2024. Available online: https://www.census.gov/construction/nrc/index.html (accessed on 22 May 2024).
2. US Energy Information Administration. U.S. Energy Facts Explained. 2023. Available online: https://www.eia.gov/energyexplained/us-energy-facts/ (accessed on 23 May 2024).
3. International Code Council. *2021 International Energy Conservation Code (IECC)*; International Code Council: Washington, DC, USA, 2021.
4. International Code Council. *2021 International Residential Code (IRC)*; International Code Council: Washington, DC, USA, 2021.
5. International Code Council. 2021 IECC: A Code on a Mission–Campaign Toolkit. 2024. Available online: https://www.iccsafe.org/products-and-services/iecc-on-a-mission-toolkit/ (accessed on 16 June 2024).
6. Building America Solution Center. 2009–2021 IECC and IRC Minimum Insulation Requirements for New Homes. 2021. Available online: https://basc.pnnl.gov/information/2009-2021-iecc-and-irc-minimum-insulation-requirements-new-homes (accessed on 29 May 2024).
7. Building America Solution Center. Table of Maximum Fenestration U-Factor Requirements for New Homes as Listed in the 2009–2021 IECC and IRC. 2021. Available online: https://basc.pnnl.gov/information/table-maximum-fenestration-u-factor-requirements-new-homes-listed-2009-2021-iecc-and (accessed on 29 May 2024).
8. US EPA. *ENERGY STAR® Program Requirements for Residential Windows, Doors, and Skylights*; US EPA: Washington, DC, USA, 2022.
9. Harris, C. *Pathway to Zero Energy Windows: Advancing Technologies and Market Adoption*; National Renewable Energy Laboratory (NREL): Golden, CO, USA, 2022.
10. Applied Building Technology Group LLC. *Installation and Performance of Flanged Fenestration Units Mounted on Walls with Foam Plastic Insulating Sheathing*; Applied Building Technology Group LLC: Madison, WI, USA, 2021.
11. Peavey, J.; Shah, N. *Performance of Windows in Walls with Continuous Insulation*; Home Innovation Research Labs: Upper Marlboro, MD, USA, 2023.
12. Lstiburek, J.; Baker, P. *Measure Guideline: Incorporating Thick Layers of Exterior Rigid Insulation on Walls*; Building Science Corporation: Westford, MA, USA, 2015.
13. Ueno, K. Residential exterior wall superinsulation retrofit details and analysis. In Proceedings of the Thermal Performance of the Exterior Envelopes of Whole Buildings XI, Clearwater, FL, USA, 5–9 December 2010.
14. Pella Windows & Doors. New Construction Installation with Nail Fin over 1 1/2″–2″ Thick Continuous Exterior Insulation Using Rough Opening Support Brackets. 2023. Available online: https://media.pella.com/professional/installation/NC_NFCI.pdf (accessed on 29 May 2024).
15. Andersen Windows & Doors. Window & Door Installation. 2024. Available online: https://www.andersenwindows.com/support/window-door-installation/ (accessed on 17 June 2024).
16. *NFRC 600*; Glossary and Terminology. National Fenestration Rating Council: Greenbelt, MD, USA, 2020.
17. *ANSI/NFRC 100*; Procedure for Determining Fenestration Product U-factors. National Fenestration Rating Council: Greenbelt, MD, USA, 2023.

18. ASHRAE. *ASHRAE Handbook—Fundamentals*; ASHRAE: Peachtree Corners, GA, USA, 2021.
19. Building America Solution Center. Continuous Rigid Insulation Sheathing. 2022. Available online: https://basc.pnnl.gov/resource-guides/continuous-rigid-insulation-sheathing (accessed on 16 June 2024).
20. Building Science Corporation. *Guide to Insulating Sheathing*; Building Science Corporation: Westford, MA, USA, 2007.
21. BASF. Neopor® GPS Smart Insulation. 2024. Available online: https://neopor.basf.us/files/technical_documents/GPS-Plus-Technical-Properties-1inch.pdf (accessed on 11 July 2024).
22. Berardi, U. The impact of aging and environmental conditions on the effective thermal conductivity of several foam materials. *Energy* **2019**, *182*, 777–794. [CrossRef]
23. *BSD-030*; Rain Control Theory. Building Science Corporation: Westford, MA, USA, 2010. Available online: https://buildingscience.com/documents/digests/bsd030-rain-control-theory (accessed on 12 July 2024).
24. *BSI-067*; Stuck on You. Building Science Corporation: Westford, MA, USA, 2013. Available online: https://buildingscience.com/documents/insights/bsi-067-stuck-on-you (accessed on 12 July 2024).
25. *BSI-085*; Windows Can Be a Pain—Continuous Insulation and Punched Openings. Building Science Corporation: Westford, MA, USA, 2015. Available online: https://buildingscience.com/documents/insights/bsi-085-windows-can-be-a-pain (accessed on 12 July 2024).
26. *ASTM Standard E783-02*; Standard Test Method for Field Measurement of Air Leakage through Installed Exterior Windows and Doors. ASTM International: West Conshohocken, PA, USA, 2018.
27. *ASTM Standard E331-00*; Standard Test Method for Water Penetration of Exterior Windows, Skylights, Doors, and Curtain Walls by Uniform Static Air Pressure Difference. ASTM International: West Conshohocken, PA, USA, 2016.
28. *ASTM Standard E283-19*; Standard Test Method for Determining Rate of Air Leakage through Exterior Windows, Skylights, Curtain Walls, and Doors Under Specified Pressure Differences Across the Specimen. ASTM International: West Conshohocken, PA, USA, 2019.
29. *ASTM Standard E330-14*; Standard Test Method for Structural Performance of Exterior Windows, Doors, Skylights and Curtain Walls by Uniform Static Air Pressure Difference. ASTM International: West Conshohocken, PA, USA, 2021.
30. *ASTM Standard E1886-19*; Standard Test Method for Performance of Exterior Windows, Curtain Walls, Doors, and Impact Protective Systems Impacted by Missile(s) and Exposed to Cyclic Pressure Differentials. ASTM International: West Conshohocken, PA, USA, 2019.
31. *ASTM Standard E779-19*; Standard Test Method for Determining Air Leakage Rate by Fan Pressurization. ASTM International: West Conshohocken, PA, USA, 2019.
32. *FMA/AAMA/WDMA 500-16*; Standard Practice for the Installation of Mounting Flange Windows into Walls Utilizing Foam Plastic Insulating Sheathing (FPIS) with a Separate Water-Resistive Barrier (WRB). American Architectural Manufacturers Association: Schaumburg, IL, USA, 2016.

energies

MDPI

Article

Energy Awareness, Energy Use, and Energy-Saving Opportunities in the Caribbean: The Island Curaçao as a Case Study

Richenel R. Bulbaai [1] and Johannes I. M. Halman [1,2,*]

1 Faculty of Engineering, University of Curaçao, Jan Noorduynweg 111, Willemstad, Curacao; richenel.bulbaai@uoc.cw
2 Department of Construction Management and Engineering, University of Twente, P.O. Box 217, 7500 AE Enschede, The Netherlands
* Correspondence: j.i.m.halman@utwente.nl

Abstract: Household energy consumption represents a significant share of global energy usage, highlighting the importance of understanding the factors that influence energy use and identifying potential strategies for conservation. The Caribbean region faces unique challenges in energy sustainability, driven by its heavy dependence on fossil fuels and rising energy demand. The primary aim of this study is to evaluate the current levels of energy awareness and energy consumption among households on the tropical Caribbean island of Curaçao and to determine practical energy-saving opportunities that can significantly reduce both energy consumption and costs. This paper is one of the first to evaluate energy awareness, energy use, and energy-saving opportunities among households in the Caribbean. The study included a literature review of key theories, concepts, and energy-saving strategies, along with a telephone survey of 382 households in Curaçao to examine household energy use, the factors shaping energy behavior, and the connections between energy consumption, behavior, and household income. The main findings of this study reveal that energy-efficient appliances are predominantly used in high-income households, with much lower adoption rates in middle- and low-income households. Cost savings, rather than environmental concerns, emerge as the primary motivation behind energy-saving behavior. Notably, the study highlights that most households in Curaçao are largely unaware of the full range of energy-efficient options available to them for reducing energy consumption. Based on the field study results, several recommendations are offered to enhance energy awareness, expand energy-saving opportunities, and ultimately reduce energy usage.

Keywords: energy awareness; energy consumption; energy-saving opportunities; sustainable energy use; energy efficiency; Caribbean SIDS

1. Introduction

Reducing energy consumption has become a critical global priority in addressing major societal challenges related to sustainability, climate change, and energy security [1,2]. The islands in the Caribbean face unique challenges in reducing energy sustainability due to their limited natural resources and isolated electricity infrastructure, unconnected to the grids of other countries, which leaves them without the option of cross-border agreements to manage intermittency. Instead, to guarantee a reliable electricity supply, expensive backup systems are needed. Electricity production on the Caribbean islands remains heavily reliant on imported fossil fuels to meet their energy needs. This results in high energy costs and significant CO_2 emissions. Raising energy awareness among consumers could significantly reduce energy consumption and encourage the adoption of renewable energy sources, helping to mitigate these vulnerabilities [3].

Since households typically consume a significant portion of around 20–30% of total final energy consumption [4], in this study we focus on energy use by households. We specifically investigate energy awareness, energy use, and the possible energy-saving opportunities for residents of the Caribbean and take the Caribbean island Curaçao as a first case study.

Several studies have been conducted in the last few decades on energy use and behavior among households [5–10]. Unfortunately, there is almost no information available about energy awareness and the adoption of renewable energy sources among households in tropical areas and more in particular in the Caribbean region. Households in tropical areas, e.g., such as the Caribbean, often have one or more air conditioners that are intensively used throughout the whole year. On the other hand, houses in the Caribbean do not need to be equipped with heating systems. This will lead to a varied composition of household appliances, along with different patterns of energy consumption and opportunities for savings. Furthermore, contrary to developed countries, many of the available appliances are often not state-of-the-art, resulting in higher energy consumption for each individual appliance [11,12]. As an initial step to address the identified gap in the literature, this paper presents a survey study involving 382 households, exploring the current state of energy awareness and consumption on the tropical Caribbean island of Curaçao. We also investigate potential differences between high-income, middle-income, and low-income households with respect to energy awareness, energy consumption, and the use of energy-efficient appliances. In addition, we investigate the per-income category, the most important drivers for residents to invest in energy-saving appliances. We further investigate to what extent residents are aware of viable energy-saving opportunities that can be implemented to reduce energy consumption and costs. The study is grounded in the context of Curaçao's unique energy landscape, which is characterized by a reliance on imported fuels, a growing interest in renewable energy sources, and the socio-economic factors influencing energy behavior.

The remainder of this paper is structured as follows: Section 2 offers a review of the literature on energy awareness, energy consumption, and opportunities for energy saving. Section 3 details the research steps taken to conduct the survey study assessing energy awareness and consumption in the residential sector of Curaçao. This is followed by Section 4. The paper concludes with Section 5, addressing the main scientific contributions, policy implications, limitations of the study, and several recommendations for future research.

2. Literature Background

Residential energy use plays a major role in global energy consumption and carbon emissions. Understanding how energy is consumed within households is essential for creating effective strategies to promote energy efficiency and conservation. This section reviews the literature on energy awareness, consumption, and saving options in the residential sector.

Energy awareness is essential for encouraging behavioral changes and fostering a culture of energy conservation within communities [13]. Energy awareness involves understanding and being conscious of energy usage, sources, and the effects of energy consumption on both the environment and the economy. It includes knowledge of energy-efficient practices, awareness of renewable energy sources, and an understanding of the personal and societal impacts of energy use [14]. In the literature, four possible options to enhance energy awareness are distinguished. This can first be done through Education and information campaigns [15], including school programs, public service announcements, and informational websites that educate the community on energy issues. The European Union Energy Efficiency Directive [16] provides measures to improve energy awareness through public awareness campaigns. Second, Feedback Mechanisms, which provide real-time feedback to residents on their energy usage through smart meters and energy dashboards, have been shown to increase energy awareness and help residents understand their consumption patterns and identify opportunities for energy savings [17,18]. Froehlich discovered that in-home feedback technology can lead to an average reduction in energy consumption by 10–15% when feedback is provided more frequently and with greater data granularity, such as detailed energy usage data for specific appliances. Casals et al. [19] demonstrated that gamification also stimulates energy savings, resulting in an electricity saving of 3.46%. A study by D'Oca et al. [20] showed that the implementation of automated home appliances timely informs users about energy consumption, uses persuasive communication, and personalizes energy-saving prompts, resulting in reducing electricity consumption in homes on average by 18% to 57% [20,21]. Third, Local initiatives and community-based programs encourage collective energy-saving behaviors [22]. Finally, through Technological interventions, the adoption of energy-efficient appliances and renewable energy technologies also contributes to greater energy awareness by making energy savings more visible and tangible [23]. However, factors such as behavioral inertia, information overload, and economic constraints can impede efforts to increase energy awareness and promote energy-saving actions [24].

As population growth and urbanization drive increased energy demand, understanding current energy consumption patterns is vital for sustainable development. Consequently, energy consumption has emerged as one of the key factors in managing development toward sustainability [25]. Residential energy consumption varies significantly across regions, influenced by factors such as climate, building design, socio-economic status, and cultural practices. According to Newell and Raimi [26], residential energy consumption represents about 25–30% of total final energy consumption worldwide. Energy consumption patterns are heavily influenced by climatic conditions, building characteristics (age, size, and insulation quality), and socio-economic factors such as income levels and access to energy-efficient technologies. Higher-income households often have more appliances and larger living spaces, leading to increased energy consumption [27]. There are numerous strategies available for reducing energy consumption in residential areas. In addition to behavioral changes, adopting energy-efficient appliances, home insulation, the integration of renewable energy, and smart home technologies represent viable options for energy saving [28].

To mitigate environmental impacts and enhance energy efficiency in households, the implementation of Energy-saving solutions in households may be considered critical. Numerous energy-saving options are available to residents, ranging from behavioral changes and technological advancements to home improvements and renewable energy integration. This has led to a stream of research showing the many opportunities to cut down on energy use in households. De Almeida et al. [29] concluded that existing technologies and improved behavior can achieve up to 48% in energy savings. Encouraging residents to adopt energy-conscious behaviors can result in significant energy savings. Simple actions, such as turning off lights when they are not in use, lowering thermostat settings, and reducing the use of high-energy appliances, can significantly reduce energy consumption. Studies have shown that behavioral changes alone can lead to energy savings of 5–15% in households [30,31]. Furthermore, adopting energy-efficient appliances and smart home technologies is one of the most effective strategies for reducing household energy consumption. Appliances such as programmable thermostats, smart meters, home energy management systems, and appliances with energy star ratings allow residents to optimize their energy consumption [32]. Improving home insulation in walls, roofs, and floors and sealing leaks and installing energy-efficient windows will decrease the need for heating and cooling, resulting in significant energy savings [33]. Passive solar design, natural ventilation, and using high-performance building materials help reduce energy requirements for heating and cooling [34]. Key additional energy-saving options include installing rooftop solar PV systems and integrating other renewable energy sources, such as solar water heaters. PV solar systems enable residents to generate their own energy, reducing dependence on grid power and lowering energy bills. Meanwhile, solar water heating systems further decrease household energy consumption and greenhouse gas emissions [35]. A significant body of the literature, such as that by [36–39], emphasizes the importance of retrofitting social housing with energy-efficient technologies to reduce overall consumption. Retrofitting involves upgrading existing buildings with improved insulation, energy-efficient windows, photovoltaics, heat pumps, and other installations. This can be particularly impactful in social households, where residents may lack the financial resources to invest in energy-saving initiatives independently.

There is also a growing recognition of the social factors that affect household energy use. These social factors encompass behaviors, cultural norms, socioeconomic status, and the roles of community and policy in shaping how energy is consumed in a home [40]. Behavioral attitudes toward energy conservation significantly impact household energy use [41]. Research has shown that implicit rules and expectations governing behavior significantly shape energy-related behaviors, such as heating, cooling, and electricity use [42]. For example, the study by Nolan et al. [43] demonstrated that normative messages emphasizing social comparisons (such as those regarding how their energy consumption compares to that of their neighbors) can be more effective in reducing energy consumption than purely informational campaigns. Energy use in households is also deeply embedded in the social interactions and dynamics within households. Family structure, gender roles, and household decision-making processes can all influence how energy is consumed [44]. Socioeconomic status also plays a critical role in shaping household energy use [45]. Lower-income households typically consume less energy overall, often due to financial constraints that restrict their ability to purchase energy-intensive appliances. In contrast, higher-income households are more likely to reside in larger homes that require more energy for heating and cooling, and they are also more inclined to adopt energy-efficient technologies [46]. The social aspects of energy use are also critical for the development and execution of energy policies. Public initiatives that focus on community-based social norms can foster more widespread adoption of energy conservation behaviors across diverse socioeconomic groups [47].

Based on the reviewed literature regarding energy awareness, energy consumption, and energy-saving options, one may conclude that a substantial decrease in household energy consumption can be realized. This is on the condition that knowledge about successful behavioral interventions and the adoption of effective energy-saving options are properly coordinated.

3. Materials and Methods

The objective of this study was to assess the current state of energy awareness and energy consumption among households on the tropical Caribbean island of Curaçao and to identify realizable energy-saving opportunities that can effectively reduce energy consumption and costs. To achieve this, a survey was conducted with the participation of 382 households. The research concept is illustrated in Figure 1.

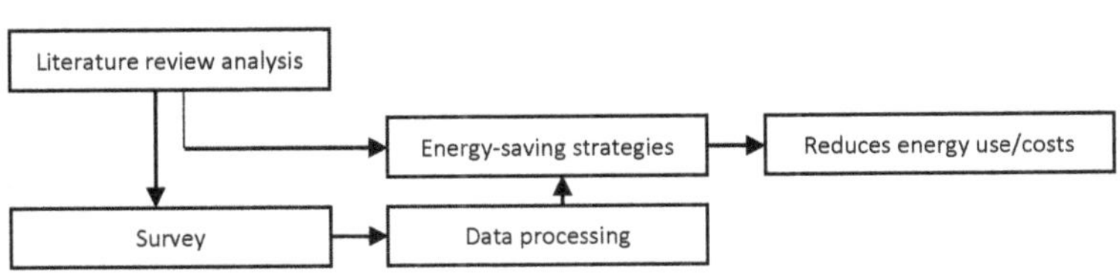

Figure 1. The research concept.

Curaçao, a Caribbean island situated in the southern Caribbean Sea, is located about 65 km north of the Venezuelan coast. It has a population of just over 150,000 residents and approximately 65,225 dwellings spread across an area of 444 km^2 [48]. Curaçao is characterized by a semi-arid to arid climate featuring distinct dry and rainy seasons. The rainy season occurs from October to January, while the dry season lasts from February to June, with July and August acting as transitional months. The island experiences warm tropical temperatures, peaking in September with an average air temperature of 27.9 °C and an average seawater temperature of 27 °C. [49]. Throughout the year, the wind predominantly blows from east to west. Curaçao experiences relative humidity levels ranging from a minimum of 76% to a maximum of 80% [34].

The Central Bureau of Statistics in Curaçao, CBS, classifies household income in Curaçao into three categories: minimum income, middle income, and maximum income. The minimum income category includes households with a monthly average income of less than USD 1125. The middle-income category encompasses households with a monthly average income between USD 1125 and USD 2808. Finally, households with a monthly average gross income exceeding USD 2808 are categorized as having maximum income.

In the initial phase of this study, a comprehensive literature review was conducted to offer an in-depth overview of the current knowledge regarding energy awareness and consumption, both in general and specifically within the Caribbean context. We focused on essential theories, concepts, and energy-saving strategies. To accomplish this, a variety of journal database search engines, including EBSCO, Emerald, Web of Science, Academia.edu, and Google Scholar, were utilized. This eventually resulted in a selection of about 90 papers for our literature review.

In the second stage, a telephone survey was conducted. Statistics indicate that telephone surveys remain one of the most significant methods of data collection [50]. A telephone survey involving 382 households in Curaçao was conducted to assess household energy consumption, the factors influencing energy behavior, and the connections between energy use, behavior, and household income. Participants were randomly selected to take part in the survey.

A questionnaire featuring eight open-ended questions (see Appendix A) was developed for our survey, which was conducted via telephone over a four-month period. Calls were made during both daytime and evening hours by students from the Faculty of Engineering at the University of Curaçao (UoC). The first author provided these students with the necessary instructions for conducting the interviews. Progress was monitored on a regular basis. The procedure of the telephone survey that was used was as follows:

1. the interviewer introduces himself/herself;
2. a short and clear description of the survey;
3. an explanation of the procedure of the survey;
4. an estimation of the time needed to complete the survey;
5. the respondent is asked to join the survey; and
6. after having completed the survey, the interviewer extends gratitude to the respondent.

A telephone survey has both advantages and disadvantages. The primary benefits noted in this survey included its accessibility, as most households in Curaçao have fixed-line telephones, and the process was quick and straightforward. However, the main drawbacks of a telephone survey are that the interviewer cannot observe the respondents' body language, the questions must be relatively simple, and respondents may be less inclined to participate if contacted at an inconvenient time [50]. In fact, during the survey, the interviewers had to call some respondents back because the initial call was made at an inconvenient time.

After the survey, the data collected from each household were processed. Subsequently, the average electricity usage of the appliances was gathered from various retailers and from Aqualectra, the government-owned provider of water and electricity in Curaçao. It is important to note that a single household may have multiple appliances of the same type.

The annual energy consumption of an appliance is calculated by multiplying the total number of appliances by the appliance's power, the daily usage time, and then multiplying that result by 365, as shown in Equation (1):

$$E = P \times t \times n \times 365 \tag{1}$$

where:

E: is the energy use of the appliance
P: is the power of the appliance in kW
t: is the time used per day
n: is the total number of appliances

Finally, based on the literature and survey results, policy recommendations were developed to reduce household energy use and realize lower household energy costs.

4. Results Findings of the Conducted Household Energy Survey

This section outlines the results and analysis of the telephone survey conducted. Table 1 provides an overview of household sizes based on the number of individuals (p) living in each residence.

Table 1. The number of persons per household (n = 382).

Household Sizes	1p	2p	3p	4p	5p	6p	>6p	Total
Number of households	65	108	88	66	36	11	8	382

In Curaçao, two-person households are the most prevalent, making up approximately 28% of all households. The average household size in Curaçao is around 2.8 individuals, which is comparable to household sizes in Europe. According to [51], the average household size in the European Union (EU) was 2.3 persons in 2022. Among European Member States, this figure ranged from 3.1 persons in Slovakia, 2.9 in Poland, and 2.7 in Croatia to 2.0 persons in Denmark, Germany, Lithuania, and Sweden, with Finland reporting the lowest average at 1.9 persons.

Table 2 summarizes the distribution of households across income categories for both the latest conducted 2011 census by the Curaçao Bureau for Statistics and the survey. As can be seen, approximately 27% of the households in the Curaçao energy survey fall into the low-income category, 38% are classified as middle-income, and 33% are considered high-income.

Table 2. Number of households per income categories.

Income Categories	Percentages and Number of Households	
	Census 2011	Survey 2023
Low income < 1125 USD	(30.0%)	115 (27.0%)
Middle income: 1125–2808 USD	(32.0%)	122 (38.0%)
High income > 2808 USD	(33.0%)	126 (33.0%)
Unknown	(5.0%)	19 (3.0%)
Total	(100%)	382 (100%)

Regarding the survey question, "Do you take actions to save energy?", 347 participants (91%) indicated that they do take measures to conserve energy, while 35 respondents reported that they do not. The participants were also asked about their motivations for saving energy. The findings showed that financial concerns were the primary reason for energy-saving actions, followed by environmental considerations (see Table 3). Notably, a higher percentage of middle-income households save energy for environmental reasons, whereas low-income households are more likely to save for financial reasons. These findings align with a study by [52], which indicated that individuals in the low-income category are less inclined to save energy for environmental reasons. Notably, a significant majority of respondents in the low-income group (79%) save energy primarily for financial reasons, compared to 36.1% in the middle-income category and 37.2% in the high-income category. Additionally, consistent with previous research by [53], 89.06% of respondents reported being aware of their household power consumption and expressed a willingness to install a home automation system to lower their electricity bills.

Table 3. Reasons for saving energy based on income categories.

No	Motives to Save Energy	Low-Income Households	Middle-Income Households	High-Income Households	Total Households
1	Financial	79.0%	36.1%	37.2%	50.1%
2	Environment	0.9%	41.5%	15.5%	19.6%
3	Environment and financial	13.1%	11.6%	32.6%	19.4%
4	No motives (do not take action)	7%	10.8%	14.7%	10.9%
5	Total	100%	100%	100%	100%

Table 4 summarizes the energy-saving practices reported in the Curaçao energy survey, along with their frequency of application by income category. When asked if they took measures to save energy, over 92% of participants in the low-income category, 89% in the middle-income category, and 90% in the high-income category responded affirmatively. The survey also inquired about specific actions taken to conserve energy. Hori et al. [54] observed that the initial step many individuals take toward more energy-efficient behavior is turning off lights. As shown in Table 4, the findings from this survey align with [54], revealing that turning off lights and appliances was the most common energy-saving action across all income categories. Despite the majority of respondents indicating they engaged in energy-saving practices, the survey results suggest that they primarily utilized basic methods for energy conservation.

Table 4. Percentage of times energy-saving methods were applied.

No	Energy-Saving Methods	Low-Income Households	Middle-Income Households	High-Income Households	Total Households
1	Turning off lights and appliances when they are not used	94.3%	96.6%	92.2%	94.3%
2	LED Lamps	82.0%	85.0%	82.9%	83.3%
3	Energy-saving air conditioner (AC) Inverter	49.0%	80.3%	89.9%	73.7%
4	LED-TV	74.0%	79.6%	79.8%	77.9%
5	Inverter refrigerator or efficient refrigerator	16.0%	54.4%	64.3%	45.7%
6	Inverter washing machine or efficient washing machine	9.40%	31.3%	50.3%	31.0%
7	Energy-saving lamps	15.1%	30.6%	33.3%	26.6%
8	Candle	0.9%	0.6%	0.7%	0.7%
9	Pool pump timer			0.7%	0.2%

The survey results indicate a positive correlation between household income and the use of energy-efficient appliances. High-income individuals are generally better positioned to purchase these products compared to their low-income counterparts, who, in turn, tend to take more proactive measures, such as turning off appliances and lights when not in use. These findings align with those of [55]. Additionally, as noted by [56], higher-income households typically live in newer and larger homes, equipped with more appliances and energy-efficient features. Conversely, low-income households are less likely to invest in energy-efficient appliances, but they do engage in other energy-saving behaviors. The respondents in this survey appeared unaware of many available energy-efficient options, such as smart power strips, inverter appliances, timers, motion sensors, and insulation. As a result, they primarily relied on basic methods for energy savings. The survey findings indicate that energy-efficient air conditioners and lamps are the most commonly utilized appliances in their homes.

Numerous studies have highlighted awareness as a key factor in promoting energy savings. For example, Hori et al. [54] propose a positive correlation between awareness and energy conservation. In our survey, we inquired whether respondents believed energy saving should be encouraged in Curaçao and their reasons for this belief. Approximately 76% of those in the low-income category and 65% in the middle-income category responded affirmatively, while about 67% of high-income respondents agreed. The predominant reason given was the need for more information about energy-saving practices. According to [29], energy awareness can be raised through labeling schemes such as the EU Energy label, awareness campaigns on TV and radio, and the expansion of energy labels for different types of products.

This study also revealed that 38% of respondents in the low-income category perceive the prices of energy-efficient appliances as extremely high, with an additional 47% indicating that the prices are high. In the middle-income category, 19% of respondents reported that prices are extremely high, while 51% considered them high. Among high-income respondents, 8% mentioned that prices are extremely high, and 35% considered them high.

Despite the higher price tags associated with energy-efficient appliances, their usage in Curaçao has risen significantly across all three income categories in the past six years [57].

Table 5 presents the types and quantities of appliances found in households in Curaçao categorized by income level, along with the total annual energy consumption of these appliances. The average electricity usage for each appliance type was sourced from various retailers and Aqualectra, the government-owned provider of water and electricity in Curaçao. It is worth mentioning that a single household may own multiple appliances of the same type. The survey results in Table 5 indicate that air conditioners (including both inverter and non-inverter models) are the most energy-intensive appliances in Curaçao's residential sector, followed by electric cooking appliances (which include electric stoves and ovens) and refrigerators with freezers.

Table 5. The quantity of appliances and their total annual energy consumption (n = 385).

No	Type of Appliances	Appliances Low-Income Households	Appliances Middle-Income Households	Appliances High-Income Households	Total Number of Appliances	Energy Use (kWh) per Year
1	Inverter air conditioner	70	224	298	592	1,608,864
2	Refrigerator with freezer	108	145	142	395	462,265
3	Non-inverter air conditioner	27	32	37	96	402,296
4	Electric oven	32	49	65	146	333,360
5	Electric stove	9	27	39	75	298,080
6	Television	158	259	314	731	294,041
7	Small electric boiler	12	54	94	160	201,600
8	Freezer	23	24	51	98	129,005
9	Router	90	127	146	363	94,090
10	TV-Box/Telecommunication company	88	132	122	342	88,646
11	Iron	108	133	133	374	84,823
12	Desktop	15	40	67	122	70,272
13	Fan	195	315	346	856	67,795
14	Indoor light bulb	66	201	242	509	65,966
15	Laptop	40	143	210	393	50,933
16	Electric dryer	8	19	27	54	44,064
17	Indoor led lamp	585	1034	1195	2814	42,548
18	Outdoor led lamp	203	482	716	1401	42,366
19	Outdoor fluorescent lamp	175	198	167	540	39,972
20	Outdoor light bulb	23	45	78	146	37,843
21	TV-box/Android	37	114	175	326	28,166
22	Microwave	60	100	103	263	26,684
23	Electrical boiler for bathing	3	10	10	23	25,308
24	Rice-cooker	75	104	112	291	20,873
25	Semi-automatic washing machine	83	64	45	192	18,931
26	Automatic washing machine	23	83	87	193	18,528
27	Electric kettle	24	74	76	174	6264
28	Indoor fluorescent lamp	67	61	27	155	6407
29	Refrigerator without freezer	2	2	4	8	2400
30	Printer	28	78	93	199	239
31	Non-automatic washing machine	0	0	0	0	0

5. Discussion

5.1. Scientific Contributions

The Caribbean islands are heavily dependent on imported fossil fuels, resulting in high electricity costs, environmental concerns, and energy insecurity. With increasing concerns about energy security and climate change, many Caribbean islands are increasingly exploring renewable energy sources and energy efficiency measures as solutions to these issues. In recent years, a number of studies [57–59] have focused on the drivers and inhibitors to develop and implement renewable energy in the Caribbean region. In addition, the studies of [33,34] have specifically examined the implementation of passive building principles for homes in Curaçao and strategies to reduce standby energy consumption in households on the island.

Our study adds to various portions of the energy efficiency literature. The studies most closely related to our paper are the ones that address energy awareness among households. Hassan et al. [5] convincingly demonstrate that increasing energy awareness through a reward system has a significant impact on reducing energy consumption. Rosak-Szyrocka and Żywiolek [10] provide an extensive literature review on household energy awareness. The results of their study among 1097 respondents in Poland indicate that the respondents possess knowledge about energy and the factors driving its increased consumption, yet they lack awareness of the importance of energy conservation and its implications for the environment. Li et al. [7] conclude, on the basis of a nationwide household survey in China, that awareness alone does not necessarily reduce energy consumption. A household's subjective attitude can greatly influence the decision to purchase more energy-efficient products and promote pro-environmental choices. Bülbül et al. [6] conclude that research on the role of Turkish households in environmental issues remains limited, highlighting the need for media campaigns to raise public awareness about carbon footprints. An interesting observation was made by Gajdzik et al. [60] on the energy behaviors of prosumers in Polish households, and they found that those who generate energy through photovoltaic panels and heat pumps tend to exhibit a general tendency toward pro-ecological behavior. They recommend prioritizing the promotion of prosumers and encouraging the use of environmentally friendly energy in the economy.

This paper is one of the first to evaluate energy awareness, energy consumption, and energy-saving opportunities among households in the Caribbean. Utilizing a survey study with participation from 382 households in Curaçao, we gathered insights into household energy use. Investigating the energy consumption and behavior on the Caribbean islands is crucial for several reasons. First, there are significant differences in device usage compared to other countries. For example, the prevalence of air conditioning per household in the Caribbean is considerably higher than in Europe. Additionally, developed countries tend to have a much greater number of devices compared to those in developing countries. Furthermore, awareness levels regarding energy use are generally higher in developed countries than in developing regions such as the Caribbean islands [12]. One of the key findings of this research is the disparity in the use of energy-efficient appliances between high-income households and those with middle to low incomes. It appears that energy-efficient appliances are predominantly utilized by high-income households, whereas middle- and low-income households tend to use them less frequently. This result highlights a significant socioeconomic aspect of energy use behaviors, where affordability is a crucial factor influencing the adoption of energy-saving technologies.

This research also indicates that financial reasons, and to a much lesser extent, environmental concerns, are the primary motivators for energy conservation. While environmental concerns are often mentioned as reasons for adopting energy-efficient practices, it is clear that in Curaçao, financial considerations are considered more important. This emphasizes the importance of presenting energy-saving projects in ways that focus on economic benefits, especially for households with limited financial resources. Additionally, by informing users about their current consumption habits and suggesting more efficient practices [61]. This research further highlights that despite the potential for substantial energy savings and cost reductions, most households in Curaçao remain unaware of the various energy-efficient alternatives available to them.

5.2. Policy Implications

The results of this study also have some specific policy implications in terms of public awareness campaigns [15], the adoption of energy-efficient building regulations [34], and financial measures such as tax incentives, subsidies, and regulatory approaches for energy efficiency [62].

Public campaign programs are needed to make households in Curaçao aware of a variety of energy-saving appliances, such as PV panels, intelligent power bars, time switches, and motion sensors. This is in addition to inverter air conditioners, inverter refrigerators, and LED lamps, of which the cost-saving benefits are already better known. The energy-efficiency-promoting campaigns may include the publication and distribution of simple and well-illustrated manuals, promotion campaigns on TV, radio, and in social media, as well as information meetings in community centers.

Significant energy savings can also be achieved by implementing passive building design principles for houses in tropical areas [33,34]. Passive building designs will increase the internal comfort by facilitating natural ventilation through windows and doors and by protecting against direct, bright sunlight. This will also decrease the energy used by air conditioners. From a policy perspective, it is recommended to adapt the existing building regulations in Curaçao by making use of passive building design principles mandatory for all new constructions.

Important barriers to adopting energy-efficient technologies include a lack of capital and insufficient information among residents, as well as households perceiving the upfront costs as too high [62]. House owners may also prioritize factors other than energy efficiency when making decisions, may lack knowledge about energy efficiency, or may be resistant to change. Therefore, policymakers need to create and implement financial measures that encourage the residential sector to become more energy efficient by removing these barriers. Examples of effective policies include import duties and subsidies that significantly enhance the demand for energy-efficient appliances.

Import duties and subsidies that significantly boost the demand for energy-efficient appliances are examples of effective policies [63–65]. Additionally, regulatory approaches such as bans, mandates, or price regulations have also proven effective. For instance, Cao et al. [66] conclude that banning incandescent lamps is one of the most effective policies for promoting the adoption of more energy-efficient lighting technologies.

Implementing these types of energy policies will not only increase energy awareness among residents in Curaçao but may consequently also lead to significant energy savings in households.

5.3. Future Research

The limitations of this study provide several avenues for future research. First, it is advised to extend the conducted survey and the estimation of appliance energy use by conducting field studies in order to derive more accurate and comprehensive methods for measuring appliance consumption and to capture actual usage patterns more effectively.

Given the noted importance of implementing energy policy measures that are focused on increasing energy awareness among energy users, we suggest monitoring the progress in developing and implementing energy policy measures and evaluating the relative effectiveness of these policy measures on a regular basis.

Curaçao's economy can be described as a relatively high-income economy within the Caribbean, featuring a well-developed infrastructure, particularly in the tourism and financial services sectors. Additionally, activities linked to the port of Willemstad, including shipping and international trade, make significant contributions to the economy. To achieve a more comprehensive understanding of energy use, behavior, and efficiency across the Caribbean region, it is advisable to expand this research to include other countries with lower living standards. It is anticipated that countries such as Cuba, Haiti, and Venezuela will have fewer electrical appliances and less advanced technology. Consequently, households in the Caribbean with lower standards of living may be expected to use less energy and demonstrate a greater willingness to save energy.

6. Conclusions

This paper is one of the first to evaluate energy awareness, consumption, and saving opportunities among households in the Caribbean, using the island of Curaçao as a case study. Following an extensive literature review on energy use, behavior, and efficiency, a survey was conducted in Curaçao to gain insights into local energy practices and efficiency.

This study identified air conditioners, followed by electric cooking appliances and refrigerators, as the highest consumers of electrical energy in households. In a survey involving 382 households, about 91% of respondents reported taking measures to save energy. Cost savings, rather than environmental considerations, seem to be the primary motivation for energy-saving behaviors. The results also indicate that many households in Curaçao are largely unaware of the various energy-efficient options available to them for reducing costs.

The survey results also indicate a positive correlation between household income and the use of energy-efficient appliances. High-income respondents are better positioned to purchase these appliances, whereas low-income participants are more likely to engage in behaviors such as turning off appliances and lights when they are not in use. This study further indicated a clear income-based difference in the perception of energy-efficient appliance prices in Curaçao. A significant majority of low-income respondents view these prices as excessively high, while this perception diminishes notably among middle- and high-income groups.

Despite the higher cost of energy-efficient appliances, their usage in Curaçao has significantly increased over the past six years. Most households depend on familiar energy-saving devices, such as energy-efficient air conditioners and lamps, while remaining unaware of other potential energy-saving options, including smart power strips, inverter appliances, timers, motion sensors, and insulation. This lack of awareness will hinder the broader adoption of energy-saving practices and highlight the urgent need for targeted education and engagement initiatives. Decreasing energy consumption through behavioral changes can also play a role in the solution, but it is crucial to understand the factors that influence energy-saving behaviors.

This study also found that the majority of respondents in all three categories concurred that energy saving should be encouraged in Curaçao.

Based on the findings from the field study, recommendations are provided to enhance energy awareness, expand energy-saving opportunities, and ultimately reduce energy consumption.

Author Contributions: Conceptualization, R.R.B. and J.I.M.H.; Methodology, R.R.B. and J.I.M.H.; Validation, R.R.B.; Formal analysis, R.R.B.; Investigation, R.R.B.; Writing—original draft, R.R.B. and J.I.M.H.; Writing—review & editing, J.I.M.H.; Project administration, R.R.B. All authors have read and agreed to the published version of the manuscript.

Funding: This research received no external funding.

Data Availability Statement: The original contributions presented in the study are included in the article, further inquiries can be directed to the corresponding author.

Conflicts of Interest: The authors declare no conflict of interest.

Appendix A Survey Questions Energy Use by Households in Curaçao

1. How many people live in your household?
2. What is the total monthly income of your household?
3. Do you practice energy saving?

4. What motivates you to save energy?
5. What methods do you use to save energy?
6. Which appliances do you utilize?
7. How do you determine the cost of energy-efficient appliances?
8. Are you seeking additional information on energy conservation?

References

1. Van Oorschot, J.A.W.H.; Halman, J.I.M.; Hofman, E. The adoption of green modular innovations in the Dutch housebuilding sector. *J. Clean. Prod.* **2021**, *319*, 128524. [CrossRef]
2. Wiatros-Motyka, M. *Global Electricity Review 2023*; Ember: London, UK, 2023; 163p. Available online: https://ember-climate.org/app/uploads/2024/05/Report-Global-Electricity-Review-2024.pdf (accessed on 28 August 2024).
3. Smith, N.; Jones, A.; Brown, T. The Role of Public Awareness in Energy Conservation: A Comparative Study. *Glob. Environ. Chang.* **2020**, *30*, 115–127.
4. International Energy Agency. *Electricity 2024, Analysis and Forecast to 2026*; IEA: Paris, France, 2024; 170p. Available online: https://www.iea.org/reports/electricity-2024 (accessed on 30 August 2024).
5. Hassan, M.G.; Hirst, R.; Siemieniuch, c.; Zobaa, A.F. The impact of energy awareness on energy efficiency. *Int. J. Sustain. Eng.* **2009**, *2*, 284–297. [CrossRef]
6. Bülbül, H.; Büyükkeklik, A.; Topal, A.; Özoğlu, B. The relationship between environmental awareness, environmental behaviors, and carbon footprint in Turkish households. *Environ. Sci. Pollut. Res.* **2020**, *27*, 25009–25028. [CrossRef] [PubMed]
7. Li, X.; Zhang, D.; Zhang, T.; Ji, Q.; Lucey, B. Awareness, energy comsumption and pro-environmental choices of Chinese Households. *J. Clean. Prod.* **2020**, *279*, 123734. [CrossRef]
8. Kumar, P.; Caggiano, H.; Cuite, C.; Andrews, C.J.; Felder, F.A.; Shwom, R.; Floress, K.; Sonya Ahamed, S.; Schelly, C. Behaving or not? Explaining energy conservation via identity, values, and awareness in U.S. suburban homes. *Energy Res. Soc. Sci.* **2022**, *92*, 102805. [CrossRef]
9. Kuai, P.; Zhang, X.; Zhang, S.; Li, J. Environmental awareness and household enery saving of Chinese residents: Unity of knowing and doing or easier said than done? *J. Asian Econ.* **2022**, *82*, 101534. [CrossRef]
10. Rosak-Szyrocka, J.; Żywiolek, J. Qualitative analysis of household energy awareness in Poland. *Energies* **2022**, *15*, 2279. [CrossRef]
11. Clement, K.; Pardon, I.; Driessen, J. Standby power consumption in Belgium. In Proceedings of the 9th International Conference on Electrical Power Quality and Utilization, Barcelona, Spain, 9–11 October 2007; pp. 1–4. [CrossRef]
12. Bulbaai, R.; Halman, J.I.M. Standby energy consumption and saving potentials in the residential sector in tropical areas: The Caribbean island Curaçao as a case study. *Energy Effic.* **2023**, *16*, 88. [CrossRef]
13. Baidoo, A.N.A.; Danquah, J.A.; Nunoo, E.K.; Mariwah, S.; Boampong, G.N.; Twum, E.; Amankwah, E.; Nyametso, J.K. Households' energy conservation and efficiency awareness practices in the Cape Coast Metropolis of Ghana. *Discov. Sustain.* **2024**, *5*, 2. [CrossRef]
14. Gadenne, D.; Sharma, B.; Kerr, D.; Smith, T. The influence of consumers' environmental beliefs and attitudes on energy saving behviours. *Energy Policy* **2011**, *39*, 7684–7694. [CrossRef]
15. Owusu, P.A.; Asumadu-Sarkodie, S. A review of renewable energy sources, sustainability issues and climate change mitigation. *Cogent Eng.* **2016**, *3*, 1167990. [CrossRef]
16. *Directive (EU) 2023/1791*; European Parliament and of the Council of 13 September 2023 on Energy Efficiency and Amending Regulation (EU) 2023/955. European Union: Brussels, Belgium, 2023. Available online: http://data.europa.eu/eli/dir/2023/1791/oj (accessed on 15 July 2024).
17. Fischer, C. Feedback on household electricity consumption: A tool for saving energy? *Energy Effic.* **2008**, *1*, 79–104. [CrossRef]
18. Geelen, D.; Mugge, R.; Silvester, S. The use of apps to promote energy saving: A study of smart meter–related feedback in the Netherlands. *Energy Effic.* **2019**, *12*, 1635–1660. [CrossRef]
19. Casals, M.; Gangolells, M.; Macarulla, M.; Forcada, N.; Fuertes, A.; Jones, R.V. Assessing the effectiveness of gamification in reducing domestic energy consumption: Lessons learned from the EnerGAware project. *Energy Build.* **2020**, *210*, 109753. [CrossRef]
20. D'Oca, S.; Corgnati, S.P.; Buso, T. Smart meters and energy savings in Italy: Determining the effectiveness of persuasive communication in dwellings. *Energy Res. Soc. Sci.* **2014**, *3*, 131–142. [CrossRef]
21. Froehlich, J. Promoting Energy Efficient Behaviors in the Home through Feedback: The Role of HumanComputer Interaction. *Biometrika* **2009**, *73*, 13–22.
22. Heiskanen, E.; Johnson, M.; Robinson, S.; Vadovics, E.; Saastamoinen, M. Low-carbon communities as context for individual behavioural change. *Energy Policy* **2010**, *38*, 7586–7595. [CrossRef]
23. Dietz, T.; Gradner, G.T.; Gilligan, J.; Vandenbergh, M.P. Household actions can provide a behavioral wedge to rapidly reduce US carbon emissions. *Proc. Natl. Acad. Sci. USA* **2009**, *106*, 18452–18456. [CrossRef]
24. Wilson, C.; Dowlatabadi, H. Models of Decision Making and Residential Energy Use. *Annu. Rev. Environ. Resour.* **2007**, *32*, 69–203. [CrossRef]
25. Gyberg, P.; Palm, J. Influencing households' energy behaviour—How is this done and on what premises? *Energy Policy* **2009**, *37*, 2807–2813. [CrossRef]

26. Newell, R.G.; Raimi, D. Global Energy Outlook Comparison Methods: 2020 Update. Resources for the Future 2020. Report 20-06. Available online: https://media.rff.org/documents/Global_Energy_Outlook_Comparison_Methods_2020.pdf (accessed on 15 July 2024).
27. Brounen, D.; Kok, N.; Quigley, J.M. Residential energy use and conservation: Economics and Demographics. *Eur. Econ. Rev.* **2012**, *56*, 931–945. [CrossRef]
28. Pérez-Lombard, L.; Ortiz, J.; Pout, C. A review on buildings energy consumption information. *Energy Build.* **2008**, *40*, 394–398. [CrossRef]
29. De Almeida, A.; Fonseca, P.; Schlomann, B.; Feilberg, N. Characterization of the household electricity consumption in the EU, potential energy savings and specific policy recommendations. *Energy Build.* **2011**, *43*, 1884–1894. [CrossRef]
30. Darby, S. *The Effectiveness of Feedback on Energy Consumption*; Environmental Change Institute, University of Oxford: Oxford, UK, 2006.
31. Stankuniene, G. Energy saving in households: A systematic literature review. *Eur. J. Interdiscip. Stud.* **2021**, *13*, 45–57.
32. Tamas, R.; O'Brien, W.; Santana Quintero, M. Developing Thermostat User Mental Models to Inform Energy-Saving Design. In *Environmental Science and Engineering, Proceedings of the 5th International Conference on Building Energy and Environment, COBEE, Montreal, QC, Canada, 25–29 July 2022*; Wang, L.L., Ge, H., Zhai, Z.J., Qi, D., Ouf, M., Sun, C., Wang, D., Eds.; Springer: Singapore, 2023. [CrossRef]
33. Sadineni, B.; Srikanth, M.; Boehm, R.F. Passive building energy savings: A review of building envelope components. *Renew. Sustain. Energy Rev.* **2011**, *15*, 3617–3631. [CrossRef]
34. Bulbaai, R.; Halman, J.I.M. Energy-efficient building design for a tropical climate: A field study on the Caribbean island Curaçao. *Sustainability* **2021**, *13*, 13274. [CrossRef]
35. Da Silva, M.G.; Zilles, E.L.; Rüther, R. The Impact of Photovoltaic Systems on Household Energy Consumption. *Energy Build.* **2012**, *50*, 90–96. [CrossRef]
36. Oorschot, J.A.W.H.; Hofman, E.; Halman, J.I.M. Upscaling large scale deep renovation in the Dutch residential sector: A case study. *Energy Procedia* **2016**, *96*, 386–403. [CrossRef]
37. Gianfrate, V.; Piccardo, C.; Longo, D.; Giachetta, A. Rethinking social housing: Behavioural patterns and technological innovations. *Sustain. Cities Soc.* **2017**, *33*, 102–112. [CrossRef]
38. Elsharkawy, H.; Rutherford, P. Energy-efficient retrofit of social housing in the UK: Lessons learned from a Community Energy Saving Programme (CESP) in Nottingham. *Energy Build.* **2018**, *172*, 295–306. [CrossRef]
39. Chomać-Pierzecka, E.; Rogozińska-Mitrut, J.; Różycka, M.; Sobón, D.; Stasiak, J. Energy innovation for individual consumers in Poland—Analysis of potential and evaluation of practical applications in selected areas. *Energies* **2023**, *16*, 5766. [CrossRef]
40. Vasseur, V.; Backhaus, J.; Fehres, S.; Goldschmeding, F. Capabilities and social practices: A combined conceptual framework for domestic energy use. *J. Clean. Prod.* **2024**, *455*, 142668. [CrossRef]
41. Gatersleben, B.; Steg, L.; Vlek, C. Measurement and determinants of environmentally significant consumer bhavior. *Environ. Behav.* **2002**, *34*, 335–362. [CrossRef]
42. Schultz, P.W.; Nolan, J.M.; Cialdini, R.B.; Goldstein, N.J.; Griskevicius, V. The constructive, destructive, and reconstructive power of social norms. *Psychol. Sci.* **2007**, *18*, 429–434. [CrossRef]
43. Nolan, J.M.; Schultz, P.W.; Cialdini, R.B.; Goldstein, N.J.; Griskevicius, V. Normative social influence is underdetected. *Pers. Soc. Psychol. Bull.* **2008**, *34*, 913–923. [CrossRef]
44. Baldini, M.; Trivella, A.; Wente, J.W. The impact of socioeconomic and behavioural factors for purchasing energy efficient household appliances: A case study for Denmark. *Energy Policy* **2018**, *120*, 503–513. [CrossRef]
45. Boardman, B. *Fixing Fuel Poverty: Challenges and Solutions*; Routledge: London, UK, 2013.
46. Chen, C.-F.; Xu, X.; Adua, L.; Briggs, M.; Nelson, H. Exploring the factors that use energy intensity across low-, middle-, and high-income households in the United States. *Energy Policy* **2022**, *168*, 113071. [CrossRef]
47. Dietz, T.; Stern, P.C.; Weber, E.U. Reducing carbon-based energy consumption through changes in household behavior. *Daedalus J. Am. Acad. Arts Sci.* **2013**, *142*, 78–89. [CrossRef]
48. Central Bureau of Statistics Curacao. (n.d.). Available online: www.cbs.cw (accessed on 8 December 2015).
49. Meteorological Department Curaçao. *Climatological Summary*; Meteoroligical Department Curaçao: Willemstad, Curaçao, 2018.
50. Szolnoki, G.; Hoffmann, D. Online, face-to-face and telephone surveys—Comparing different sampling methods in wine consumer research. *Wine Econ. Policy* **2013**, *2*, 57–66. [CrossRef]
51. *Housing in Europe—2023 Interactive Edition*; Eurostat: Luxembourg, 2023. Available online: https://ec.europa.eu/eurostat/web/interactive-publications/housing-2023 (accessed on 8 April 2024).
52. Owen, A.L.; Videras, J. Civic cooperation, pro-environment attitudes, and behavioral intentions. *Ecol. Econ.* **2006**, *58*, 814–829. [CrossRef]
53. Ahmed, M.S.; Mohamed, A.; Homod, R.Z.; Shareef, H.; Khalid, K. Awareness on energy management in residential buildings: A case study in Kajang and Putrajaya. *J. Eng. Sci. Technol.* **2017**, *2*, 1280–1294.
54. Hori, S.; Kondo, K.; Nogata, D.; Ben, H. The determinants of household energy-saving behavior: Survey and comparison in five major Asian cities. *Energy Policy* **2013**, *52*, 354–362. [CrossRef]
55. Yue, T.; Long, R.; Chen, H. Factors influencing energy-saving behavior of urban households in jiangsu province. *Energy Policy* **2013**, *62*, 665–675. [CrossRef]

56. Dennehy, E.; Howley, M. *Energy in the Residential Sector 2013*; Sustainable Energy Authority of Ireland: Dublin, Ireland, 2013; 104p. Available online: http://www.seai.ie/publications/Energy-in-the-Residential-Sector-2013.pdf (accessed on 8 April 2024).
57. Bulbaai, R.R. Toward 100% Sustainable Energy Production and a Structural Decrease in Energy Demand: Curacao, as a Case Study of Small Island Developing States. Ph.D. Thesis, University of Twente, Enschede, The Netherlands, 2019. [CrossRef]
58. Ince, D.; Vredenbrug, H.; Liu, X. Drivers and inhibitors of renewable energy: A qualitative and quantitative study of the Caribbean. *Energy Policy* **2016**, *98*, 700–712. [CrossRef]
59. Chen, R.; Steinbuks, J. Assessing the potential or energy efficiency improvements in Latin America and Caribbean. *Energy Policy* **2024**, *92*, 114224. [CrossRef]
60. Gajdzik, B.; Jaciow, M.; Wolniak, R.; Wolny, R.; Grebski, W.W. Energy behaviors of prosumers in example of Polish households. *Energies* **2023**, *16*, 3186. [CrossRef]
61. Bonino, D.; Corno, F.; De Russis, L. Home energy consumption feedback: A user survey. *Energy Build.* **2012**, *47*, 383–393. [CrossRef]
62. Hesselink, L.X.W.; Chappin, E.J.L. Adoption of energy efficient technologies by households—Barriers, policies and agent-based modelling studies. *Renew. Sustain. Energy Rev.* **2019**, *99*, 29–41. [CrossRef]
63. Galarraga, I.; Abadie, L.M.; Kallbekken, S. Designing efficient schemes for promoting energy-efficient appliances: A new methodology and a case study for Spain. *Energy Policy* **2016**, *90*, 24–36. [CrossRef]
64. Bertoldi, P. Policies for energy conservation and sufficiency: Review of existing policies and recommendations for new and effective policies in OECD countries. *Energy Build.* **2022**, *262*, 112075. [CrossRef]
65. Shi, X. Application of best preactice for setting minimum energy efficiency standards in technically disadvantaged countries: Case study of air conditioners in Brunei Darussalam. *Appl. Energy* **2015**, *157*, 1–12. [CrossRef]
66. Cao, J.; Choi, C.H.; Zhao, F. Agent-based modeling of the adoption of high-efficiency lighting in the residential sector. *Sustain. Energy Technol. Assess.* **2017**, *19*, 70–78. [CrossRef]

energies

MDPI

Article

Utilizing Wastewater Tunnels as Thermal Reservoirs for Heat Pumps in Smart Cities

Fredrik Skaug Fadnes [1,2] and Mohsen Assadi [1,*]

1 Department of Energy and Petroleum, University of Stavanger, 4021 Stavanger, Norway; fredrik.s.fadnes@uis.no
2 Department of Energy and Smart Technology, Norconsult AS, 1338 Sandvika, Norway
* Correspondence: mohsen.assadi@uis.no

Abstract: The performance of heat pump systems for heating and cooling heavily relies on the thermal conditions of their reservoirs. This study introduces a novel thermal reservoir, detailing a 2017 project where the Municipality of Stavanger installed a heat exchanger system on the wall of a main wastewater tunnel beneath the city center. It provides a comprehensive account of the system's design, installation, and performance, and presents an Artificial Neural Network (ANN) model that predicts heat pump capacity, electricity consumption, and outlet temperature across seasonal variations in wastewater temperatures. By integrating domain knowledge with the ANN, this study demonstrates the model's capability to detect anomalies in heat pump operations effectively. The network also confirms the consistent performance of the heat exchangers from 2020 to 2024, indicating minimal fouling impacts. This study establishes wastewater heat exchangers as a safe, effective, and virtually maintenance-free solution for heat extraction and rejection.

Keywords: wastewater heat pump; ANN; monitoring and fault detection; fouling; COP; SPF

1. Introduction

As urban populations grow, with projections indicating that nearly 70% of the world will reside in cities by 2050, the impact of urban areas on global environmental challenges becomes increasingly significant [1]. Cities account for about 70% of the global CO_2 emissions and are major economic centers, contributing 80% of the world's Gross Domestic Product (GDP). This positions them as key players in efforts to reduce carbon footprints.

As global energy and climate targets highlight the need for energy efficiency and renewable energy production [2], the International Energy Agency (IEA) identifies heat pumps as a key technology for thermal energy production in buildings [3]. Heat pumps enable the simultaneous production of heating and cooling [4], meeting thermal demands with minimal energy input [5]. However, compared to conventional heaters and chillers, heat pump systems exhibit increased complexity, requiring careful planning and management of multiple temperature settings. For building owners, acquiring a heat pump involves not only understanding its advanced mechanisms but also integrating it successfully with the heat sources and sinks [6].

In urban environments, identifying suitable thermal reservoirs for heat pumps presents multiple challenges [7]. Ambient air, the most widely used option globally [8], is favored for its cheap and simple installation. However, these systems often underperform during peak demand periods, especially in cold climates [8], leading to both high electricity consumption for the heat pump itself and costly peak load heating [9]. Alternatives such as geothermal boreholes and seawater offer more reliable performance and efficiency [10] but are significantly more expensive to install [11]. The installation can be complicated by local geographical and environmental conditions, such as proximity to suitable seawater depths [7] or the thermal properties of the ground [8]. Additionally, the land footprint requirement for boreholes makes them more difficult to install in retrofitting projects within urban areas [10]. While geothermal boreholes and seawater serve as excellent thermal reservoirs where available, exploring alternatives is essential as the urgency to meet climate targets intensifies.

Acknowledging wastewater as a renewable heat source, the EU Directive 2018/2001 highlights its potential to significantly meet heating demands throughout Europe [12]. Wastewater systems, which are fundamental components of urban infrastructure [13], can serve as stable thermal reservoirs for heat pump systems [14]. This approach is exemplified by Norway's largest heat pump system in Oslo, which utilizes wastewater to produce district heating [15]. Recent advancements in heat exchanger technology simplify the installation of new wastewater systems, featuring prefabricated pipes with integrated heat exchangers and retrofitting existing wastewater tunnels with heat plate collectors [14].

In 2014, the Norwegian city of Stavanger joined the EU-funded Triangulum initiative under the Horizon 2020 framework, designed to demonstrate future solutions through the innovative integration of energy, mobility, and information technology [16]. This lighthouse project aimed to address societal challenges and enhance the sustainability of growing urban environments, marking the beginning of Stavanger's exploration of smart technology. As part of this initiative, the Municipality of Stavanger refurbished a thermal energy plant, installing heat pumps connected to the main municipal wastewater tunnel through heat exchanger plates. A brine solution circulates between the heat exchangers and the heat pumps, transferring low-temperature heat between the reservoir and the evaporator [17]. This paper offers valuable insights into the design and operational phases of the energy plant and wastewater heat exchanger system, presenting knowledge on an alternative to traditional thermal reservoirs such as air, geothermal, and seawater. Among the 114 wastewater heat exchanger installations produced by UHRIG between 2007 and 2023, this 360 kW system is the only one installed in Norway and is the twelfth largest in terms of capacity [18]. Figure 1 shows the number of installations from UHRIG sorted by country, along with the minimum, maximum, and median design capacities for both heating and cooling. Notably, while all systems are designed for heat extraction, 25 of them are also utilized for cooling. The capacities range from 2 kW to 1200 kW for heating and from 17 kW to 6000 kW for cooling, demonstrating the wide applicability and scalability of these systems.

Type	Country	Number of installations	Minimum [kW]	Median [kW]	Maximum [kW]
Heating	Austria	6	22	174	1 200
Cooling	Austria	3	275	530	6 000
Heating	Belgium	1		177	
Cooling	Belgium	1		260	
Heating	Denmark	2	22	29	36
Cooling	Denmark	0	-	-	-
Heating	France	18	50	140	450
Cooling	France	1		200	
Heating	Germany	81	2	108	1 000
Cooling	Germany	19	17	250	1 000
Heating	Netherlands	3	23	76	120
Cooling	Netherlands	0	-	-	-
Heating	Norway	1		360	
Cooling	Norway	1		440	
Heating	Switzerland	2	50	60	69
Cooling	Switzerland	0	-	-	-

Figure 1. Key figures for the 114 systems installed by UHRIG from 2007 to 2023.

Two review articles serve as foundational introductions to the knowledge of wastewater heat exchanger technologies within urban energy frameworks. In 2015, Culha et al. published a key review of wastewater heat exchangers, emphasizing their potential for heating and cooling applications. They identify fouling and corrosion as significant challenges and recommend focusing on bio-fouling prevention and performance optimization in future research [14]. In a comprehensive review, Nagpal et al. (2021) explored the technological and economic benefits of wastewater heat recovery at scales ranging from individual components to complete wastewater treatment plants. They discuss the temperature and flow dynamics of wastewater systems, the environmental impacts, and the legal complexities of wastewater heat recovery. Focusing on component, building, and wastewater network levels, they present the current technological landscape while calling for more in-depth economic analyses and improved integration methods for these systems [12].

An ideal location for heat recovery from wastewater is at the wastewater treatment plant itself. Bartnicki et al. (2022) performed an analysis of the potential for heat recovery in wastewater treatment facilities and developed comprehensive guidelines for selecting the optimal site and system for heat recovery [19]. Similarly, Kowalik et al. explored the feasibility of heat extraction from wastewater at a small treatment plant in Świętokrzyskie, Poland, examining monthly temperature fluctuations and the amount of heat that could be extracted by a heat pump [20]. In addition, Łokietek investigated the integration of heat pump systems at the Mokrawica wastewater treatment plant in Poland across various stages of the treatment process [21]. Moreover, Cecconet et al. (2019) presented a study assessing wastewater heat recovery for heating and cooling a building in Brno, Czech Republic, showing the potential for a 59% energy reduction compared to a conventional grid-connected heating and cooling system. A year-long study of historical wastewater data revealed that the temperature changes from the heat recovery had a negligible impact on downstream wastewater treatment biological processes [22].

While wastewater treatment plants offer clear opportunities for heat recovery, the concept can also be applied across urban areas. Aprile et al. (2019) examined the efficiency and economic feasibility of a district heating and cooling network in Milan that combines sewage heat pumps with a photovoltaic system. Their study found a levelized cost of 79 €/MWh for the combined system, substantially lower than the 96 €/MWh for a comparable system using independent reversible air-to-water heat pumps. They highlighted the economic advantages of integrating photovoltaics-generated electricity with sewage heat recovery, despite higher initial and maintenance costs [23]. Xu et al. investigated the use of a sewage source heat pump and micro-cogeneration system in a large hotel, employing TRNSYS simulations to devise an economical operation strategy tailored for hot water loads. Their findings revealed a 37% decrease in peak power consumption, lower operating costs with a six-year payback period, and significant emission reduction [24]. Chen et al. developed a model to assess urban wastewater heat recovery by integrating sewage characteristics and building heat demands. Tested in Osaka, the model recommended focusing on larger buildings and clusters for effective heat recovery implementation [25].

Fouling in wastewater heat pump plants, frequently highlighted in academic research, occurs when unwanted materials such as biological growths and scale accumulate on heat exchanger surfaces. This accumulation can degrade the performance of the heat pumps, leading to increased operational and maintenance costs and significant downtime [26]. Several factors influence fouling rates, including the properties and flow of the fluid, the condition of the heat exchanger plates, temperature variations, and periods of non-operation [27]. In a 2023 study, Zhuang et al. investigated a raw sewage source heat pump system in Qingdao, China, implemented in a 28,000 m^2 office building. Over the year, the sewage temperature fluctuated between 12 °C and 24 °C. The system demonstrated substantial energy savings compared to traditional coal-fired boilers and conventional chillers. However, fouling in the heat exchangers reduced their effectiveness by about 50%, significantly impacting system performance and increasing maintenance requirements [28].

A research initiative, based on data from a Danish district heating system, explored predictive maintenance strategies for sewage heat exchangers in a two-stage ammonia heat pump system [27]. Initially, fouling management depended on irregular chemical cleanings based on operator experience rather than on systematic analysis. In this study, machine learning methods, specifically linear regression and radial basis function networks, were employed to predict the progression of fouling and its impact on system efficiency. Integrating these predictive models with operational data and a thermodynamic model allowed for more accurate maintenance scheduling [27]. Wang et al. utilized a two-layer Long Short-Term Memory neural network, enhanced with an attention mechanism, to predict fouling thickness in heat exchangers [29]. As in the study from Denmark, the goal of this research was to facilitate maintenance by ensuring that fouling remains within safe operational thresholds. Comparing thermal reservoirs, Kim et al. found that ground-source heat pumps consistently outperformed sewage water-source heat pumps, primarily due to fouling issues in the latter [30]. Their study also presented a predictive model from long-term operational data, which indicated potential improvements in the sewage heat pumps through targeted fouling reduction.

Contrary to the experience presented in the existing literature, fouling was not considered a major concern during the design and installation phase of the heat exchanger system investigated in this study. This assumption was based on two key factors: (a) the heat exchangers were designed with overcapacity, implying that a newly installed system would have superior heat transfer capabilities compared to operational systems [31]; and (b) historical observations by the wastewater tunnel operators suggested that the high flow rates were effective in preventing significant accumulation of dirt on the tunnel walls at the installation point.

Within the paradigm of smart cities and smart technologies, capturing and utilizing data are essential for technological advancement. The Organization for Economic Co-operation and Development (OECD) defines smart cities as "cities that leverage digitalization and engage stakeholders to improve people's well-being and build more inclusive, sustainable, and resilient societies" [32]. In such cities, digitalization can significantly enhance the energy efficiency of heating and cooling networks through optimized performance and continuous monitoring [1]. The thermal energy plant in Stavanger is ideally positioned within this framework, equipped with a comprehensive sensor setup for collection of temperature and pressure, as well as thermal and electrical energy meters that track all energy flows in the system. Consequently, this project is not just "smart" due to its utilization of wastewater as a thermal reservoir but also through the strategic integration of the measured data into the local academic community's research on thermal energy and data utilization [33].

Artificial Intelligence (AI) and Machine Learning (ML) are core concepts within the smart technology framework. A review of recent advances in ML approaches for heat exchanger modeling concluded that Artificial Neural Networks (ANNs) were predominant, favored for their high prediction accuracy and robust processing capabilities. Notably, ANNs have featured in 56% of the surveyed literature [34]. The versatility of ANNs makes them ideal for modeling various thermodynamic properties and operational conditions of heat exchangers. For instance, Starzec demonstrated that ANNs effectively predict the performance of greywater heat exchangers by leveraging data from experimental tests [35].

This study utilizes historical data collected from the Municipal Energy Plant in Stavanger to conduct a comprehensive review of its wastewater heat exchanger plate system and the heat pump operations. The paper adds to the field by presenting a detailed analysis of advanced technology in a large-scale operational context. It introduces an ANN model that evaluates the assumption of minimal fouling impact. The direct involvement of one of the authors in the system's planning and installation offers unique perspectives on the technology's benefits and challenges.

The paper is structured as follows: Section 2 introduces the energy plant case study, focusing on the wastewater heat exchangers. It further outlines the methodologies used to evaluate the operation of the heat pumps and heat exchangers, defining key performance parameters and relating them to the plant's energy meters and sensors. Additionally, the ANN modeling approach is detailed. Section 3 presents historical data on energy production, consumption, and the calculated performance parameters, along with the outcomes of applying the ANN model to a test dataset from the case study. The discussion in Section 4 reflects on the findings and broadens the discussion to a general evaluation of the use of wastewater as a thermal reservoir, drawing on experiences from this specific project. Here, the temperature of the wastewater is compared to ambient air to clearly illustrate the advantages of wastewater as a thermal reservoir. The paper concludes with a summary of the findings and recommendations for future research.

2. Materials and Methods

2.1. Case Study Description

The case study plant and the Municipality of Stavanger's contribution to Triangulum project, detailed in a previous work [33], are highly ambitious EU-funded thermal energy initiatives. Operational since 2017, the plant utilizes wastewater heat pumps and biogas boilers to produce 1.5–2.5 GWh of thermal energy annually, serving three municipal buildings with heating and cooling.

Wastewater was chosen as the most feasible thermal reservoir for the project after a thorough evaluation that balanced investment and operational costs, CO_2 emission reduction, and practical implementation. In the densely built urban areas, alternatives such as geothermal boreholes and seawater were deemed unsuitable due to challenging local conditions. Located approximately 100 m directly from the energy plant, a main municipal storm and sewage water tunnel run through rock beneath Stavanger, Norway. This nearly circular tunnel, about 4 km long and 3.3 m in diameter, was drilled through the bedrock in the 1980s. The tunnel starts at an elevation of 2.4 m above sea level and ends at 1.6 m, with the section near the plant being about 2.0 m high, located 7 m below the plant's floor.

The wastewater plate heat exchanger system was identified through an internet-based, non-academic search and subsequently developed in collaboration with a potential technology supplier. Key design parameters of this system include the wastewater flow rate and temperature, the geometry of the tunnel, and the specifications of the heat pump and brine system, such as flow rate and design temperature levels.

To determine the design flow rate, historical measurements of the wastewater flow rate were correlated with rainfall data, as illustrated in Figure 2. The figure represents daily values averaged over 24 h for flow, rainfall, and the resulting water height in the tunnel, based on data from 2015. From these historical data, the baseline wastewater flow rate for the heat exchanger design was set to 250 L per second. However, the data indicated that this flow rate can increase significantly following rainfall events. Historical wastewater temperatures had been observed to vary between +7 °C and +16 °C, and the design temperature levels for the brine system were set to +1 °C at the inlet and +5 °C at the outlet of the heat exchangers in heating mode. To calculate the brine flow rate required to achieve the 360 kW design heat extraction, the following formula was used [36]:

$$\dot{Q} = \dot{m} \times c_p \times (T_{out} - T_{in}), \quad (1)$$

where $\dot{Q}$ (in kW) represents the net rate of heat transfer from the wastewater to the heat pump brine, or vice versa, $\dot{m}$ (in kg/s) is the mass flow rate of the heat pump brine, c_p (in kJ/kg·K), is the specific heat capacity of the heat pump brine, here specified for MEG20 (a 20% solution of Monoethylene Glycol), and T_{in} and T_{out} (in K), are the temperatures of the heat pump brine entering and exiting the heat exchangers, respectively.

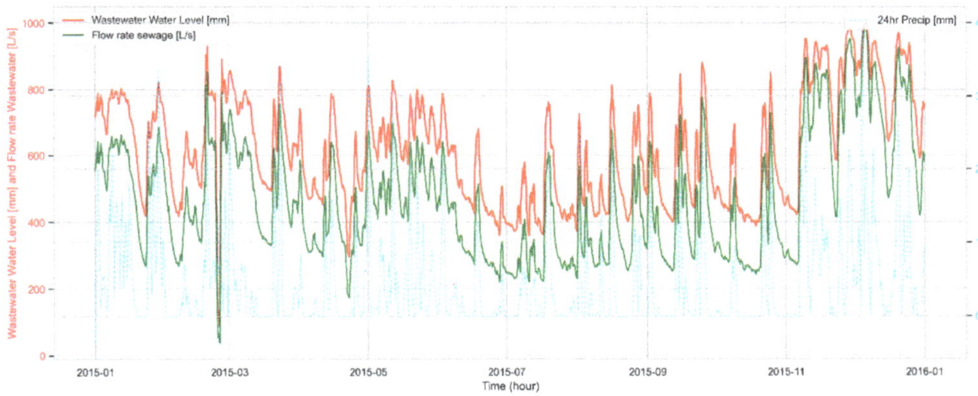

Figure 2. Daily averages of flow, rainfall, and water height in the tunnel (2015). Based on data provided by the municipality of Stavanger.

Through a public procurement process, several European suppliers were invited to submit their proposals and project costs based on the specified design parameters. Given that the tunnel is sealed during wastewater operations and the installation point is far from the nearest entry (see Section 4 for details), the municipality requested a maintenance-free system. A team consisting of Dansk Kloak RenoveringsTeknik [37] and UHIRG [17] was selected to install UHRIG's custom-built stainless steel heat exchanger system, named Therm-Liner, directly on the tunnel wall. The Therm-Liner system, characterized by its lack of moving parts and absence of electrical components, minimizes maintenance needs.

The final configuration of the heat exchanger system, as shown in Figure 3, included 108 heat exchanger plates, each weighing 100 kg and measuring 1.0 m in length, shaped according to the design sketch. To ensure equal distribution of the brine fluid across all heat exchangers, the return pipe was reversed.

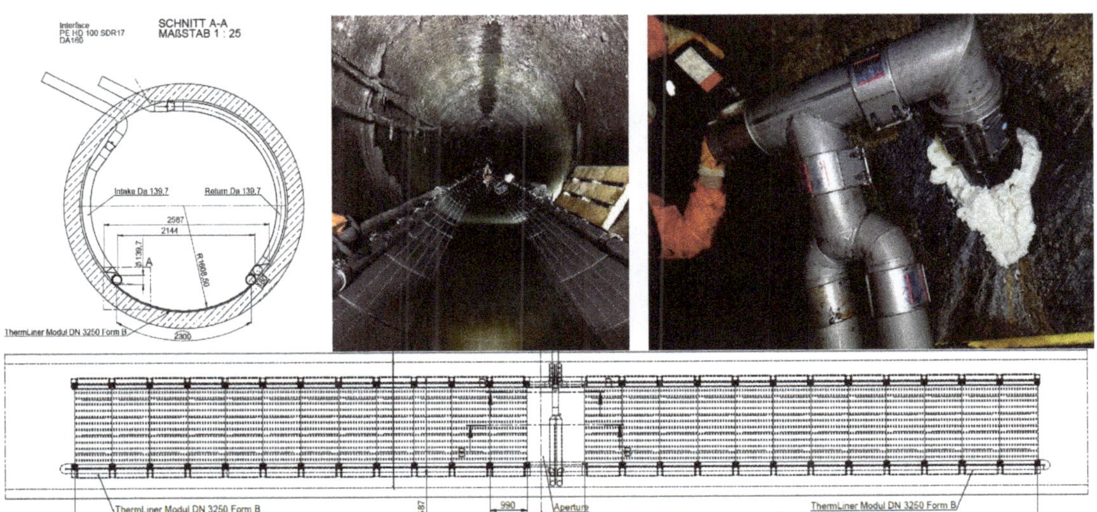

Figure 3. (**Top left**) design sketch of the heat exchanger system showing a cross-sectional view. (**Top center** and **right**) photographs taken during the system installation. (**Bottom**) overhead design sketch of the system layout above the tunnel floor. Photos by Uhrig/Municipality of Stavanger.

Three tunnels were drilled through the mountain to connect the energy plant with the wastewater tunnel: two are used for the supply and return of energy brine pipes, and one houses utilities such as fiber cables and a temperature sensor for monitoring wastewater temperature.

Figure 4 presents an aerial view diagram of the energy plant building and its connections to the wastewater tunnel. The red and blue lines show the heating and cooling distribution pipes from the plant to neighboring buildings, while the brown line approximates the location of the wastewater tunnel. The solid green line indicates the tunnels and pipes from the plant to the wastewater, and the dashed green line denotes the buildings included in the project. In Section 4, further elaboration on challenges during the planning and installation phases is given.

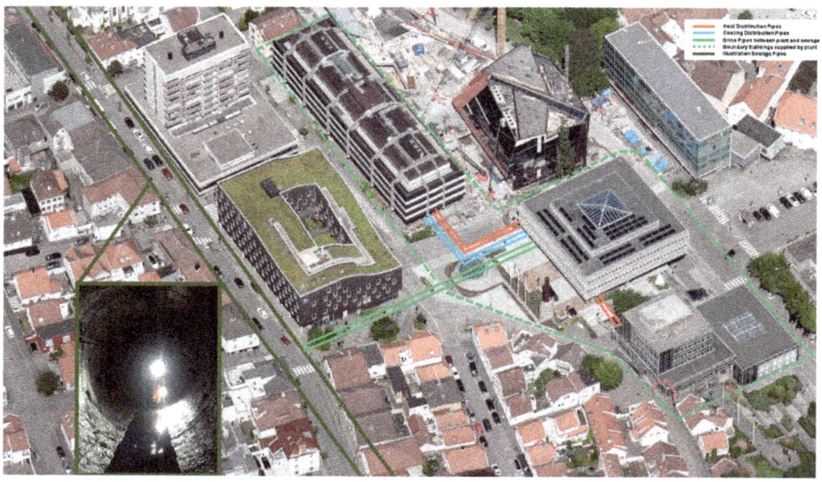

Figure 4. Thermal energy plant and surrounding buildings in relation to the wastewater tunnel.

The main design targets for the project related to wastewater heat pumps are presented in Table 1 [33]:

Table 1. Annual design targets heat pump system in study case.

Indicator	Target Value
Heat Production Heat Pumps [kWh/yr]	1,692,000
Electricity Consumption for Heating [kWh/yr]	483,000
Seasonal Coefficient of Performance Heating *	3.5
Heat Extraction at Evaporator [kWh/yr]	1,209,000
Cooling Production [kWh/yr]	187,000
Electricity Consumption for Cooling [kWh/yr]	18,700
Seasonal Coefficient of Performance Cooling *	10.0
Heat Rejection at Condenser [kWh/yr]	205,700
Gas Boiler Contribution Peak Load Heating [kWh/yr]	66,000

* Defined in next subchapter.

2.2. *Methodology for Evaluating the Performance of the Heat Pumps and Wastewater Heat Exchangers*

The primary goal of this evaluation was to investigate the long-term performance of the heat pumps and wastewater heat exchangers while identifying any short-term issues that suggest opportunities for improvement.

Historical operational data were collected and processed to calculate the key performance parameters. Tables summarizing several years of operational data were compared against the design of the targets. Duration curves were developed to detail the thermal energy production, including contributions from wastewater heat, electricity used for compressors, gas for boilers, and recovered heat from cooling production. Section 4 presents a statistical analysis of key parameters, along with a series of scatter plots from the two heat pumps, to visualize relationships and performance trends.

While cooling production and seasonal cooling parameters were calculated in this study, the detailed analysis of heat pump operation excludes the cooling mode. This exclusion is due to the relatively minor contribution of cooling to the overall thermal energy production and the challenges presented by rapid ON-OFF operation cycles. For further discussion on the cooling production, readers are referred to previous work [33].

2.2.1. System Design and Relevant Sensors

Figure 5 illustrates a schematic of the integrated system. The system consists of two heat pumps, tagged as IK001 and IK002, connected in series on the condenser side and in parallel on the evaporator side. Both heat pumps have a nominal heat capacity of 250 kW, with four semi-hermetic reciprocating compressors, two of which are equipped with capacity control to manage load demands effectively. The design capacity allows for a high base load heat contribution and meets the maximum cooling demand. The machines have two operational modes to adapt to varying thermal demands.

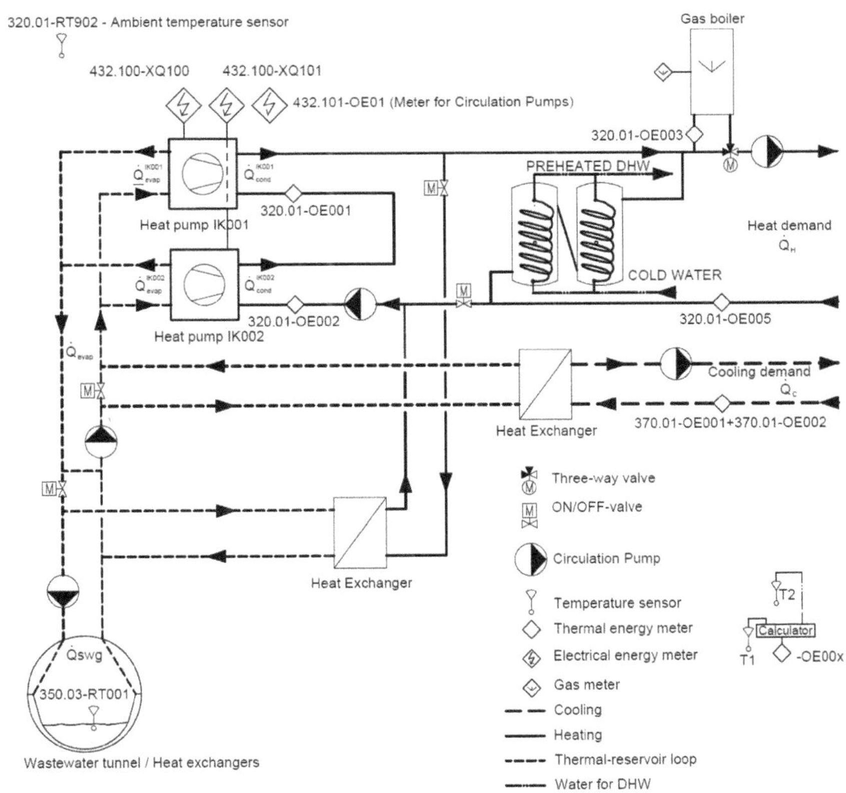

Figure 5. Schematic of the energy plant system with relevant sensors and meters.

In heating mode, the operation is controlled by outlet temperature setpoints on the condenser water side, with the first heat pump in the series set to operate at a temperature that is 5K lower than the second one. The heat pumps are connected to two accumulator tanks on the condenser side, serving as a zero-pressure junction between the heat pumps and the heat distribution loop. A gas boiler acts as the peak load and backup heating unit. Low-temperature heat is primarily extracted from the wastewater, while also utilizing any excess heat from simultaneous cooling production.

Cooling mode is defined based on a general assumption, that there is no demand for heating in this mode. The heat pumps are managed by outlet temperature setpoints at each evaporator, normally set equal to 10 °C. Excess heat from the cooling production is rejected to the wastewater via the condenser and a rejection heat exchanger. Despite the assumption of no heating demand, the gas boiler can be activated to provide heating. In both modes, the flow rates across each condenser and evaporator are close to constant.

All sensors utilized to monitor system performance are presented in Figure 5. Thermal energy meters are installed at each condenser, at the gas boiler, and within the heat and cooling distribution systems. Each thermal energy meter is equipped with a flow meter and two calibrated temperature sensors. Additionally, three meters are installed for measurement of electricity consumption: one at each heat pump condenser and one for other electrical equipment, primarily circulation pumps.

2.2.2. Data Capture

Data for this analysis were obtained from the thermal energy plant's control system, Citech Scada [38], covering the period from September 2020 to May 2024. These data were manually captured at varying points in time, with a resolution varying from 5 to 60 min. To ensure analytical consistency, data recorded at five-minute intervals were aggregated into 60 min mean values. For the performance evaluation, only data from two full years, 2022 and 2023, were available and used.

2.2.3. Performance Parameters

In this section, key evaluation parameters based on the energy meters shown in Figure 5 are defined. These parameters establish the baseline for all evaluations conducted in this work. In the analysis, both instantaneous values and accumulated data were examined. Instantaneous values were represented by hourly averages.

The Coefficient of Performance (COP) is a primary performance measure for the heat pump, indicating its performance by comparing the ratio of heating or cooling output to electrical energy consumed [39]. The heat pump can operate in either heating or cooling mode, each affecting the COP calculation. For heating and cooling, the COP is determined as follows:

$$\mathrm{COP}_{\mathrm{heat}} = \frac{\dot{Q}_{cond}}{\dot{W}_{hp}} \tag{2}$$

$$\mathrm{COP}_{\mathrm{cool}} = \frac{\dot{Q}_{evap}}{\dot{W}_{hp}} = \mathrm{EER} \tag{3}$$

where $\dot{Q}_{evap}$ is the heat extracted at the evaporator, $\dot{Q}_{cond}$ is the heat output at the condenser and $\dot{W}_{hp}$ is the electrical input to the heat pump, all measured in kWh/h. The cooling COP is also known as the Energy Efficiency Ratio (EER). When the system operates in heating mode, it may produce both heating and cooling simultaneously, utilizing low-temperature excess heat from cooling as a heat source. If the cooling demand is lower than the heat extracted at the evaporator, the total COP of the heat pump system is defined as follows:

$$\mathrm{COP}_{\mathrm{tot}} = \frac{\dot{Q}_{cond} + \dot{Q}_{cool}}{\dot{W}_{hp}}, \tag{4}$$

where $\dot{Q}_{cool}$ is the actual cooling demand, measured within the cooling distribution system. In cooling mode, all excess heat produced at the condenser is rejected to the wastewater.

Since there is no thermal energy meter on the evaporator side of the system, the analysis relies on the following well-known simplification to estimate the cooling production at the evaporators:

$$\dot{Q}_{evap} = \dot{Q}_{cond} - \dot{W}_{hp}, \tag{5}$$

This formula is based on the premise that the heat removed at the evaporator can be calculated by subtracting the work done by the heat pump from the heat rejected at the condenser. This is a common practice in thermodynamic calculations where direct measurements are not available [39].

The following energy meters are utilized to describe the system's heating and cooling production:

- Heat production is measured by the heat distribution loop energy meter, $\dot{Q}_{heat}$ 320.01-OE005.
- Cooling production is measured by the sum of the cooling distribution loop energy meters, $\dot{Q}_{cool} = \text{370.01-OE001} + \text{370.01-OE002}$.

To calculate the COP and EER for the heat pumps, the following configurations of energy meters are utilized:

$$\text{COP}_{\text{heat}}^{\text{IK001}} = \frac{\text{320.01-OE001}}{\text{432.100-XQ100}}, \ \text{EER}_{\text{cool}}^{\text{IK001}} = \frac{\text{320.01-OE001-432.100-XQ100}}{\text{432.100-XQ100}},$$

$$\text{COP}_{\text{heat}}^{\text{IK002}} = \frac{\text{320.01-OE002}}{\text{432.100-XQ101}}, \text{EER}_{\text{cool}}^{\text{IK002}} = \frac{\text{320.01-OE002-432.100-XQ101}}{\text{432.100-XQ101}},$$

$$\text{COP}_{\text{heat}}^{\text{heat pumps}} = \frac{\text{320.01-OE001} + \text{320.01-OE002}}{\text{432.100-XQ100} + \text{432.100-XQ101}},$$

$$EER_{cooling}^{heat\ pumps} = \frac{\text{370.01-OE001} + \text{370.01-OE002}}{\text{432.100-XQ100} + \text{432.100-XQ101}},$$

$$\text{COP}_{\text{total}}^{\text{heat mode}} = \frac{\text{320.01-OE001} + \text{320.01-OE002} + \text{370.01-OE001} + \text{370.01-OE002}}{\text{432.100-XQ100} + \text{432.100-XQ101}},$$

The heat extracted at the evaporators is estimated using Equation (5) and the following energy meter combinations:

$$\dot{Q}_{evap}^{IK001} = \text{320.01-OE001-432.100-XQ100}$$

$$\dot{Q}_{evap}^{IK002} = \text{320.01-OE002-432.100-XQ101}$$

$$\dot{Q}_{evap} = \dot{Q}_{evap}^{IK001} + \dot{Q}_{evap}^{IK002} \tag{6}$$

In heat mode, the heat pumps operate to meet the temperature setpoints at the condensers. However, there may still be a demand for cooling, in which case any excess heat is diverted to the evaporator. This process is known as free cooling. Free cooling is prioritized over extracting heat from the wastewater; therefore, the wastewater heat extraction process is calculated as follows:

$$\dot{Q}_{ww} = \dot{Q}_{evap} - \dot{Q}_{cool}, \tag{7}$$

and using the energy meters, the wastewater heat extraction is determined from:

$$\begin{aligned}\dot{Q}_{ww} &= (\text{320.01-OE001} + \text{320.01-OE002}) - (\text{432.100-XQ100} + \text{432.100-XQ101}) \\ &\quad - (\text{370.01-OE001} + \text{370.01-OE002})\end{aligned}$$

In cooling mode, heat is rejected to the wastewater and calculated as follows:

$$\dot{Q}_{ww} = \text{320.01-OE001} + \text{320.01-OE002}$$

For assessing seasonal performance, the definitions of performance metrics align with those used for momentary evaluations but rely on accumulated data collected over a defined seasonal period instead of instantaneous values. The Seasonal Coefficient of Performance (SCOP) measures the performance of a heat pump over one year or a specific heating or cooling season. It takes into account variations in the COP under different operating conditions encountered throughout the year [40]. Here, each 'season' is defined as a year, consisting of 8760 h. For example, Seasonal Coefficient of Performance for heating for the heat pump ($SCOP_{heat}$) is defined as follows:

$$SCOP_{heat} = \frac{Q_{cond}}{W_{hp}}, \tag{8}$$

where Q_{cond} is the total heat produced at the heat pump condenser over a season, and W_{hp} is the total electricity input to the heat pump during the same season. The total plant performance of a year, the Seasonal Performance Factor (SPF), is defined as follows:

$$SPF_{total} = \frac{Q_{heat} + Q_{cool}}{W_{hp} + W_{gas} + W_{pumps}} \tag{9}$$

where Q_{heat} represent the total heat production, Q_{cool} is the total cooling production, W_{gas} accounts for gas consumption and W_{pumps} represents the electricity consumption for circulation pumps. Using the energy meters, the SPF_{total} can be calculated from actual readings as follows:

$$SPF_{total} = \frac{320.01\text{-OE001} + 320.01\text{-OE002} + 320.01\text{-OE003} + 370.01\text{-OE001} + 370.01\text{-OE002}}{432.100\text{-XQ100} + 432.100\text{-XQ101} + 320.01\text{-OE003} + 432.101\text{-OE01}}$$

Note that the heat pump system is connected to two thermal accumulators equipped with internal heat exchanger coils for pre-heating Domestic Hot Water (DHW). In the calculation of COP and the SPF above, the heat pump's contribution to DHW is factored in.

To evaluate the efficiency of the heat pump process itself, the System Efficiency Index (SEI) [40], sometimes known as the Carnot efficiency, is used. The SEI is calculated as the ratio of the actual COP to the COP of an ideal, reversible Carnot process (COP_C). This ideal COP serves as a theoretical benchmark, rooted in the laws of thermodynamics, for a process that transfers heat energy to a higher temperature level. For heating (h) and cooling (c), the Carnot COP can be expressed as follows:

$$COP_{heat,C} = \frac{T_{h,ref}}{T_{h,ref} - T_{c,ref}}, \tag{10}$$

$$COP_{cooling,C} = \frac{T_{c,ref}}{T_{h,ref} - T_{c,ref}}, \tag{11}$$

where $T_{h,ref}$ and $T_{c,ref}$ are reference temperatures for the two reservoirs that the heat pump operates between, represented by the average between the inlet and outlet temperatures on the condenser and evaporator, respectively. The temperature difference, $T_{h,ref} - T_{c,ref}$, is defined as the heat pump temperature lift for future evaluations. The design or measured COP is then divided by the ideal COP, and this ratio, less sensitive to changes in temperatures and flow rates than the COP alone, equals the SEI. The SEI calculations for systems supplying heat are as follows:

$$SEI_{heat} = \frac{COP_{heat}}{COP_{heat,C}}, \tag{12}$$

According to the report Method and Guidelines to Establish System Efficiency Index during Field Measurements on Air Conditioning and Heat Pump Systems [40], SEI values for heat are categorized as follows for assessing performance quality:

- 0–0.2: Unacceptable
- 0.2–0.35: Poor
- 0.35–0.45: Good
- >0.45: Excellent

To evaluate the operational efficiency of heat pumps under varying load conditions, a straightforward metric known as the Electrical Load Factor (ELF) is defined by the following formula:

$$\text{ELF}\ (\%) = \left(\frac{Actual\ Electricty\ Consumption\ of\ Heat\ Pump}{Maximum\ Elecrictiy\ Consumption\ of\ Heat\ Pump} \right) \times 100 \tag{13}$$

2.2.4. Limitations

The key limitations identified in the analysis are as follows:

- Gas boiler contribution: The energy contribution from the gas boiler used in the performance calculations is measured by the thermal energy meter 320.01-OE003, which is positioned between the gas boiler and the heat distribution system. However, actual gas consumption data from the gas company was unavailable due to data capture errors. Previous studies have indicated that the boiler's efficiency is below expectations, but this error is not attributed to the heat pump system design, but rather to the control strategy implemented in this specific part of the system. Consequently, the SPF values reported here may be higher than the real values, as more gas was used than measured at 320.01-OE003.
- Reduced demand due to refurbishment: The plant was originally designed to supply three buildings with thermal energy. During the data collection period, one of these buildings had been temporarily removed from the system for refurbishment. Thus, during the whole measurement period, the heat pumps have had an overcapacity relative to the maximum demand. Consequently, the utilization rate of the heat pump may appear disproportionately high when compared to typical systems designed to balance both base and peak load units. Additionally, the design production numbers presented in Table 1 are expected to be higher than those measured.

2.3. *Statistical Evaluation Using Correlation Analysis*

Correlation analysis was used to evaluate how the operational parameters affect the heat pump. Pearson's coefficient, r, was utilized to measure and quantify the strength and direction of linear relationships between variables [41]:

$$r = \frac{\sum(x_i - \overline{x})(y_i - \overline{y})}{\sqrt{\sum(x_i - \overline{x})^2 \sum(y_i - \overline{y})^2}}, \tag{14}$$

where:

- x_i and y_i are the individual sample points indexed i,
- $\overline{x}$ and $\overline{y}$ are the means of the x and y data sets.
- The result, r, ranges from -1 to $+1$, where:
- An r-value of +1 indicates a perfect positive linear relationship,
- An r-value of -1 indicates a perfect negative linear relationship,
- An r-value of 0 indicates no linear relationship between the variables.

All statistical analyses were performed using Python, utilizing libraries such as *Pandas* for data manipulation, *NumPy* for numerical operations, and *Statsmodels* for performing statistical tests and regression analyses [41].

2.4. *Artificial Neural Networks for Evaluating the Heat Pump Performance*

To evaluate the performance of heat exchangers over time, Artificial Neural Networks (ANNs), an ML method with substantial popularity in various fields such as mathematics and engineering [42], were utilized. ANNs are favored for their ability to model complex relationships and predict outcomes from large datasets. The methodology adopted for this study is detailed in previous work [43]. Readers seeking a deeper understanding of the specific technique are encouraged to consult the relevant literature in the field of ML [41].

2.4.1. Model Structure and Development

The ANN model was designed to predict heat pump performance based on inlet conditions and setpoint temperatures. As shown in Figure 6, the model considers the two heat pumps as a single production unit with one inlet and one outlet on the condenser side. Model inputs include the water temperature entering the first condenser and the production setpoint of the second heat pump, while the wastewater temperature serves as the input for the evaporator side. The model outputs are total heat production, electricity consumption, and the system's outlet temperature.

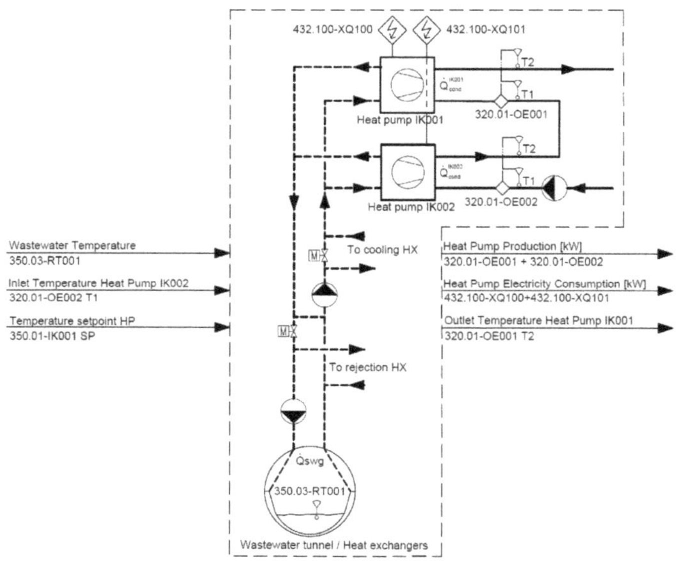

Figure 6. Model configuration of wastewater heat pump ANN.

2.4.2. Training, Validation, and Test Data with Emphasis on Fouling Assessment

Data from September 2020 to June 2024 were utilized to develop the ANN, organized into distinct sets to specifically determine the impact of fouling on system performance:

- Training Set: Data from 2020 to 2022 represented the training set, with 20% reserved for validation during the training phase to fine-tune the model.
- Data from 2023 were used for "visual validation," evaluating the model configuration, testing various input/output parameters, and adjusting hyperparameters. This stage was important for identifying potential faulty operations and providing a practical check against real-world conditions.
- Test Set: Data from 2024, referred to as "unseen" data, were used for final testing to confirm the model's effectiveness. The test aimed to verify that the model, trained on data from earlier years, could accurately predict system performance under current conditions. A successful outcome would indicate that the system's performance has remained consistent over the years, free from significant deviations due to fouling or other inefficiencies. Positive results could also suggest the model's potential for ongoing monitoring and diagnostic applications.

2.4.3. Data Preparation

To ensure the quality and relevance of the training data, thorough data processing was performed before developing the ANN. Initially, all rows with missing values were removed to guarantee consistency in the dataset. Then, outlier detection was performed using a Z-score approach, which measures how far each data point deviates from the mean in terms of standard deviations [44]. Data points with a Z-score above 3 were considered outliers and excluded. This removed 3223 rows of the dataset, initially consisting of 25,242 rows.

The dataset was further processed using a Savitzky-Golay filter, a method that involves using a moving window to fit a polynomial among the points within that window [45]. A second-order polynomial was selected to smooth segments of eleven consecutive data points, effectively capturing fluctuations throughout the day. This approach preserves critical features such as peaks and minima through its polynomial fitting technique. A visual representation of the filtering for heat production, electricity consumption, and wastewater temperature is provided in Figure 7.

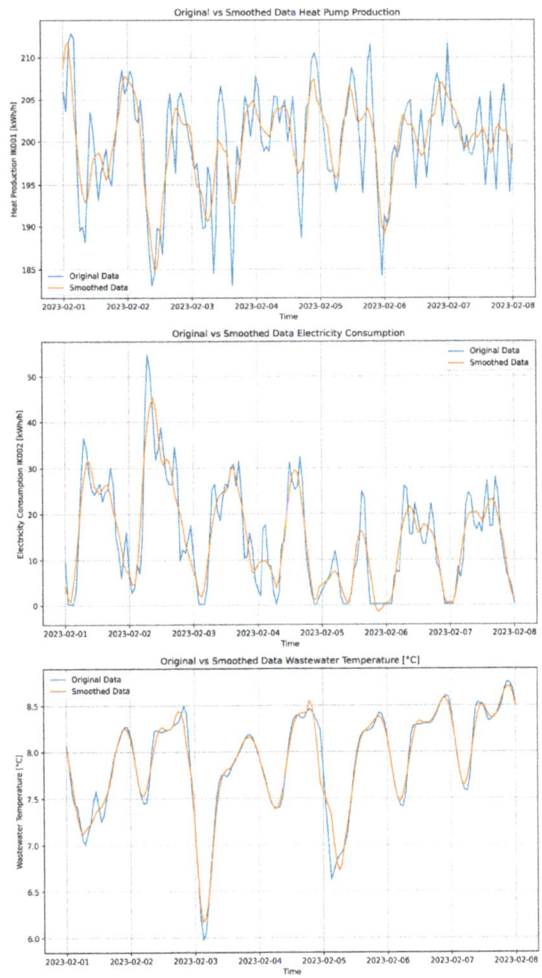

Figure 7. Examples of data smoothing using the Savitzky-Golay filter for Heat Production (**top**), Electricity Consumption (**middle**) and Wastewater Temperature (**bottom**).

Next, a more hands-on evaluation was conducted to ensure the dataset reflected healthy operational conditions. Initially, rows where the COP exceeded a threshold of 5.0 were removed to filter out instances where a small amount of heat was recorded after the heat pump had shut down, eliminating a total of 170 rows for the heat pump combined.

Then, erroneous operations of the heat pumps, initially identified through manual examination of time series data and using the visual validation data actively, were excluded. Note that this was a coarse manual procedure, and there may be erroneous instances within the final data set. Specifically, instances where the temperature difference between the outlet temperature and the setpoint was high while the power output was lower than a threshold were filtered out. These situations indicated that one or several of the compressors were out of order. Additionally, there were cases where heat pump IK002 was significantly more active than IK001, which, due to active setpoint configurations, suggested operational errors with IK001. These filtration steps led to the removal of 8515 rows.

The final filtration step involved excluding data from the peak summer months, June, July, and August, to focus on the heating season. Through the filtration steps, the dataset was reduced to 10,481 entries from an initial count of 25,242. Notably, the removal of 8515 rows due to erroneous operations is particularly significant as it represents almost a full year's worth of data where one or both heat pumps had faulty operation. This not only underscores the importance of the data cleaning process but also highlights the critical need for consistent monitoring and maintenance of these systems, given the frequency of operational errors. This study was performed without access to maintenance logs. Had these logs been available, they could have enabled more precise identification of operational errors, thereby making the data cleaning more systematic than the current approach.

2.4.4. Model Construction and Training

After cleaning, the training dataset was separated into the features and labels as defined in Figure 6. Both features and labels were scaled using a StandardScaler [41] to normalize the data, ensuring no feature dominated the model due to its scale. The model was structured using a sequential layout consisting of an input layer, three hidden layers, and an output layer. Each layer employed a Rectified Linear Unit (ReLU) activation function, except for the output layer, which used linear activation [41].

Training was conducted using the Adam optimizer and the Mean Squared Error loss function. The model underwent training for 5000 epochs, with early stopping implemented to prevent overfitting. Early stopping monitored the validation loss and halted training if no improvement was seen for 50 consecutive epochs. Model checkpoints were utilized to save the best-performing model based on validation loss [41].

The selected approach ensured a robust and thoroughly trained ANN, with specific steps taken to prevent overfitting. Table 2 summarizes the hyperparameters and training settings used in the model's development.

Table 2. Summary of hyperparameters and training settings for ANN.

Parameter	Value
Network Architecture	(50, 75, 150)
Activation Functions	['ReLu', 'ReLu', 'ReLu', 'linear']
Loss Function	Mean Squared Error
Optimizer	Adam
Batch Size	150
Epochs	5000
Validation Split	0.2
Early Stopping	Enabled
Patience	50
Batch Size	150
Save Best Model	Yes

2.4.5. Performance Metrics

The performance of the ANN was assessed using the 2024 test set, which was separated from the training data to provide an unbiased evaluation of the model's predictive accuracy. The same performance metrics were used during the visual validation phase. Mean Absolute Error (MAE) quantifies the average magnitude of errors in the model's predictions [41]. It is calculated as follows:

$$MAE = \frac{1}{n}\sum_{i=1}^{n}|y_i - \hat{y}_i|, \tag{15}$$

where n represents the number of data points and y_i and $\hat{y}_i$ are actual and predicted values of parameters. MAE provides a straightforward measure of error magnitude without considering direction.

Root Mean Square Error (RSME) measures the overall magnitude of errors, emphasizing larger deviations due to the squaring of each error [41]. RMSE is particularly sensitive to outliers and provides a more conservative estimate of model performance:

$$RSME = \sqrt{\frac{1}{n}\sum_{i=1}^{n}(y_i - \hat{y}_i)^2} \tag{16}$$

Mean Absolute Percentage Error (MAPE) estimates the average percentage error between the model's predictions and observed data, giving a sense of error in relative terms [46]. MAPE is especially useful when comparing the performance of models across different scales or units. However, it should be used with caution when the actual values are close to zero, as it can lead to disproportionately high errors and may distort the overall performance assessment:

$$MAPE = \frac{1}{n}\sum_{i=1}^{n}\left|\frac{y_i - \hat{y}_i}{y_i}\right|, \tag{17}$$

Together, these metrics offer a comprehensive view of model accuracy, with MAE providing a baseline average error, RMSE highlighting larger errors, and MAPE offering a percentage-based evaluation. Additionally, the Maximum Absolute Error is reported, which captures the single largest error across all predictions, helping to identify the worst-case scenarios in model performance.

2.5. Manuscript Preparation and Editorial Assistance

In addition to the technical methodologies, during the development of this manuscript, the OpenAI GPT-4 model was employed for editorial assistance. Specifically, GPT-4 aided in refining sentence structures and providing word choices, enhancing the clarity and readability of the text. It also played a role in explaining and summarizing complex sections from the referenced literature.

3. Results

3.1. Evaluation of Heat Pump Performance

The annual energy results for the plant are presented in Table 3 for the years 2022 and 2023. Additionally, duration curves for the gas boiler and the components contributing to heat pump production for the same years are displayed in Figures 8 and 9. These duration curves are based on sorted values of heat production from maximum to minimum, with corresponding data for gas and electricity consumption, wastewater heat, and excess heat from cooling, all linked to their contributions to the maximum production levels.

Table 3. Accumulated values for plant thermal energy production and energy consumption.

	2022		2023	
	Energy [kWh/yr]	**Power [kW]**	**Energy [kWh/yr]**	**Power [kW]**
Heat production	1,342,000	450	1,372,000	430
Heat Production—IK001	1,159,000	244	1,041,000	242
Electricity Consumption—IK001	321,000	71	291,000	71
SCOP IK001 [-]	3.61		3.58	
Heat Production—IK002	177,000	231	321,000	248
Electricity Consumption—IK002	52,000	66	91,000	67
SCOP IK002 [-]	3.40		3.52	
Heat Pump Production	1,336,000	450	1,362,000	430
Electricity consumption	373,000	131	382,000	130
SCOP Heat [-]	3.58		3.57	
Heat extracted at evaporator Qevap	963,000	320	980,000	302.0
Cooling to Heat	128,000	68	123,000	118.0
Wastewater Heat	835,000	304	858,000	283.0
Gas Boiler Load	5700	190	10,000	156.0
Cooling Production	34,000	270	44,000	233
Electricity Consumption Cooling	14,000	100	15,000	81
SEER [-]	2.43		2.93	
Electricity Consumption Pumps	102,000	19	110,000	19
SPF Total [-]	2.78		2.74	

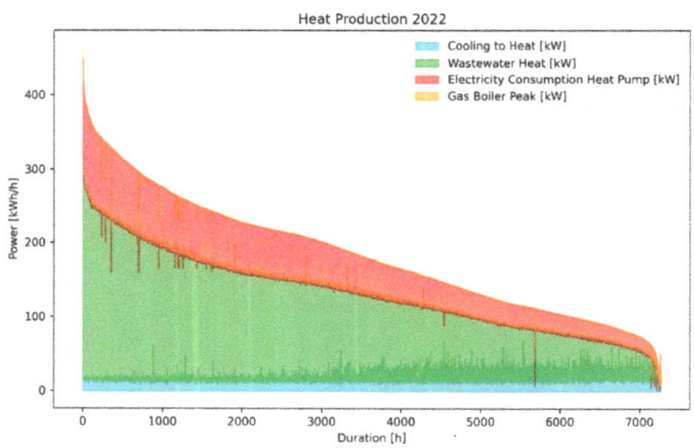

Figure 8. Duration curve heat production 2022.

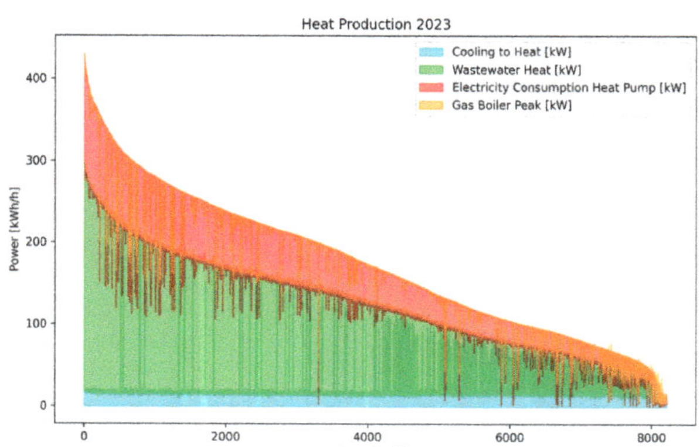

Figure 9. Duration curve heat production 2023.

From the accumulated energy results, the following can be observed:

- The system for heating and cooling production, excluding peak heating for DHW, has produced its energy with an SFP between 2.7 and 2.8, which is considered highly satisfactory.
- The heat pumps have met most of the thermal demand for the two operational buildings, with the gas boiler contributing minimally. This outcome aligns with expectations and contrasts with the period of 2019 to 2020, when three buildings were operational [33] and both the heat pump and gas boiler had significantly higher contributions. It is important to note that data from 2019 to 2020 are not as detailed as those presented in this study.
- There have been no significant peaks in gas boiler usage, and the boiler has primarily served as a backup unit during these years.
- Wastewater heat has been the predominant low-temperature heat source, contributing to more than 60% of the total heat produced in both evaluated years, indicating that the heat exchangers are performing in line with expectations.
- While the power contribution of excess heat from cooling is small, averaging about 14 kW, it has been consistent throughout the years. Though not as important in a system where the heat extraction does not significantly influence the source temperature, a steady contribution of 14 kW, equivalent to 120,000 kWh/yr, could significantly benefit a geothermal heat pump system.
- The production from the two heat pumps has been highly uneven; IK001 has produced 87% and 75% of the heat in the respective years, while IK002 has produced 13% and 25%. The SCOP values for IK001 and IK002 were 3.6/3.6 and 3.4/3.5, respectively, perfectly in line with design expectations. Given that IK001, as the second pump in the series, has been set to produce a temperature 5K above that of IK002 and still achieved a higher SCOP, this suggests that the operational strategy and set-point scheme for IK002 should be re-evaluated.

3.2. Prediction of Heat Production, Electricity Consumption, and Outlet Temperature Using ANN

The results of the ANN model are detailed in the figures and tables that follow. The model was initially trained on data from 2020 to 2022. During the training process, the model results were continuously visually evaluated using data from 2023, which served as an aid through data processing, alongside standard validation principles. Finally, data from a month in 2024 were used to test the final model configuration.

Figure 10 illustrates an example of the input data used for the visual validation of the final model configuration. Figures 11 and 12 display the model's predictions alongside the actual values for heat production and outlet temperature in the same period, respectively. These figures also include the error, calculated as actual minus predicted values. The results of the electricity consumption follow a similar pattern as the heat production.

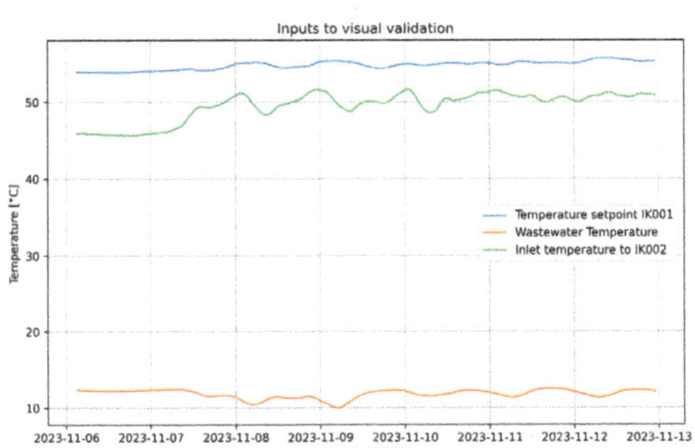

Figure 10. Input values used during visual validation.

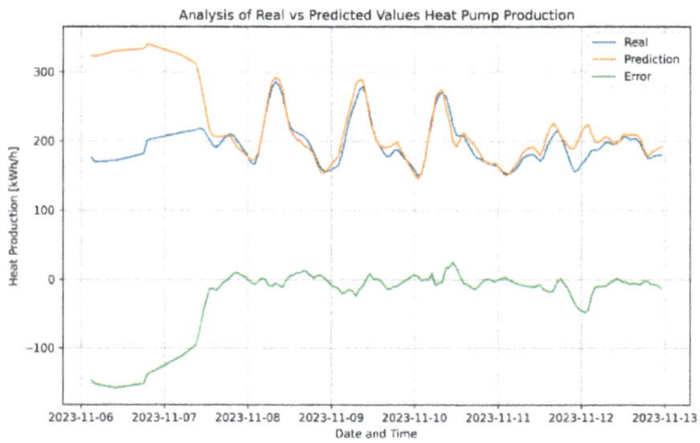

Figure 11. Results from visual validation, heat production both heat pumps.

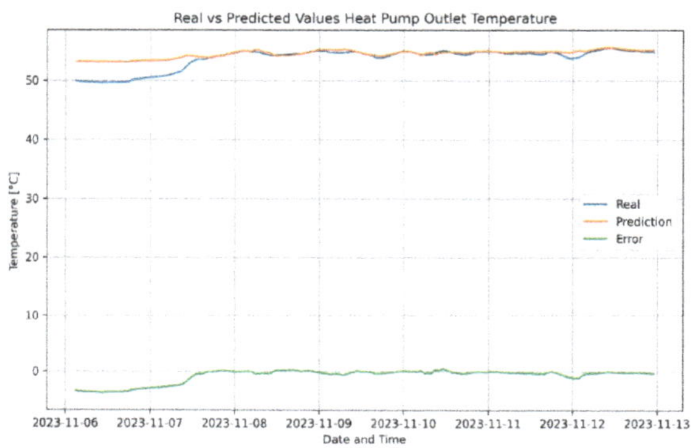

Figure 12. Results from visual validation, outlet temperature from IK001.

During visual validation, the model exhibited significantly higher errors during specific periods. These included the initial days and a brief period on 12 November, as highlighted in the figures. Notably, these instances coincided with the malfunctioning of one of the compressors in heat pump IK001.

In Table 4, the error metrics are summarized for the visual validation. The table shows results both for the complete week and after erroneous data were removed, demonstrating that the model accurately predicted the final heat production and electricity consumption within a 4% MAPE and outlet temperature within 0.3% when erroneous data were removed.

Table 4. Evaluation of visual validation—Error metrics with and without faulty operation.

Parameter	MAE	RMSE	Max Absolute Error	MAPE
		Including Errors due to Faulty Operation of IK001		
Heat Pump Production [kWh/h]	16.3	34.2	157.9	8.5%
Electricity Consumption [kWh/h]	4.3	9.6	45.0	8.5%
Outlet Temperature Heat Pump [°C]	0.4	0.8	3.5	5.3%
		Excluding Errors due to Faulty Operation of IK001		
Heat Pump Production [kWh/h]	6.2	9.2	24.8	3.7%
Electricity Consumption [kWh/h]	1.8	2.4	6.9	3.3%
Outlet Temperature Heat Pump [°C]	0.2	0.2	0.6	0.3%

Continuing with the final model configuration, the model was evaluated using test data from 2024. The inputs for a month of this test are shown in Figure 13, while

Figures 14–16 compare the model's predictions against the actual values along with the errors for heat production, electricity consumption, and outlet temperature. The error metrics for this testing interval are presented in Table 5. From Figures 14–16, it is clear that there are periods when the errors are significantly higher than during the rest of the operation. Both these periods and periods without errors have been isolated in Table 5, documenting that outside the erroneous periods, the model predicts very well. A discussion is provided in Section 4.3.

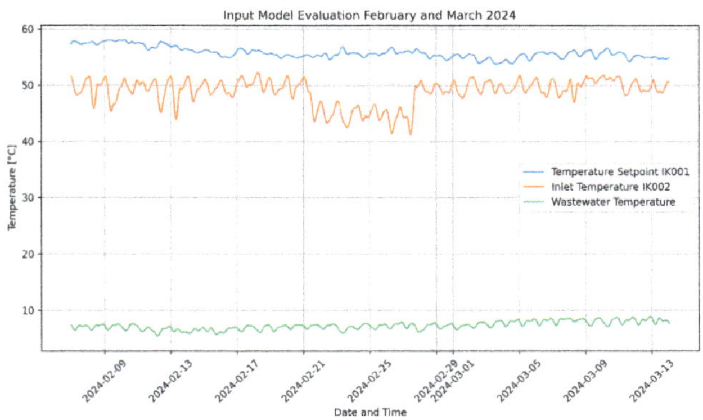

Figure 13. Input data for the ANN applied on 2024 test data.

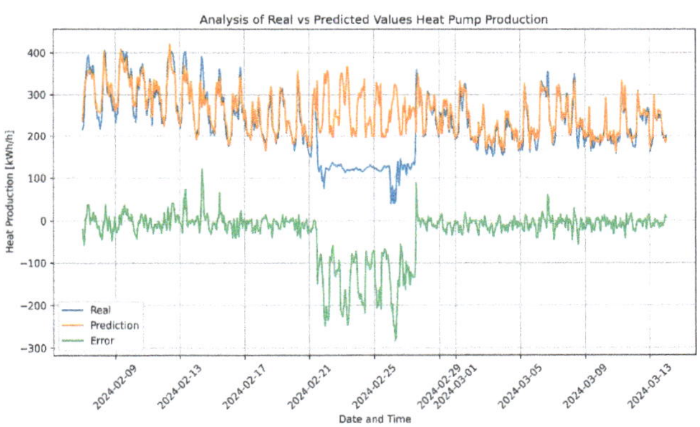

Figure 14. Predicted vs. actual heat production for 2024 test data.

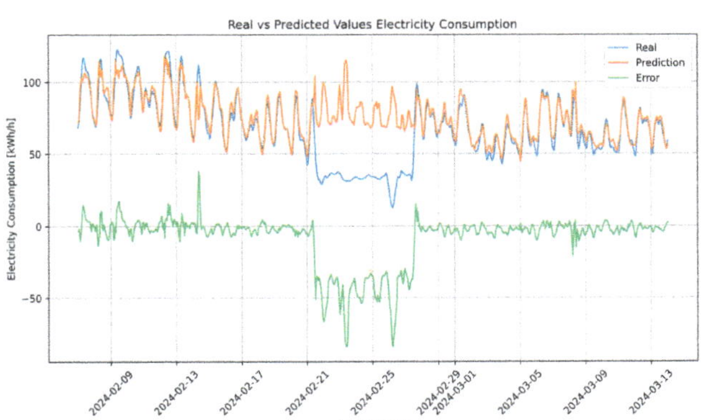

Figure 15. Predicted vs. actual electricity consumption for 2024 test data.

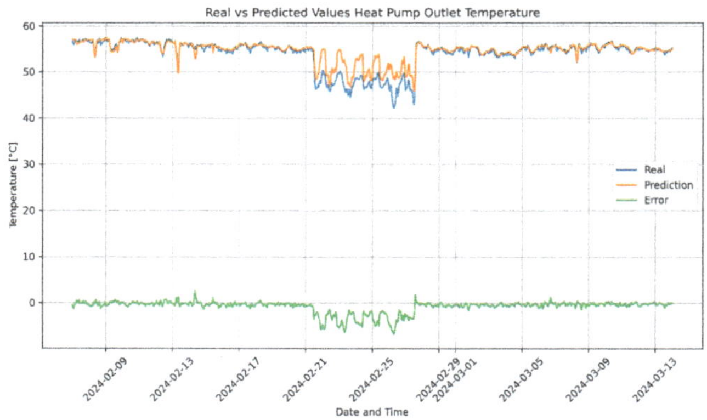

Figure 16. Predicted vs. actual outlet temperature for 2024 test data.

Table 5. Error metrics for 2024 testing interval, complete and segregated by operational status (without and with faulty operation).

Parameter	MAE	RMSE	Max Absolute Error	MAPE
	Complete results including period with significant error. 7 February 2024 to 14 March 2024			
Heat Pump Production [kWh/h]	33.7	63.6	260.1	25.8%
Electricity Consumption [kWh/h]	9.7	18.3	72.6	26.3%
Outlet Temperature Heat Pump [°C]	0.8	1.5	6.1	1.6%
	Result excluding period with significant error. 7 February 2024 to 21 February 2024 and 27 February 2024 to 14 March 2024			
Heat Pump Production [kWh/h]	12.2	17.0	111.6	5.0%
Electricity Consumption [kWh/h]	3.6	5.1	38.2	5.1%
Outlet Temperature Heat Pump [°C]	0.3	0.4	2.4	0.5%
	Results period with significant error. 21 February 2024 to 27 February 2024			
Heat Pump Production [kWh/h]	140.4	150.7	260.1	129.4%
Electricity Consumption [kWh/h]	40.0	43.1	72.6	132.2%
Outlet Temperature Heat Pump [°C]	3.3	3.5	6.1	7.0%

4. Discussion

4.1. Wastewater as a Thermal Reservoir: Evaluating Temperature and Other Influences on Heat Pump Performance

The results show that the operational SCOP of the heat pump system met the initial design targets in both evaluated years, indicating that the system is functioning as intended. This section delves deeper into the factors influencing the efficiency of the heat pump system, focusing on both the Coefficient of Performance (COP) and System Efficiency Indicator (SEI). The aim is to identify which parameters most significantly affect the COP and to assess the resulting SEI, determining if, despite satisfactory COP figures on paper, there is room for improvement or specific operational conditions that notably improve or weaken the SEI.

The most significant factors influencing the COP of a building heat pump system are the temperature lift between the heat source and sink and performance variations during part-load conditions, both of which fluctuate with seasonal and ambient temperature changes [47]. To analyze these influences, correlation matrices for relevant parameters were developed using Pearson's correlation [41]. The parameters analyzed include Wastewater Temperature, Electrical Load Factor (ELF), Temperature Lift, COP, and SEI. The correlation matrices in Figure 17 provide detailed insights into the operations of heat pump systems IK001 and IK002. Specifically:

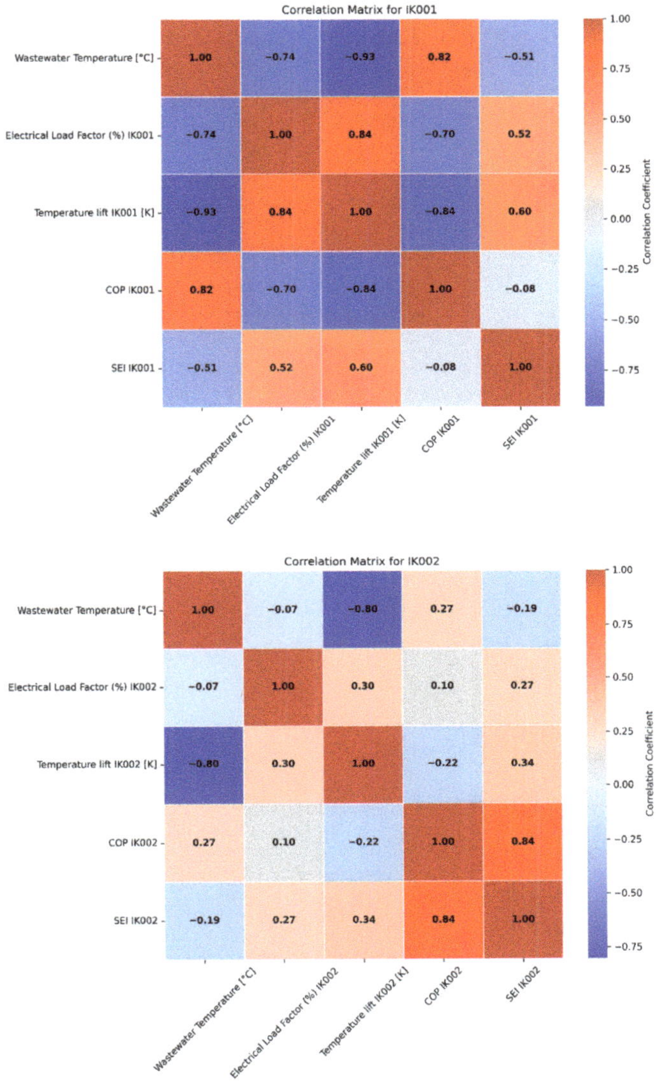

Figure 17. Correlation Matrices for IK001 (**top**) and IK002 (**bottom**).

IK001: A weak correlation (−0.08) between COP and SEI indicates that COP alone does not fully reflect the system's efficiency. It is a well-established principle in heat pump theory that an increase in temperature lift leads to a decrease in COP. When the ambient temperatures are low, the wastewater temperature generally decreases as well (see Section 4.4 for further details). Under colder ambient conditions, the setpoint temperature for heat distribution is typically at its highest. This scenario, coupled with low source temperature, results in a greater temperature lift between the condenser and evaporator. The inverse relationship between COP and temperature lift is demonstrated in practice by a correlation of −0.84.

Additionally, a negative correlation between the ELF and wastewater temperature indicates that the heat pump operated at higher capacities at lower source temperatures, consuming more energy. This expected behavior reflects how the heat pumps typically respond to increased heating demands during colder periods. Despite higher energy usage and lower COP when the ELF was high, a positive correlation between the ELF and SEI suggests that the heat pump may still achieve higher efficiency when operating close to maximum capacity.

IK002: The correlation matrix for heat pump IK002 requires careful interpretation, as this unit has been significantly less active compared to IK001, often serving primarily as a peak heater with brief periods of operation. To prevent bias in the analysis from the unit's frequent start-stop cycles, all data points with energy consumption below 10 kW were removed, leaving a dataset of 6566 rows for analysis. This filtering process affects the robustness of data correlations.

For this heat pump, SEI and COP were strongly correlated, with a coefficient of 0.84, contrasting sharply with IK001. This unit's COP showed less sensitivity to variations in temperature lift, wastewater temperature, and ELF compared to IK001.

To provide a deeper understanding of how each heat pump operates, scatter plots between relevant parameters have been created, with a color index highlighting key trends. These are presented for heat pumps IK001 and IK002 in Figures 18 and 19, respectively. These visuals help illustrate the correlations discussed earlier, demonstrating the dynamic relationships between variables such as COP, ELF, and wastewater temperature at various operational conditions of the heat pumps.

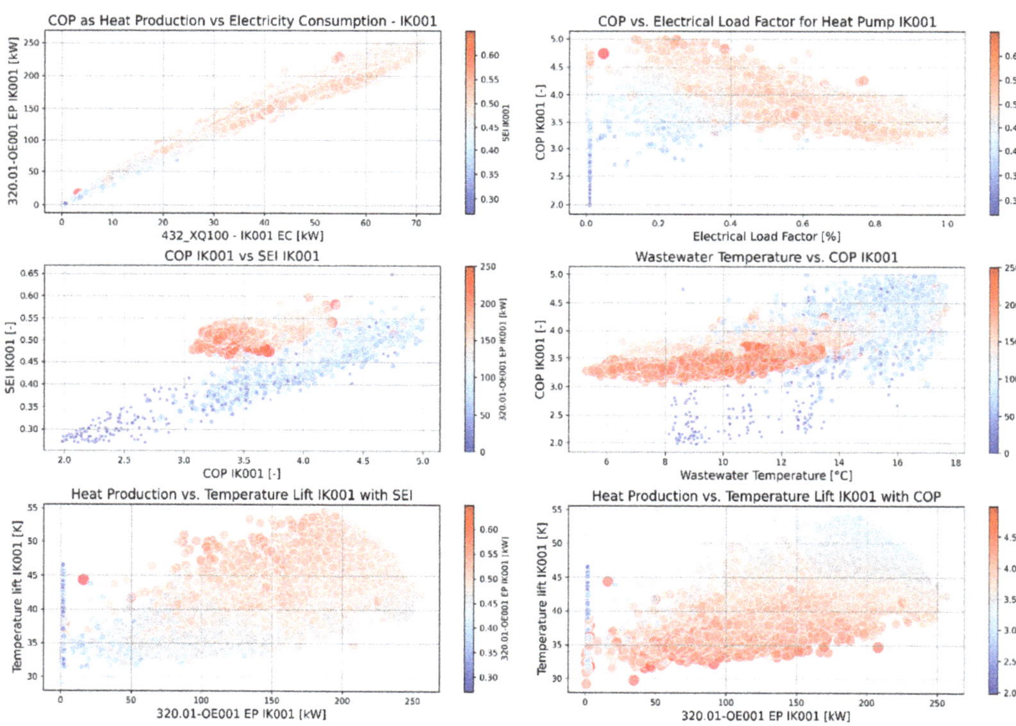

Figure 18. Comprehensive visualization of heat pump performance metrics for IK001, based on 21,800 rows of data. (**Top Left**) heat production vs. electricity consumption, depicted with a color index representing SEI. (**Top Right**) COP vs. electrical load factor, with SEI as the color index. (**Middle Left**) SEI plotted against COP, with heat production serving as the color index. (**Middle Right**) COP in relation to wastewater temperature, colored by heat production. (**Bottom Left**) heat production vs. temperature lift with SEI as the color index. (**Bottom Right**) heat production vs. temperature lift with COP as the color index.

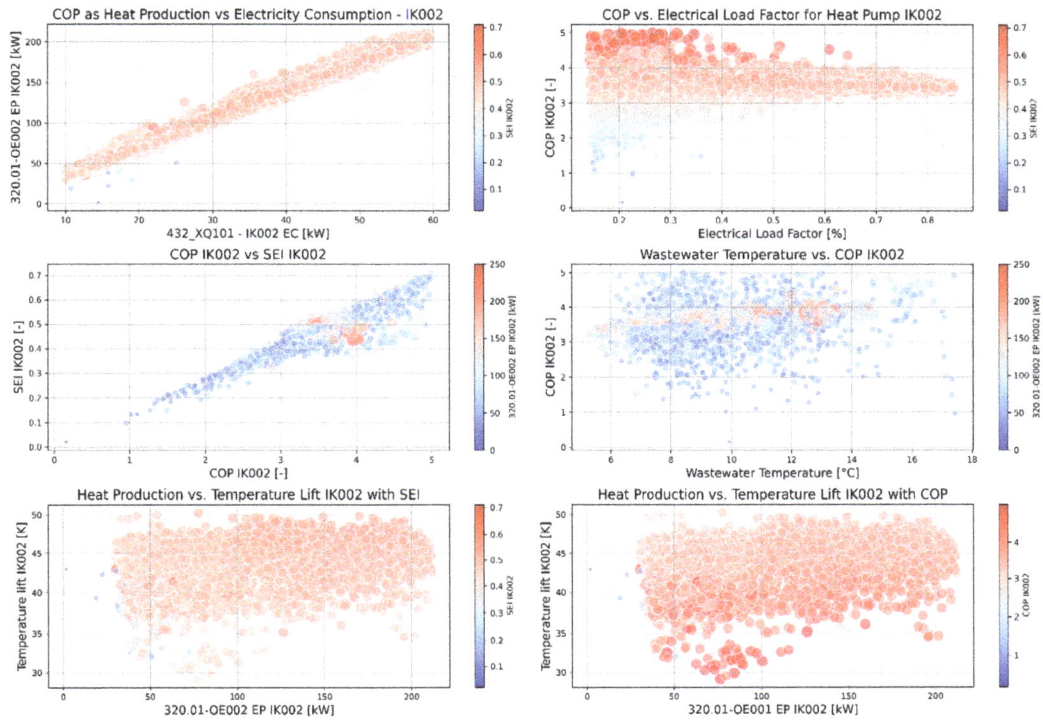

Figure 19. Comprehensive visualization of heat pump performance metrics for IK002, based on 6566 rows of data. Visualizations: same as Figure 18, with datasets corresponding to IK002.

Observations from the correlation matrix and scatter plots provide detailed insights into the operational dynamics of the heat pumps. Since IK001 has significantly more stable operation data, it serves as a more reliable benchmark for evaluating overall system performance and identifying optimal operational strategies.

For both heat pumps, the relationship between heat production and electricity consumption is represented as a near-linear line, seen in the upper left figure, with the slope of the line indicating COP. A slight change in the slope, as heat production increases, suggests a minor decrease in COP at higher production levels.

In the case of IK001, plotting COP against the ELF with SEI as the color index reveals that, while COP decreases with increasing Electrical Load Factor, the SEI remains above 0.45, indicating excellent operation when the ELF is above 40%. Even at 20–40% ELF, the SEI stays within the 'good' range most of the time.

This trend is further confirmed in the middle-left figure, which plots SEI vs. COP, with heat production as the color index. For IK001, two distinct patterns emerge: a linear-shaped relationship, represented by a blue line at lower heat production, and a concentrated cluster of red dots at higher heat production levels. This suggests that the heat pump performs more efficiently at higher capacity. Both heat pumps are equipped with four semi-hermetic stable compressors: two are controlled by inverters and two operate on an on/off basis. When the capacity exceeds a certain threshold, both on/off compressors are activated, and the inverter-controlled compressors adjust to fine-tune the production. The blue line likely represents periods when only the inverter-controlled compressors are operating, while the red dots indicate periods where at least one of the on/off compressors is running, consistently achieving excellent SEI values. For IK002, this pattern is less obvious due to fewer data points. However, when energy production is high, both COP and SEI remain above the thresholds for optimal operation. The SEI vs. COP scatter plots illustrate different correlation patterns for the two heat pumps. IK001 displays a more complex pattern, with a linear relationship at lower capacities and a more stable pattern at higher capacities. In contrast, IK002, having fewer data points at high capacity, shows a trend closer to linear. This simpler pattern explains why the correlation between SEI and COP is stronger for this heat pump.

The right-side middle figures plot COP against wastewater temperature, with heat production serving as the color code. The chart consistently shows COP values above 3.0, confirming that the system has operated within expected levels. For IK001, the parts of the data form a red pattern resembling a rotated ellipse, highlighting high-capacity operations. At lower temperatures around 5 °C, COP is about 3.2–3.3. As wastewater temperature increases to around 13 °C, COP peaks at 3.6. Beyond this temperature, as capacities decrease, COP varies more. The plot suggests that lower wastewater temperatures, while significant, do not directly correlate with the lowest COP values, likely because these figures do not account for temperature lift. The bottom figures, which plot Energy Production against Temperature Lift with SEI and COP as color indices, show that temperature lift significantly influences COP: higher production with lower temperature lift results in higher COP. Additionally, these figures demonstrate the differences between SEI and COP, indicating that while COP decreases, SEI values generally increase with higher temperature lifts, signaling more efficient operation at higher lifts.

Overall, with COP values mostly above 3.0 and SEI values above 0.4, the system's operation ranges from good to excellent. Even though COP decreases at high production levels, this is expected due to the higher temperature lifts involved. The main challenge appears to be the uneven operation between IK001 and IK002, where IK002 is less efficient than IK001, mainly due to its frequent starts and stops. Adjusting the operational hours of the machines, with IK001 operating less and IK002 more, could potentially extend the system's lifespan and improve overall efficiency. This adjustment can be explored manually by changing the setpoint in the control system or as part of an academic modeling exercise. The wastewater heat exchanger system performs as anticipated, contributing to the strong COP and SEI values, even at the lowest wastewater temperatures.

4.2. Comparing Wastewater and Ambient Air as Thermal Reservoirs

To evaluate wastewater as a thermal reservoir, its temperature is compared to the corresponding ambient air temperatures. Historical data for wastewater temperature from 2021 to 2023 is shown on the top in Figure 20, displaying a clear seasonal pattern. The lowest temperatures occur in winter and the highest in summer, aligning with the estimated temperature ranges used for system design.

In the bottom, Figure 20 presents a time series from January 2021 to December 2023, showcasing both wastewater and ambient temperatures. Figure 21 plots the duration curve for each year's ambient temperature alongside the corresponding wastewater temperature for the same hours. These visualizations clearly demonstrate that the wastewater temperature is generally more stable than the ambient temperature.

A correlation analysis between wastewater and ambient air temperatures reveals a strong positive relationship, with correlations of 0.79 for 2021, 0.73 for 2022, and 0.80 for 2023. These values suggest that as ambient temperatures rise or fall, wastewater temperatures generally follow. Despite the clear correlation, Figure 21 shows the significant stability of wastewater temperatures. For instance, even as the ambient temperature drops to nearly −10 °C, the wastewater temperature never falls below +5 °C. The wastewater temperature remains stable because it mixes stormwater with warmer household wastewater and continuously flows through an underground tunnel insulated by surrounding rocks. The duration curves further highlight the advantage of wastewater compared to ambient air, consistently showing that wastewater temperatures remain higher than ambient air when there is a demand for heat and lower when cooling is required.

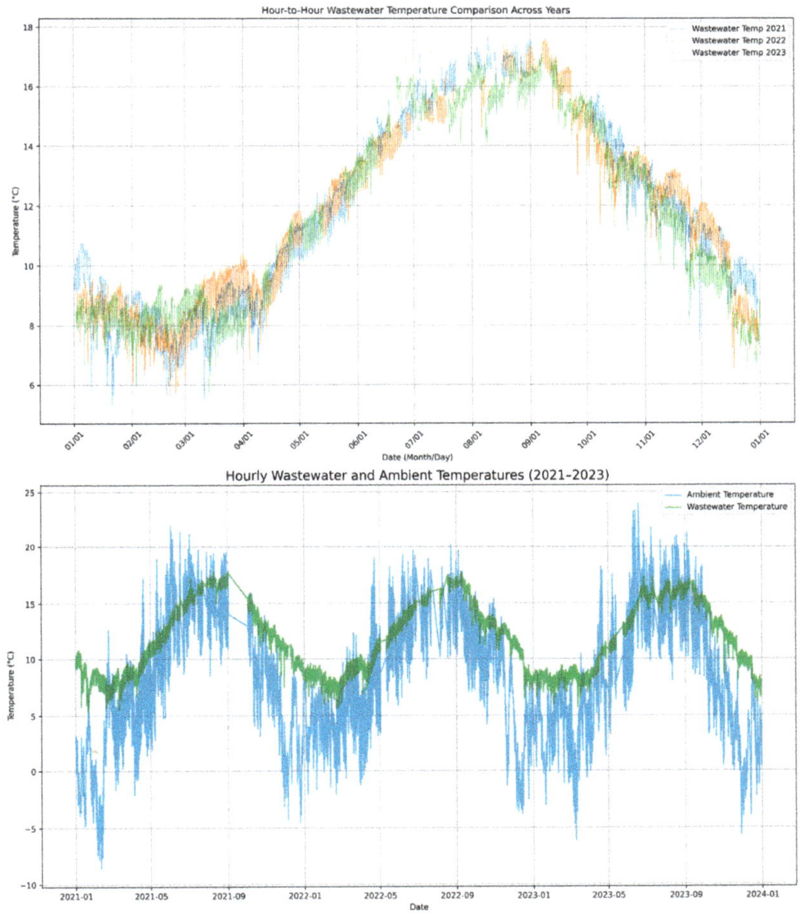

Figure 20. Historical data for the wastewater temperature for the years 2021, 2022, and 2024. Comparison of wastewater temperature and ambient temperature—2021–2023.

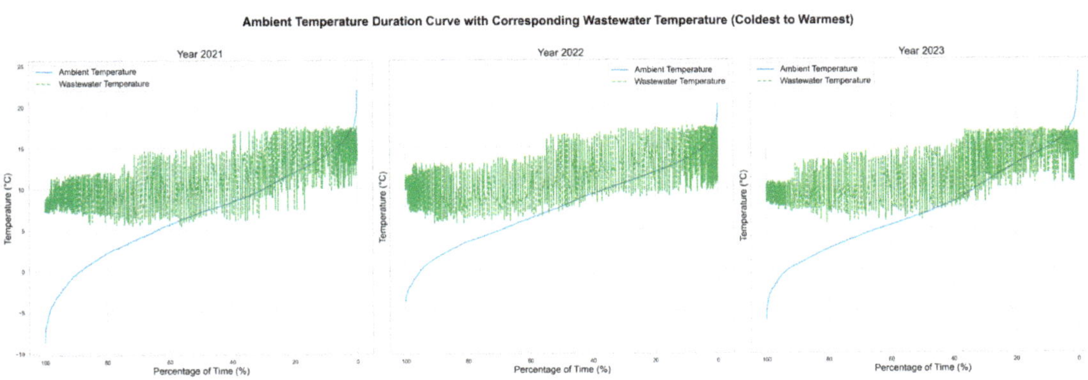

Figure 21. Sorted duration curve for ambient temperature with corresponding wastewater temperatures for the years 2021, 2022, and 2023.

4.3. ANN for Monitoring and Evaluating the Heat Pump System and Fouling

Previously, results from both visual validation and test data analysis of the ANN representing the heat pump system were reported. The visual validation identified periods of high error, particularly in the initial days and notably on 12 November. Closer examination during these times indicated that the errors originated from a malfunction in one of the compressors of heat pump IK001. This discovery led to refining the data cleaning criteria, removing similar erroneous data points from the final training dataset. Utilizing a dataset that extends beyond standard validation or test sets, an approach not typical in conventional machine learning practices, provided the flexibility to adjust the dataset based on domain knowledge.

In the unseen test set, the results of the ANN model demonstrate a MAPE of about 5% for heat production and electricity consumption and 0.5% for the outlet temperature for most of the test period, which is considered satisfactory. However, an exception occurs during a four-day period, 21 February 2024 to 25 February 2024, where the errors are significantly higher. A potential issue can be assumed by investigating the input data in Figure 13, which shows that the inlet temperature is noticeably lower than during other periods.

The ANN model was designed to correlate wastewater temperature and inlet conditions with the combined production and consumption of the two heat pumps. By plotting a time series of the output from each heat pump separately, along with the gas boiler contribution, as shown in Figure 22, the source of these errors in predictions becomes clearer. Normally, heat pump IK001 operates as the base load unit, while IK002 has a peak load functionality. However, during the specific four-day period, IK001 was shut off, likely due to a malfunction or scheduled maintenance. Consequently, IK002 automatically took over as the base load unit. Since IK002 is set to produce a temperature 5 K lower than that of IK001, the resulting outlet temperature was lower than normal. This affected the inlet temperature of the heat pumps and caused the gas boiler to compensate. This led to increased usage of expensive gas, even though IK002 had the capacity to meet a larger share of the demand.

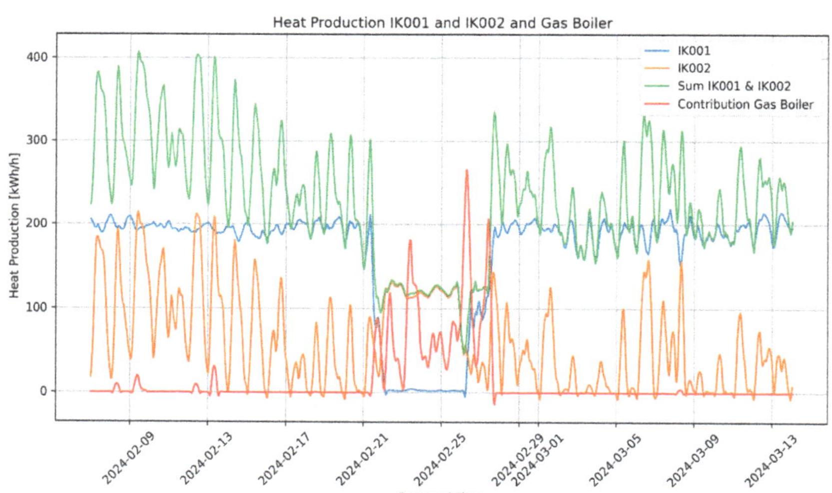

Figure 22. Evaluation of heat pump operation during test interval 2024.

A significantly higher prediction error during faulty operation is expected since similar data were excluded from the training dataset. This scenario demonstrates the model's ability to detect operations that deviate from expected behavior, highlighting potential issues. Had there been an actual malfunction, the system would have triggered an immediate alarm, and while a model trained on hourly data does not support real-time monitoring, the model is robust enough to identify unusual operational patterns, which enhances the data cleaning beyond manual methods. This is particularly useful when retraining the model with a larger dataset, making it a practical tool for proactive maintenance and efficient management.

When assessing whether any significant fouling has occurred between the training data from 2020 to 2022 and the testing data from 2024, the low error rates on the healthy operational data suggest that the system's capability of extracting heat from the wastewater has remained stable. Despite the test data being from the period of typically low wastewater temperatures, the model's performance in 2024 reflects similar patterns observed in previous years. It should be noted that the error rates for the test set are higher than those from the visual validation but still fall within an acceptable range, indicating no significant fouling issues. Since the visual validation set was actively used to refine the model and dataset, lower error rates in this set, compared to the test set, are expected.

The ANN is specifically trained on fixed operational conditions. Significant changes in this study case system, such as variations in the setpoint regime of the heat pumps or modifications to the circulation pump control, would affect the model's reliability. The robustness of the ANN validated between 2020 and 2024 depends on its training under stable operational conditions. While ANNs and deep learning systems are capable of processing and learning from large datasets, they require ongoing monitoring and retraining to adapt to new operational conditions.

Furthermore, in a scenario where fouling does occur in the heat exchangers, the ANN's predictions would likely deviate as heat extraction efficiency decreases. Rather than training the model on fouling data, it would be preferable to initiate actions to improve operation and prevent or address fouling effectively.

4.4. Assessing Wastewater as a Thermal Reservoir from the Perspective of the Municipal Energy Plant Project

The evaluation of temperature conditions within the wastewater system and its significant contribution to heat pump production demonstrate that wastewater is a stable and predictable low-temperature reservoir suitable for both heating and cooling. The ANN modeling suggests minimal impact from fouling over the years, confirming the supplier's claims from the design and installation phases.

The major challenges in replicating a similar project involve accessing the wastewater, both physically and through regulatory means. The regulatory issues include ownership rights, permissions for installation, and requirements from the wastewater treatment company. In this project, the wastewater tunnel is owned by the municipality, simplifying ownership discussions compared to many other projects. If a private building were to use a public wastewater tunnel, there is potential for a charge for accessing the low-temperature energy, making the system less appealing. A significant challenge was the need to reroute the wastewater flow during installation, which involved temporarily discharging it untreated into the sea. This action required approval from county management, which was granted without major objections but required a detailed plan outlining the duration of the installation phases. The project calculations indicated a maximum temperature drop in the wastewater of about 0.5 K, a change considered negligible from the perspective of wastewater operators. However, the temperature of the wastewater entering the treatment plant remains a critical factor, potentially a dealbreaker for larger implementations.

Accessing the installation site within the wastewater system was challenging, as the nearest entry point was about 1 km from the actual installation site. A small electric vehicle was employed to transport the 108 plates, each weighing 100 kg, through the tunnel. Before transportation could begin, approximately 75,000 kg of accumulated dirt at the entry point of the tunnel had to be cleared, delaying installation by a week, increasing costs, and extending the period of untreated wastewater discharge. Working far away from the nearest exit in a confined and isolated space significantly heightened safety concerns, leading to strict evacuation procedures, gas detection measures, and the provision of a small rubber boat for emergency use.

The transportation and installation of the heat exchangers began on a Monday morning and concluded by Thursday evening. The highly trained team worked 15–16 h per day to speed up the process and minimize the untreated wastewater discharge period, likely also motivated by a desire to reduce their time at the site.

The drilling process was challenging, requiring precise alignment of three tunnels to hit the wall of the wastewater tunnel, 100 m away. This phase of the project received bids from only one drilling company, resulting in significantly higher costs than anticipated and impacting the overall budget.

A preliminary life-cost analysis compared the Levelized Cost of Energy (LCOE) for this wastewater system with those of geothermal and seawater heat pump systems. While the performance of the wastewater system was comparable to these alternatives, the significant costs associated with drilling and dirt removal did raise the overall installation costs. Nevertheless, the project is regarded as a success by the Municipality of Stavanger. It met the objectives of the EU project within the estimated budget, and importantly, the most uncertain aspect, utilizing wastewater as a heat source, has operated flawlessly.

A significant challenge for the long-term performance and reliability of the system is accessing the heat exchangers. As humorously highlighted in Figure 23 with a "see you later" sign left at the tunnel exit by the installers, the system is located 1000 m away, sealed within the wastewater tunnel. There is no straightforward means for re-access. Although the system is designed to be maintenance-free on paper, the difficulty of accessing it poses real challenges in the event of a malfunction. Accessing the system would require shutting down the wastewater tunnel again, disrupting water transportation and releasing the untreated wastewater into the sea.

Figure 23. A sign mounted on the door entry to the wastewater tunnel by Uhrig, reading "Careful! Heat Exchangers" in Danish.

Moreover, the custom design of the heat exchangers and the challenging conditions at the installation site significantly complicate the replacement or repair of malfunctioning elements. The energy plant is equipped with full backup options for heat production, allowing for potential shutdowns during the winter season, if necessary. However, these interventions are complex and require careful planning and consideration, with increased operational costs as well as the cost of the new equipment. Notably, if there is no backup for cooling and a malfunction occurs in the heat exchanger system, it could lead to significant comfort issues during the summer.

5. Conclusions

This study has presented a detailed description and analysis of an advanced wastewater heat pump system for heating and cooling production. The system's performance was evaluated, and an ANN was employed to model the heat pump operations, confirming minimal deterioration due to fouling over the last four years. Key conclusions from this study include the following:

- The project is considered successful by those responsible for its specification, design, and operation, despite substantial challenges. The wastewater system has proven to be an effective thermal reservoir, maintaining higher temperatures than ambient air during winter for heating operations and colder temperatures during summer for cooling. The consistent temperature stability, never dropping below +5 °C, ensures a reliable heat source during the coldest days. Additionally, the innovative design of the wastewater heat exchanger plates, which are flexible and adaptable to various configurations, makes them ideal for both new and existing wastewater systems.
- There is room to improve the control strategy of the two heat pumps. Notably, heat pump IK001, which operates more frequently than IK002, achieves a higher SCOP despite being set to produce heat at a higher temperature. Re-evaluating the setpoint scheme is recommended, possibly through manual adjustments or by using the ANN model for optimization.
- The ANN has confirmed that the heat exchangers have not experienced degradation due to fouling. Moreover, it has effectively identified operational errors, pinpointing areas for improvement in heat pump management. This demonstrates the model's utility in guiding operational adjustments. Integrating physics-based modeling with the ANN could further enhance the model's operational range.
- The main challenges associated with the technology involve accessing the wastewater, addressing issues of ownership, tariffs, and wastewater temperature before it reaches the treatment plant, in addition to the physical installation and establishment of the wastewater heat pump system.
- Future work on this project could aim to refine the control systems of the heat pumps and develop an enhanced fault detection mechanism. Using information from the current manual maintenance logs, more detailed information on the sources of heat pump faults could be extracted and utilized within the machine learning framework. The analysis clearly indicates that the system lacks an automatic response to correct errors as they occur, leading to subsequent issues in other parts of the plant. Therefore, developing a methodology that combines practical knowledge with ML could be a valuable direction for future research.
- Looking ahead more broadly, future studies could investigate the utilization of wastewater as a thermal resource within urban planning, promoting the development of larger integrated systems that utilize this sustainable energy source.

Author Contributions: Conceptualization, F.S.F. and M.A.; methodology, F.S.F.; validation, F.S.F.; formal analysis, F.S.F.; data curation, F.S.F.; writing—original draft preparation, F.S.F.; writing—review and editing, M.A.; visualization, F.S.F.; supervision, M.A.; project administration, F.S.F.; funding acquisition, F.S.F. and M.A. All authors have read and agreed to the published version of the manuscript.

Funding: This research was partially funded by the Norwegian Research Council (project 311269) and Norconsult Norge AS (project 5195400).

Data Availability Statement: The data presented in this study are available on request to the corresponding author.

Acknowledgments: The authors would like to thank the municipal representative in Stavanger for discussions, access to data, and advice. The authors appreciate the feedback and suggestions received from colleagues and friends. The OpenAI GPT-4 model was employed for editorial assistance.

Conflicts of Interest: Author F.S.F. is employed by the Norwegian Consultant Engineering Company, Norconsult Norge AS, which partly funds his industrial Ph.D. project. The remaining author declares that research was conducted in the absence of any commercial or financial relationships that could be construed as potential conflicts of interest.

Abbreviations

AI	Artificial Intelligence
ANN	Artificial Neural Network
COP	Coefficient of Performance
DHW	Domestic Hot Water
EER	Energy Efficiency Ratio
ELF	Electrical Load Factor
IEA	International Energy Agency
IK001	Identifier for the first heat pump in the system
IK002	Identifier for the second heat pump in the system
LCOE	Levelized Cost of Energy
MAE	Mean Absolute Error
MAPE	Mean Absolute Percentage Error
ML	Machine Learning
MEG20	20% Monoethylene Glycol solution
OECD	Organization for Economic Co-operation and Development
ReLU	Rectified Linear Unit
RSME	Root Mean Square Error
SCADA	Supervisory Control and Data Acquisition
$SCOP$	Seasonal Coefficient of Performance
SEI	System Efficiency Index
SPF	Seasonal Performance Factor
Symbols and Variables	
c_p	Specific Heat Capacity (in kJ/kgK)
m	Mass flow rate (in kg/s)
$\dot{Q}$	Rate of heat transfer (in kW)
r	Pearson's correlation coefficient
T	Temperature
$\dot{W}_{hp}$	Electrical input to the heat pump (in kWh/h)

References

1. IEA. *Empowering Cities for a Net Zero Future: Unlocking Resilient, Smart, Sustainable Urban Energy Systems*; IEA: Paris, France, 2020.
2. IEA. *Net Zero by 2050*; IEA: Paris, France, 2021.
3. IEA. *Heat Pumps*; IEA: Paris, France, 2020.
4. Byrne, P. Modelling and Simulation of Heat Pumps for Simultaneous Heating and Cooling, a Special Issue. *Energies* **2022**, *15*, 5933. [CrossRef]
5. Rosenow, J.; Gibb, D.; Nowak, T.; Lowes, R. Heating up the global heat pump market. *Nat. Energy* **2022**, *7*, 901–904. [CrossRef]
6. Madani, H.; Claesson, J.; Lundqvist, P. Capacity control in ground source heat pump systems. *Int. J. Refrig.* **2011**, *34*, 1338–1347. [CrossRef]
7. Lund, R.; Persson, U. Mapping of potential heat sources for heat pumps for district heating in Denmark. *Energy* **2016**, *110*, 129–138. [CrossRef]
8. Blázquez, C.S.; Nieto, I.M.; García, J.C.; García, P.C.; Martín, A.F.; González-Aguilera, D. Comparative Analysis of Ground Source and Air Source Heat Pump Systems under Different Conditions and Scenarios. *Energies* **2023**, *16*, 1289. [CrossRef]
9. Klein, K.; Huchtemann, K.; Müller, D. Numerical study on hybrid heat pump systems in existing buildings. *Energy Build.* **2014**, *69*, 193–201. [CrossRef]
10. Carroll, P.; Chesser, M.; Lyons, P. Air Source Heat Pumps field studies: A systematic literature review. *Renew. Sustain. Energy Rev.* **2020**, *134*, 110275. [CrossRef]
11. IEA. *The Future of Heat Pumps*; IEA: Paris, France, 2022.
12. Nagpal, H.; Spriet, J.; Murali, M.; McNabola, A. Heat Recovery from Wastewater—A Review of Available Resource. *Water* **2021**, *13*, 1274. [CrossRef]
13. Patil, V.; Kadam, A. Problems and Perspectives of the Urban Sewage System: A Geographical Review. *Res. Rev. Int. J. Multidiscip.* **2019**, *4*, 2815–2819.
14. Culha, O.; Gunerhan, H.; Biyik, E.; Ekren, O.; Hepbasli, A. Heat exchanger applications in wastewater source heat pumps for buildings: A key review. *Energy Build.* **2015**, *104*, 215–232. [CrossRef]
15. Klimaetaten Oslo. Bringing You Heat That's Been Extracted from Your Sewage. Available online: https://www.klimaoslo.no/district-heating-from-sewage/ (accessed on 28 May 2024).

16. Seehus, G.; Vigre, E. What Is Triangulum? Available online: https://triangulum.no/about-triangulum/?lang=en (accessed on 21 July 2024).
17. Helmut UHRIG Straßen- und Tiefbau GmbH. UHRIG Product: Therm-Liner. 2020. Available online: https://www.uhrig-bau.eu/en/division/heat-from-wastewater/product-therm-liner/ (accessed on 21 July 2024).
18. Helmut UHRIG Straßen- und Tiefbau GmbH. References UHRIG Energy from Wastewater, Therm-Liner, Last Update: 31.03.2023. Available online: https://www.uhrig-bau.eu/wp-content/uploads/2020/11/230331-references-uhrig-energy-from-wastewater.pdf (accessed on 21 July 2024).
19. Bartnicki, G.; Ziembicki, P.; Klimczak, M.; Kalitka, A. The Potential of Heat Recovery from Wastewater Considering the Protection of Wastewater Treatment Plant Technology. *Energies* **2022**, *16*, 227. [CrossRef]
20. Kowalik, R.; Bąk-Patyna, P. Analysis of Heat Recovery from Wastewater Using a Heat Pump on the Example of a Wastewater Treatment Plant in the ŚwiĘtokrzyskie Voivodeship in Polish. *Struct. Environ.* **2021**, *13*, 90–95. [CrossRef]
21. Łokietek, T.; Tuchowski, W.; Leciej-Pirczewska, D.; Głowacka, A. Heat Recovery from a Wastewater Treatment Process—Case Study. *Energies* **2022**, *16*, 44. [CrossRef]
22. Cecconet, D.; Raček, J.; Callegari, A.; Hlavínek, P. Energy Recovery from Wastewater: A Study on Heating and Cooling of a Multipurpose Building with Sewage-Reclaimed Heat Energy. *Sustainability* **2019**, *12*, 116. [CrossRef]
23. Aprile, M.; Scoccia, R.; Dénarié, A.; Kiss, P.; Dombrovszky, M.; Gwerder, D.; Schuetz, P.; Elguezabal, P.; Arregi, B. District Power-To-Heat/Cool Complemented by Sewage Heat Recovery. *Energies* **2019**, *12*, 364. [CrossRef]
24. Xu, T.; Wang, X.; Wang, Y.; Li, Y.; Xie, H.; Yang, H.; Wei, X.; Gao, W.; Lin, Y.; Shi, C. Integration of sewage source heat pump and micro-cogeneration system based on domestic hot water demand characteristics: A feasibility study and economic analysis. *Process Saf. Environ. Prot.* **2023**, *179*, 796–811. [CrossRef]
25. Chen, W.-A.; Lim, J.; Miyata, S.; Akashi, Y. Methodology of evaluating the sewage heat utilization potential by modelling the urban sewage state prediction model. *Sustain. Cities Soc.* **2022**, *80*, 103751. [CrossRef]
26. Aguilera, J.J.; Meesenburg, W.; Markussen, W.B.; Zühlsdorf, B.; Elmegaard, B. Real-time monitoring and optimization of a large-scale heat pump prone to fouling—Towards a digital twin framework. *Appl. Energy* **2024**, *365*, 123274. [CrossRef]
27. Meesenburg, W.; Aguilera, J.J.; Kofler, R.; Markussen, W.B.; Brian, E. Prediction of fouling in sewage water heat pump for predictive maintenance. In Proceedings of the 35th International Conference on Efficiency, Cost, Optimization, Simulation and Environmental Impact of Energy Systems 2022, Copenhagen, Denmark, 3–7 July 2022.
28. Zhuang, Z.; Zhao, J.; Mi, F.; Zhang, T.; Hao, Y.; Li, S. Application and Analysis of a Heat Pump System for Building Heating and Cooling Using Extracting Heat Energy from Untreated Sewage. *Buildings* **2023**, *13*, 1342. [CrossRef]
29. Wang, J.; Sun, L.; Li, H.; Ding, R.; Chen, N. Prediction Model of Fouling Thickness of Heat Exchanger Based on TA-LSTM Structure. *Processes* **2023**, *11*, 2594. [CrossRef]
30. Kim, M.-H.; Kim, D.-W.; Han, G.; Heo, J.; Lee, D.-W. Ground Source and Sewage Water Source Heat Pump Systems for Block Heating and Cooling Network. *Energies* **2021**, *14*, 5640. [CrossRef]
31. Helmut UHRIG Straßen- und Tiefbau GmbH. Energy from Wastewater with UHRIG Therm-Liner Description of the Heat Exchanger System. Available online: https://www.uhrig-bau.eu/wp-content/uploads/2021/04/en-system-description-uhrig-energy-from-wastewater-eu-211210-1.pdf (accessed on 21 July 2024).
32. OECD. *Measuring Smart Citities Performance*; OECD: Paris, France, 2020.
33. Fadnes, F.S.; Olsen, E.; Assadi, M. Holistic management of a smart city thermal energy plant with sewage heat pumps, solar heating, and grey water recycling. *Front. Energy Res.* **2023**, *11*, 1078603. [CrossRef]
34. Zou, J.; Hirokawa, T.; An, J.; Huang, L.; Camm, J. Recent advances in the applications of machine learning methods for heat exchanger modeling—A review. *Front. Energy Res.* **2023**, *11*, 1294531. [CrossRef]
35. Starzec, M.; Kordana-Obuch, S.; Piotrowska, B. Evaluation of the Suitability of Using Artificial Neural Networks in Assessing the Effectiveness of Greywater Heat Exchangers. *Sustainability* **2024**, *16*, 2790. [CrossRef]
36. Çengel, Y.A. *Heat and Mass Transfer: A Practical Approach*, 3rd ed.; McGraw-Hill Science Engineering: Blacklick, OH, USA, 2006.
37. DKRT. Om DKRT—Dansk Kloak RenoveringsTeknik ApS. Available online: https://kloakshop.dk/om-os/ (accessed on 21 July 2024).
38. Schneider Electric. *Citect SCADA 2018 Installation and Configuration Guide*; Schneider Electric: Rueil-Malmaison, France, 2018.
39. Andresen, T.; Nekså, P.; Stene, J. *Heat Pumps in Smart Energy-Efficient Buildings A State-of-the-Art Report*; NTNU and SINTEF: Trondheim, Norway, 2002.
40. Lane, A.-L.; Benson, J.; Eriksson, L.; Fahlén, P.; Nordman, R.; Haglund Stignor, C.; Berglöf, K.; Hundy, G. *Method and Guidelines to Establish System Efficiency Index during Field Measurements on Air Conditioning and Heat Pump Systems*; SP Technical Research Institute of Sweden: Borås, Sweden, 2014.
41. Géron, A. *Hands-On Machine Learning with Scikit-Learn, Keras, and TensorFlow*, 2nd ed.; Tache, R.R.a.N., Ed.; O'Reilly Media, Inc.: Sebastopol, CA, USA, 2019.
42. Abida, A.; Richter, P. HVAC control in buildings using neural network. *J. Build. Eng.* **2023**, *65*, 105558. [CrossRef]
43. Fadnes, F.S.; Banihabib, R.; Assadi, M. Using Artificial Neural Networks to Gather Intelligence on a Fully Operational Heat Pump System in an Existing Building Cluster. *Energies* **2023**, *16*, 3875. [CrossRef]
44. Witte, R.S.W.; John, S. *Statistics*, 11th ed.; John Wiley & Sons, Inc.: Hoboken, NJ, USA, 2017.
45. Russo, R. *Stop Using Moving Average to Smooth Your Time Series*; BIP xTech: Rome, Italy, 2024.

46. de Myttenaere, A.; Golden, B.; Le Grand, B.; Rossi, F. Mean Absolute Percentage Error for regression models. *Neurocomputing* **2016**, *192*, 38–48. [CrossRef]
47. Bogdanov, D.; Satymov, R.; Breyer, C. Impact of temperature dependent coefficient of performance of heat pumps on heating systems in national and regional energy systems modelling. *Appl. Energy* **2024**, *371*, 123647. [CrossRef]

energies

Article

Advanced Fuel Based on Semi-Coke and Cedarwood: Kinetic Characteristics and Synergetic Effects

Andrey Zhuikov [1,*], Lily Irtyugo [1], Alexander Samoilo [1], Yana Zhuikova [2], Irina Grishina [1], Tatyana Pyanykh [1] and Stanislav Chicherin [3,4]

[1] Polytechnic School, Siberian Federal University, 79, Svobodny Avenue, Krasnoyarsk 660041, Russia; lirtugo@sfu-kras.ru (L.I.); asamoylo@sfu-kras.ru (A.S.); igrishina@sfu-kras.ru (I.G.); tpyanykh@sfu-kras.ru (T.P.)

[2] Research School of High-Energy Physics, National Research Tomsk Polytechnic University, 30, Lenin Avenue, Tomsk 634050, Russia; yvz12@tpu.ru

[3] Thermo and Fluid Dynamics (FLOW), Faculty of Engineering, Vrije Universiteit Brussel (VUB), Pleinlaan 2, 1050 Brussels, Belgium; stanislav.chicherin@vub.be

[4] Brussels Institute for Thermal-Fluid Systems and Clean Energy (BRITE), Vrije Universiteit Brussel (VUB) and Université Libre de Bruxelles (ULB), 1050 Brussels, Belgium

* Correspondence: azhuikov@sfu-kras.ru

Abstract: This paper presents the results of analytical studies of the combustion process of semi-coke, cedar sawdust, and their mixtures using the TGA method at three different heating rates with the determination of the main characteristics of heating: the presence of synergetic interaction between the components of the mixture affecting the maximum rate of combustion and kinetic parameters. Calculations of activation energy and pre-exponential multiplier of the Arrhenius equation by the Friedman and Ozawa–Flynn–Wall priori methods for initial combustibles and their mixtures have been carried out. Semi-coke was obtained by thermal treatment of brown coal at 700–900 °C to remove volatile substances, which makes it more environmentally friendly than the original coal. Semi-coke has a higher heat of combustion than biomass, and biomass has a higher reactivity than semi-coke. The combustion process of biomass occurs in a lower temperature range, and adding biomass to semi-coke shifts the combustion process to a lower temperature range than such for biomass. Adding at least 50% of biomass to semi-coke increases the combustion index by at least 1.1 times. Regardless of the heating rate of mixtures, synergetic interaction between the mixture's components increases the maximum combustion rate of coke residue by 20%.

Keywords: semi-coke; biomass; cedar sawdust; co-combustion; synergistic effects; TGA; kinetic analysis

1. Introduction

The consumption of solid fossil fuels for heat and electricity generation in the world reaches 40% compared to other energy fuels [1,2]. Reducing coal consumption and improving environmental performance is currently an urgent scientific and practical task. One of the available ways to realize this task is the addition of biomass to coal, which allows for the reduction of coal consumption, reduced harmful emissions (sulfur oxides and nitrogen oxides), reduced CO_2 emissions, reduced emissions of fine ash particles, and does not require large-scale reconstruction of equipment [3–5].

Considering the issue of a feasibility study of the transition to coal co-combustion (semi-coke produced from coal), it can be noted that biomass is considered waste from any production, for example, in the wood processing industry, and is conditionally free fuel due to the fact that the enterprise needs to utilize its waste at its own expense. In this case, the cost of biomass will depend only on the distance of its delivery to the heat power facilities, so biomass will be cheaper than coal, which will improve the technical and economic performance of the boiler house. In addition, it is proved that the cost of reconstruction of a coal-fired boiler house will be lower than the cost required for the construction of a new biomass-fired boiler house [6]. If payments for harmful emissions and CO_2 emissions are taken into account for the technical and economic indicators of the boiler house, these payments will be reduced when switching to the combustion of biomass-based mixtures due to the fact that biomass is a carbon-neutral fuel and less harmful emissions, such as sulphur oxides and nitrogen oxides, are emitted during combustion [7].

Semi-coke produced in the process of the thermal treatment of coal by gasification or pyrolysis is obtained as waste or as a product. In the case of synthesis gas production for the chemical industry, semi-coke is waste with low calorific value [8] and is stored in special landfills. Such waste is sometimes used to produce thermal energy, but there are a number of problems associated with its combustion in power plants. Most of the problems with the combustion of semi-coke are related to the low content of volatile substances, which reduces the maneuverability of power plants due to the high ignition and burnout temperature of semi-coke. Semi-coke, produced as high-calorie furnace fuel for the metallurgical industry, is not used as energy fuel for boilers. The reason for this is that the process of heat energy production becomes more expensive as the cost of energy fuel increases due to the process of thermal treatment before its combustion in boilers. Therefore, semi-coke obtained as waste is expediently burned in a mixture with highly reactive coals or biomass [9], and semi-coke obtained for the metallurgical industry [10] and having a high calorific value is expediently partially burned together with free biomass waste.

In the process of investigating the co-combustion of semi-coke and different types of biomass (corn stalk, rice stalk, and pine wood), it was found that the addition of biomass has an effect on reducing the ignition and burnout temperature of the mixture [11]. Liu H.-P. et al. [12] investigated the co-combustion of waste from the thermal treatment of oil shale and torrefied corn stalks and found that the change in activation energy was affected by increasing the proportion of biomass in the mixture. During the combustion of a mixture based on coal and char, the presence of synergetic effects affecting the ignition temperature due to an increase in volatile substances in the mixture was found, as well as an increase in the average combustion temperature of fuel particles, which affects the improvement in combustion efficiency of the mixture [13]. Qin H. et al. [14], in the study of co-combustion of semi-coke and biomass using thermo-gravimetric analysis, found that biomass burns more efficiently than semi-coke and that the heating rate (too low or too high) affects the reaction time, which adversely affects combustion, and they also noted the presence of synergistic effects. When combusting semi-coke and hard coal together, the proportion of semi-coke in the mixture should not exceed 45%. The addition of semi-coke to coal leads to a decrease in the combustion index of the mixture and an increase in the activation energy [15]. The NO content of co-combustion of semi-coke and hard coal decreases as the proportion of coal in the mixture increases [16,17]. Zhao R. et al. [18] investigated the co-combustion of lignite and semi-coke and found that increasing the proportion of lignite in the mixture affects the reduction in CO and CO_2, while NO emissions increase and semi-coke has a suppressive effect on nitrogen and sulfur oxide emissions.

The purpose of this study is to comprehensively investigate the combustion of industrial semi-coke produced for the metallurgical industry and forest biomass, taking into account flue gas analysis and synergistic effects. For the first time, the influence of heating rate on the interaction of mixture components with each other was analyzed, taking into account the main combustion characteristics. The results of the study can be applied in the design of power plants and in CFD modeling of furnace devices and processes.

2. Materials and Methods

2.1. Materials and Sample Preparation

The following fuels and their mixtures (by mass) were selected as objects of research:

No. 1—semi-coke obtained from brown coal by gasification under conditions of oxidizer deficiency at a temperature of 700–900 °C, Russia.

No. 2—cedar sawdust, biomass waste obtained at a woodworking enterprise, Russia;

No. 3—a mixture based on semi-coke 75% + cedar sawdust 25%;
No. 4—a mixture based on semi-coke 50% + cedar sawdust 50%;
No. 5—a mixture based on semi-coke 25% + cedar sawdust 75%.

Visualization of the fuels is presented in Figure 1. Semi-coke is produced for use as an energy fuel in aluminum production or as sorbents in other industries. Semi-coke is not used as an energy fuel for heat generation due to its minimal content of volatile substances, which makes it less reactive, so it is advisable to burn it with highly reactive fuel, for example, biomass.

(a) (b)

Figure 1. Type of fuels under study: (**a**)—semi-coke; (**b**)—cedar sawdust.

Cedar is used to produce furniture, sports equipment, and construction material; after its processing, it leaves a large amount of wood waste (sawdust), which must be disposed of in special landfills, as storage in the open air can lead to fire and, in the process of long storage, decomposing sawdust can harm the environment.

The fuels were studied after they reached the air-dry state. Coal and sawdust were separately ground in a Retsch DM200 (Haan, Germany), and then the dispersion of fuel particles 53–200 μm was obtained using a Retsch AS200 (Haan, Germany).

The calorimeter C6000 (IKA, Staufen, Germany) was used to determine the combustion heat; a Vario MACRO cube device (Elementar Analysensysteme GmbH, Langenselbold, Germany) was used to determine the content of carbon, hydrogen, and nitrogen; a humidity analyzer MA-150 (Sartorius, Göttingen, Germany) was used to determine the humidity; a muffle furnace Snol was used to determine the yield of volatile substances and ash content 7.2/1300 (AB "Umega", Utena, Lithuania). Technical and elemental analyses were carried out according to the following standards: ISO 11722:1999, Solid mineral fuels—Bituminous coal—Determination of moisture in a sample for general analysis by drying in nitrogen; ISO 1171:2010, Solid mineral fuels—Determination of ash; ISO 562: 2010, Bituminous coal and coke—Determination of volatile matter; ISO 1928: 2009, Solid mineral fuels—Determination of gross calorific value by the bomb calorimetric method and calculation of net calorific value; ASTM D5373-14e1, Standard Test Methods for Determination of Carbon, Hydrogen and Nitrogen in Analysis Samples of Coal and Carbon in Analysis Samples of Coal and Coke, ASTM International, West Conshohocken, PA, 2014 [19–23]. The results of technical and elemental analyses of semi-coke (No. 1) and cedar sawdust (No. 2) are summarized in Table 1.

Table 1. Proximate and ultimate analysis of tested samples.

No.	Proximate Analysis/%				Ultimate Analysis/%				
	MC^a	A^d	VC^{daf}	HHV	C^{daf}	H^{daf}	N^{daf}	S^{daf}	O^{daf}
	%	%	%	MJ/kg	%	%	%	%	%
1	0.8	9.1	8.4	32.1	91.2	2.4	2.2	0.2	4.0
2	6.4	0.2	80.2	19.2	51.3	5.4	0.3	–	43.0

Notes: ^{a}—analytical state; ^{d}—a dry state; ^{daf}—a dry, ash-free state.

The combustion of fuels was investigated using a synchronous thermal analyzer SDT Q600 (TA Instruments Inc., New Castle, DE, USA). The experiments were carried out in airflow with a flow rate of 50 mL/min at heating rates of 10, 20, and 30 °C min^{-1}; the weight of the sample was 5–6 mg. Universal Analysis 2000 software (Software v5.5.24, TA Instruments Inc., New Castle, DE, USA) was used to process the results of thermo-gravimetry (TG) and differential thermo-gravimetry (DTG). The experiments were repeated at least 2 times to achieve repeatability.

2.2. Combustion Characteristics

The TG results were used to determine the main combustion characteristics, including the fuel combustion index (*S*) [24–26], which was determined according to Formula (1). This quantitative characteristic is used in analyzing the combustibility of different fuels and takes into account the temperature at which ignition occurs, mass loss rates, and burnout temperature. A high value of the combustion index indicates that the fuel ignites at lower temperatures and has a higher combustion rate, which in turn affects the conditions for completing the combustion process at lower temperatures. When calculating the combustion index, the temperature at which carbon ignites (T_i) and the temperature at which the combustion process is completed (T_b) were used [27–30]. The temperatures at which the fuel ignition occurs and the combustion process is completed were determined using the curve crossing method.

The combustion index is calculated using the following formula:

$$S = \frac{R_{DTG} \cdot R_{mean}}{T_i^2 \cdot T_b}, \quad (1)$$

where R_{DTG}—maximum rate of fuel mass loss, % min^{-1}; R_{mean}—average rate of fuel mass loss from ignition to complete burnout of its carbon residue, % min^{-1}; T_i and T_b—temperatures corresponding to ignition and carbon burnout, °C; *S*—combustion index, min^{-2} °C^{-3}.

2.3. Estimation Methods of Synergy

To analyze the influence of components in the combustion of a mixture, experimental (exp) and calculated (est) data were compared. The calculated data were obtained using Formula (2) [18,31,32]:

$$DTG_{est} = x_1 DTG_1 + x_2 DTG_2, \quad (2)$$

where DTG_1 and DTG_2—values of maximum rate of mass loss for each fuel (DTG_1—semi-coke; DTG_2—sawdust), % min^{-1}; x_1 and x_2—values of fuel content in the mixture, their sum should be equal to one.

2.4. Kinetic Analysis

Kinetic analysis was performed on TGA data using NETZSCH Thermokinetics software (NETZSCH-Geraetebau GmbH, Selb, Germany). The values of such kinetic parameters as activation energy (E_a) and pre-exponential multiplier (A) were determined using Friedman and Ozawa–Flynn–Wall (OFW) models.

These models are based on the kinetic equation derived from the law of acting masses, which defines the reaction rate $d\alpha/dt$ as the product of the rate constant (k) and the concentration of the starting substance to a degree equal to the reaction order (f (α)). In turn, the rate constant is a function of temperature, described by the Arrhenius Equation (3):

$$k = A \cdot \exp\left(-E_a/RT\right), \tag{3}$$

where R is the gas constant, and T is the temperature. Thus, the basic kinetic equation of the heterogeneous process is described in expression 4 as follows:

$$\frac{d\alpha}{dt} = k(T) \cdot f(\alpha), \tag{4}$$

where α is the degree of transformation of the substance.

The Friedman and Ozawa–Flynn–Wall models refer to isoconversion methods of kinetic analysis, which assumes that each point of the experimental TGA curve corresponds to a certain value of the degree of conversion (x), proportional to the degree of transformation of the substance during the chemical reaction. The calculation of x is carried out according to Expression (5):

$$x_i = \frac{m(t_s) - m(t_i)}{m(t_s) - m\left(t_f\right)}, \tag{5}$$

where xi is the degree of conversion at time t_i, $m(t_s)$ is the signal at the initial time t_s, $m(t_i)$ is the signal at time t_i, and $m(f_t)$ is the signal at the final time t_f.

Friedman [33] proposed to use the logarithm of the rate of change of conversion d_x/d_t as a function of the corresponding temperature, represented in Expression (6):

$$\ln \frac{dx}{dt}_{x=x_i} = \ln A - \frac{Ea}{RT} + \ln f(x_i), \tag{6}$$

Considering that f (x) is constant for a given xi, the dependence in coordinates $\ln d_x/d_t = f\ (1/T)$ is described by a straight line with slope $m = -E_a/R$.

The pre-exponential multiplier is evaluated assuming that f (x) = $(1 - x_i)$, which is true for the first-order reaction, in which case A is calculated from Expression (7):

$$lnA = ln\frac{dx}{dt}_{x=x_i} + \frac{Ea}{RT} + \ln(1 - x_i), \tag{7}$$

Independently of each other, Ozawa [34] and Flynn and Wall [35] developed a method for determining the activation energy from data from a series of dynamic measurements with different heating rates (β). If the heating rate is constant in time $\beta = d_T/d_t$, expression (4) is transformed into Expression (8):

$$\frac{d\alpha}{dT} = \frac{1}{\beta}k(T) \cdot f(\alpha), \tag{8}$$

Taking into account (3), this expression, when integrating, takes the form of Expression (9):

$$\int_0^\alpha \frac{d\alpha}{f(\alpha)} = \frac{A}{\beta} \cdot \int_{T_0}^{T} exp\left(-\frac{Ea}{RT}\right) dT = G_\alpha, \tag{9}$$

where G_a is the integral conversion function, which is constant at a constant value of xi.

After logarithmizing (9), the equation is represented by Expression (10):

$$\ln G_{\alpha} = \ln \frac{A \cdot Ea}{R} - \ln \beta + \ln p_{z}, \tag{10}$$

where $p_z = \frac{\exp(-z)}{z} - \int_{-\infty}^{z} \frac{\exp(-z)}{z} dz$, $z = Ea/RT$. Using Doyle's approximation [36], it is obtained that $\ln p_z = -5.3305 - 1.052 \cdot z$ and substituting this value into (10) gives Expression (11):

$$\int_{0}^{\alpha} \frac{d\alpha}{f(\alpha)} = \frac{A}{\beta} \cdot \int_{T_0}^{T} exp\left(-\frac{Ea}{RT}\right) dT = G_{\alpha}, \tag{11}$$

Considering that G_a is constant for a given x_i, the dependence in coordinates $\ln \beta = f(1/T)$ is described by a straight line with slope $m = -1.052 \cdot E_a/R$.

When averaged over all heating rates, equation (10) leads to the determination of the values of the pre-exponential multiplier assuming a first-order reaction when G_{α} in Expression (12):

$$\ln A = \ln(-\ln(1 - x_i)) - \ln \frac{Ea}{R} + \ln \beta - \ln p_z \tag{12}$$

2.5. SEM

Scanning electron microscopy (SEM) was performed on a TM-4000 microscope (HITACHI High-Technologies Corporation, Chiba, Japan) to analyze the surface texture of particles of solid fuels (semicoke and sawdust). The main characteristics of the microscope: magnification from ×10 to ×100,000 times; depth of field 0.5 mm; accelerating voltage from 5 kV to 15 kV; maximum sample size up to 80 mm in diameter and up to 50 mm in height; minimum displacement step is 65 nm. The TM-4000 microscope is equipped with a microanalysis system for Hitachi TM4000Plus benchtop microscope (HITACHI High-Technologies Corporation, Chiba, Japan): silicon-drift detector with a working area of 30 mm2; guaranteed energy resolution: 137 eV (Mn Ka); electron source is a pre-centered tungsten cathode. The main functionality of the TM-4000 microscope is to obtain and process magnified images of the sample surface in backscattered electrons (BSE) and secondary electrons (SE).

Figure 2 shows SEM images showing the surface area of semi-coke and biomass fuel particles. Generally, the specific surface area of the coal particle is small compared to biomass because the presence of pores, cracks, and channels in the fuel particles increases the specific surface area. In its structure, the biomass particle (Figure 2b,d) consists of a large number of different pores and crack channels through which, in the life process, fluid flows from the roots to the upper edge, nourishing the whole tree. High specific surface area primarily affects the ignition and combustion process of the fuel particle because, through the channels, pores, and cracks, the oxidizer (air) penetrates faster into the particle and reacts with carbon.

Unlike biomass, the surface of coal particles, especially bituminous coal and anthracite, may have no pores, cracks, or channels at all, while brown coal sometimes has small cracks. This, in turn, is one of the factors affecting the reactivity of the fuel, so the reactivity of coal is lower than that of biomass, but other factors must be taken into account.

Gasification of coal in the reactor at a temperature of 700–900 °C resulted in highly porous carbonizate differing from the original coal with a low content of volatile substances, high ash content, and high heat of combustion, which makes it particularly attractive for use as an energy fuel. When gaseous volatile substances escape from the depth of the particle during thermal treatment of coal, the surface of the semi-coke particle is ruptured, forming a large number of pores, cracks, and channels (Figure 2a,c).

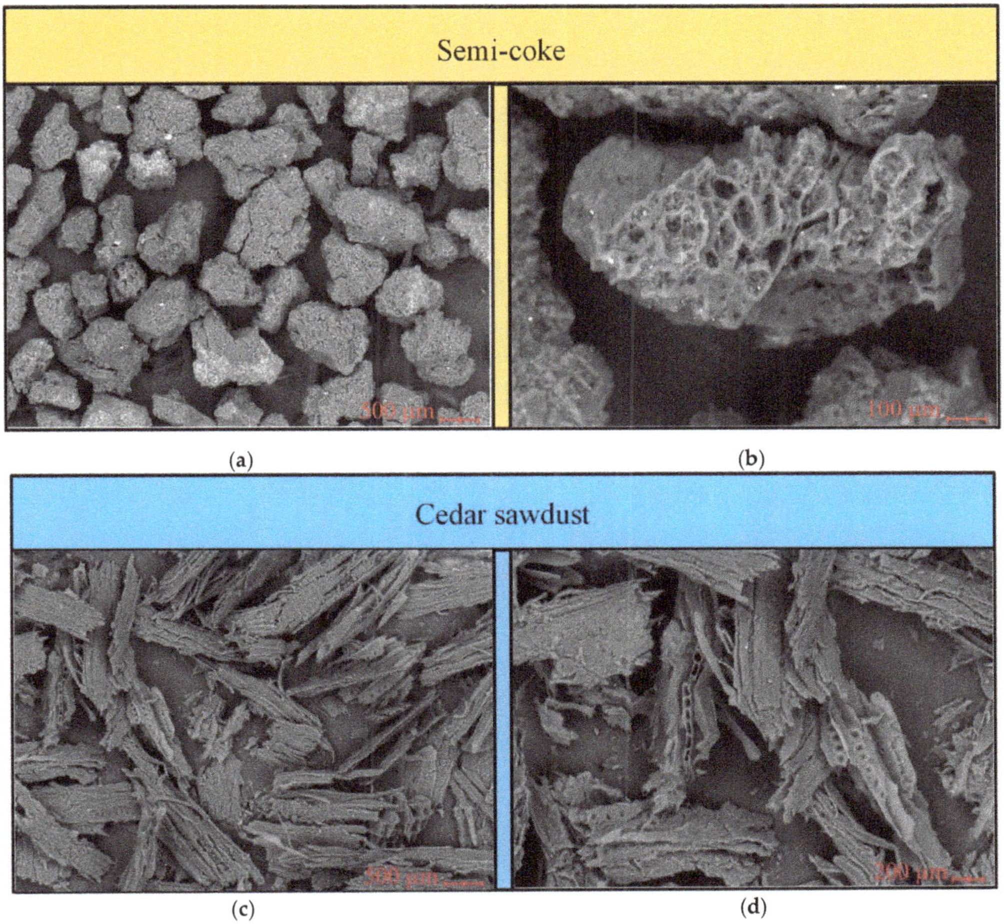

Figure 2. SEM images: (**a**)—semi-coke 100×; (**b**)—semi-coke 500×; (**c**)—cedar sawdust 100×; (**d**)—cedar sawdust 200×.

2.6. Ash Analysis

The elemental composition of ash residue was analyzed as follows. The fuel with a mass of 2 g in a porcelain pot was placed in a muffle furnace, Heraeus K114 (Thermo Fisher Scientific Inc., Waltham, MA, USA), preheated to a temperature of 1000 °C. The holding time at this temperature was 1 h. The values of basic oxides included in the ashes of fuels No.1 and 2 are presented in Table 2.

Since semi-coke was obtained from brown coal, the chemical composition of the mineral part of ash is mainly represented by silicon oxide 46.1% and aluminum oxide 10% as well as iron oxide 13.7% and calcium oxide 23% (see Table 2). High content of these elements can intensify at high temperatures the process of slagging of heating surfaces on the basis of ferruginous deposits in the boiler furnace; therefore, this coal grade belongs to high slagging. In wood biomass, according to Table 2, high content of calcium oxide and potassium oxide in the ash is noted; these elements can also intensify the contamination of heating surfaces on the basis of active alkalis, which is characteristic of wood biomass. It is noted that the high SiO_2 content of 10.5% is not characteristic of woody biomass and is most likely obtained in the form of fine sand during its storage or transportation. Detailed studies on the propensity of this type of coal and pine sawdust are presented in [37].

Table 2. Ash analysis of samples.

Oxides, %	No.1—Semi-Coke	No.2—Cedar Sawdust
SiO_2	50.5	10.5
Al_2O_3	10.0	1.3
Fe_2O_3	13.7	1.1
CaO	23.0	55.1
MgO	4.5	4.0
TiO_2	0.1	0.1
Na_2O	0.2	0.6
K_2O	0.3	19.2
SO_3	6.0	2.3
P_2O_5	0.04	3.1
ZnO	0.05	0.9
Cl	0.01	0.3
MnO	0.05	1.5

The heating process of individual fuels and fuel mixtures is shown below. Heating of fuels can be divided into three main stages: at the first stage of heating, there is evaporation of moisture; the second stage corresponds to the beginning of thermal decomposition, which develops into ignition and combustion of volatile substances contained in fuels; at the third stage, there is ignition and combustion of coke residue to the temperature corresponding to the completion of the combustion process of the carbon part of fuel particles, after which only unburnable ash residue remains. Only the second and third heating stages of fuels can be referred to as the combustion process in thermo-gravimetric analysis; the first heating stage usually takes place in the temperature range from the initial heating temperature to 110–130 °C, and the mass reduction in fuels is minimal due to the fact that the analytical moisture content is minimal (see Table 1). In real conditions, the working moisture content of semi-coke and biomass can be many times higher since the specific surface area formed by a large number of pores, cracks, and channels in both fuels is quite high, which will negatively affect the delivery and storage of these fuels in the open air, presenting an opportunity to increase the moisture content due to precipitation.

3. Results

This section presents the temperature ranges and time intervals of the second and third stages of combustion of fuels/fuel mixtures and the main combustion characteristics of individual fuels/fuel mixtures.

3.1. Individual Combustion

The onset of thermal decomposition of semi-coke at a heating rate of 10 °C min^{-1} occurs in the temperature range of 295–405 °C accompanied by the release of volatile substances (Figure 3a,b).

The ignition of coke residue occurs at 405 °C. The third stage of heating takes place in the temperature range of 406–653 °C and is characterized by the combustion of coke residue (Table 3), expressed by one large exothermic peak (see Figure 3b) with a maximum mass loss rate equal to 15.5% min^{-1} at a temperature of 436 °C. The combustion of semi-coke is completed at a temperature of 653. The combustion index of semi-coke was 6.5 min^{-2} $°C^{-3}$.

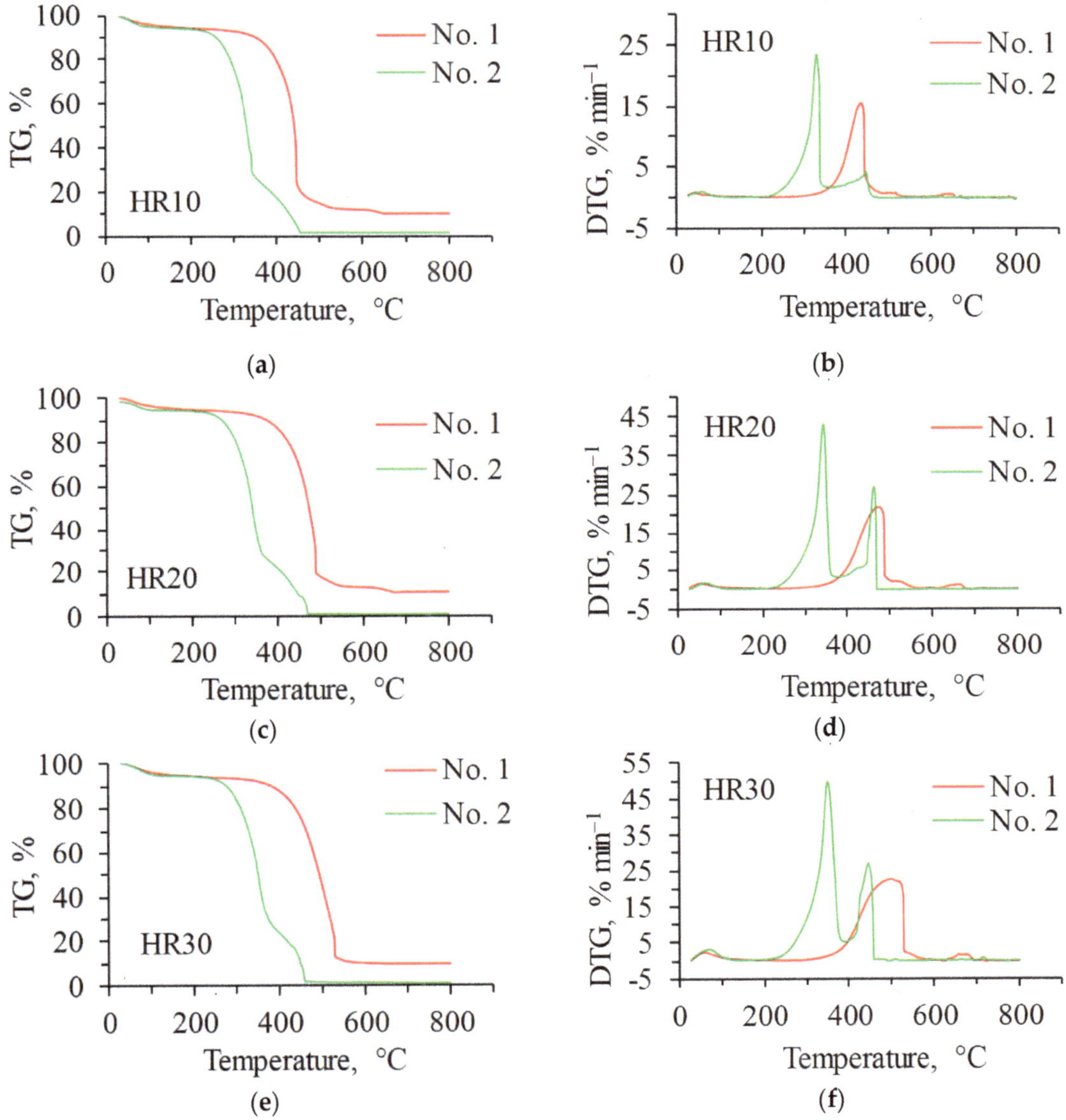

Figure 3. Combustion profiles of semi-coke (No. 1) and cedar sawdust (No. 2): (**a**)—TG curves at heating rate 10 °C min^{-1}; (**b**)—DTG curves at heating rate 10 °C min^{-1}; (**c**)—TG curves at heating rate 20 °C min^{-1}; (**d**)—DTG curves at heating rate 20 °C min^{-1}; (**e**)—TG curves at heating rate 30 °C min^{-1}; (**f**)—DTG curves at heating rate 30 °C min^{-1}.

When the heating rate is increased two and three times, the temperature range of the second heating stage shifts to higher temperatures up to 440 °C (see Figure 3c–f). In turn, this leads to an increase in the ignition temperature of coke residue up to 335–440 °C. Burning of coke residue, which occurs at the third stage of heating, shifts to the region of higher temperatures with increasing heating rate, and the process time decreases more than twice. The burnout temperature of semi-coke increases as the heating temperature increases. Increasing the ignition and burnout temperature did not affect the decrease in the combustion index; on the contrary, increasing the heating rate more than doubled the combustion index due to an increase in the maximum mass loss rate (Table 4).

Table 3. Temperature ranges of the main combustion stages of individual fuels and fuel mixtures.

Samples	HR, °C min^{-1}	Temperature Interval Stage II, °C	Stage II, min	Temperature Interval Stage III, °C	Stage III, min	Burning, min
No. 1	10	295–405	9.5	406–653	26.5	36.0
	20	310–435	5.1	436–672	13.1	18.2
	30	290–440	4.2	441–690	9.2	13.4
No. 2	10	201–299	9.4	300–461	16.7	26.1
	20	202–311	5.2	312–469	8.2	13.4
	30	202–318	3.8	319–458	4.7	8.5
No. 3	10	240–349	21.2	350–644	30.0	51.2
	20	230–401	8.0	402–669	14.0	22.0
	30	240–406	5.1	407–689	9.9	15.0
No. 4	10	233–301	6.6	302–669	37.2	43.8
	20	220–313	4.6	314–665	17.7	22.3
	30	229–318	2.9	319–675	12.0	14.9
No. 5	10	216–301	8.0	302–625	33.1	41.1
	20	204–311	5.4	312–456	7.4	12.8
	30	206–316	3.5	317–489	5.9	9.4

Table 4. Combustion performance of mixed fuel under different mixing ratios.

Samples	HR, °C min^{-1}	R_{DTG}, % min^{-1}	T_i, °C	T_{DTG}, °C	T_b, °C	$S \times 10^{-7}$, min^{-2} °C^{-3}
No. 1	10	295–405	9.5	406–653	26.5	36.0
	20	310–435	5.1	436–672	13.1	18.2
	30	290–440	4.2	441–690	9.2	13.4
No. 2	10	201–299	9.4	300–461	16.7	26.1
	20	202–311	5.2	312–469	8.2	13.4
	30	202–318	3.8	319–458	4.7	8.5
No. 3	10	240–349	21.2	350–644	30.0	51.2
	20	230–401	8.0	402–669	14.0	22.0
	30	240–406	5.1	407–689	9.9	15.0
No. 4	10	233–301	6.6	302–669	37.2	43.8
	20	220–313	4.6	314–665	17.7	22.3
	30	229–318	2.9	319–675	12.0	14.9
No. 5	10	216–301	8.0	302–625	33.1	41.1
	20	204–311	5.4	312–456	7.4	12.8
	30	206–316	3.5	317–489	5.9	9.4

Combustion of biomass volatiles at a heating rate of 10 °C/min occurs in the temperature range of 201–299 °C. Ignition of the coke residue takes place at a temperature of 299 °C. Burning of the coke residue takes place in the temperature range of 300–461 °C. The maximum mass loss rate was 23.5%/min. The burnout temperature was 461 °C. In general, it can be noted that the combustion of semi-coke and biomass takes place in different temperature ranges. The key factor here is the content of volatile substances, which is many times higher in biomass than in semi-coke (see Table 1). The combustion index of biomass is three times higher than that of semi-coke (Table 4).

3.2. Co-Combustion Characteristics of Blends

The heating process of the mixtures at different heating rates is represented by the profiles of the TG and DTG curves in Figure 4.

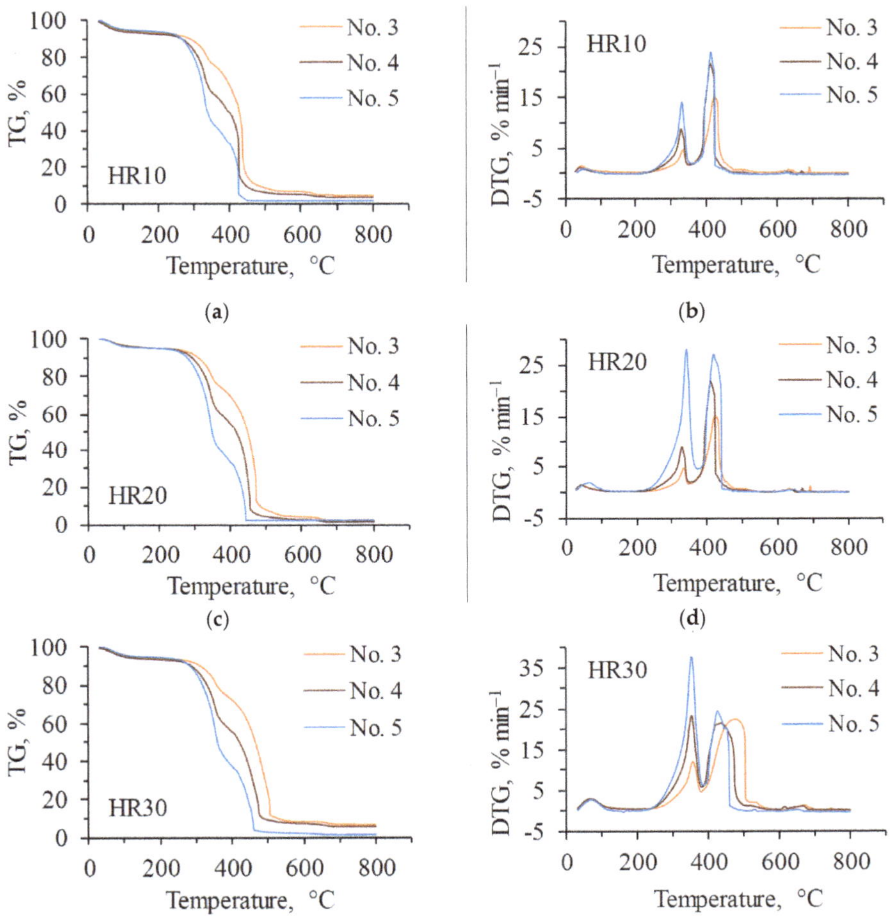

Figure 4. Thermal curves of processes occurring during the heating of solid fuel mixtures: (**a**)—TG curves at heating rate 10 °C min^{-1}; (**b**)—DTG curves at heating rate 10 °C min^{-1}; (**c**)—TG curves at heating rate 20 °C min^{-1}; (**d**)—DTG curves at heating rate 20 °C min^{-1}; (**e**)—TG curves at heating rate 30 °C min^{-1}; (**f**)—DTG curves at heating rate 30 °C min^{-1}.

The combustion process of mixtures No. 3–5 is expressed by two DTG maxima corresponding to the combustion of volatile substances of biomass and semi-coke residue. At the content of 25% of the biomass in the mixture (No. 3), the first maximum DTG is located in the temperature range of 240–349 °C and is characteristic of the combustion of volatile substances of biomass and part of the coke residue; the duration of the second stage was 21.2–5.1 min, depending on the heating rate (Table 3). The second maximum of DTG located in the temperature range of 350–644 °C is characteristic of the combustion of semi-coke residue and biomass; the duration of the third stage was 30.0–9.9 min. The total combustion time of mixture No. 3 was 51.2–15.0 min. The temperature at which the coke residue ignition occurred was 349–406 °C depending on the heating rate (Table 4), the burnout temperature was 644–689 °C, and the combustion index was 2.5–18.3 min^{-2} $°C^{-3}$. The decrease in combustion index compared to semi-coke at heating rates of 10 and 20 °C min^{-1} is explained by the fact that the maximum rate of mass loss (R_{DTG}) decreases, which is an indicator of fuel reactivity; the higher the R_{DTG} value, the more reactive, and thus better burning, the fuel.

Increasing the share of biomass in the mixture up to 50% (No. 4) affects the decrease in the duration of the second stage of combustion by 6.6–2.9 min at different heating rates and shifts the temperature range of the second stage to lower temperatures of 233–301 °C. The duration of the third stage increased and amounted to 37.2–12.0 min. The total combustion time of the No. 4 mixture was 43.8–14.9 min (Table 3). The ignition temperature decreased and amounted to 301–318 °C due to an increase in the volatile content of the mixture. The burnout temperature was 669–675 °C. The combustion index at different rates was 7.2–16.6 min^{-2} $°C^{-3}$ (Table 4).

In the mixture containing 75% of biomass (No. 5), the duration of the second stage (combustion of cellulose and hemicellulose contained in biomass) located in the temperature range of 216–301 °C was 8.0–3.5 min. The third stage took place in the temperature range of 302–625 °C with a duration of 33.1–5.9 min at different heating rates. The total combustion time of mixture No. 5 was 41.1–9.4 min, which was shorter than that of mixtures No. 3 and 4 (Table 3). The ignition temperature was 301–316 °C, and the burnout temperature was 625–489 °C. The combustion index of mixture No. 5 increased to 12.3–53.7 min^{-2} $°C^{-3}$ due to an increase in the maximum rate of mass loss.

The addition of biomass to semi-coke had a positive effect on the reduction in ignition and burnout temperature. The addition of more than 25% biomass influences the increase in the combustion index of semi-coke due to the increase in volatile matter content in the mixture, in turn influencing its ignition at lower temperatures compared to semi-coke.

3.3. Interaction between Blend Components—Synergistic Effects

In this section, only the second and third stages of heating fuel mixtures at three heating rates will be considered. The analysis of the interaction of the mixture of component particles on each other is presented in Figure 5 in the form of DTG curve profiles. Comparisons of DTG_{exp} (values obtained during the experiment) and DTG_{est} (values obtained by calculation) curve profiles show the presence of additive combustion or the presence of synergetic effects expressed in the change of the maximum combustion rate at two combustion stages: Stage II corresponds to the temperature region of biomass volatile combustion; Stage III corresponds to the temperature region of coke residue combustion of mixture components. The results of DTG_{exp} and DTG_{est} at different heating rates and stages are presented in Table 5.

Table 5. DTG_{exp} and $DTGest$ results at different heating rates and stages.

	Blends	Stage II		Stage III	
		DTG_{exp}, % min^{-1}	DTG_{est}, % min^{-1}	DTG_{exp}, % min^{-1}	DTG_{est}, % min^{-1}
Heating rate 10 °C min^{-1}	No. 3	4.5	6.4	15.1	12.4
	No. 4	8.8	12.1	21.7	9.4
	No. 5	14.3	17.7	24.1	6.4
Heating rate 20 °C min^{-1}	No. 3	9.4	11.6	21.5	22.5
	No. 4	16.8	22.0	23.7	24.0
	No. 5	28.1	32.5	27.2	25.4
Heating rate 30 °C min^{-1}	No. 3	11.8	13.6	22.3	20.2
	No. 4	23.4	25.7	21.5	22.4
	No. 5	37.7	37.8	24.6	24.8

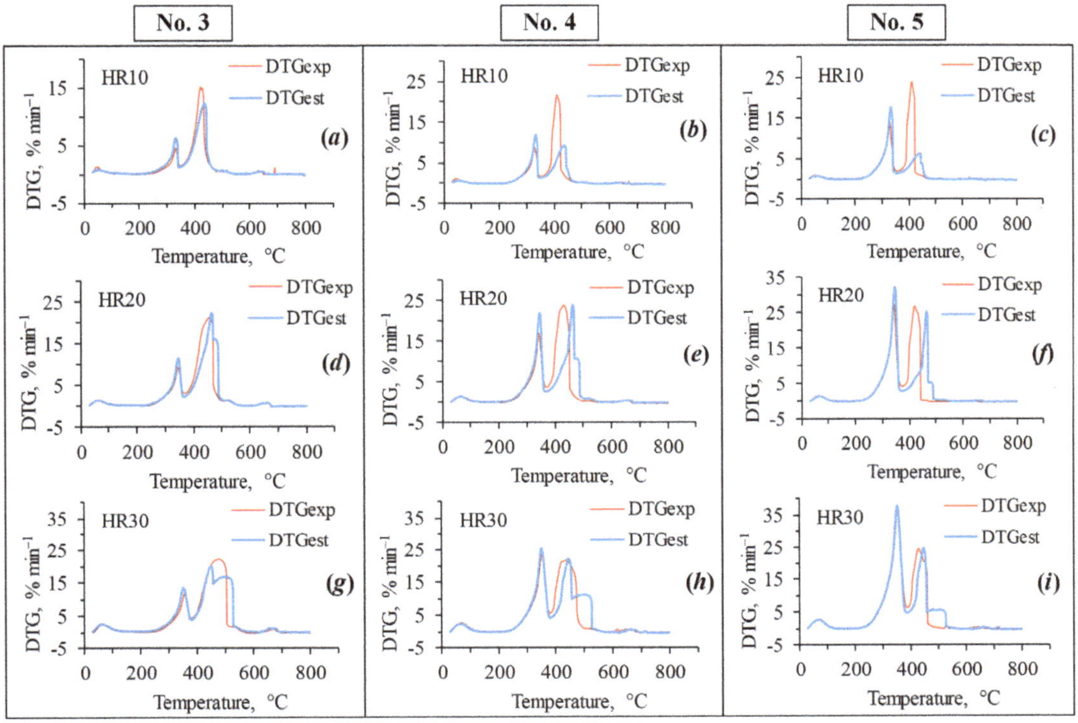

Figure 5. Comparison of DTG curve profiles obtained by experimental (DTG_{exp}) and calculated (DTG_{est}) methods: (**a**)—mixture No. 3 at HR 10; (**b**)—mixture No. 4 at HR 10; (c)—mixture No. 5 at HR 10; (**d**)—mixture No. 3 at HR 20; (**e**)—mixture No. 4 at HR 20; (**f**)—mixture No. 5 at HR 20; (**g**)—mixture No. 3 at HR 30; (**h**)—mixture No. 4 at HR 30; (**i**)—mixture No. 5 at HR 30.

In mixture No. 3 (Figure 5a), the synergetic effect is manifested at Stage II and has a negative effect on the combustion process of volatile substances at a heating rate of 10 °C min^{-1}, reducing the maximum combustion rate by 1.9% min^{-1}; unburned volatile substances finish combustion at Stage III having a positive synergetic effect on the combustion of biomass coke residue and semi-coke. This is evidenced by an increase in the maximum combustion rate by 2.7% min^{-1} (Table 5). Increasing the heating rate of mixture No. 3 up to 20 °C min^{-1} (Figure 5d) leads to the strengthening of the negative synergistic effect expressed by the decrease in the maximum combustion rate in the experiment for combustion of volatile substances by 2.2% min^{-1} for combustion of biomass coke residue and semi-coke by 1% min^{-1}. At a combustion rate of 30 °C min^{-1} (Figure 5g) at Stage II, the synergistic effect reduces the maximum combustion rate of volatile substances by 1.8% min^{-1} while enhancing the synergistic interaction of the mixture components between themselves expressed in the increase in the maximum combustion rate of Stage III by 2.1% min^{-1} (Table 5).

Analyzing the interaction of the components of mixture No. 4 between each other, it was found that, as well as in mixture No. 3, there is no additive combustion at both stages, and there is a synergetic interaction of mixture components between each other. At Stage II, there is a decrease in the maximum burning rate of volatiles by 3.3% min^{-1} (Figure 5b); at Stage III, the synergistic interaction increases the maximum burning rate of coke residue by 2.3 times (Table 5). By doubling the heating rate, the maximum volatile combustion rate decreases by 5.2% min^{-1} and runs in the same temperature range as the calculated values. At Stage III (Figure 5e), the experimental and calculated values do not differ significantly, only by 0.3% min^{-1} (Table 5), but the temperature interval in the experiment shifted to lower temperatures, thus affecting the reduction in the burn-up temperature. When the heating rate was increased to 30 °C min^{-1} (Figure 5h), there was a slight decrease in the maximum burning rate of volatiles by only 2.3% min^{-1}, the profiles of DTG_{exp} and DTG_{est} curves coincide up to the peak, indicating the presence of additive combustion of volatiles. In coke residue combustion, the synergistic effects had a negative effect, reducing the maximum heating rate by 0.9% min^{-1} (Table 5).

In mixture No. 5 (Figure 5c), synergistic interactions between particle components were negatively affected during volatile combustion, reducing the maximum combustion rate by 3.4% min^{-1}. In Stage III, the synergistic effects increased the maximum burning rate of the coke residue by 3.8 times, while the combustion region moved to lower temperatures compared to the calculated values, which also had a positive effect on the combustion process. Increasing the heating rate up to 20 °C min^{-1} (Figure 5f), in Stage II, there was a decrease in DTG_{exp} by 4.4% min^{-1}, and in Stage III, as a consequence of synergetic interactions of mixture components, the maximum heating rate increased by 1.8 and shifted to lower temperatures, which favorably affected the combustion of mixture No. 5. At a heating rate of 30 °C min^{-1} (Figure 5i), Stage II demonstrates additive combustion (i.e., the profiles of curves DTG_{exp} and DTG_{est} completely coincided). At Stage III, the maximum DTG_{exp} and DTG_{est} values differ by only 0.2% min^{-1}, but the curve profiles did not coincide, indicating no additive combustion of biomass coke residue and semi-coke.

The analysis of the interaction between the particles of the mixture components has shown that the heating rate does not affect the synergetic effects. At increasing speed, synergetic effects in the combustion process of mixtures can be both positive and negative, affecting the change in the maximum combustion rate. It was found that in all the studied mixtures presented in Figure 4 on Stage II at combustion of volatile substances, the maximum burning speed is higher at calculated values; at experiment, it is lower.

3.4. Kinetic Analysis

3.4.1. Kinetic Analysis of Individual Fuels

The data of kinetic analysis of combustion of semi-coke and cedar sawdust show the complex nature of this process. Friedman isoconversion curves for the combustion process of sample No. 1 show two closely located peaks (Figure 6a), which characterize the presence of at least two stages occurring at degrees of conversion α = 0–0.7 and α = 0.7–1, corresponding to Stage II and Stage III. However, the stages of thermal decomposition and combustion of coke residue are poorly separated and practically merge at high heating rates.

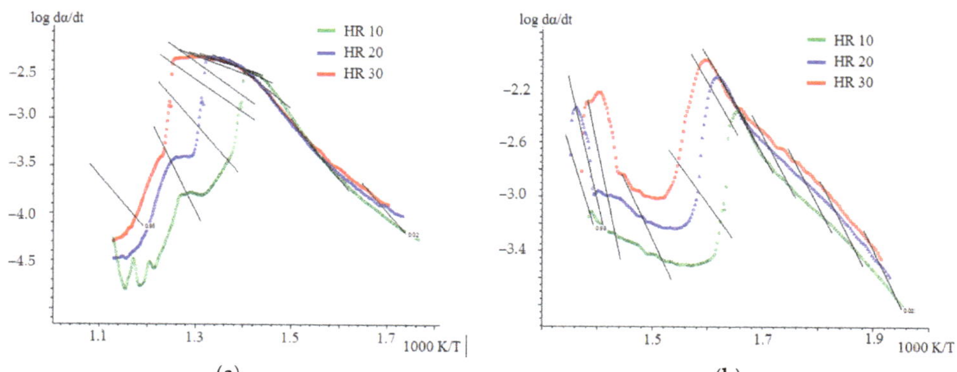

Figure 6. Friedman method isoconversion curves for combustion of semi-coke (sample No. 1) (**a**) and cedar sawdust (sample No. 2) (**b**). Black line—lines connecting points with the same degree of transformation (α) on isoconversion curves with different heating rates.

In the combustion of cedar sawdust, clearly separated stages of thermal decomposition and combustion of coke residue are observed according to TG data. The Friedman model isoconversion curves confirm the thermograms, distinguishing the first stage at α = 0–0.6 and the second at α = 0.6–1 (Figure 6b).

The implicit separation of stages in semi-coke combustion does not show any difference in E_a values for thermal decomposition and ignition stages. Data on the values of activation energy and pre-exponential multipliers calculated by Friedman and Ozawa–Flynn–Wall models using NETZSCH Thermokinetics software for semi-coke combustion are presented in (Figure 7a and 7b), respectively.

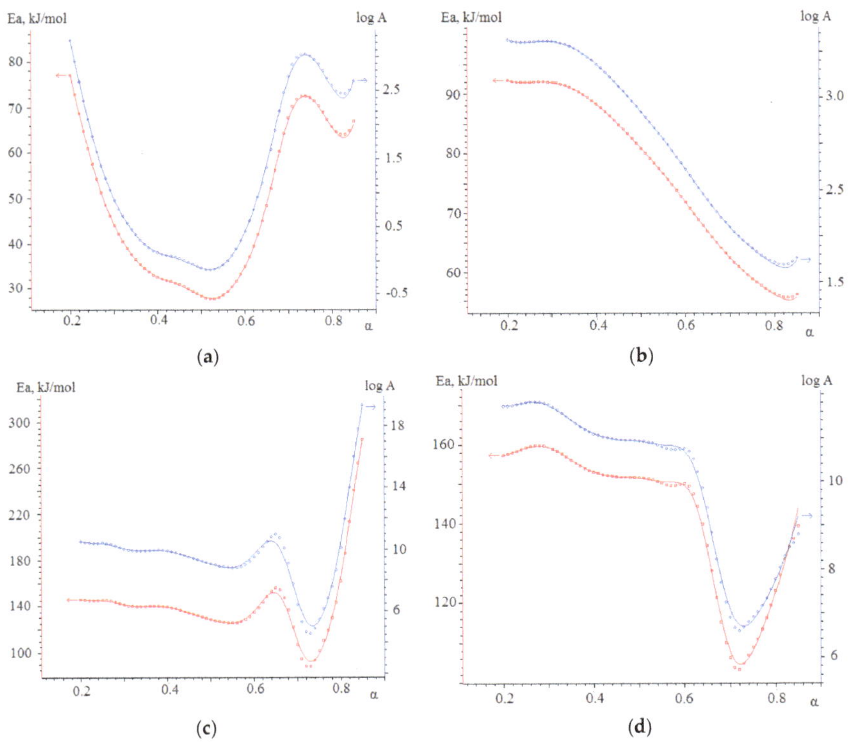

Figure 7. Dependence of E_a (red line) and A values on α (blue line) for semi-coke combustion: (**a**)—Friedman model, (**b**)—OFW model and for cedar sawdust combustion, (**c**)—Friedman model, (**d**)—OFW model.

The values of activation energy and pre-exponential multiplier for the combustion reaction of cedar sawdust calculated by Friedman and Ozawa–Flynn–Wall models are shown in (Figure 7c,d).

The averaged values of E_a of the combustion process of initial combustibles are presented in Table 6.

Table 6. Values of E_a and A for different stages of combustion of initial combustibles.

	Friedman Model E_a, **kJ/mol**	**OFW Model** E_a, **kJ/mol**	**Friedman Model** E_a, **kJ/mol**	**OFW Model** E_a, **kJ/mol**
Stage II	n/a	n/a	140.1	155.1
Stage III	n/a	n/a	113.5	120.9
average	63.6	76.5	n/a	n/a

The obtained data of activation energy for the semi-coke combustion process insignificantly differ from those for the combustion of Kansko-Achinsk brown coal [38], which is the source of raw material for the analyzed sample No. 1. During the combustion of Borodino coal, Stages II and III also proceed almost simultaneously, with the average value of E_a = 38.4 kJ/mol. It should be noted that the obtained average values of the activation energy of combustion of semi-coke are higher than for the original coal, which may be due to the low content of volatile components compared to the original material.

The activation energy values for cedar sawdust combustion significantly exceed similar data for semi-coke combustion, which is an interesting fact since literature data more often indicate the opposite.

Stage III for cellulosic substances usually has a lower value of activation energy compared to E_a of Stage II, associated with a greater heat release at Stage II, which facilitates the combustion process. The calculated data of activation energy on combustion of sample No. 2 confirm this fact; there is a decrease in activation energy during the transition from thermal decomposition to the process of ignition of coke residue, which is confirmed by both calculation methods having a close value.

Relatively high values of the activation energy of Stage II cause a high fraction of the degree of transformation attributable to this stage in the individual fuels combustion process: 0.7 and 0.6 for sample No. 1 and sample No. 2, respectively.

3.4.2. Kinetic Analysis of Co-Combustion

Isoconversion curves of the Friedman model for combustion of the studied mixtures are shown in Figure 8.

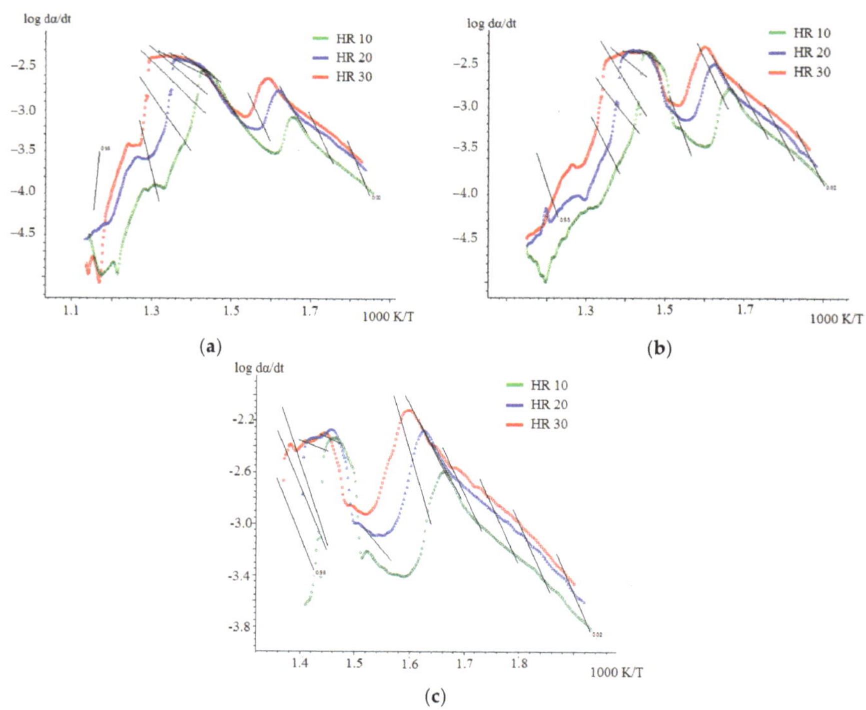

Figure 8. Isoconversion curves of the Friedman model for the combustion process of mixtures: (**a**)—No. 3, (**b**)—No. 4, (**c**)—No. 5. Black line—lines connecting points with the same degree of transformation (α) on isoconversion curves with different heating rates.

As the Friedman model isoconversion curves calculated with the NETZSCH Thermokinetics software show, the mechanism of the combustion process of mixtures is more complicated than for the combustion of initial combustibles: semi-coke and cedar sawdust. In samples No. 3 and No. 4 with high SC content, the profiles of isoconversion curves are similar to each other; from them, it is possible to distinguish three stages occurring at the following degrees of conversion: for sample No. 3, α = 0–0.3; α = 0.3–0.7; α = 0.7–1 and for composition No. 4, α = 0–0.4; α = 0.4–0.7; α = 0.7–1. For composition No. 5, three consecutive stages can also be distinguished: α = 0–0.5; α = 0.5–0.7; and α = 0.7–1.

For the combustion process of all three mixtures, the first stage corresponds to the thermal decomposition of Stage II biomass—sample No. 2, proceeding at a lower temperature for all heating rates than the combustion of semi-coke—sample No. 1.

Stages II and III for samples No. 3 and No. 4 are similar to the profile of the isoconversion curve for combustion of pure semi-coke. These stages also occur at close temperatures and are poorly separated; however, increasing the heating rate does not cause these peaks to merge since the second stage in the isoconversion curves corresponds to the combination of Stage III combustion of cedar sawdust coke residue and Stage II thermal decomposition of semi-coke, which should facilitate the thermal decomposition of sample No. 1 and allow it to complete at a lower temperature. The third stage, occurring at α = 0.7–1, corresponds to the combustion of the coke residue of sample No. 1 and, for mixture No. 3, has a higher intensity compared to mixture No. 4 due to the larger amount of semi-coke present in the sample.

The profile of the isoconversion curve of sample No. 5 is identical to the similar curve for the combustion of cedar sawdust; the difference is Stage 2 for sample No. 5. This stage occurs in a small range of the degree of conversion α = 0.5–0.7, has a small intensity, smooths out with increasing heating rate, and corresponds to the process of thermal decomposition of semi-coke, occurring with a lower E_a than biomass combustion and present in sample No. 5 in a smaller amount than biomass. The third stage for mixture No. 5 combines the stages of the combustion of coke residues and biomass and semi-coke.

It is possible to note an increase in the fraction of the substance participating in the first stage of the combustion process from α = 0.3 to α = 0.5 with increasing biomass fraction in the mixtures, which is explained by the large contribution to the thermal decomposition reaction of sample No. 2 with the highest E_a value.

The values of activation energy and pre-exponential multiplier calculated by NETZSCH Thermokinetics software using Friedman and Ozawa–Flynn–Wall models for the combustion reaction of mixtures are shown in (Figure 9).

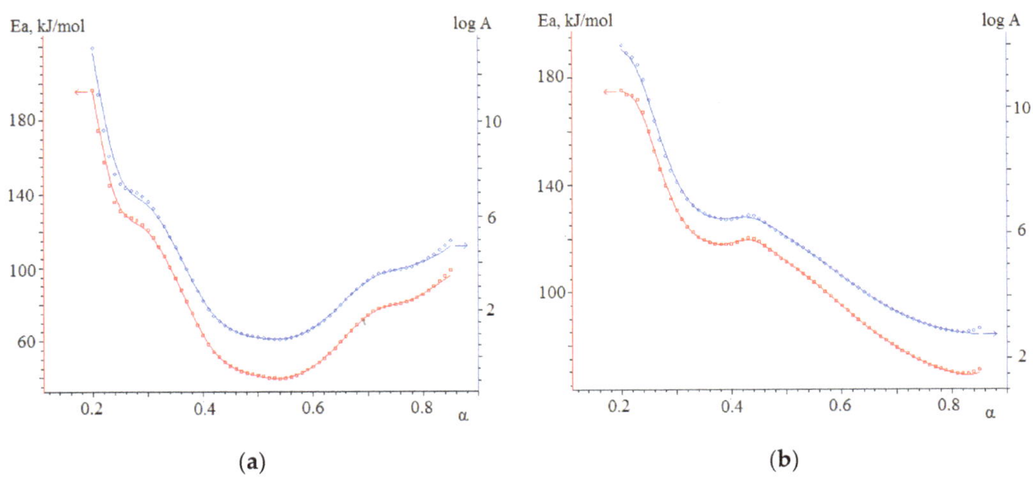

Figure 9. *Cont.*

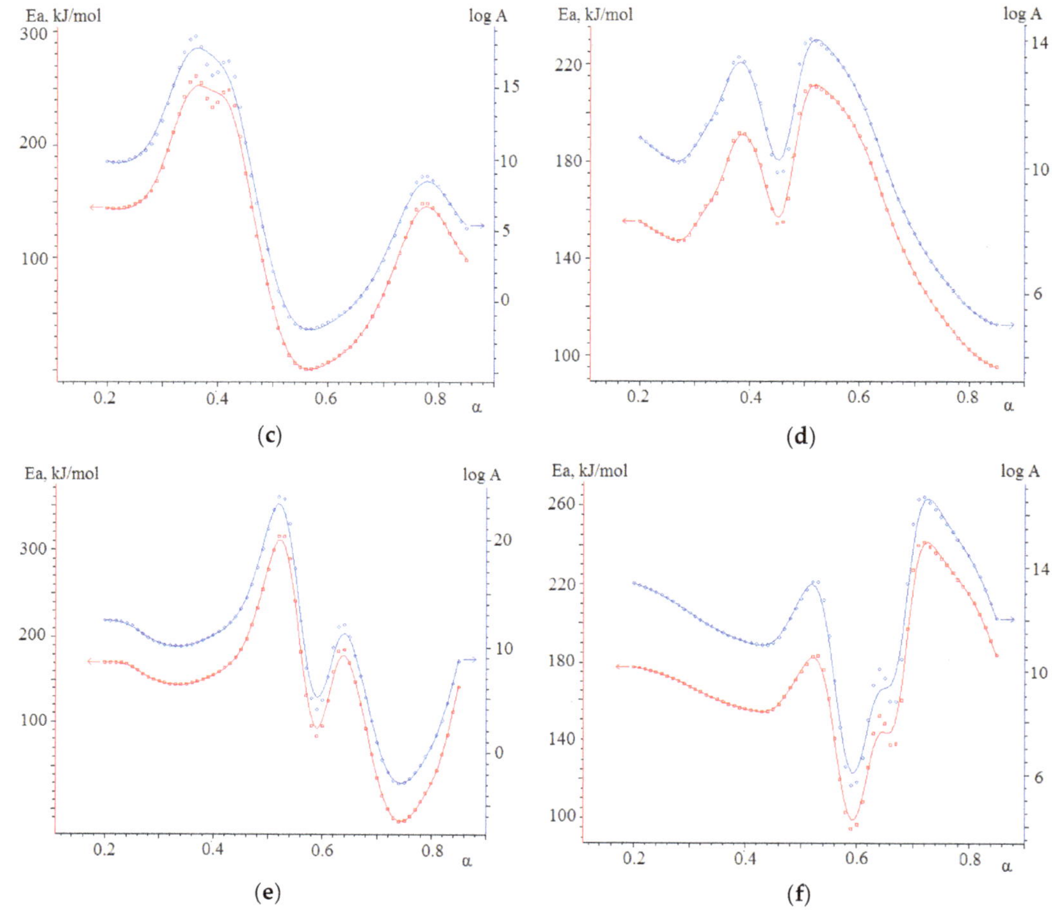

Figure 9. Dependence of E_a (red line) and A values on α (blue line): sample No. 3. (**a**)—Friedman model, (**b**)—OFW model; sample No. 4 (**c**)—Friedman model, (**d**)—OFW model; sample No. 5 (**e**)—Friedman model, (**f**)—OFW model.

The averaged values of activation energy for different stages of combustion of the mixtures are presented in Table 7.

Table 7. Values of Ea for different stages of combustion of mixtures.

Sample	Transformation Degree	Friedman Model E_a, kJ/mol	OFW Model E_a, kJ/mol
No. 3	α = 0–0.3	141.7	157.0
	α = 0.3–0.7	58.8	107.8
	α = 0.7–1	87.1	77.9
No. 4	α = 0–0.4	176.1	159.0
	α = 0.4–0.7	67.4	179.4
	α = 0.7–1	120.0	114.0
No. 5	α = 0–0.5	166.6	165.0
	α =0.5–0.7	164.5	143.2
	α = 0.7–1	104.5	158.9

The activation energy of the first stage of combustion of sample No. 3, corresponding to the thermal decomposition of cedar sawdust, has the same value as for the pure initial combustible sample No. 2 for both calculation methods; also, there is a consistency of data on the values of E_a for the third stage relating to the combustion of coke residue of sample No. 1 (Table 6). It follows that these stages are individual stages of the combustion process of samples No. 1 and No. 2 and do not interact with each other when co-combusted at composition semi-coke 75% + cedar sawdust 25%.

The calculated E_a values for the second stage combining simultaneous combustion of biomass coke residue and thermal decomposition of semi-coke show different values obtained by different methods, but in both cases, there is a tendency to decrease E_a during the combustion of coke residue of sample No. 2 due to the presence of a large amount of semi-coke in the system, the activation energy of thermal decomposition of which is much lower than for Stage III of the cedar sawdust combustion process.

During combustion of sample No. 4, containing the same amount of semi-coke and cedar sawdust, the calculated values of E_a for the degrees of transformation $\alpha = 0$–0.4 are similar in value to the data for samples No. 3 and No. 2, which indicate Stage II thermal decomposition of mixture No. 2, occurring at this stage of combustion and the lack of influence of semi-coke on this process. For the subsequent stages of combustion of sample No. 4, the Friedman model describes the combustion process similarly to sample No. 3: the second stage has a reduced value of E_a due to the combined occurrence of Stage III of sample No. 2 and Stage II of sample No. 1; an increase in the activation energy for the degree of transformation $\alpha = 0.7$–1, related to the burnout of the coke residue of sample No. 1, but with a higher value than for pure sample No. 1, indicating the influence of biomass additives on this process. It should be noted that these stages proceed with a higher E_a value than mixture No. 3 due to the larger amount of biomass having higher activation energy values. The OFW method shows close results to the Friedman model for stages 1 and 3, but the calculated E_a values for the second stage do not show a decrease in activation energy relative to the first stage, although the energy curve profile (Figure 9d) has a well-defined minimum at $\alpha \approx 0.5$, which corresponds to a similar relationship calculated by the Friedman method. The high values of E_a in the OFW method are compensated by higher values of the pre-exponential multiplier, differing by a factor of 10 compared to the Friedman method.

For sample No. 5, the large amount of biomass present in the mixture and burning with a high E_a value allows describing the energetics of the process with values close to the E_a values of the combustion of pure sample No. 2. The very narrow range of the degree of transformation of the second stage, related to the thermal decomposition of sample No. 1 at $\alpha = 0.5$–0.7 does not allow us to calculate a significant decrease in activation energy for this stage; however, at the degree of transformation $\alpha = 0.6$, the Friedman method and the OFW method show minimum and very close values of E_a equal to 95.0 and 96.7 kJ/mol, respectively.

The kinetic analysis determined that the activation energy values for the combustion process of the initial substances are very different. Sample No. 2 burns with a higher value of activation energy than sample No. 1. The combustion of the mixtures of initial fuels for compositions No. 3 and No. 4 are more described by the combustion energy of the initial semi-coke and sample No. 5 by the combustion energy of cedar sawdust. For all mixtures, Stage II combustion of cedar sawdust has a significantly separated stage by temperature and cannot participate in the synergy of the combustion process of mixtures. As the amount of biomass in the mixtures increases, there is a successive overlap of Stage III combustion of the coke residue of sample No. 2 and Stage II thermal decomposition of fuel No. 1 in samples No. 3 and No. 4 and Stage III thermal decomposition of both No. 1 and No. 2 in sample No. 5. A noticeable decrease in E_a occurs with the symbiosis of Stage III combustion of sample No. 2 and Stage II of sample No. 1 in samples No. 3 and No. 4, but the low presence of volatile components in sample No. 3 does not reveal a clear synergistic effect for this composition.

4. Conclusions

In this paper, we have researched the combustion process of semi-coke obtained in the process of gasification of brown coal at temperatures of 700–900 °C, cedar sawdust, and their mixtures using a thermogravimetric method at heating rates of 10, 20, and 30 °C min^{-1} in an oxidizing environment. The main results of the work are as follows:

(1) The obtained semi-coke has a low volatile matter content of 8.4%, which may have an adverse effect on its combustion in the boiler furnace, and a high calorific value of 32.1 MJ/kg. Adding biomass with high volatile matter content (80.2%) to semi-coke will increase the volatile matter content of the mixture, which will have a positive effect on the combustion of the mixtures.

(2) According to the results of the thermal analysis, the main combustion characteristics were established for the investigated fuels and mixtures. The ignition temperature of semi-coke is 38% higher than that of biomass, the burnout temperature is 45% higher, and the combustion index is five times lower than that of biomass. At least 50% of biomass should be added to semi-coke; there is a 7% increase in combustion index compared to semi-coke; further increase in biomass content in the mixture will increase the combustion index, which will have a positive effect on the combustion of the mixture.

(3) Both positive and negative synergetic interactions between mixture components are observed during the combustion of mixtures. Synergetic effects reducing the maximum heating rate at all heating rates are mainly observed in the combustion of biomass volatiles. Synergetic effects positively influencing the combustion process were observed in the combustion of biomass coke residue and semi-coke. There is no dependence between the heating rate of the studied fuels and the synergetic effects occurring between the components of the mixtures influencing the combustion process.

(4) The results obtained in the determination of kinetic parameters show higher activation energy values for biomass combustion (113.5 kJ/mol) compared to semi-coke (76.5 kJ/mol). The kinetic analysis found that the combustion of mixtures overlaps different stages of combustion processes of individual fuels, resulting in lower activation energy values for such joint processes. Thus, the mixture based on 75% semi-coke and 25% cedar sawdust has the lowest activation energy value, high values of the pre-exponential multiplier, sufficient amount of volatile components, and, in our case, is a composition with a large synergetic effect.

Author Contributions: Conceptualization, A.Z. and L.I.; methodology, A.Z.; software, A.Z.; validation, A.Z., A.S. and S.C.; formal analysis, A.Z.; investigation, A.Z.; resources, A.Z.; data curation, A.Z.; writing—original draft preparation, A.Z.; writing—review and editing, I.G.; visualization, T.P.; supervision, Y.Z. All authors have read and agreed to the published version of the manuscript.

Funding: This research received no external funding.

Data Availability Statement: The data presented in this study are available upon request from the corresponding author. The data are not publicly available due to confidentiality reasons.

Conflicts of Interest: The authors declare no conflicts of interest.

References

1. Gür, T.M. Carbon Dioxide Emissions, Capture, Storage and Utilization: Review of Materials Processes and Technologies. *Prog. Energy Combust. Sci.* **2022**, *89*, 100965. [CrossRef]
2. Overland, I.; Loginova, J. The Russian coal industry in an uncertain world: Finally pivoting to Asia? *Energy Res. Soc. Sci.* **2023**, *102*, 103150. [CrossRef]
3. Baxter, L. Biomass-Coal Cofiring: An Overview of Technical Issues. *Green Energy Technol.* **2011**, *28*, 43–73. [CrossRef]
4. Variny, M.; Varga, A.; Rimár, M.; Janošovský, J.; Kizek, J.; Lukáč, L.; Jablonský, G.; Mierka, O. Advances in biomass co-combustion with fossil fuels in the European context: A review. *Processes* **2021**, *9*, 100. [CrossRef]
5. Pazheri, F.R.; Othman, M.F.; Malik, N.H. A review on global renewable electricity scenario. *Renew. Sust. Energ. Rev.* **2014**, *31*, 835–845. [CrossRef]

6. Sahu, S.G.; Chakraborty, N.; Sarkar, P. Coal-biomass co-combustion: An overview. *Renew. Sust. Energ. Rev.* **2014**, *39*, 575–586. [CrossRef]
7. Al-Mansour, F.; Zuwala, J. An evaluation of biomass co-firing in Europe. *Biomass Bioenergy* **2010**, *34*, 620–629. [CrossRef]
8. Ding, G.; He, B.; Yao, H.; Cao, Y.; Su, L.; Duan, Z. Co-combustion behaviors of municipal solid waste and low-rank coal semi-coke in air or oxygen/carbon dioxide atmospheres. *J. Therm. Anal. Calorim.* **2021**, *143*, 619–635. [CrossRef]
9. Wang, P.; Wang, C.; Wang, C.; Du, Y.; Che, D. Experimental investigation on co-combustion characteristics of semi-coke and coal: Insight into synergy and blending method. *Process Saf. Environ. Prot.* **2023**, *175*, 290–302. [CrossRef]
10. Zhou, H.; Wang, K.; Ni, J.; Wu, J.; Ji, P.; Zeng, W.; Li, J.; Zhao, B.; Kou, M. Numerical simulation of co-combustion characteristics of semicoke and coke breeze in an ironmaking blast furnace. *Fuel* **2023**, *335*, 127113. [CrossRef]
11. Liu, Y.; Tan, W.; Liang, S.; Pan, X. Study on the co-combustion behavior of semi-coke and typical biomass: Combustion, NO emission and ash characteristics analysis. *Fuel* **2024**, *358*, 130068. [CrossRef]
12. Liu, H.-P.; Liang, W.-X.; Qin, H.; Wang, Q. Synergy in co-combustion of oil shale semi-coke with torrefied cornstalk. *Appl. Therm. Eng.* **2016**, *109*, 653–662. [CrossRef]
13. Qi, H.; Sun, R.; Peng, J.; Meng, X.; Cao, Z.; Wang, Z.; Ren, X.; Yuan, M.; Zhang, L.; Ding, S. Experimental investigation on the ignition and combustion characteristics of pyrolyzed char and bituminous coal blends. *Fuel* **2020**, *281*, 118732. [CrossRef]
14. Qin, H.; Wang, W.; Liu, H.; Zhang, L.; Wang, Q.; Shi, C.; Yao, K. Thermal behavior research for co-combustion of furfural residue and oil shale semi-coke. *Appl. Therm. Eng.* **2017**, *120*, 19–25. [CrossRef]
15. Zheng, S.; Hu, Y.; Wang, Z.; Cheng, X. Experimental investigation on ignition and burnout characteristics of semi-coke and bituminous coal blends. *J. Energy Inst.* **2020**, *93*, 1373–1381. [CrossRef]
16. Zhang, J.; Jia, X.; Wang, C.; Zhao, N.; Wang, P.; Che, D. Experimental investigation on combustion and NO formation characteristics of semi-coke and bituminous coal blends. *Fuel* **2019**, *247*, 87–96. [CrossRef]
17. Hu, L.; Zhang, Y.; Chen, D.; Fang, J.; Zhang, M.; Wu, Y.; Zhang, H.; Li, Z.; Lyu, J. Experimental study on the combustion and NOx emission characteristics of a bituminous coal blended with semi-coke. *Appl. Therm. Eng.* **2019**, *160*, 113993. [CrossRef]
18. Zhao, R.; Qin, J.; Chen, T.; Wu, J. TG-FTIR study on co-combustion of bituminous coal semicoke and lignite. *J. Therm. Anal. Calorim.* **2022**, *147*, 1849–1858. [CrossRef]
19. *ISO 11722:1999*; Solid Mineral Fuels—Hard Coal—Determination of Moisture in the General Analysis Test Sample by Drying in Nitrogen. International Organization for Standardization: Geneva, Switzerland, 1999.
20. *ISO 1171:2010*; Solid Mineral Fuel—Determination of Ash. International Organization for Standardization: Geneva, Switzerland, 2010.
21. *ISO 562:2010*; Hard Coal and Coke—Determination of Volatile Matter. International Organization for Standardization: Geneva, Switzerland, 2010.
22. *ISO 1928:2009*; Solid Mineral Fuels—Determination of Gross Calorific Value by the Bomb Calorimetric Method and Calculation of Net Calorific Value. International Organization for Standardization: Geneva, Switzerland, 2009.
23. *ASTM D5373-14e1*; Standard Test Methods for Determination of Carbon, Hydrogen and Nitrogen in Analysis Samples of Coal and Carbon in Analysis Samples of Coal and Coke. ASTM International: West Conshohocken, PA, USA, 2014.
24. Oladejo, J.M.; Adegbite, S.; Pang, C.H.; Liu, H.; Parvez, A.M.; Wu, T. A novel index for the study of synergistic effects during the co-processing of coal and biomass. *Appl. Energy.* **2017**, *188*, 215–225. [CrossRef]
25. Moon, C.; Sung, Y.; Ahn, S.; Kim, T.; Choi, G.; Kim, D. Effect of blending ratio on combustion performance in blends of biomass and coals of different ranks. *Exp. Therm. Fluid Sci.* **2013**, *47*, 232–240. [CrossRef]
26. Liu, Z.; Quek, A.; Hoekman, S.K.; Srinivasan, M.P.; Balasubramanian, R. Thermogravimetric investigation of hydrochar-lignite co-combustion. *Bioresour. Technol.* **2012**, *123*, 646–652. [CrossRef] [PubMed]
27. Zhuikov, A.V.; Glushkov, D.O.; Kuznetsov, P.N.; Grishina, I.I.; Samoilo, A.S. Ignition of two-component and three-component fuel mixtures based on brown coal and char under slow heating conditions. *J. Therm. Anal. Calorim.* **2022**, *147*, 11965–11976. [CrossRef]
28. Wang, C.; Wang, F.; Yang, Q.; Liang, R. Thermogravimetric studies of the behavior of wheat straw with added coal during combustion. *Biomass Bioenergy* **2009**, *33*, 50–56. [CrossRef]
29. Raza, M.; Abu-Jdayil, B.; Al-Marzouqi, A.H.; Inayat, A. Inayat Kinetic and thermodynamic analyses of date palm surface fibers pyrolysis using Coats-Redfern method. *Renew. Energy* **2022**, *183*, 67–77. [CrossRef]
30. Isaac, K.; Bada, S.O. The co-combustion performance and reaction kinetics of refuse derived fuels with South African high ash coal. *Heliyon* **2020**, *6*, e03309. [CrossRef]
31. Yuan, Y.; Zuo, H.; Wang, J.; Gao, Y.; Xue, Q.; Wang, J. Co-combustion behavior, kinetic and ash melting characteristics analysis of clean coal and biomass pellet. *Fuel* **2022**, *324*, 124727. [CrossRef]
32. Armakan, S.; Civan, M.; Yurdakul, S. Determining co-combustion characteristics, kinetics and synergy behaviors of raw and torrefied forms of two distinct types of biomass and their blends with lignite. *J. Therm. Anal. Calorim.* **2022**, *147*, 12855–12869. [CrossRef]
33. Friedman, H.L. Kinetics of thermal degradation of char-forming plastics from thermogravimetry. Application to a phenolic plastic. *J. Polym. Sci. Part C Polym. Symp.* **1964**, *6*, 183–195. [CrossRef]
34. Ozawa, T. A New Method of Analyzing Thermogravimetric Data. *Bull. Chem. Soc. Japan* **1965**, *38*, 1881–1886. [CrossRef]
35. Flynn, J.H.; Wall, L.A. A quick, direct method for the determination of activation energy from thermogravimetric data. *J. Polym. Sci. Part B Polym. Lett.* **1966**, *4*, 323–328. [CrossRef]

36. Doyle, C.D. Estimating isothermal life from thermogravimetric data. *J. Appl. Polym. Sci.* **1962**, *6*, 639–642. [CrossRef]
37. Glushkov, D.O.; Zhuikov, A.V.; Nurpeiis, A.E.; Paushkina, K.K.; Kuznechenkova, D.A. Ignition behavior of a mixture of brown coal and biomass during the movement of fine particles in a hot air flow. *Fuel* **2024**, *363*, 131010. [CrossRef]
38. Kuznetsov, P.N.; Kuznetsova, L.I.; Bimer, J.; Salbut, P.; Gruber, R.; Brodzki, D. Quantitative relation between the macromolecular characteristics of brown coal and its reactivity in conversion with tetralin. *Fuel* **1997**, *76*, 189–193. [CrossRef]

energies

MDPI

Article

An End-to-End Relearning Framework for Building Energy Optimization

Avisek Naug [1,†], Marcos Quinones-Grueiro [2,†] and Gautam Biswas [2,*,†]

[1] Hewlett Packard Labs (HPE), Milpitas, CA 95035, USA; avisek.naug@hpe.com
[2] Institute for Software Integrated Systems, Vanderbilt University, Nashville, TN 37235, USA; marcos.quinones.grueiro@vanderbilt.edu
[*] Correspondence: gautam.biswas@vanderbilt.edu
[†] These authors contributed equally to this work.

Abstract: Building HVAC systems face significant challenges in energy optimization due to changing building characteristics and the need to balance multiple efficiency objectives. Current approaches are limited: physics-based models are expensive and inflexible, while data-driven methods require extensive data collection and ongoing maintenance. This paper introduces a systematic relearning framework for HVAC supervisory control that improves adaptability while reducing operational costs. Our approach features a Reinforcement Learning controller with self-monitoring and adaptation capabilities that responds effectively to changes in building operations and environmental conditions. We simplify the complex hyperparameter optimization process through a structured decomposition method and implement a relearning strategy to handle operational changes over time. We demonstrate our framework's effectiveness through comprehensive testing on a building testbed, comparing performance against established control methods.

Keywords: energy consumption; reinforcement learning; relearning; nonstationary systems

1. Introduction

Autonomous control of non-stationary cyber–physical systems (CPSs) that combine sensing, computation, and actuation has been an area of active research in recent years [1,2]. It involves the development of control strategies without human-in-the-loop that can adapt to dynamic changes in plant models either due to external factors or internal model reconfiguration. For a non-stationary CPS, time-dependent characteristics may drive the system to unexpected states for the same actuation and sensing conditions [3]. Therefore, self-adaptation, i.e., making decisions depending on the context and coping with the inherent uncertainty of the real world, becomes a crucial aspect of autonomous control. In this work, we focus on buildings as a case study of autonomous control for non-stationary CPS.

Optimal control methods for dynamical systems focus on developing policies through minimizing user-defined cost functions that encapsulate specific design objectives [4]. Classical optimal control approaches generally define policies before deployment and necessitate complete knowledge of the system dynamics. Consequently, they cannot handle uncertainties and changes in the system dynamics not considered at the design stage, limiting their applicability for non-stationary CPSs. Adaptive control techniques, which can adjust their actuations in response to these changes, are required to overcome this limitation. Data-driven control techniques,which do not rely on analytical models of a system, like model-free reinforcement learning (RL) [5], have emerged as powerful tools for adaptive control. However, classic RL methods do not guarantee adequate performance for non-stationary CPSs because of the time-varying nature of the system dynamics [3].

Traditionally, non-stationary behaviors have been modeled as a hybrid system with well-defined transitions between the operating modes [6]. However, in real-world systems, where the energy behavior of the building depends on internal operational models and environmental parameters, it is difficult to establish operating modes and transitions between modes in advance. Therefore, we adopt a data-driven modeling approach that continually adjusts to the non-stationary changes in the system for accurate predictions and forward simulation to support controller relearning, i.e.,: reformulate the control strategy completely in response to changes in plant model dynamics. However, data-driven model learning may suffer from low performance due to the slow adaptation speed. Many samples are needed to relearn data-driven models, but sufficient data may not be available for timely relearning to support decision-making without significant degradation in performance. To address the above problems, we develop an autonomous relearning framework [7] augmented with a systematic hyperparameter selection approach and analyze the robustness of the proposed approach over long periods of operation.

The rest of the paper is organized as follows. Section 2 reviews the relevant literature. Section 3 outlines the problem statement and assumptions governing our relearning approach. Section 5 presents a solution to data-driven offline learning and relearning. Section 4 provides the complete framework and a detailed discussion of the individual components. We evaluate the performance of our approach on a standard ASHRAE 5 zone testbed and a real building in Sections 6 and 7, respectively. Finally, we discuss the conclusions, limitations, and future work in Section 8.

2. Related Work

Researchers have explored traditional control methods, MPC [8,9], and deep RL [7,10–12] or hybrid approaches [13] for climate control in buildings and form a basis for benchmarking in our experiments. Apart from testbed experiments using these approaches, building practitioners frequently refer to the ASHRAE Guideline 36 [14,15] for implementing building control, which we also consider during our benchmarking experiments. These methods have achieved partial success, but end-to-end data-driven methodologies for non-stationary operating conditions have not been developed.

Traditional control algorithms such as PID (Proportional-Integral-Derivative) controllers are not capable of handling changes in the system dynamics [16]. Researchers have explored advanced control methods such as Model Predictive Control (MPC) with model adaptation to account for dynamic changes in building conditions and optimize the control strategy [8,9,17,18]. However, most authors acknowledged that their approaches rely on accurate models of the building's dynamics, which can be challenging to obtain for non-stationary systems, especially for online deployment.

RL has been applied to HVAC control in buildings and tested with simulated physics-based models. However, they have had varying degrees of success. For example, [19] employed a Demand Response-aware RL controller during demand response periods, reducing power consumption by 50% on a weekly basis compared to the default controllers. Several works have pointed out that taking actions on every instant may be detrimental and instead suggested event-driven decision-making using RL [20] showing improved performance when considering energy savings and thermal comfort violations compared to earlier works. However, these approaches always seem to be fine-tuned or ad hoc for the particular application. A universal approach that works across different weather conditions and internal building behavior seems to be missing. This is primarily due to the difficulty in modeling the non-stationary behavior in these systems. Moreover, none of these approaches are end-to-end that can be readily applied to any building HVAC and fail to discuss how to address the sim-to-real gap. Some work in the direction of a generalized end-to-end approach has been recently studied in [21]. However, they focus on the transfer learning aspect of the work without any emphasis on the widespread application under varying building conditions.

Recent work has used data-driven models to train RL agents for HVAC control. Kontes et al. [22] used Gaussian process models to simulate building energy consumption and train a control strategy using Dyna-Q, achieving comparable energy savings to an MPC-based approach. Constanzo et al. [23] applied Q-learning to a data-driven model of a building created using a combination of neural networks and an ensemble of extreme learning machines (ELMs) models, achieving results within 10% of the true optimum. However, like physics-based models, these methods require building-specific data for training and are not end-to-end approaches that can be readily applied to any building HVAC system. Overall, while RL has shown promise for HVAC control in buildings, there is a lack of end-to-end data-driven methodologies that can be easily applied across varying operating conditions of buildings.

Creating end-to-end data-driven relearning approaches for climate control in non-stationary building environments has been challenging for several reasons. First, building HVAC systems are complex and highly nonlinear [24]. Moreover, according to [25], their behavior is influenced by several factors such as weather conditions, occupancy patterns, and equipment performance. The difficulty of developing a unified or cascade of models that capture factors and their interactions in a complete way across multiple data-driven thermal modeling for buildings has been discussed in [26]. Second, building conditions are highly variable and can change rapidly over time; therefore, any model or control strategy must adapt and be responsive to these changes, while certain building-specific transfer learning approaches may be used to address these changes [27]. Deploying this for real-time applications requires sufficient real-time data and feedback. It may be challenging to obtain and recondition the model and adapt the control during operations. Third, deploying end-to-end approaches in real systems requires hyperparameter tuning of large models, a topic rarely discussed in current literature. Intuitively, building a cascaded computational architecture for monitoring, modeling, and control makes the hyperparameter optimization problem infeasible [28,29]. Furthermore, most of these works lack a principled approach to moving towards real-world deployment since that involves an end-to-end pipeline that can handle the non-stationary exogenous variables, a highly efficient adaptive control approach, and dynamic model updates. Most importantly, these updates need to occur efficiently in real time so that the building can operate as optimally as possible while it transitions to a new operating regime.

3. Problem Formulation

This section presents a formal problem statement for the end-to-end relearning problem for energy optimization in dynamic environments. The problem is modeled as a Non-stationary Markov Decision Process, encapsulating the complexities of building energy optimization.

Definition 1 (Non-Stationary Markov Decision Process [30] (NS-MDP)). *A non-stationary Markov decision process is defined as a 5-tuple:* $M = \{S, A, \mathcal{T}, (p_t)_{t \in \mathcal{T}}, (r_t)_{t \in \mathcal{T}}\}$. *S represents the set of possible states the environment can reach at decision epoch t. A is the action space.* $\mathcal{T} = \{1, 2, ..., N\}$ *is the set of decision epochs with* $N \leq +\infty$. $p_t(s'|s, a)$ *and* $r_t(s, a, s')$ *represent the transition function and the reward function at decision epoch* $t \in \mathcal{T}$, *respectively.*

The time-varying nature of the control problem requires the optimal solution to be a set of policies π_t^* whose selection depends on the transition function at each decision epoch. Our proposed framework is designed to update the control policy efficiently as the system dynamics change. This involves two steps: (1) detecting the onset of a non-stationary behavior change and (2) updating the policy. The non-stationary behavior is assumed to be driven by changes in the system parameters and/or exogenous variables. Exogenous state variables and rewards may impede the reinforcement learning (RL) controller by introducing unregulated fluctuations into the reward function [31]. The proposed updating framework, defined by transition function changes, is bounded in time, making the adaptation process feasible. This is a natural assumption for most physical systems, as abrupt changes do not occur frequently; therefore, the transitions satisfy the Lipschitz Continuity (LC) condition on the NS-MDP [30]: i.e.,: there is an upper bound to the rate of change in the dynamics of the system.

Although the agent does not know the true NSMDP model, it can learn a quasi-optimal policy by interacting with temporal slices of the NSMDP, assuming the LC property. In other words, the agent learns a stationary MDP from the environment data at epoch t, implying the trajectory generated by an LC-NSMDP $\{s_0, r_0, ..., s_k\}$ is assumed to be generated by a sequence of stationary MDPs $\{MDP_{t_0}, ..., MDP_{t_0+k-1}\}$, each of which can be considered to be an individual learning task [30].

4. End-to-End Relearning Framework

Using the LC-NS-MDP problem formulation in the previous section, we develop a detailed description of the proposed end-to-end relearning framework [32,33]. (The associated hyperparameter tuning methods will be described in the next section.) The first step of the relearning process is captured at a high level by a two-step process shown in Figure 1. We start with a high-level overview of the two-step process that includes self-monitoring and relearning. Then, we discuss the components of the approach in more detail. Finally, we summarize how these components work in tandem.

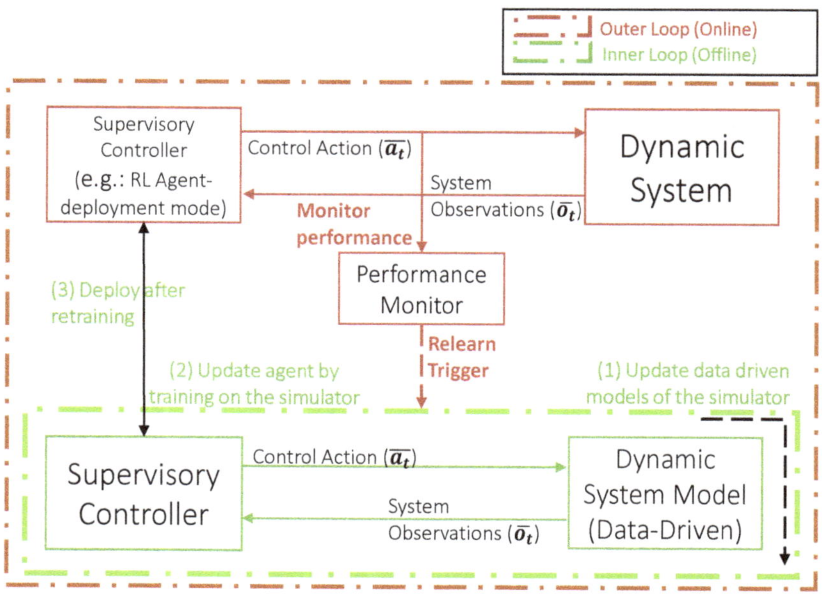

Figure 1. Overview of the solution using an inner and outer loop schema.

The proposed framework, as depicted in Figure 1, consists of two iterative processes: (i) an **Outer loop**, where a Performance Monitor assesses the reward per interaction during the deployment phase; and (ii) an **Inner Loop** that is activated when degradation of system performance attributed to non-stationary changes in system performance leads to relearning the dynamic system model for a new system configuration.

4.1. Outer Loop: Online Operation and Performance Monitoring

The purpose of the outer loop is to generate supervisory control actions given the current system state, self-monitor performance, and detect non-stationary alterations in the system and its environment. This change triggers data-driven relearning of a new system model and a corresponding control policy. The monitoring focuses on the reward signal during the interaction of the Supervisory RL Controller with the actual system, as illustrated in Figure 2. For simplicity, this reward formulation can be identical or an augmented form of the reward function used for the Lipschitz Continuous NS-MDP formulation. We assume that whenever the controller performance deteriorates, it is reflected as an overall negative trend in the reward signal. Since the reward is a simple scalar time-series signal, we estimate the fit of the negative trend using the technique described in [34]. The trend is statistically significant if the R^2 coefficient of determination is greater than 0.65 and the p-value is less than 0.05. Although more intricate non-linear trend detection techniques are available and have been applied in recent studies ([35]), the efficacy of this module is contingent upon the window size W_{pm_i}, where $i \geq 1$ is used to evaluate the reward. The window size is generally correlated with the temporal dynamics of the non-stationary changes.

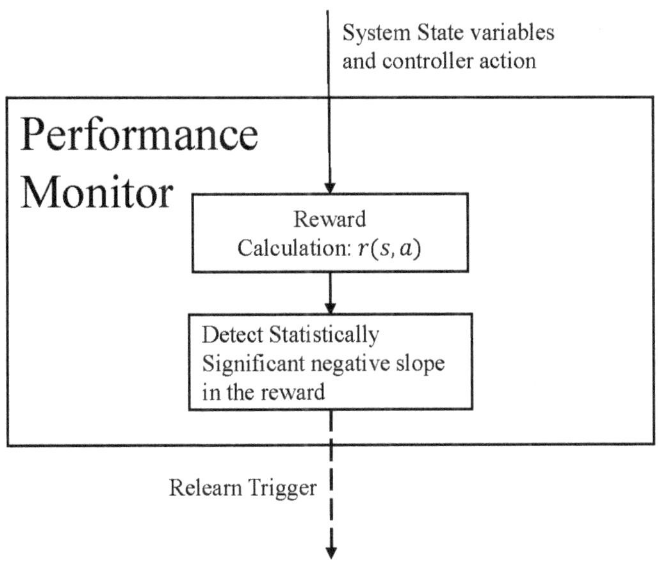

Figure 2. Performance monitor module.

4.2. Inner Loop: Update and Relearning

Our solution architecture for the inner loop includes simulating the real system using multiple data-driven models that can predict relevant state variables in the LC-NSMDP.

4.2.1. Modeling of the Dynamic Systems

Due to the complexity and associated costs of developing precise physics-based models for large systems ([36]), our approach utilizes a set of data-driven models. These models predict the next state, $\bar{s}_{t+1}$ based on the current state $\bar{s}_t$, exogenous variables $\bar{d}_t$, and control inputs $\bar{u}_t$ given by the actions of the RL controller $\bar{a}_t$. Figure 3 shows the framework of our data-driven strategy for constructing a state space model of the dynamic system. To simulate the state variables accurately, our architecture integrates two sequential components: (1) Long Short Term Memory (LSTM) networks to encapsulate temporal dependencies between inputs and outputs, and (2) a Fully Connected Neural Network (FCNN) to model the non-linear interactions among variables. The precise architecture of each deep learning model is derived through a hyperparameter optimization process, which we discuss in a later section.

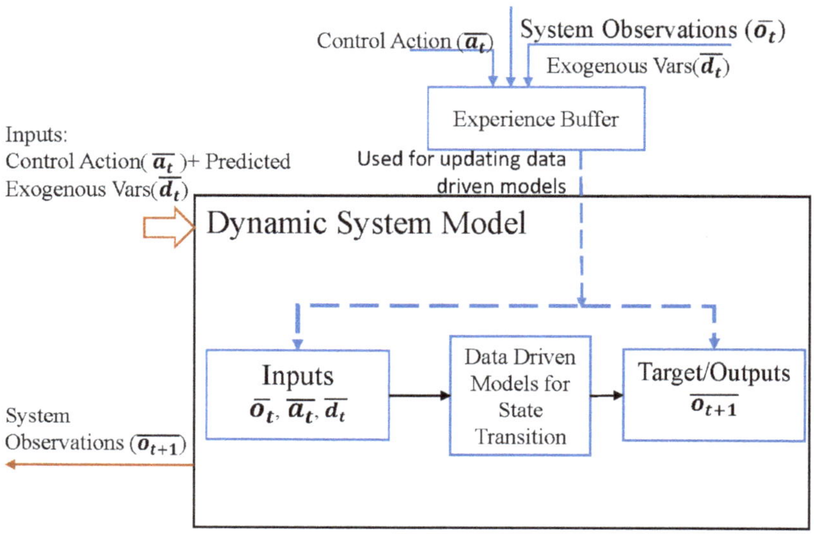

Figure 3. Dynamic system models. The dashed lines represent any interfacing operation between the component itself and external components.

Furthermore, given the non-stationary behaviors in the operating regimes of our system, it is necessary to retrain/relearn these models. Retraining with the limited amounts of data available after the non-stationary change may result in overfitting and, therefore, cause catastrophic forgetting. To avoid this, we adopt a regularization process termed Elastic Weight Consolidation (EWC) proposed in [37]. This process effectively retains previously learned behavior from older data while avoiding long learning times.

4.2.2. Exogenous Variable Prediction Models

In addition to the models required to simulate the system transition, we propose to develop a set of data-driven models to simulate the future behavior of exogenous variables. We name these the Exogenous Variable Predictors. These models simulate the system behavior into the future, and they help us address the problem of potentially limited data available after a non-stationary change is detected. The derived models are used to relearn the RL controller to make it optimal for the system's future behavior.

The schematic of the generic exogenous variable predictor module is shown in Figure 4. We develop Exogenous Variable Predictors to predict the weather, thermal load, and occupancy schedules for our building's application. Our models use the current sequence of past inputs of length K for the exogenous variables $\bar{d}_{t-K:t}$ and predict the value of the exogenous variable at the next time instant as $\hat{d}_{t+1}$. For forecasting over a horizon of length N, we use the output at the $t+1^{th}$ instant and append it to the input sequence. Both K

and N are hyperparameters that are fine-tuned for the specific application. The LSTM models capture the temporal sequence relations in these variables, and FCNN captures the non-linearity of the processes. The specific network architecture is also obtained through hyperparameter search. Further, depending on the application domain, the training can be continual, as newer batches of data are acquired, or conditional, i.e., when certain system non-stationary behavior is detected.

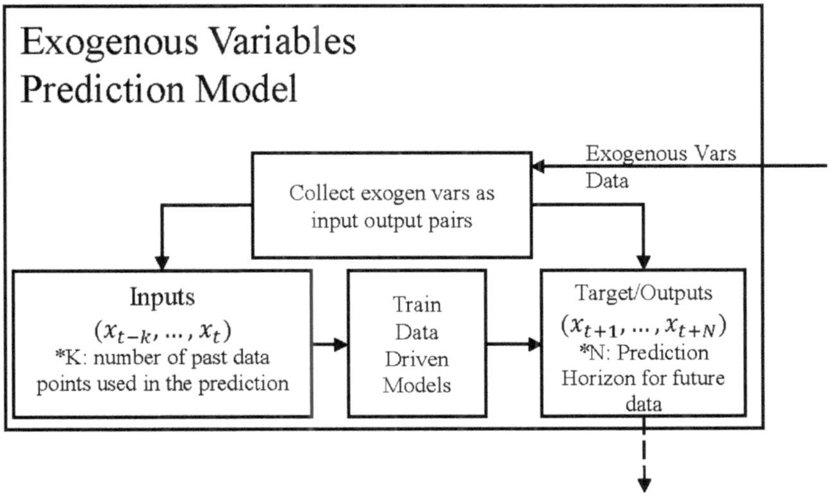

Figure 4. Exogenous variable prediction module. The dashed lines represent any interfacing operation between the component itself and external components. *K and *N represent ideal values for the past and future horizon respectively.

For data-driven modeling, the training data needs to include input variables to capture accurate modeling of system behavior. This includes variables, such as $\bar{a}_t$, $\bar{s}_t$ and $\bar{d}_t$, as well as the data to estimate the next state $\bar{s}_{t+1}$ in the Exogenous Variable Prediction module. In our approach, we collect and use real data of system operations based on the actual pre-existing controller-system interactions. These data are collected at a pre-determined rate and stored in an Experience Buffer (Figure 3) modeled as a FIFO queue with queue length M_e. The Experience Buffer helps us retain the latest data from the real system to adapt the models to the latest system behavior. Choosing an optimal value for M_e is an important step in the overall approach.

4.2.3. Deep Reinforcement Learning Controller

We develop a policy gradient-based RL algorithm to design and implement the controller π_t^* to interact with the real system [38]. The Policy Network, parameterized by the vector θ, takes as input the current state of the NS-MDP, $\bar{s}_t$, which comprises observations $\bar{o}_t$ from the system and certain exogenous variables in $\bar{d}_t$ that support the decision-making process. The network outputs an action $\bar{a}_t$ in response. In other words, it collects a set of tuples of information $(\bar{s}_t, \bar{a}_t, \bar{a}_{t+1}, r(s_t, a_t))$, which is then used to optimize a loss function J_θ. Depending on the algorithm used to update the loss function, the obtained DRL agent might be the result of a classic policy gradient network like REINFORCE, an actor-critic network like A2C, or an advanced actor-critic algorithm like Proximal Policy Optimization (PPO) [39] or Deep Deterministic Policy Gradient(DDPG) [40].

We summarize our relearning in Algorithm 1. Based on the inputs, the conditional online deployment loop with monitoring runs indefinitely. The Offline Relearn Phase is triggered conditionally.

Algorithm 1: End-to-End Relearning algorithm

Input ← $\mathcal{D}$; Exogenous Variables Source
Input ← $\mathcal{M}$; Real Dynamic System
Input ← P_θ ; Pre-trained RL Controller
Input ← PM ; Performance Monitor: $Window = W_{pm}$
Input ← EB ; Experience Buffer: $MemorySize = M_e$
Input ← D_p ; Exogenous Var Predictor: $OutputSequenceLength = N$
Input ← DSM ; Dynamic System Model
while *True* **do**
    Deploy P_θ on $\mathcal{M}$
    Monitor reward $r(s_t, a_t)$ using PM
    Update D_p models using $\mathcal{D}$ and Online Learning
    Add (s, a, s') to EB
    if *PM triggers* **then**
        Offline Relearn Phase()
Offline Relearn Phase
    update DSM models with EB using EWC
    Create a copy of P_θ as $P_\theta^{'}$
    Optimize $J_\theta^{'}$ using parallel roll-outs on DSM
    Update deployed controller: $P_\theta \leftarrow P_\theta^{'}$

5. Hyperparameter Selection

The end-to-end relearning framework discussed in the previous section has a large number of parameters across multiple systems. The joint optimization of these hyperparameters is computationally intractable. Hence, we develop a set of methods to decompose the hyperparameter space to reduce the complexity of the tuning process.

5.1. HPO: Problem Formulation

Let us assume that an ensemble A of models (not limited to machine learning models) is used to solve a problem associated with a complex system, D. The ensemble has an associated set of hyperparameters $H = (H_1, H_2, \ldots, H_j)$. The performance of the ensemble associated with D is defined by multiple metrics, $L = (L_1, L_2, \ldots, L_k)$. Our task is to identify the values for the set of hyperparameters, H^*, that allows us to achieve the best performance given the metrics, L. This is mathematically formulated as hyperparameter optimization of the ensemble model A with respect to the metrics in L:

$$H^* = argmin_{h \in H} \mathcal{L}(A, D; h), \quad (1)$$

where $\mathcal{L}$ can be a single scalar evaluated as a weighted sum of the metrics in L or a set of individual equations if the elements in L depend on different subsets of H. If the cardinality of H is large, the joint hyperparameter optimization problem becomes computationally complex and sometimes, intractable. We propose an approach for systematically decomposing the hyperparameter space into independent subsets of hyperparameters to optimize each subset individually.

5.2. Decomposition of Hyperparameter Space

We adopt a Bayes Net approach for characterizing the hyperparameter space as a graph, where the links in a graph capture the directed relations between corresponding hyperparameters and the evaluation metrics they influence. The crux of our approach then uses the concept of d-separation to determine the conditionally independent subsets of hyperparameters to be optimized independently.

Using the knowledge of the ensemble of models and the relations among performance metrics in the application domain, we derive the Bayes Net structure that captures the relations between the model hyperparameters and their corresponding evaluation metrics. Adopting the method discussed in [41], we construct the Bayes Net using a topological order (cause precedes effects) to link all $H_i \in H$ to the corresponding performance variables, $L_k \in L$, such that the order matches the directed graph structure. This helps to establish the Markov blanket, i.e., $P(X_i|X_1, X_2, X_n) = P(X_i|Parents(X_i))$, where $X = \{X_1, X_2, \cdots X_n\} = H \cup L$. Below, we describe the guiding principle to generate this graph structure.

5.2.1. Metric-Based Decomposition

We first simplify the HPO problem by classifying the hyperparameters associated with the metrics of the ensemble models into two primary groups: (1) local and (2) global.

Definition 2 (Local and Global Metrics). *For an ensemble of data-driven models A associated with a system D, the evaluation metrics in L may be decomposed into two classes. The metrics whose computation depends on an individual data-driven model are called local metrics, L_l. The metrics affecting multiple models' computations are called global metrics, L_h.*

Next, the set of hyperparameters is divided according to the specific metrics each one influences, as detailed below.

Definition 3 (Decomposition of Hyperparameter space). *For an ensemble of data-driven models, A associated with a system, D, the existing hyperparameter set, H can be decomposed into two main subsets H_h and H_l using the causal structure of a derived Bayes net [42]. Hyperparameters linked to at least one global metric, L_h, are termed global and associated with the set, H_h. Hyperparameters that are only linked to the local metrics L_l are termed local and associated with H_l.*

5.2.2. Separation of Hyperparameters: Connected Components and D-Separation

Given a Bayes Net that captures the relations between hyperparameters and metrics, we apply the concepts of connected components and d-separation [43] to identify the independent hyperparameter groupings. A graph, G, is said to be connected if every vertex of the graph is reachable from every other vertex. We can use a simple Breath-First, Search approach to identify the connected components for the directed acyclic graph (DAG) representation of the Bayes Net. Once we identify the connected components, we apply d-separation by making all links undirected and then establish if a set of variables, X, in the graph is independent of a second set of variables, Y, given a third set, Z (conditional independence). There are **four primary rules** that can be used to test the independence relation.

1. Indirect Causal Effect $X \rightarrow Z \rightarrow Y:$ X can influence evidence Y if Z has not been observed.
2. Indirect Evidential Effect $Y \rightarrow Z \rightarrow X:$ Evidence X can influence Y if Z has not been observed.
3. Common Cause $X \leftarrow Z \rightarrow Y$: X can influence Y if Z has not been observed.
4. Common Effect $X \rightarrow Z \leftarrow Y:$ X can influence Y only if Z has been observed. Otherwise, they are independent.

In our formulation of the ensemble models, we encounter the following cases based on the above rules.

1. The evaluation of local metrics blocks the effect of the local hyperparameters on global metrics (Rule 1). Therefore, any two models affecting the same global metric will not have their hyperparameters related via a common effect (Rule 4).
2. Assume that Z is the set of global hyperparameters, while X and Y represent local hyperparameter sets associated with individual models. If they belong to the same connected component (sub-graph), we will have to jointly optimize the hyperparameters of the individual models, thus increasing the computational complexity of the optimization process.
   Instead, we can consider a two-level optimization process: First, we chose candidate values for the global hyperparameters in Z. Given the values of the variables in Z, we can independently optimize the hyperparameters connected to components X and Y, thus decomposing the hyperparameter space further by applying Rule 3.
3. In many cases, all global hyperparameters are linked to the global metrics, and then they have to be jointly optimized following Rule 4.

Subsequently, during each trial of the hyperparameter optimization process, we consider the following steps:

- Choose candidate values of global hyperparameters H_h.
- With the chosen values of H_h, optimize the hyperparameters in H_l associated with each model in the ensemble by using the corresponding model performance as the objective function.
- Evaluate the performance of subsets in H_h on L_h using the set of Equation (1).

5.2.3. Bayesian Optimization for Hyperparameter Tuning

We adopt a model-based black box optimization method called Sequential Model-Based Optimization (SMBO) [44]. This method offers several advantages over gradient-based or derivative-free optimization techniques. Unlike gradient-based optimization, SMBO can handle non-convex surfaces, making it preferable when the hyperparameter space includes discrete variables. Unlike other derivative-free methods, SMBO also maintains a history of past evaluations of candidate hyperparameter settings. It uses this information to form and update a prior, thereby selecting hyperparameter values that potentially improve upon the best choices identified thus far.

The optimization process itself then includes three iterative steps that we run until a termination criterion is satisfied: (1) Using the surrogate probability model and the selection function, choose the best-performing hyperparameter; (2) Apply the hyperparameters to the fitness function $\mathbf{L}$; and (3) Update the surrogate model incorporating the new trial results. The termination criterion is based on the improvement of the metric of interest. For example, in Bayesian optimization for the HVAC problem, we look at improving detection time to non-stationarity, total relearning time, model errors, and agent reward. The details of these are provided in Section VI−D. We terminate the optimization when the expected improvement from the best hyperparameter candidate is below a threshold ϵ. We applied the Bayes rule on the surrogate probability model and then used the Tree Parzen Estimator (TPE) [44] to obtain a generative model to construct the hyperparameter distribution.

6. Experimental Settings

This section describes the settings we adopted for our relearning algorithm and the associated hyperparameter tuning approach we applied to a 5-zone building testbed.

6.1. System Description

The five-zone building testbed shown in Figure 5, developed by a Lawrence Berkeley National Labs team, is a frequently used physics-based dynamic simulation model. For our work, we exported the compiled testbed from Modelica to a Functional Mockup Unit (FMU) and used the PyFMI library to interact with the system model in Python 3.9. The FMU comprises an HVAC system, a building envelope model that includes air flow and leakage through open doors, and other building components. For a further detailed description involving the equations for modeling this building testbed, we refer the reader to [45]. Exogenous factors such as weather, occupancy, and human-induced local setpoint changes introduce non-stationary building behavior. Our approach aims to maintain operational efficiency in the face of these changes.

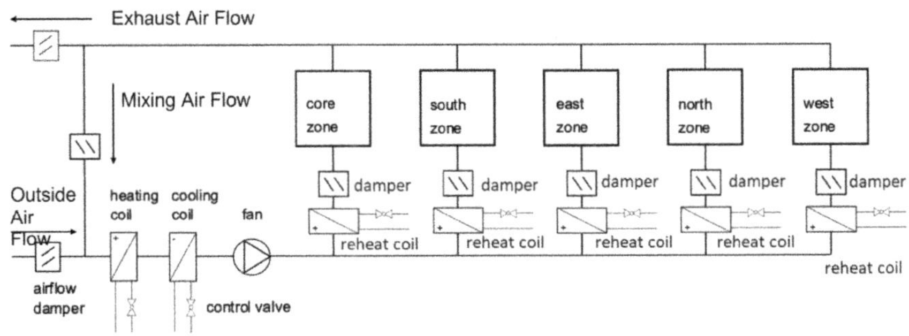

Figure 5. Schematic of the five zone testbed. Source: [45].

6.2. Reinforcement Learning Definitions

Table 1 outlines the various components of the testbed as a non-stationary MDP. Recommendations from building managers inform the selection of variables and are partially influenced by pertinent studies discussed in the literature review.

Table 1. Description of the testbed Dynamic System Model as a non-stationary MDP.

Component	Variables
State $\bar{s}_t$	1. Outside Air Temperature(oat) 2. Outside Air Relative Humidity(orh) 3. Five Zone Temperatures($T_z, z = 1\ldots5$) 4. Total Energy Consumption(E_{tot}) 5. AHU Discharge Air Temperature (T_{disch})
Action: $\bar{a}_t$	AHU Discharge Temperature Set-point (T_{dsp})
Reward $r(s_t, a_t)$	$r_{energy} + r_{cmft} + r_{vav}$ where $r_{energy} = -E_{tot}$ $r_{cmft} = -\sum_{z\in zones}$ $max((T_z - ub_{z,t}), 0, (lb_{z,t} - T_z))$ $r_{vav} = -\sum_{z\in zones} \lvert v_{\%,z,t} - v_{\%,z,t-1}\rvert$
Non-stationary Transition Model($p_t(s', s_t, a_t)$)	1. Total Energy Consumption Model(M_{energy}) 2. Zone Temperature Model($M_{T,zone}$) 3. VAV Damper Percentage Model($M_{vav\%}$)

As components of the reward function, r_{energy} optimizes energy efficiency, r_{cmft} penalizes zone comfort violations, and r_{vav} penalizes frequent changes in the controller actions T_{dsp}, as the zone VAV dampers tend to actuate aggressively in response. Here, $ub_{z,t}$ and

$lb_{z,t}$ represent the upper and lower comfort bounds for the temperature in each zone z at time t. $v_{\%,z,t}$ denotes the VAV damper valve percentage in zone z at time t. The transition and reward functions are assumed to be locally Lipschitz continuous due to the large time constants in building thermodynamics.

6.3. Implementation of the Solution

We discuss the different components of our approach specific to our testbed. The Results section provides details regarding the architecture of the individual models, hyperparameter values, performance evaluation procedures, and the corresponding results.

6.3.1. Dynamic System Model

The transition model ($p(s', s_t, a_t)$) predicts values for the following observations ($\bar{o}_t$) at the next time step: Total Energy Consumption (E_{tot}), the zone temperatures ($T_z, z = 1\ldots5$), and the VAV damper opening percentages ($v_{\%,z}, z = 1\ldots5$). Accordingly, we create a model M_{energy} for predicting energy consumption, a model $M_{T.zone}$ for predicting all the zone temperatures, and 5 individual models ($M_{vav\%,z}, z = 1\ldots5$) that predict the VAV damper opening percentages for the five zones. The ensemble of these models constitutes the Dynamic System Model. The discharge temperature model for predicting $T_{d,t}$ is modeled as

$$T_{d,t} = T_{dsp,t-1} + N(0, \sigma_{disch}).$$

We observed that the discharge temperature was always close to the setpoint specified by the Action: $a = T_{dsp}$. σ_{disch} is chosen to be 0.1^oF to account for non-deterministic effects.

6.3.2. Experience Buffer

The Buffer's optimal memory size M_e is determined by hyperparameter optimization.

6.3.3. Supervisory Controller

The DRL-based Supervisory Controller was implemented as a simple Multi-Actor Critic framework [46]. This formulation helped us determine whether our framework provided improvements compared to a standalone state-of-the-art online algorithm like PPO [39]. Given the training resources, we trained in $n = 10$ parallel environments to generate diverse samples (similar to [47]), accounting for uncertainties in measurement and resulting model inaccuracies in the Dynamic System Models. We did not specify maximum training steps, as we incrementally trained to detect performance degradation, using callbacks to stop training when the reward no longer improved, assuming convergence was achieved.

6.3.4. Exogenous Variable Predictors

For the testbed, we needed to predict ambient dry bulb temperature (oat) and relative humidity (orh). We used Long Short-Term Memory Neural Network (LSTM) models (adapted from [48]) with fine-tuning to fit our specific location's data. The Exogenous variable predictor models were learned continuously in a batched online fashion. For zone setpoint schedules and thermal load-based exogenous variables, models used simple rules to look up current schedules or values in the system and set them for the required prediction horizon N.

6.3.5. Performance Monitor Module

For the Performance Monitor, we tracked the presence of a negative trend in the deployment phase using $i = 2$ windows W_{pm1} and W_{pm2} in parallel. This helped us track slow-moving non-stationarities due to weather using W_{pm1}, and fast-moving non-stationarities due to zone temperature or load changes using W_{pm2}.

6.4. Hyperparameter Selection

The framing of the hyperparameter optimization problem is presented below and the results are discussed in the next section.

6.4.1. Bayes Net

The set of hyperparameters for the ensemble models is broadly summarized in the first column of Table 2. The set of performance metrics included in the Bayes Net are: (1) time to detect non-stationarity after occurrence ($L_{\Delta t_d}$), (2) total relearning time ($L_{\Delta t_r}$), (3) individual data-driven models errors (L_{me}), and (4) RL agent reward (L_{rwd}). The resulting Bayes Net is depicted in Figure 6. The links, representing the cause-effect relations of the ensemble structure, are derived from the local versus global labeling of the variables.

Table 2. Hyperparameters of the ensemble–CPS pair, the metrics they affect and the classification of the hyperparameters as global or local.

Hyperparameter(s)	Metric Affected	Global/Local
Performance Monitor Module Window sizes: W_{pm1}, W_{pm2}	$L_{\Delta t_d}$	Global
Memory Buffer Size: M_e	L_{me}, $L_{\Delta t_r}$	Global
Forecast Horizon Length: N	L_{me}, L_{rwd}. $L_{\Delta t_r}$	Global
Exogenous Variable Predictor: *Nodes, Layers, Activations*	L_{me}	Local
Dynamic System Model(s): *Nodes, Layers, Activations*	L_{me}	Local
RL Agent Policy Network: *Nodes, Layers, Activations*	L_{rwd}	Local
RL Agent Value Network: *Nodes, Layers, Activations*	L_{rwd}	Local
Discount Factor: γ	L_{rwd}	Local
Episode Length: l_e	L_{rwd}	Local

To identify the set of global and local hyperparameters, we first classified the metrics as global and local. For the ensemble approach and the five-zone testbed, the time to detect a non-stationary change after occurrence ($L_{\Delta t_d}$) and total relearning time ($L_{\Delta t_r}$) were labeled as global metrics, as they were influenced by multiple models and represented overall ensemble performance. The individual data-driven model errors (L_{me}) and RL agent losses (L_{rwd}) were labeled as local performance metrics. Accordingly, Table 2 lists the metrics affected by the hyperparameters and shows their classification as global and local in the last column.

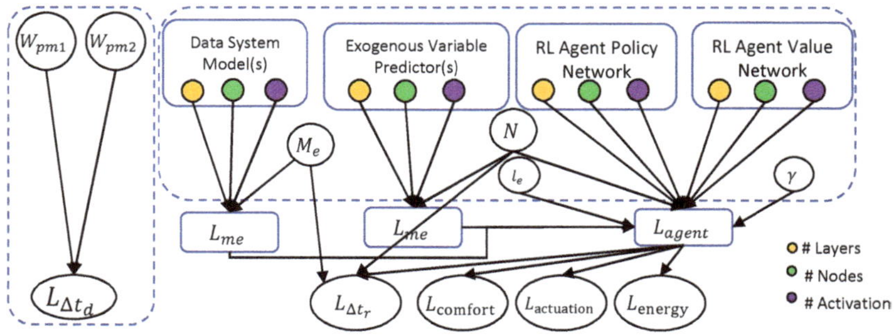

Figure 6. Bayes net for the relearning approach applied to the 5 zone testbed.

6.4.2. Separation of Hyperparameters

Given the Bayes Net structure in Figure 6, we identified W_{pm1} and W_{pm2} to be related via common effect (Rule 4). However, not being connected to other nodes, they were independent of the other variables. The nodes M_e and N were connected via the common effect rule (Rule 4) through the node $L_{\Delta t_r}$. Given the two-level hyperparameter optimization, the individual model hyperparameters in the dynamic system, exogenous variable predictors, the agent actor, and critic networks were independent of each other via the common cause (Rule 3). The hyperparameters inside individual models were dependent on each other due to the common effect rule (Rule 4). The nodes l_e and γ were jointly optimized with the agent hyperparameters because of common cause (rule 4) since they affected L_{rwd}. Finally, the individual model hyperparameters did not affect the global metrics due to the blocking effect of the local metrics L_{me}. Hence, the hyperparameter space could be decomposed as follows: (1) (W_{pm1}, W_{pm2}), and (2) (M_e, N, H_l) where subsets of H_l. Each could be optimized independent of the other. Here, H_l comprises all the hyperparameters of individual data-driven models.

6.4.3. Two-Step Hyperparameter Optimization

Given the separation of hyperparameters, we independently optimized the values of (W_{pm1}, W_{pm2}) using the metric $L_{\Delta t_d}$. For the other subset including (M_e, N, H_l), we performed two-level optimization, where we chose candidate values of (M_e, N) and then optimized the subsets of H_l independently. The independent subsets included hyperparameters of the Exogenous Variable Predictor, Dynamic System Model(s), and RL Agent Policy Network, Value Network, l_e and γ. We considered four types of building non-stationary changes: (1) Weather based: ambient temperature and ambient relative humidity, (2) Changes in zone set-points (3) Changes in thermal load due to changes in occupancy, and (4) a combination of the first 3 cases. For cases 2 and 3, weather-related non-stationary changes were also present. This two-step optimization approach was performed across all possible non-stationary changes.

6.4.4. Global and Local Hyperparameter Choices

The candidate choices for the global and local hyperparameters are described in Tables 3 and 4, respectively. These ranges were selected based on existing building energy optimization problems in the literature, while we primarily used discrete choices for the hyperparameter values, separating the hyperparameters helped simplify the search space. For the dynamic system neural network-based models, the exogenous variable predictor models, and the actor-critic networks, we restricted the number of hidden layers to four to avoid computational intractability.

Table 3. Ranges of the global hyperparameters.

Hyperparameter	**Search Space (Range)**
W_{pm1} (Performance Monitor Module)	$\{1, 2, \ldots, 12\}$ h
W_{pm2} (Performance Monitor Module)	$\{15, 30, \ldots, 165, 180\}$ min
M_e (Experience Buffer)	$\{24, 48, \ldots, 144, 168\}$ h
N(Exogenous Variable Predictor and Dynamic System Model)	$\{24, 48, 72, 96\}$ h

Table 4. Ranges of the local hyperparameters.

Hyperparameter	**Search Space (Range)**
Dynamic System Model Weights (M_{energy}, $M_{T,zone}$, $M_{vav\%,z}$)	$W \in \{8, 16, 32, \ldots, 256\}$
Dynamic System Model Activation (M_{energy}, $M_{T,zone}$, $M_{vav\%,z}$)	$a \in \{linear, relu, sigmoid, tanh\}$
Exogenous Variable Model Weights	$W \in \{8, 16, 32, \ldots, 256\}$
Exogenous Variable Model Activation	$a \in \{linear, relu, tanh\}$
Actor(π_θ) Critic (V_ϕ) Network weights	$W \in \{64, 128, 256, 512\}$
Actor(π_θ) Critic (V_ϕ) Network Activation	$a \in \{linear, relu, tanh\}$
γ	$\{0.99, 0.95, \ldots, 0.80\}$
l_e	$\{1, 2, 3\}$ days

The selection and separation of the hyperparameters emphasize that we do not rely on the physics of the approach but allow the system's information to dictate the hyperparameter values through tuning.

7. Results and Discussion

We present the results of the hyperparameter tuning followed by the relearning algorithm application on the five-zone testbed. We discuss the optimized model architectures and the evaluation metrics. The distributed two-step hyperparameter optimization utilized Ray-Tune [49], which was applied across four types of building non-stationarities. Specifically, our hyperparameters are optimized to enhance the online performance of our deep relearning RL algorithm. No additional training is conducted during online operations.

7.1. Results on Tuned Model Architecture and Model Evaluation

In this subsection, we provide the details of the tuned model architectures and the results of evaluating the models on the standard five-zone testbed.

7.1.1. Dynamic System Model

Our model evaluation used the predicted output from timestep $t-1$ as the input for prediction at time step t over prediction horizon N. We assessed model performance across 100 different $N = 48$ h intervals throughout the year. We calculated the Coefficient of Variation of the Root Mean Square Error (CVRMSE) and evaluated temperature and zone VAV predictors with the Mean Absolute Error (MAE).

7.1.2. Experience Buffer

The following values (in hours) were obtained for the size of the Experience Buffer M_e: (1) Weather: 36; (2) Zone Set Point: 18; (3) Thermal Load: 18; and (4) Combined: 18.

7.1.3. Supervisory Controller

The controller is modeled as an Actor Critic framework [46]. The inputs to the actor-network are the state variables in $\bar{s}_t$ described in Table 1 and the output is the mean a_μ and standard deviation a_σ from which an action $\bar{a}_t$ is sampled. The critic network is a Q-network that takes as input the current state $\bar{s}_t$ and action $\bar{a}_t$. It is then used to estimate the Advantage using Equation (2).

$$A(s_t, a_t) = Q(s_t, a_t) - \sum_{a_t \in A} \pi(a_t|s_t) \times Q(s_t, a_t) \tag{2}$$

Typically, advantages are normalized for better convergence during agent training. There is less confidence in future estimated returns for parameters like weather with slow non-stationary changes with high uncertainty. Hence, we used low values of γ for weather. In contrast, the opposite was true for non-stationarities related to zone setpoint and thermal load changes as they tended to sustain values or maintain the same schedule in the future and not change very often.

7.1.4. Exogenous Variable Predictor Models

We developed models for predicting outside air temperature and relative humidity as a sequence prediction problem. Given K past inputs, we predicted future values over a horizon N, adapting the approach of [48] to Nashville's weather. Lacking future labeled data for sequence-to-sequence prediction, we utilized a for loop during prediction, feeding the previous output ($\bar{o}_t$), cell state ($\bar{c}_t$), and network state ($\bar{h}_t$) from the last LSTM into the next time-step predictions ($\bar{h}_t$), using recurrent neural network translation techniques [50]. The resulting encoder-decoder network was pre-trained on one year of Nashville data, predicting over a horizon of length, N using past $K = 12$ h inputs at half-hour intervals. The test dataset consisted of 100 samples with $N = 48$-h horizons at similar intervals. The optimal K and N values for various non-stationarities are listed in Table 5.

Table 5. Tuned values of the input sequence length K and the prediction horizon N under different conditions of non-stationarity.

Non-Stationarity	**Weather**		**Zone Set Point**		**Thermal Load**		**Combined**	
Hyperparameter	K	N	K	N	K	N	K	N
Value (h)	18	72	6	72	6	72	12	48

The tuning of the output horizon length N is considered a weighted metric that includes model error, relearning time, energy consumption, actuation frequency, and comfort performance. Our approach struck a balance between producing sufficient future samples for expedited reinforcement learning agent training and convergence, and minimizing the impact of modeling errors stemming from uncertainties in future return estimates G_t.

7.1.5. Performance Monitor Module

We tuned the values of the two windows for detecting negative trends over (1) small intervals due to faster relatively non-stationarities; and (2) large intervals for slow-moving non-stationarities. The tuned values for W_{pm1} and W_{pm2} are shown in Table 6.

Table 6. Tuned values W_{pm1} and W_{pm2}.

Non-Stationarity	**Weather**		**Zone Setpoint**	
Hyperparameter Value (h)	W_{pm1} 6	W_{pm2} 2	W_{pm1} 3	W_{pm2} 2
Non-stationarity	**Thermal Load**		**Combined**	
Hyperparameter Value (h)	W_{pm1} 3	W_{pm2} 2	W_{pm1} 6	W_{pm2} 3

7.2. Benchmark Experiments

We assessed the performance of our relearning algorithm by implementing it online in the five-zone testbed and comparing it against benchmark algorithms using established building literature metrics.

Energy Consumption E_{tot}: A lower energy consumption under similar conditions indicates better energy efficiency.

Average Zone Temperature Deviation: $T_D = \sum_{z \in Z} max(T_z - ub_z, 0, lb_z - T_z)$ or $\sum_{z \in Z} |T_z - T_{z,sp}|$. Lower deviations from indicated setpoints imply better thermal comfort. Z represents the total number of zones, T_z is the temperature in zone z, $T_{z,sp}$ is the set-point for zone z, and ub_z and lb_z are lower and upper comfort bounds. One of the two choices can be selected as a proxy for comfort, depending on whether the bounds are predefined or not for each zone of the building.

Actuation Rate: The actuation rate is given by $A_s = \sum_{t=0}^{T} \sum_{z \in Z} |A_{t+1,z} - A_{t,z}|$, where A is the VAV damper opening state (percentage). Lesser actuation on aggregate implies that the controller can enforce smoother control such that the wear on the actuator is less in the long run.

7.3. Results

We conducted experiments to assess the impact of varying weather conditions, zone set-point values, and thermal loads, utilizing three months of data for pre-training to learn building dynamics and derive the initial supervisory controller. Subsequently, we tested our framework for a year with Nashville weather data. Weather-related changes include sudden increases and decreases in the outside air temperature and relative humidity, e.g., sudden short warm spells during spring mostly occurring in February and March 2021 and sudden cold spells in August and October 2021. Zone set-point adjustments altered temperature bounds by 4^0F to 6^0F and increased thermal loads mimicked events with high occupancy.

We detected 24 instances of weather changes, 14 set-point modifications, 11 thermal load increases, and 26 combined scenarios. Our framework's performance was benchmarked against Guideline-36 [14] and compared with PPO [39], DDPG [40], and a data-driven MPC [51] using MPPI with periodic model updates. All algorithms shared the same reward function, state space, and control actions. The DRL approaches ran online. PPO updated policies every 12 h, DDPG sampled from its Replay Buffer weekly, and MPPI maintained consistent prediction horizons across non-stationarities, with weekly model refreshes as in [47].

To compare our approach's performance after non-stationary changes occurred, we examined metrics over a week following detection and considered the maximum interval for building response alteration. Figure 7 shows these results as bar plots, demonstrating our method's superior performance to rule-based control and PPO and DDPG's online deployment. Our results are also comparable or better than MPPI. Next, we analyze individual metric performance.

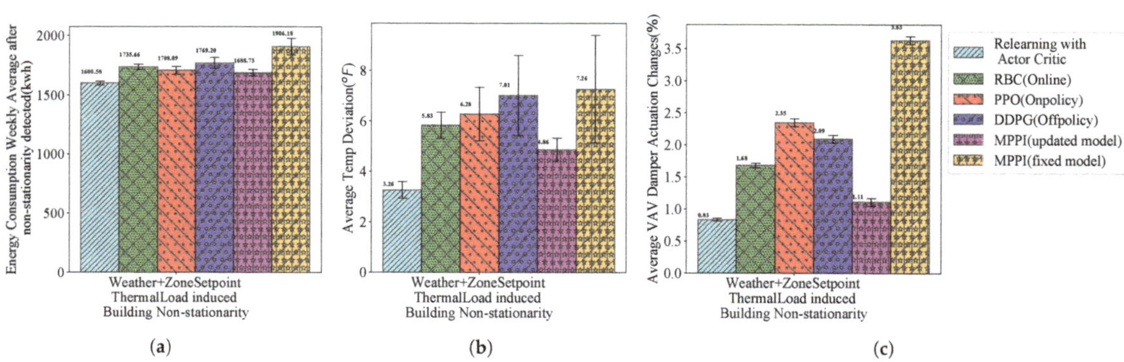

Figure 7. Performance of Rule-Based, PPO, DDPG, MPPI, and Relearning Approach deployed on the testbed and simulated for a period of 1 year. Benchmarking is done across all types of non-stationarity changes. Metrics are recorded for a week after detection of non-stationarity using the Performance Monitor Module. Energy performance is aggregated for a week as in figure (**a**). Temperature deviation in figure (**b**) and Actuation rates in figure (**c**) are aggregated on a per-hour basis.

Our approach yields significantly better energy savings E_{tot} compared to other methods during non-stationary changes. This is attributed to the accelerated adaptation process. This speed-up is due to multiple actors generating experiences and predictive models facilitating quicker future behavior simulation, that outpaces fully online methods that rely on data from the testbed in real time. The rule-based online (RBC), on policy (PPO) and off policy(DDPG) approaches perform significant amount of exploratory behavior under non-stationary system behavior, leading to suboptimal performance for a significant duration of time. This leads to faster convergence, which we discuss later in the context of adaptation time. MPPI also performs well using testbed models for offline planning and online execution. However, as we have discussed earlier, its performance suffers from less reliable state estimates as MPPI with updated models performs better than one without model updates.

Regarding comfort, measured by temperature deviation T_D, our method outperformed others, with PPO and DDPG performing worse than RBC due to their exploratory behavior in non-stationary conditions. PPO's impact was less severe due to conservative updates. Guideline 36 also underperformed, as its abrupt operational changes increased energy use and compromised temperature control. MPPI's frequent setpoint adjustments, termed "hunting" behavior, caused discomfort in spite of making optimal choices. Our RL agent in the relearning loop used the models to generate and sample many experiences over a short time period. Sudden changes were penalized by the reward formulation, leading to superior performance compared to Guideline-36, PPO, and DDPG. The relearning agent's performance was on par with MPPI.

The VAV Damper actuation rate of the relearning framework was also better than the other approaches due to similar reasons as above. This led us to investigate the duration of operation where each of these methods were performing suboptimally. This would provide further inside in to the differences in the behavior. Hence, we compared the time taken to relearn $\Delta T_{relearn}$ compared to the online algorithms PPO and DDPG in Figure 8. $\Delta T_{relearn}$ indicates the time it took from the start of the relearning trigger to the time until the controller training converged. We measured this for our approach as well as PPO and DDPG using a callback during the training process that told us whether the episode reward over the last 10 episodes was within 2 standard deviations of the average of the past 100 episode rewards.

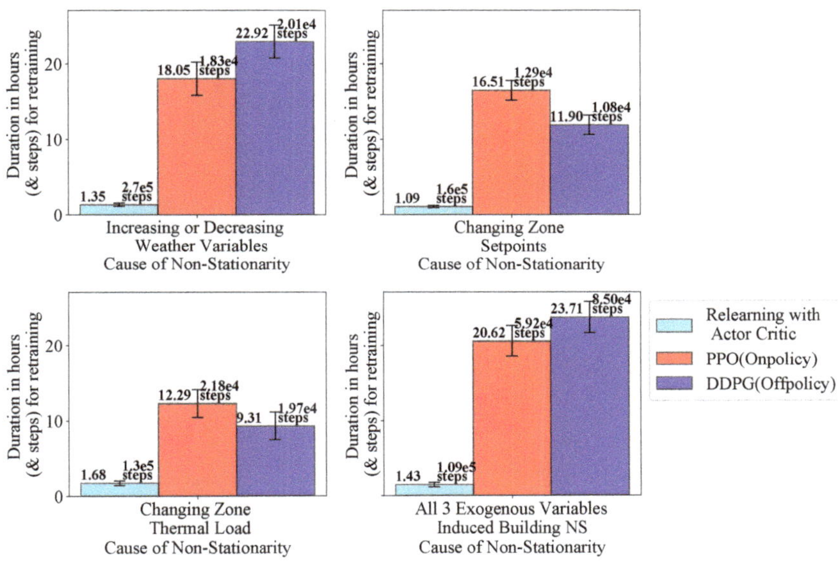

Figure 8. Time to adapt under each DRL based approach across four different types of non-stationary behavior.

Specifically, we observe that the dual loop controller approach takes 60% to 80% less time than the online approaches proposed in [52–54] using PPO and DDPG while using much more samples (10 times more samples) across parallel environments. This speed up is a major advantage to addressing the challenges of having a suboptimal policy under non-stationary behavior conditions when the system dynamics is slow.

Next, the seasonal reward analysis, shown in Figure 9, revealed optimal spring performance due to stable temperature and humidity conditions, which were close to comfortable values. Autumn and winter faced challenges due to frequent weather shifts, with autumn being particularly problematic in Nashville due to frequent changes in its weather. This required frequent sampling of the real data used as input for the simulation. Figure 10 shows the number of relearning phases in a year, highlighting the true causes of non-stationarity. Weekly activations were reasonable; they ranged from 8 to 16, and were predominantly triggered by user preference changes because weather and occupancy patterns were more predictable. The consistent average number of relearning phases suggests the framework's limited retention capacity, pointing to future research on hybrid automata to reduce relearning frequency.

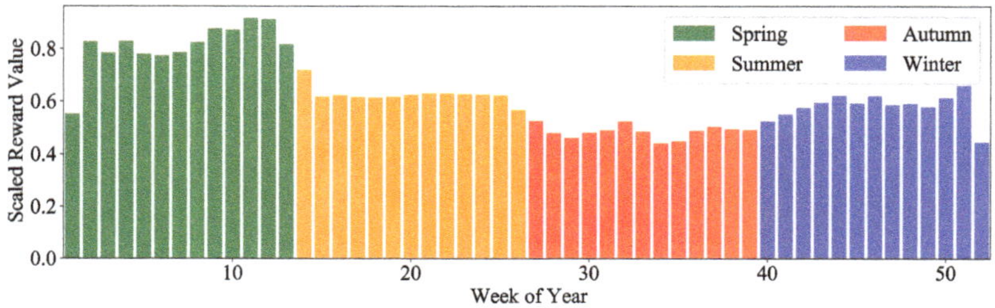

Figure 9. Total reward obtained for our approach depending on the week and season of the year.

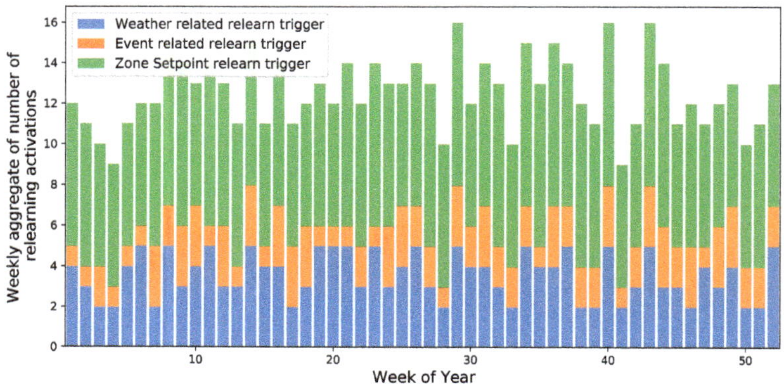

Figure 10. Total number of relearning phases triggered for our approach depending on the week of the year.

8. Conclusions and Future Work

This study introduced a relearning framework tailored for non-stationary system control, exemplified by a building energy optimization case. The framework enables end-to-end data-driven control suitable for practical applications. We also established a systematic hyperparameter optimization strategy that efficiently manages complex hyperparameter spaces to avoid computational burdens. We demonstrated the relearning framework's performance on a five-zone building testbed and benchmarked it against Guideline-36, PPO, DDPG, and MPPI algorithms under similar operating conditions. Our relearning algorithm is stable across seasons and consistent in its relearning triggers, which underscore its robustness. Future efforts will aim to enhance model retention post-convergence to reduce relearning frequency. Another important aspect of this work is how we can extend this framework to a real building. This involves adding contingency plans to the framework that can withstand multiple robustness considerations on top of the performance challenges we addressed. It includes sensor information loss, default safety logic, constant monitoring to ensure building comfort for the occupants, and actual energy comparison under nominal conditions that have to be studied. Hence, we separately published a real world implementation of this approach in [55]. Our goal is to ensure that the framework can be deployed on any HVAC system configuration. Hence, in the future, we plan to study the generalizability of our approach across different manufacturer specifications for HVAC components as well as different weather conditions. We also plan to consider cost optimization as one of the objectives in our framework.

Author Contributions: Conceptualization, M.Q.-G. and G.B.; Methodology, A.N., M.Q.-G. and G.B.; Software, A.N.; Formal analysis, M.Q.-G. and G.B.; Investigation, A.N.; Data curation, A.N.; Writing—original draft, A.N.; Writing—review & editing, M.Q.-G. and G.B. All authors have read and agreed to the published version of the manuscript.

Funding: This research received no external funding.

Data Availability Statement: The data presented in this study are openly available in GitHub: https://github.com/AvisekNaug/ah_deployment.

Conflicts of Interest: The authors declare no conflicts of interest.

Abbreviations

The following abbreviations are used in this manuscript:

HVAC	Heating, Ventilation, and Air Conditioning
CPS	Cyber Physical Systems
MPC	Model Predictive Control
ML	Machine Learning
RL	Reinforcement Learning
EWC	Elastic Weighted Consolidation
ASHRAE	American Society of Heating, Refrigerating and Air-Conditioning Engineers
MDP	Markov Decision Process
LC-NSMDP	Lipschitz Continuous Non Stationary Markov Decision Process
LSTM	Long Short Term Memory
FCNN	Fully Connected Neural Network
FIFO	First, In First, Out Queue
OOD	Out of Distribution Error
HPO	Hyperparameter Optimization
DAG	Directed Acyclic Graph
SMBO	Sequential Model Based Optimization
FMU	Functional Mockup Unit
VAV	Variable Air Volume Unit
MPPI	Model Predictive Path Integral Control
PPO	Proximal Policy Optimization
DDPG	Deep Deterministic Policy Gradient

References

1. Cassandras, C. Chapter 3—Online Control and Optimization for Cyber-Physical Systems. In *Cyber-Physical Systems*; Song, H., Rawat, D.B., Jeschke, S., Brecher, C., Eds.; Intelligent Data-Centric Systems; Academic Press: Boston, MA, USA, 2017; pp. 31–54.
2. Al-Ali, R.; Bulej, L.; Kofroň, J.; Bureš, T. A guide to design uncertainty-aware self-adaptive components in Cyber–Physical Systems. *Future Gener. Comput. Syst.* **2022**, *128*, 466–489. [CrossRef]
3. Padakandla, S.; J, P.K.; Bhatnagar, S. Reinforcement learning algorithm for non-stationary environments. *Appl. Intell.* **2020**, *50*, 3590–3606. [CrossRef]
4. Lewis, F.L.; Vrabie, D.L.; Syrmos, V.L. *Optimal Control*; John Wiley & Sons, Ltd.: Hoboken, NJ, USA, 2012.
5. Sutton, R.S.; Barto, A.G. *Reinforcement Learning: An Introduction*; MIT Press: Cambridge, MA, USA, 2018.
6. Branicky, M.S. Introduction to hybrid systems. In *Handbook of Networked and Embedded Control Systems*; Springer: Berlin/Heidelberg, Germany, 2005; pp. 91–116.
7. Naug, A.; Quinones-Grueiro, M.; Biswas, G. Deep reinforcement learning control for non-stationary building energy management. *Energy Build.* **2022**, *277*, 112584. [CrossRef]
8. Kim, D.; Lee, J.; Do, S.; Mago, P.J.; Lee, K.H.; Cho, H. Energy modeling and model predictive control for HVAC in buildings: A review of current research trends. *Energies* **2022**, *15*, 7231. [CrossRef]
9. Zhang, H.; Seal, S.; Wu, D.; Bouffard, F.; Boulet, B. Building energy management with reinforcement learning and model predictive control: A survey. *IEEE Access* **2022**, *10*, 27853–27862. [CrossRef]
10. Fu, Q.; Han, Z.; Chen, J.; Lu, Y.; Wu, H.; Wang, Y. Applications of reinforcement learning for building energy efficiency control: A review. *J. Build. Eng.* **2022**, *50*, 104165. [CrossRef]
11. Fang, X.; Gong, G.; Li, G.; Chun, L.; Peng, P.; Li, W.; Shi, X.; Chen, X. Deep reinforcement learning optimal control strategy for temperature setpoint real-time reset in multi-zone building HVAC system. *Appl. Therm. Eng.* **2022**, *212*, 118552. [CrossRef]

12. Li, F.; Du, Y. Intelligent multi-zone residential HVAC control strategy based on deep reinforcement learning. In *Deep Learning for Power System Applications: Case Studies Linking Artificial Intelligence and Power Systems*; Springer: Berlin/Heidelberg, Germany, 2023; pp. 71–96.
13. Arroyo, J.; Manna, C.; Spiessens, F.; Helsen, L. Reinforced model predictive control (RL-MPC) for building energy management. *Appl. Energy* **2022**, *309*, 118346. [CrossRef]
14. Guideline 36: Best in Class HVAC Control Sequences. 2025. Available online: https://www.ashrae.org/professional-development/all-instructor-led-training/catalog-of-instructor-led-training/guideline-36-best-in-class-hvac-control-sequences (accessed on 26 February 2025).
15. Yoon, Y.; Amasyali, K.; Li, Y.; Im, P.; Bae, Y.; Liu, Y.; Zandi, H. Energy performance evaluation of the ASHRAE Guideline 36 control and reinforcement learning–based control using field measurements. *Energy Build.* **2024**, *325*, 115005. [CrossRef]
16. Lee, Y.M.; Horesh, R.; Liberti, L. Optimal HVAC Control as Demand Response with On-site Energy Storage and Generation System. *Energy Procedia* **2015**, *78*, 2106–2111. [CrossRef]
17. D'Ettorre, F.; Conti, P.; Schito, E.; Testi, D. Model predictive control of a hybrid heat pump system and impact of the prediction horizon on cost-saving potential and optimal storage capacity. *Appl. Therm. Eng.* **2019**, *148*, 524–535. [CrossRef]
18. Luzi, M.; Vaccarini, M.; Lemma, M. A tuning methodology of Model Predictive Control design for energy efficient building thermal control. *J. Build. Eng.* **2019**, *21*, 28–36. [CrossRef]
19. Azuatalam, D.; Lee, W.L.; de Nijs, F.; Liebman, A. Reinforcement learning for whole-building HVAC control and demand response. *Energy AI* **2020**, *2*, 100020. [CrossRef]
20. Fu, Q.; Li, Z.; Ding, Z.; Chen, J.; Luo, J.; Wang, Y.; Lu, Y. ED-DQN: An event-driven deep reinforcement learning control method for multi-zone residential buildings. *Build. Environ.* **2023**, *242*, 110546. [CrossRef]
21. Fang, X.; Gong, G.; Li, G.; Chun, L.; Peng, P.; Li, W.; Shi, X. Cross temporal-spatial transferability investigation of deep reinforcement learning control strategy in the building HVAC system level. *Energy* **2023**, *263*, 125679. [CrossRef]
22. Kontes, G.D.; Giannakis, G.I.; Sánchez, V.; Agustin-Camacho, D.; Romero-Amorrortu, A.; Panagiotidou, N.; Rovas, D.V.; Steiger, S.; Mutschler, C.; Gruen, G.; et al. Simulation-based evaluation and optimization of control strategies in buildings. *Energies* **2018**, *11*, 3376. [CrossRef]
23. Costanzo, G.T.; Iacovella, S.; Ruelens, F.; Leurs, T.; Claessens, B.J. Experimental analysis of data-driven control for a building heating system. *Sustain. Energy Grids Netw.* **2016**, *6*, 81–90. [CrossRef]
24. Di Natale, L.; Svetozarevic, B.; Heer, P.; Jones, C.N. Physically Consistent Neural Networks for building thermal modeling: Theory and analysis. *Appl. Energy* **2022**, *325*, 119806. [CrossRef]
25. Balali, Y.; Chong, A.; Busch, A.; O'Keefe, S. Energy modelling and control of building heating and cooling systems with data-driven and hybrid models—A review. *Renew. Sustain. Energy Rev.* **2023**, *183*, 113496. [CrossRef]
26. Shah, S.F.A.; Iqbal, M.; Aziz, Z.; Rana, T.A.; Khalid, A.; Cheah, Y.N.; Arif, M. The Role of Machine Learning and the Internet of Things in Smart Buildings for Energy Efficiency. *Appl. Sci.* **2022**, *12*, 7882. [CrossRef]
27. Pinto, G.; Wang, Z.; Roy, A.; Hong, T.; Capozzoli, A. Transfer learning for smart buildings: A critical review of algorithms, applications, and future perspectives. *Adv. Appl. Energy* **2022**, *5*, 100084. [CrossRef]
28. Morteza, A.; Yahyaeian, A.A.; Mirzaeibonehkhater, M.; Sadeghi, S.; Mohaimeni, A.; Taheri, S. Deep learning hyperparameter optimization: Application to electricity and heat demand prediction for buildings. *Energy Build.* **2023**, *289*, 113036. [CrossRef]
29. Boutahri, Y.; Tilioua, A. Machine learning-based predictive model for thermal comfort and energy optimization in smart buildings. *Results Eng.* **2024**, *22*, 102148. [CrossRef]
30. Lecarpentier, E.; Rachelson, E. Non-stationary Markov decision processes, a worst-case approach using model-based reinforcement learning. *Adv. Neural Inf. Process. Syst.* **2019**, *32*, 7214–7223.
31. Trimponias, G.; Dietterich, T.G. Reinforcement Learning with Exogenous States and Rewards. *arXiv* **2023**, arXiv:2303.12957.
32. Glasmachers, T. Limits of end-to-end learning. In Proceedings of the Asian Conference on Machine Learning, PMLR, Nagoya, Japan, 15–17 November 2017; pp. 17–32.
33. Ring, M.B. Continual Learning in Reinforcement Environments. Ph.D. Thesis, University of Texas at Austin, Austin, TX, USA, 1994.
34. Bryhn, A.C.; Dimberg, P.H. An operational definition of a statistically meaningful trend. *PLoS ONE* **2011**, *6*, e19241. [CrossRef]
35. Deng, X.; Zhang, Y.; Qi, H. Towards optimal HVAC control in non-stationary building environments combining active change detection and deep reinforcement learning. *Build. Environ.* **2022**, *211*, 108680. [CrossRef]
36. Stripping off the Implementation Complexity of Physics-Based Model Predictive Control for Buildings via Deep Learning. Online. 2019. Available online: https://s3.us-east-1.amazonaws.com/climate-change-ai/papers/neurips2019/34/paper.pdf (accessed on 22 September 2021).
37. Kirkpatrick, J.; Pascanu, R.; Rabinowitz, N.; Veness, J.; Desjardins, G.; Rusu, A.A.; Milan, K.; Quan, J.; Ramalho, T.; Grabska-Barwinska, A.; et al. Overcoming catastrophic forgetting in neural networks. *Proc. Natl. Acad. Sci. USA* **2017**, *114*, 3521–3526. [CrossRef]

38. Sutton, R.S.; McAllester, D.A.; Singh, S.P.; Mansour, Y. Policy gradient methods for reinforcement learning with function approximation. *Adv. Neural Inf. Process. Syst.* **2000**, *12*, 1057–1063.
39. Schulman, J.; Wolski, F.; Dhariwal, P.; Radford, A.; Klimov, O. Proximal Policy Optimization Algorithms. *arXiv* **2017**, arXiv:1707.06347.
40. Lillicrap, T.P.; Hunt, J.J.; Pritzel, A.; Heess, N.; Erez, T.; Tassa, Y.; Silver, D.; Wierstra, D. Continuous control with deep reinforcement learning. *arXiv* **2016**, arXiv:1509.02971.
41. Russell, S.; Norvig, P. *Artificial Intelligence: A Modern Approach*, 4th ed.; Pearson Education, Inc.: Hoboken, NJ, USA, 2021.
42. Bowers, R.I.; Salmon, C. Causal Reasoning. In *Encyclopedia of Evolutionary Psychological Science*; Springer: Cham, Switzerland, 2017; pp. 1–17. [CrossRef]
43. Geiger, D.; Verma, T.; Pearl, J. d-separation: From theorems to algorithms. In *Machine Intelligence and Pattern Recognition*; Elsevier: Amsterdam, The Netherlands, 1990; Volume 10, pp. 139–148.
44. Bergstra, J.; Bardenet, R.; Bengio, Y.; Kégl, B. Algorithms for hyperparameter optimization. *Adv. Neural Inf. Process. Syst.* **2011**, *24*, 2546–2554.
45. Buildings.Examples.VAVReheat. 2021. Available online: https://simulationresearch.lbl.gov/modelica/releases/v4.0.0/help/Buildings_Examples_VAVReheat.html (accessed on 15 July 2021).
46. Zaytar, A.; Amrani, C.E. Sequence to Sequence Weather Forecasting with Long Short-Term Memory Recurrent Neural Networks. *Int. J. Comput. Appl.* **2016**, *143*, 7–11.
47. Ding, X.; Du, W.; Cerpa, A.E. MB2C: Model-Based Deep Reinforcement Learning for Multi-zone Building Control. In *BuildSys '20: Proceedings of the 7th ACM International Conference on Systems for Energy-Efficient Buildings, Cities, and Transportation*; Association for Computing Machinery: New York, NY, USA, 2020; pp. 50–59. [CrossRef]
48. Karevan, Z.; Suykens, J.A.K. Transductive LSTM for time-series prediction: An application to weather forecasting. *Neural Netw.* **2020**, *125*, 1–9. [CrossRef]
49. Liaw, R.; Liang, E.; Nishihara, R.; Moritz, P.; Gonzalez, J.E.; Stoica, I. Tune: A Research Platform for Distributed Model Selection and Training. *arXiv* **2018**, arXiv:1807.05118.
50. A Ten-Minute Introduction to Sequence-to-Sequence Learning in Keras. 2020. Available online: https://blog.keras.io/a-ten-minute-introduction-to-sequence-to-sequence-learning-in-keras.html (accessed on 27 February 2022).
51. Nagabandi, A.; Finn, C.; Levine, S. Deep Online Learning via Meta-Learning: Continual Adaptation for Model-Based RL. *arXiv* **2018**, arXiv:1812.07671.
52. Wei, T.; Wang, Y.; Zhu, Q. Deep reinforcement learning for building HVAC control. In Proceedings of the 54th Annual Design Automation Conference 2017, Austin, TX, USA, 18–22 June 2017; pp. 1–6.
53. Barrett, E.; Linder, S. Autonomous hvac control, a reinforcement learning approach. In *Proceedings of the Joint European Conference on Machine Learning and Knowledge Discovery in Databases*; Springer: Berlin/Heidelberg, Germany, 2015; pp. 3–19.
54. Zhang, Z.; Chong, A.; Pan, Y.; Zhang, C.; Lam, K.P. Whole building energy model for HVAC optimal control: A practical framework based on deep reinforcement learning. *Energy Build.* **2019**, *199*, 472–490. [CrossRef]
55. Naug, A.; Quinones-Grueiro, M.; Biswas, G. Reinforcement learning-based HVAC supervisory control of a multi-zone building-A real case study. In Proceedings of the 2022 IEEE Conference on Control Technology and Applications (CCTA), Trieste, Italy, 23–25 August 2022; pp. 1172–1177. [CrossRef]

energies

MDPI

Article

Experimental Study on Heat Transfer Coefficients in an Office Room with a Radiant Ceiling During Low Heating Loads

Piotr Michalak

Department of Power Systems and Environmental Protection Facilities, Faculty of Mechanical Engineering and Robotics, AGH University of Krakow, al. A. Mickiewicza 30, 30-059 Krakow, Poland; pmichal@agh.edu.pl; Tel.: +48-12-617-35-79

Abstract: Estimation of the heating or cooling capacity of radiant systems requires selecting appropriate internal heat transfer coefficients by convection (CHTCs) and radiation (RHTCs). Due to practical reasons, their measurement during the normal use of buildings is very troublesome. This study attempts to present the results of measurements of CHTCs and RHTCs taken in an office room located in a passive building with a heated concrete ceiling. Special attention was paid to the proper choice of reference temperatures. For better accuracy, view factors for radiant heat exchange were calculated using Matlab. Average values of CHTCs and RHTCs calculated from measurements amounted to 0.80 W/m^{2}K and 5.66 W/m^{2}K. RHTCs showed a significant correlation against the ceiling temperature, with the coefficient of determination being R^2 = 0.96. Finally, the total heat transfer coefficient of 6.47 W/m^{2}K was obtained. These values are comparable with other studies and standards and confirm that measurements were performed correctly.

Keywords: heat transfer coefficient; convection; radiation; heat flux measurement; concrete ceiling heating

1. Introduction

Water-based radiant heating and cooling systems have become increasingly popular in recent decades due to their positive features as good indoor climate and effective cooperation with low-temperature sources such as heat pumps [1,2].

The ISO 11855 standard [3] categorises these systems into several groups. Depending on construction and geometry, they are labelled from A to G. Among them, an interesting solution is the Type E (named Thermally Activated Building System—TABS) in which pipes are embedded in a massive concrete layer of a floor or a ceiling, and heat is transferred to both adjacent zones, below and above it. When located in a given zone as a ceiling, it can operate as radiant ceiling cooling (RCC) or radiant ceiling heating (RCH). The first solution was analysed in numerous theoretical and experimental works [4–6]. However, as recently stated in [7,8], radiant ceiling heating (RCH) was rarely studied in the literature. If so, the authors focused mainly on energy consumption [9], indoor comfort [10], or economic aspects [11].

To estimate the cooling or heating capacity of such systems, heat transfer coefficients by convection (CHTC) and radiation (RHTC) are necessary. Several authors have published their works on indoor heat transfer in buildings with radiant ceiling systems recently.

Causone et al. [12] measured heat transfer coefficients of a radiant ceiling in an environmental chamber (floor area of 11.6 m^2) acting as an office room. Using heated cylinders and cooled surfaces they simulated heat gains and losses, respectively. Tests were performed both in cooling and heating modes, at various working water flow rates and supplying temperatures. The authors emphasised the important role of the reference temperature in the calculations of heat transfer coefficients.

Rahimi and Sabernaeemi [13] studied heat transfer by radiation and free convection from a heated ceiling to other internal surfaces of a cubical (edge length of 2.4 m) test chamber. Based on their measurements, they concluded that over 90% of the heat was transferred from the ceiling to the zone interior by radiation. However, heat transfer coefficients were not evaluated.

Cholewa et al. [14] used a small laboratory room (floor area of 2.43 m^2) to measure heat transfer coefficients for the surface of a cooled and heated radiant floor. They recommended the correction of CHTCs from other models due to the high (24%) difference between their results and the literature data.

Yu et al. [15] presented tests of heating and cooling of a concrete ceiling with and without a ceiling panel in a test chamber under steady-state conditions. Natural ventilation with a diffuse ceiling inlet was used. Obtained heat transfer coefficients were compared with other references, showing visible differences in the case with a ceiling panel.

Koca and Gürsel [16] integrated hydronic ceiling heating with an additional heated wall to cover peak heating loads in cold climates. Then, they evaluated thermal characteristics and heat transfer coefficients for different configurations of this system. They also found that radiant heat exchange dominated with a share of 72% and 87% for the heated wall and heated ceiling cases, respectively.

In [17], experiments in a test room with heated radiant ceiling panels, made of gypsum board, water pipes, and thermal insulation, were described. The authors evaluated the heat transfer characteristics of this system under its different configurations in a room in 28 test cases. In the next paper [7], they enriched their investigation withCFD simulations. Then, experimental and simulation data were used as input for the artificial neural network (ANN) analysis. The predicted values of CHTCs and RHTCs were within the ±15% deviation range.

In [18], a radiant ceiling system in a test chamber was tested experimentally in both heating and cooling modes. Heat transfer coefficients were calculated and compared with values reported in the literature. The authors suggested using lower values of total heat transfer coefficients for the heating mode than those reported in the literature.

Based on this review, several outcomes can be formulated. At first, all the above experiments were performed in the laboratory, steady-state conditions with thoroughly controlled parameters. This way, high accuracy and reliability were maintained, the number of uncertainty sources was reduced, and the impact of various ambient factors was limited. The question then becomes how such an RHC system will behave in real-life conditions during operation in a building in daily use. Will it be possible to measure CHTCs and RHTCs under these conditions? If so, will the values obtained be comparable to those recommended by various standards and the literature?

What is more, all presented studies were carried out in rather small areas when compared to real spaces in residential or office buildings. Ceilings were made as 20 cm TABS with air cavities [15], 1.5 cm gypsum boards [7,16,17], or 2 cm granoliths [18], which are not typical construction materials in buildings. Therefore, these facts confirm the need to examine this type of radiant system in real facilities.

This study is an attempt to answer these questions and to give some new insights into the operation of radiant ceiling heating during its normal daily use. It also providesa chance to indicate the limitations of such experiments and to formulate possible measures to improve their quality in the future.

The paper is structured as follows: First, the studied object is presented, and measurement equipment is described. Then, the calculation procedure is given in detail. Next, the results of calculations of radiant, convective, and total heat transfer coefficients are presented. The results are compared with the data from the literature. Finally, concluding remarks are given.

2. Materials and Methods

2.1. Building Description

The research was conducted in a passive office building (Figure 1). This object is located in Katowice in south Poland and it was presented in [19,20]. It has a total and usable area of 8100 m^2 and 7500 m^2, respectively. Energy-efficient solutions were used in this object, such as triple-glazed external windows with external blinds, photovoltaic modules mounted on the roof and on the facade, and the three trackers in front of the building. Heating and cooling are provided mainly by a thermally activated building system (TABS) in the form of concrete ceiling heating and cooling and additional floor heating in the basement. It is supplied by a set of three cascade-connected two-compressor heat pumps. For energy monitoring purposes, the building management system (BMS) is used.

Figure 1. Southwest view of the building.

An office room (Figure 2), located on the west side of the second floor of the building, was used during the research. It is 7.95 m long, 5.80 m wide, and 3.1 m high.

Figure 2. General view of the studied room.

The measurements started on 31 October at 18:00 and ended on 10 November at 18:00. During this period, the outdoor air temperature (Figure 3) varied from 1.9°C (at 7:00 on 9 November) to 17.7°C (at 15:00 on 2 November). The weather was cloudy, and solar irradiance was low (Figure 4). When considering the external, west-facing wall with a window, it was up to 97 W/m^2 (at 16:00 on 5 November).

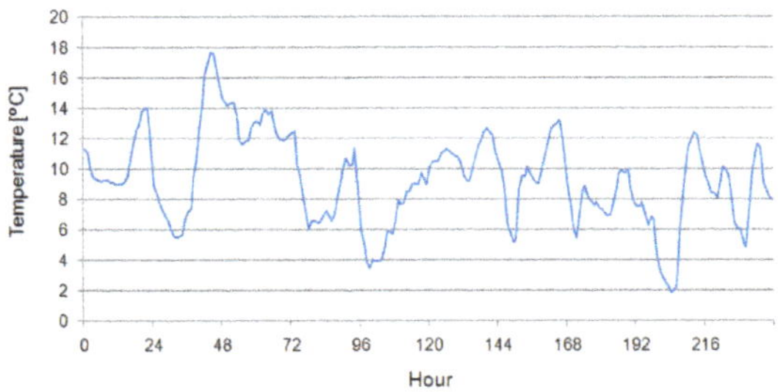

Figure 3. Outdoor air temperature during measurements.

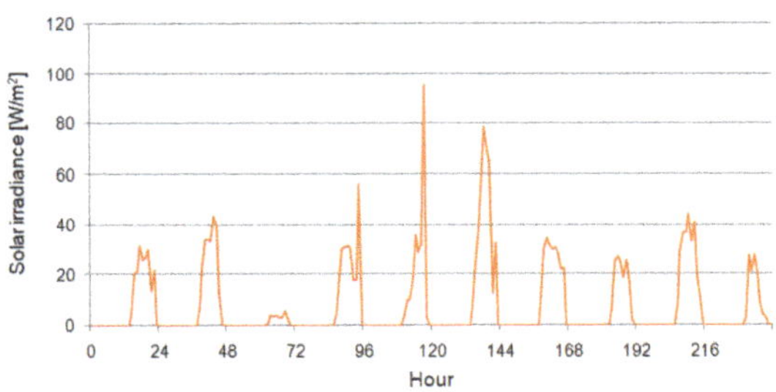

Figure 4. Global solar irradiance incident on the west-facing wall during measurements.

2.2. Experimental Setup

The measurement system was set from various sensors (Table 1). Platinum resistance sensors were used to measure the temperatures of internal and ambient air and the internal surfaces of all vertical walls, windows, ceilings, and floors. Global solar irradiance incident on the external wall was measured by the pyranometer. In the centre of the room, a tripod was placed with three cylindrical air temperature sensors (diameter 3 mm) at heights of 0.55 m, 1.5 m, and 2.2 m above the floor level. All sensors were connected to the Fluke 2638A data logger. Their locations are shown in Figure 5.

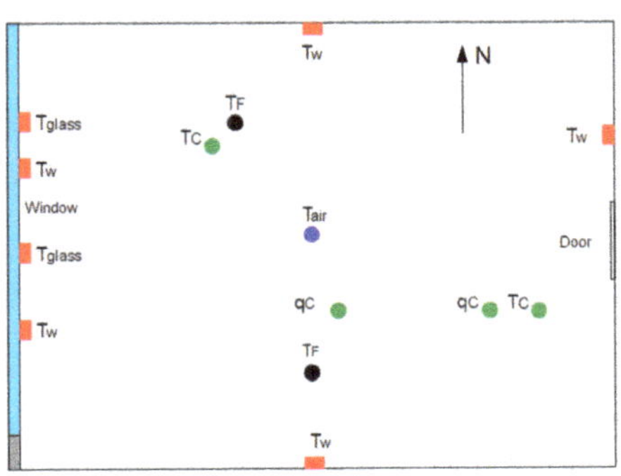

Figure 5. Location of measurement sensors (C—ceiling; F—floor; w—wall).

Table 1. The main metrological parameters of the measuring devices used.

Device	Manufacturer	Measured Variable	Measurement Range	Accuracy
Pt100 resistance sensor	Limatherm Sensor, Poland	Room air temperature	−50 °C ÷ +150 °C	Class AA [1]
Pt100 resistance sensor	Ampero Thermo-Est, Poland	Surface temperature	−50 °C ÷ +150 °C	Class AA [1]
Pt1000 resistance sensor	Apator, Poland	Ambient air temperature	−50 °C ÷ +150 °C	Class A [1]
LP PYRA03	Delta Ohm, Italy	Solar irradiance	0 ÷ 2000 W/m^2	Spectrally Flat Class C [2]
HFP01	Hukseflux, Netherlands	Heat flux	−2000 ÷ 2000 W/m^2	±3%
HFP03	Hukseflux, Netherlands	Heat flux	−2000 ÷ 2000 W/m^2	±6%
Fluke 2638A data logger	Fluke, U.S.A.	Voltage	0÷100 mV	0.0025% MV + 0.0035% FS + 2 μV [3]
Fluke 2638A data logger	Fluke, U.S.A.	Temperature	−50 °C ÷ +150 °C	0.038 °C at 0 °C, 0.073 °C at 300 °C

[1] According to EN 60751 [21]. [2] According to ISO 9060 [22] and IEC 61724 [23]. [3] MV—measured value; FS—full scale.

The ceiling heat flux was measured (Figure 6) by the HFP03 (white, on the left) and HFP01 (red coloured, on the right) heat flux sensors. This first sensor is an ultra-sensitive heat flux sensor. The manufacturer states that its nominal sensitivity is 500 μV/(W/m^2). It was chosen due to low expected values of ceiling heat flux. The second heat flux sensor, HFP01, has a ten-times-lower nominal sensitivity. It had also one important role. Due to its dimensions, HFP03 is larger and heavier than HFP01. Consequently, even if adhesive tape is used according to the manufacturer's instructions, it may dry and peel off from the ceiling more easily during measurement than the much lighter HFP01. By comparing the results from both sensors, one can easily capture such situations.

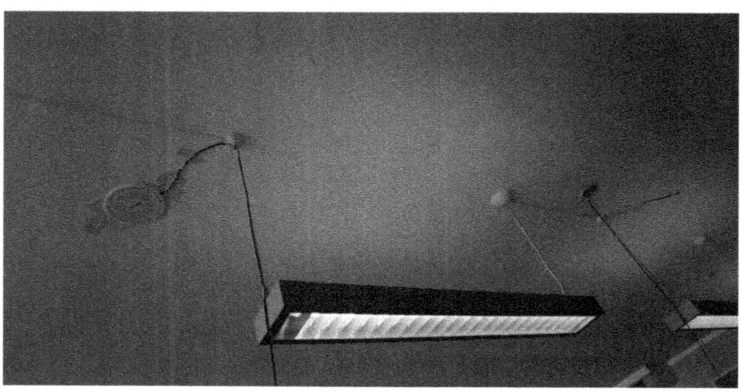

Figure 6. Measurement sensors mounted on the ceiling.

In this study, the internal surface temperature of each wall was measured with two temperature sensors. However, a vertical temperature gradient can adversely affect results based on the assumption of temperature uniformity. An analysis of the room was therefore carried out with the Testo 883 thermal imaging camera before the tests, which showed that there were no noticeable temperature differences on the internal surfaces. For example, Figure 7 shows a view of a window section and corner on the southwest side. Temperature differences are only visible on the window frame, but no longer on the walls.

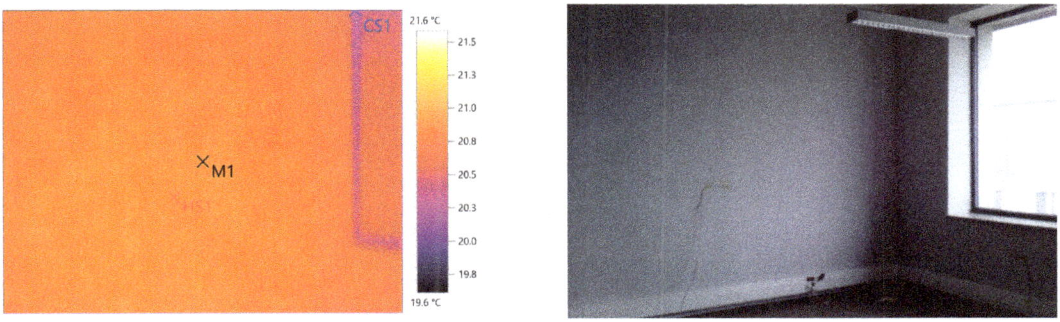

(**a**) (**b**)

Figure 7. View of the southwest side of the room: (**a**) thermal imaging photo; (**b**) real view.

2.3. Calculation Procedure

The total heat flux flowing through the ceiling surface (q_{tot}) and measured by the heat flux sensor is the sum of radiant (q_r) and convective (q_c) fluxes entering an interior space of the room:

$$q_{tot} = q_r + q_c. \tag{1}$$

Radiant heat transfer between the ceiling and other internal surfaces in the room creates a closed system. To obtain the RHTC, the average unheated surface temperature (AUST) is computed first [16,17]:

$$\text{AUST} = \sqrt[4]{\sum_{j=1}^{n}\left(F_{c-j}T_j^4\right)}. \tag{2}$$

These values can be obtained from the relevant view factors and surface temperatures. The view factor between the surface of interest (in this case, the ceiling, assigned by the "c" subscript) and j-th surface is given by

$$F_{c-j} = \frac{1}{A_c}\int_{A_c}\int_{A_j}\frac{\cos\theta_c\cos\theta_j}{\pi R^2}. \tag{3}$$

Then, the radiant heat transfer coefficient is obtained from

$$h_r = \varepsilon\sigma\frac{q_r}{\text{AUST} - T_c}. \tag{4}$$

Radiant heat flow exchanged by the ceiling and surrounding surfaces is expressed by the following relationship:

$$q_r = \sum_{j=1}^{n}\sigma F_{\varepsilon_{c-j}}\left(T_c^4 - T_j^4\right), \tag{5}$$

with the following radiation interchange factor

$$F_{\varepsilon_{c-j}} = \frac{1}{\frac{(1-\varepsilon_c)}{\varepsilon_c} + \left(1/F_{c-j}\right) + \left(A_c/A_j\right)\left(\frac{(1-\varepsilon_j)}{\varepsilon_j}\right)}. \tag{6}$$

As this method is computationally demanding [24], simpler ways have been developed to obtain radiant heat flux in a zone. If surface emissivities are equal within a studied enclosure, the area-weighted radiant temperature can be used [25,26]:

$$T_{rad} = \frac{\sum_{j=1}^{n}(A_j T_j)}{\sum_{j=1}^{n} A_j}. \quad (7)$$

Then, Equation (5) may be simplified to the well-known form commonly used in building calculations:

$$q_r = h_r(T_c - T_{rad}). \quad (8)$$

with

$$h_r = \varepsilon\sigma\frac{T_c^4 - T_r^4}{T_c - T_r} = \varepsilon\sigma(T_c + T_{rad})\left(T_c^2 + T_{rad}^2\right). \quad (9)$$

Further, if the difference between surface temperatures within a zone is small enough and the mean temperature of all surfaces accounts for T_m, the equation can be written as [27,28]

$$h_r = 4\varepsilon\sigma T_m^3. \quad (10)$$

It should be noted that Equation (10) is also used in the EN ISO 6946 standard [29].

When q_r is known, then, from Equation (1), q_c can be obtained. On the other hand, q_c is given by

$$q_c = h_c(T_c - T_{air}). \quad (11)$$

From the above, an unknown convective heat transfer coefficient can be computed.

The last examined parameter is the total heat transfer coefficient. It takes into account both radiant and convective heat transfer between the considered surface and its surroundings. In such a case as the reference variable, the operative temperature is used:

$$T_{op} = (h_c T_{air} + h_r AUST)/(h_c + h_r). \quad (12)$$

Then,

$$h_{tot} = q_{tot}/(T_c - T_{op}). \quad (13)$$

2.4. Selected Correlations for CHTC Calculations

During the last several decades, many experimental models have been developed to obtain CHTCs for surfaces of various orientations [8,30]. Among them, some relationships can be used for a heated ceiling to compare with other measurements.

Awbi and Hatton [31] conducted a series of experiments on convection in a test chamber (2.78 × 2.78 × 2.3 m) and a small box (1.05 × 1.01 × 1.05 m) under steady-state conditions. The internal surfaces of both objects were covered with aluminium plates to minimise radiant heat flux. In the case of a heated ceiling in the chamber, they proposed the following relationship:

$$h_c = \frac{0.704}{D^{0.601}}(\Delta T)^{0.133}, \quad (14)$$

The ASHRAE handbook [32] gives a correlation for a downward-facing heated small plate with the length L:

$$h_c = 0.59\left(\frac{\Delta T}{L}\right)^{0.25}, \quad (15)$$

The ASHRAE handbook of HVAC [33] gives correlations developed by Min [34] in a room 3.66 m long, 7.74 m wide, and 1.5 m above its floor. For natural convection from heated ceiling panels, when room size cannot be ignored,

$$h_c = 0.20|T_c - T_{air}|^{0.25}/D^{0.25}, \quad (16)$$

with D being the equivalent diameter of a panel (4× area/perimeter).

In a simpler form,

$$h_c = 0.134|T_c - T_{air}|^{0.25}. \quad (17)$$

In [16], the authors cited a relationship given in the CIBS guide:

$$h_c = 1.32\left(\frac{|T_c - T_{air}|}{L}\right)^{0.25}. \quad (18)$$

3. Results and Discussion

3.1. Radiant Heat Transfer Coefficient

Following the first calculation method of the RHTC, presented in Section 2.3, view factors were calculated from Equation (3). For this purpose, Matlab R2017b code was used. The resulting values are given in Table 2.

Table 2. View factors between the ceiling and other surfaces in the room.

Surface Number	Surface Name	$F_{c\text{-}j}$ [–]
1	East wall	0.116039641
2	North wall	0.163240031
3	External (west) wall	0.033180406
4	External window	0.082859227
5	South wall	0.163240030
6	Floor	0.441440661

The average unheated surface temperature (Figure 8) was from 21.0°C (at 9:00 on 9 November) to 22.32°C (at 16:00 on 1 November) with 21.56°C on average. During the whole study, it was lower than the ceiling temperature, which varied from 21.34°C (at 22:00 on 7 November) to 22.68°C (at 6:00 on 1 November) with 21.85°C on average.

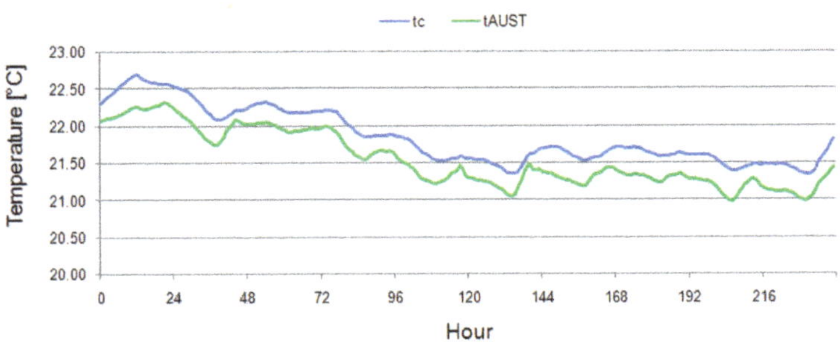

Figure 8. AUST and ceiling surface (t_c) temperatures.

The difference between them (Figure 9) was from 0.10°C (at 15:00 on 2 November) to 0.42°C (at 6:00 on 1 November) with 0.30°C on average. It was very low, which means uniform thermal conditions in the room. In the next step, the area-weighted radiant temperature was calculated. Its comparison with AUST resulted in very small differences, with a maximum of 0.041 K (Figure 10), which can be treated as negligible.

Therefore, both methods (involving AUST and T_{rad}) were employed to compute the RHTC. In the first method, the resulting RHTC varied (Figure 11) from 5.621 W/m^{2}K (at 8:00 on 6 November) to 5.718 W/m^{2}K (at 21:00 on 31 October) with 5.661 W/m^{2}K on average.

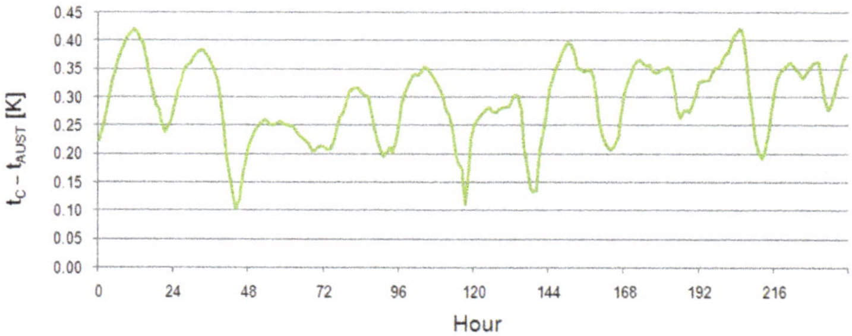

Figure 9. Difference between ceiling and AUSTs.

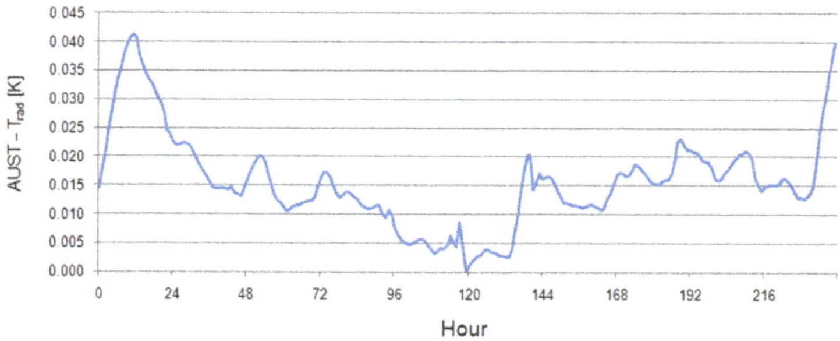

Figure 10. Difference between AUST and area-weighted radiant temperature.

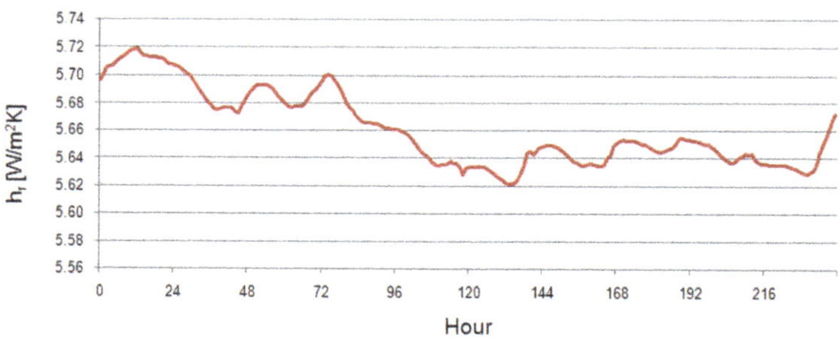

Figure 11. Radiant heat transfer coefficient from measurements.

RHTCs were calculated from the simplified relationship (Equation (10)) at the average temperature t_{mn} = 21.7 °C and emissivity ε = 0.95, h_r = 5.523 W/m^{2}K, which is very close to the obtained average value of 5.661 W/m^{2}K.

In the experimental study, it should also be noted that measurement error may influence the difference between AUST and T_c. This difference is in the denominator of Equation (4) used to compute h_r. Therefore, the resulting radiant heat transfer coefficient is very sensitive to any inaccuracies. However, despite small differences between AUST and T_c (below 0.5 K), the resulting values of RHTCs, depending on the ceiling temperature, have the correct view (Figure 12).

The obtained correlation is very strong, with the calculated coefficient of determination R^2 = 0.959, which means that over 97.9% of the variation in RHTCs is explained by the model. At the same, when comparing hourly values of RHTCs calculated from both presented methods, the correlation between them is also very strong, with R^2 = 0.912.

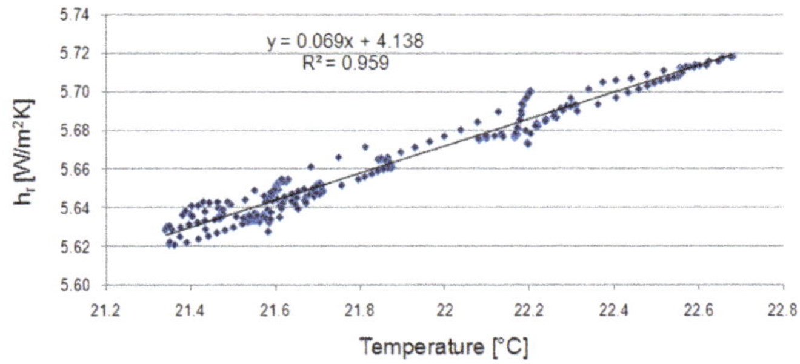

Figure 12. Radiant heat transfer coefficient from measurements (AUST method).

The presented results confirm the applicability of the simplified method to obtain RHTCs in indoor building applications when the differences between internal surface temperatures are small. The details on the calculation of measurement uncertainties are given in Appendix A.

3.2. Convective Heat Transfer Coefficient

During the measurements, indoor air temperature showed very good vertical uniformity. It varied from 20.93°C to 22.37°C, from 20.92°C to 22.35°C, and from 20.92°C to 22.36°C at heights of 0.55 m, 1.5 m, and 2.2 m above the floor (Figure 13) with the hourly difference between the maximum and minimum values ranging from 0 to 0.08 K. Its average value was from 20.92°C (at 9:00 on 9 November) to 22.35°C (at 16:00 on 1 November) and was lower than the ceiling surface temperature from 0.04°C (at 15:00 on 2 November) to 0.47°C (at 8:00 on 9 November). This temperature difference was then of a similar order as the difference between the ceiling and AUST, which created comfortable indoor conditions.

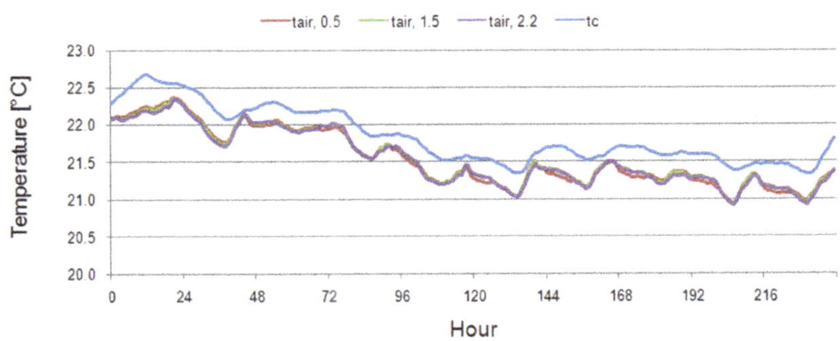

Figure 13. Indoor air temperatures at three heights and their ceiling temperatures.

Calculations showed that CHTCs varied from 0.01 W/m^{2}K (at 11:00 on 4 November) to 2.51 W/m^{2}K (at 21:00 on 31 October) with the average value being0.801 W/m^{2}K. But, when excluding the first day of measurements which may have been influenced by various factors (equipment assembling, personal control, etc.), the average h_c = 0.639 W/m^{2}K. Its daily averaged values are given in Figure 14.

Variability of CHTC can be mainly attributed to measurement errors which tend to be higher at low heat flows. A significant dispersion of experimentally obtained CHTCs in real conditions was observed in [35]. Despite these problems, a comparison of the average value of h_c with other references (Table 3) reveals that the obtained values are comparable at the same average temperature difference of 0.31 K. The same also refers to the convective heat transfer coefficient, given in EN ISO 6946 [26], for a horizontal wall with downward heat flow.

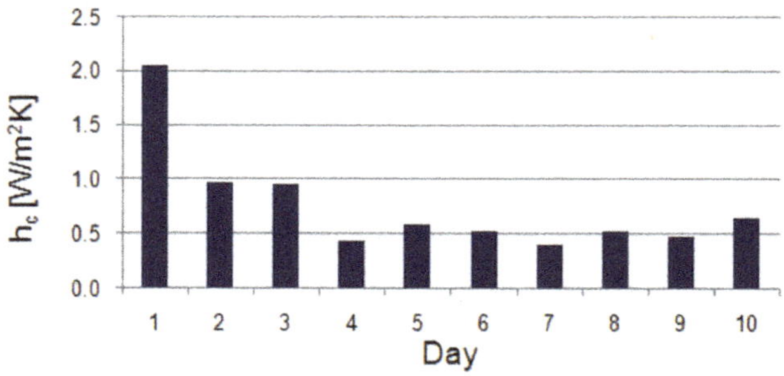

Figure 14. Daily heat transfer coefficient by convection obtained from measurements.

Table 3. Convective heat transfer coefficients for downward-facing heated surfaces.

Reference	h_c [W/m^{2}K]	Comments
This study	0.80	Whole period
[31]	0.19	Equation (14)
[32]	0.26	Equation (15)
[33]	0.09	Equation (16)
[33]	0.10	Equation (17)
[16]	0.59	Equation (18)
[29]	0.70	Horizontal wall with downward heat flow
[16]	0.82	T_c—T_{air} = 10.8 K
[12]	0.0 . . . 0.60	T_c—T_{air} = 6.3 . . . 11.1 K, T_{air} at 1.1 m
[18]	0.0 . . . 0.13	T_c—T_{air} = 1.32 . . . 8.29 K, T_{air} at 1.1 m
[36]	1.25	Validated TRNSYS model

3.3. Total Heat Transfer Coefficient

Obtained values of the radiant and convective heat transfer coefficients were used to calculate the operative temperature. It varied from 20.97°C to 22.32°C. The resulting total heat transfer coefficient was from 5.625 W/m^{2}K (at 9:00 on 6 November) to 8.218 W/m^{2}K (at 21:00 on 31 October), with 6.473 W/m^{2}K on average. It showed a positive correlation with total heat flux (Figure 15). However, the resulting correlation was rather moderate, with R^2 = 0.211, which means that about 46% of the dependent variables were explained by this model.

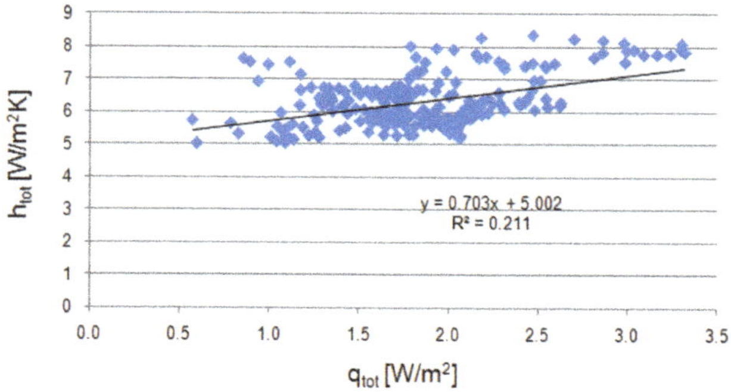

Figure 15. The total heat transfer coefficient in relation to total heat flux.

Finally, daily averaged values of the main variables that were measured and calculated are given in Table 4. It can easily be noticed that the heating heat flux is low when compared to popular radiant water-based floor heating systems in residential buildings when values of 20–70 W/m^2 are commonly met and differences between indoor air and floor surface temperatures are more significant. However, in passive buildings, these capacities can be significantly lower, which makes measurements more demanding.

Table 4. Daily average values of the measured variables.

Variable	Unit	1	2	3	4	5	6	7	8	9	10
T_c	°C	22.54	22.26	22.22	21.99	21.65	21.50	21.63	21.65	21.50	21.48
T_{air}	°C	22.20	21.98	21.97	21.74	21.36	21.25	21.33	21.32	21.18	21.13
AUST	°C	22.21	21.98	21.99	21.73	21.37	21.25	21.32	21.32	21.18	21.14
T_{op}	°C	22.21	21.98	21.98	21.76	21.34	21.26	21.31	21.32	21.16	21.14
q_r	W/m^2	1.88	1.62	1.35	1.44	1.58	1.40	1.76	1.85	1.83	1.91
h_r	W/m^{2}K	5.71	5.69	5.69	5.68	5.64	5.63	5.64	5.65	5.64	5.64
q_c	W/m^2	0.70	0.29	0.24	0.13	0.12	0.12	0.11	0.17	0.15	0.24
h_c	W/m^{2}K	2.05	0.97	0.96	0.45	0.59	0.54	0.40	0.53	0.50	0.65
q_{tot}	W/m^2	2.58	1.84	1.59	1.51	1.62	1.52	1.76	2.02	1.94	2.14
h_{tot}	W/m^{2}K	7.77	6.66	6.64	6.13	6.23	6.17	6.05	6.18	6.14	6.29

Variation in the daily averaged RHTCs was negligible, between 5.63 and 5.71 W/m^{2}K. CHTCs changed more significantly, from 0.40 to 2.05 W/m^{2}K. The total heat transfer coefficient was from 6.14 to 7.77 W/m^{2}K. These values show that radiation dominated heat exchange between the ceiling and the zone (Figure 16). Its share varied in the consecutive days from 72.8% (day 1) to 93.9% (day 7) with 88.6% on average.

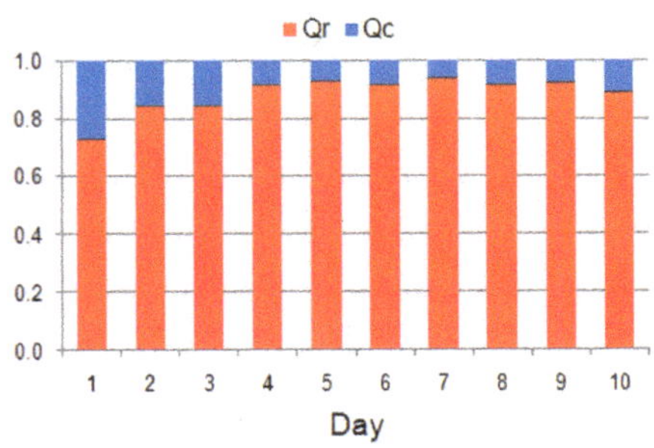

Figure 16. Heat transfer between the ceiling and the room.

Rahimi and Sabernaeemi [13] used a test chamber with a heated ceiling and reported an average share of a radiant heat transfer of 96.2%. The next study [16] on a heated ceiling with a gypsum board placed in a 4 × 4 × 3 m test chamber reported an 87% share of radiant transfer. But when wall heating was also used, it decreased to 72%. Causone et al. [12] used a test box with a 15 cm thick plasterboard radiant ceiling. Radiant heat transfer in their case varied from 90.2% to 100%. In [18], the authors used a ceiling with a 2 cm thick granolite filling. They reported that, in one case, radiant heat transfer was over 98% of the total heat flow. However, in the next eight cases, it was over 100%, which might result from measurement errors.

3.4. Comparison of Results

Obtained resulting values of heat transfer coefficients, given in previous sections, should be compared to other sources to obtain a more complete view (Table 5). Radiant, convective, and total heat transfer coefficients were reported by several authors. Also, ISO 11855 provides recommended values for the design purposes of radiant systems.

Variation can be seen in the presented values. The smallest dispersion is observed for h_r. However, its values below 5.0 W/m²K are rather surprising in building applications. CHTCs in experimental works are lower than 1.0 W/m²K and these values are in agreement with the findings presented here. The total heat transfer coefficient is also within acceptable range.

It is also worth noting that for horizontal surfaces with downward heat flow, the EN ISO 6946 standard suggests the value h_c = 0.7 W/m²K, and for the total surface thermal resistance, the suggested value is R_{si} = 0.17 m²K/W. For the obtained h_r and h_c, R_{si} = 0.154 m²K/W is the resulting value.

Table 5. Convective, radiant and total heat transfer coefficients for downward-facing heated surfaces.

Ref.	h_c [W/m²K]	h_r [W/m²K]	h_{tot} [W/m²K]
Present study	0.40–2.05	5.53–5.71	6.05–7.77
[7]	0.9	5.3	7.0
[12]	0.3	5.6	5.8
[16]	0.82	5.70	7.28
[18]	0–0.13	5.21–5.64	4.94–5.90
[17]	0.5–1.0	4.6–5.5	6.1–6.9
[3]	–	–	6.5

4. Conclusions

In the presented study, convective (h_c), radiant (h_r), and total (h_{tot}) heat transfer coefficients were calculated for the heated concrete ceiling during the period of the heating load. This resulted in low values of the temperature difference between the ceiling surface and other internal surfaces facing the room and indoor air. This situation is very comfortable for the occupants, but much less beneficial for measurement accuracy.

Other experiments were conducted in specially designed test chambers with stable internal conditions and thermal isolation reducing the impact of ambient factors and under steady-state thermal conditions during tests. Also, sufficiently large differences between the temperatures of conditioned and unconditioned internal surfaces and indoor air were maintained. Consequently, the impact of the main sources of errors could be reduced. That is why their outcomes can be treated as a reference.

However, in real buildings, during their everyday use, such laboratory conditions are impossible to obtain. During measurements in the studied object, the heating load was low. Therefore, high-sensitivity sensors were successfully used for the precise measurement of heat flux. Accurate temperature measurements were made possible by using sensors with a high-accuracy class. Further improvements in the accuracy of the tests carried out would be possible after additional calibration of the temperature sensors using special certified calibration equipment. It is also advisable to measure the temperature of each wall at several heights to determine the uniformity of its distribution.

Nevertheless, despite the mentioned limitations, the results presented in this study are comparable with other experiments in zones with heated ceilings and confirm the validity of the tests performed.

Funding: This research project was partly supported by the programme "Excellence initiative—research university" for the AGH University of Science and Technology.

Data Availability Statement: The raw data supporting the conclusions of this article will be made available by the author upon request.

Conflicts of Interest: The author declares no conflicts of interest.

Symbols

AUST	average unheated surface temperature, K
h_c	convective heat transfer coefficient, W/m^2K
h_r	radiant heat transfer coefficient, W/m^2K
h_{tot}	total heat transfer coefficient, W/m^2K
k	coverage factor,
q_c	convective heat flux, W/m^2
q_r	radiant heat flux, W/m^2
q_{tot}	total heat flux, W/m^2
t	temperature (general), °C
u_c	combined uncertainty,
R^2	coefficient of determination,
T_{air}	internal air temperature, K
T_{rad}	area-weighted radiant temperature, K
T_c	ceiling surface temperature, K
T_{op}	operative temperature, K
U	expanded uncertainty,
ε	surface emissivity,
σ	Stefan–Boltzmann constant, $\sigma = 5.6697\ 10^{-8}\ W/m^2K^4$

Appendix A

In the present study, heat transfer coefficients are computed indirectly from formulas given by Equations (4) and (10), or Equation (11). Therefore, they are based on physical variables measured with various accuracies.

In the case of indirect measurement of a physical quantity, y, being a function of independent measurements $x_1, x_2, \ldots, x_n$,

$$y = f(x_1, x_2, \ldots, x_n) \tag{A1}$$

The standard combined uncertainty u_c of y can be obtained using the propagation model of uncertainty [37]:

$$u_c(y) = \sqrt{\left(\frac{\partial y}{\partial x_1}u(x_1)\right)^2 + \left(\frac{\partial y}{\partial x_2}u(x_2)\right)^2 + \ldots + \left(\frac{\partial y}{\partial x_n}u(x_n)\right)^2}. \tag{A2}$$

Then, the expanded uncertainty of the measured quantity is computed from

$$U = ku_c(y) \tag{A3}$$

where k is the coverage factor; for a 95% confidence level, the uncertainty of k = 2.

Using the procedure described in the previous section, at first, the uncertainty of the RHTC is derived. Inserting Equation (4) into Equation (11), we can obtain an equation describing the standard combined uncertainty of the measured RHTC. It has three independent variables: q_r, T_c and AUST. Consequently,

$$u_c(h_r) = \sqrt{\left(\frac{\partial(h_r)}{\partial q_r}u(q_r)\right)^2 + \left(\frac{\partial(h_r)}{\partial T_c}u(T_c)\right)^2 + \left(\frac{\partial(h_r)}{\partial AUST}u(AUST)\right)^2}. \tag{A4}$$

with the following partial derivatives,

$$\frac{\partial(h_r)}{\partial q_r} = \varepsilon\sigma\frac{1}{T_c - AUST}, \tag{A5}$$

$$\frac{\partial h_r}{\partial T_c} = \varepsilon\sigma\frac{q_r}{(T_c - AUST)^2}, \tag{A6}$$

$$\frac{\partial h_r}{\partial AUST} = -\varepsilon\sigma\frac{q_r}{(T_c - AUST)^2}. \tag{A7}$$

Uncertainty of the ceiling temperature measurement, $u(T_c)$, consists of two elements: accuracy of a temperature sensor and accuracy of the data logger.

$$u(T_c) = \sqrt{(u_{sens,c})^2 + \left(u_{logger,c}\right)^2}, \tag{A8}$$

Here, "sens" and "logger" subscripts refer to a sensor and a logging device, respectively. They can be easily obtained from the manufacturers' data given in Table 1.

To estimate uncertainties of radiant heat flux and AUST, there are necessary additional calculations. When inserting Equation (5) into Equation (A2), we obtain

$$u_c(q_r) = \sqrt{\left(\frac{\partial(q_r)}{\partial T_k}u(T_k)\right)^2}. \tag{A9}$$

with T_k being the temperatures of all k-th surfaces facing the zone. Partial derivative of radiant flux is then given by:

$$\frac{\partial(q_r)}{\partial T_k} = \frac{\partial\left(\sum_k \sigma F_{\varepsilon_{c-j}}\left(T_c^4 - T_j^4\right)\right)}{\partial T_k}. \tag{A10}$$

By writing out the numerator of the right side of Equation (A10), we obtain

$$\sum_k\left(\sigma F_{\varepsilon_{c-j}}\left(T_c^4 - T_j^4\right)\right) = \sum_{j=1}^{n}\sigma F_{\varepsilon_{c-j}}T_c^4 - \sum_{j=1}^{n}\sigma F_{\varepsilon_{c-j}}T_j^4. \tag{A11}$$

And finally,

$$\frac{\partial(q_r)}{\partial T_k} = \sum_{j=1}^{n}4\sigma F_{\varepsilon_{c-j}}\left(T_c^3 - T_j^3\right) \tag{A12}$$

To simplify the calculations, it can be assumed that the temperatures of all surfaces are measured by the same sensors. Therefore, we can write that $u(T_k)$ in Equation (A9) is the same for all considered partitions.

The last component of RHTC uncertainty is AUST. This variable is computed from the complex summation formula. After rewriting Equation (2), we obtain

$$AUST = \left(\sum_{j=1}^{n}\left(F_{c-j}T_j^4\right)\right)^{1/4}. \tag{A13}$$

The partial derivative of AUST with respect to all unheated surfaces (T_j) is as follows:

$$\frac{\partial(AUST)}{\partial T_j} = \frac{\partial\left(\left(\sum_{j=1}^{n}\left(F_{c-j}T_j^4\right)\right)^{1/4}\right)}{\partial T_j}. \tag{A14}$$

And finally,

$$\frac{\partial(\text{AUST})}{\partial T_j} = \frac{\sum_{j=1}^{n}\left(F_{c-j}T_j^3\right)}{\left(\sum_{j=1}^{n}\left(F_{c-j}T_j^4\right)\right)^{3/4}}. \tag{A15}$$

As can be seen, this procedure is complicated. Therefore, the second one, based on Equation (9), can be used for convenience. After inserting Equation (9) into Equation (A2), we obtain three derivatives, as follows:

$$\frac{\partial h_r}{\partial \varepsilon} = \sigma\left(T_c^3 + T_c T_{rad}^2 + T_{rad} T_c^2 + T_{rad}^3\right), \tag{A16}$$

$$\frac{\partial h_r}{\partial T_{rad}} = \varepsilon\sigma\left(2T_c T_{rad} + T_c^2 + 3T_{rad}^2\right), \tag{A17}$$

$$\frac{\partial h_r}{\partial T_c} = \varepsilon\sigma\left(3T_c^2 + T_{rad}^2 + 2T_c T_{rad}\right). \tag{A18}$$

In the case of the simple model, given by Equation (10), only one derivative can be written:

$$\frac{\partial h_r}{\partial T_m} = 12\varepsilon\sigma T_m^2. \tag{A19}$$

In the case of the heat transfer coefficient by convection, the uncertainty assessment is simpler. After rearranging Equation (7), we obtain

$$h_c = q_c/(T_c - T_{air}). \tag{A20}$$

After inserting Equation (11) into Equation (A2), we obtain

$$u_c(h_c) = \sqrt{\left(\frac{\partial(h_c)}{\partial q_c}u(q_c)\right)^2 + \left(\frac{\partial(h_c)}{\partial T_i}u(T_{air})\right)^2 + \left(\frac{\partial(h_c)}{\partial T_s}u(T_c)\right)^2}. \tag{A21}$$

with the following partial derivatives:

$$\frac{\partial h_c}{\partial q_c} = \frac{1}{T_c - T_{air}}, \tag{A22}$$

$$\frac{\partial h_c}{\partial T_s} = \frac{-q_c}{(T_c - T_{air})^2}, \tag{A23}$$

$$\frac{\partial h_c}{\partial T_i} = \frac{q_c}{(T_c - T_{air})^2}. \tag{A24}$$

The uncertainty components due to the measurement of indoor air temperature $u(T_{air})$ and surface temperature $u(T_c)$ can be derived similarly, as in the previous case on the basis of Equation (A8).

Because of stable thermal conditions in the room during the experiment and the operational temperature of heat flux sensors close to the calibration temperature, only an additional 2% uncertainty was also included because of the non perfect contact of a sensor with a ceiling. This means that for the maximum measured heat flux of 2.5 W/m^2, the resulting uncertainty $u(q_c) = 0.175\ W/m^2$.

To give the reader a better view of this analysis, the results of the calculations of partial derivatives are given by Equations (A5)–(A7) and (A19).

For the first method of RHTC calculation, based on AUST, the following average conditions were used: AUST = 294.699 K, T_c = 294.992 K, and q_r = 1.655 W/m^2. Then, the results presented in Table A1 were obtained. The average uncertainty $u_c(h_r) = 1.10 \times 10^{-7}$

W/m^2K is very small and is comparable with findings presented in other studies on radiant heating systems [16,17]. This is because radiant heat flux was computed analytically from the detailed model.

Table A1. Uncertainties in RHTC measurement.

Uncertainty	Value	Unit
$u(q_r)$	0.017	W/m^2
$u(T_c)$	0.050	K
u(AUST)	0.648	K
$\frac{\partial(h_r)}{\partial q_r}$	-1.966×10^{-7}	W/m^2K
$\frac{\partial h_r}{\partial T_c}$	1.113×10^{-6}	W/m^2K^2
$\frac{\partial h_r}{\partial AUST}$	1.113×10^{-6}	W/m^2K^2

When applying the simple method to evaluate RHTCs (Equation (10)), only the average mean radiant temperature T_m = 294.850 K was used. Then, from Equation (A19), $12\varepsilon\sigma T_m^2$ = 0.065 W/m^2K, and, from Equation (10), h_r = 5.523 W/m^2K.

The last computed variable was the heat transfer coefficient by convection (Table A2). The relevant derivatives, given by Equations (A22), (A23) and (A24), were computed for the following average conditions: T_i = 21.555 °C, T_c = 21.861°C, and q_c = 0.245 W/m^2. For these conditions, uncertainty $u(h_c)$ = 0.189 W/m^2K for the whole period.

Table A2. Uncertainties in CHTC measurement.

Uncertainty	Value	Unit
$u(q_c)$	0.012	W/m^2
$u(T_i)$	0.05	K
$u(T_C)$	0.05	K
$\frac{\partial(h_c)}{\partial q_c}$	3.268	W/m^2K
$\frac{\partial(h_c)}{\partial T_i}$	−2.617	W/m^2K^2
$\frac{\partial(h_c)}{\partial T_C}$	2.617	W/m^2K^2

The obtained uncertainty of CHTCs is high and comparable with the calculated value of CHTCs. This is the most important problem in this study. However, when considering other experimental studies on internal heat transfer coefficients in buildings with various radiant systems, it was commonly noticed that measured CHTCs were influenced by uncertainties significantly higher than RHTCs [16,17]. The accuracy of experimentally measured CHTCs was estimated from about 20% [38,39] to 30% or even 35% at $\Delta T \approx 1$ K [35]. These are the outcomes of the methods applied. The measurement uncertainty of CHTCs is determined by the experimental method (Equation (11)). Therefore, the results are very sensitive to the difference between the surface (ceiling) and internal air temperatures (Equations (A22)–(A24)).

In this study, highly sensitive heat flux sensors and precise temperature sensors were used. Therefore, the next step to improve the accuracy of the obtained results is the additional calibration of the temperature sensors using the special certified calibration equipment, as in the experimental study presented in [40].

References

1. Junasová, B.; Krajčík, M.; Šikula, O.; Arıcı, M.; Šimko, M. Adapting the construction of radiant heating and cooling systems for building retrofit. *Energy Build.* **2022**, *268*, 112228. [CrossRef]

2. Krajčík, M.; Šimko, M.; Šikula, O.; Szabó, D.; Petráš, D. Thermal performance of a radiant wall heating and cooling system with pipes attached to thermally insulating bricks. *Energy Build.* **2021**, *246*, 111122. [CrossRef]
3. *ISO 11855–1:2021.*; Building Environment Design. Embedded Radiant Heating and Cooling Systems. Part 2: Determination of the Design Heating and Cooling Capacity. International Organization for Standardization: Geneva, Switzerland, 2021.
4. Sinacka, J.; Szczechowiak, E. An Experimental Study of a Thermally Activated Ceiling Containing Phase Change Material for Different Cooling Load Profiles. *Energies* **2021**, *14*, 7363. [CrossRef]
5. Aryal, A.; Chaiwiwatworakul, P.; Chirarattananon, S. An experimental study of thermal performance of the radiant ceiling cooling in office building in Thailand. *Energy Build.* **2023**, *283*, 112849. [CrossRef]
6. Shi, S.; Merabtine, A.; Bennacer, R. Radiant systems and solar-driven overheating: A comprehensive literature analysis over a decade. *Build. Environ.* **2024**, *259*, 111659. [CrossRef]
7. Karakoyun, Y.; Acikgoz, O.; Çebi, A.; Koca, A.; Çetin, G.; Dalkilic, A.S.; Wongwises, S. A comprehensive approach to analyze the discrepancies in heat transfer characteristics pertaining to radiant ceiling heating system. *Appl. Therm. Eng.* **2021**, *187*, 116517. [CrossRef]
8. Hu, R.; Sun, S.; Liang, J.; Zhou, Z.; Yin, Y. A Review of Studies on Heat Transfer in Buildings with Radiant Cooling Systems. *Buildings* **2023**, *13*, 1994. [CrossRef]
9. Liao, W.; Wen, C.; Luo, Y.; Peng, J.; Li, N. Influence of different building transparent envelopes on energy consumption and thermal environment of radiant ceiling heating and cooling systems. *Energy Build.* **2022**, *255*, 111702. [CrossRef]
10. Dogan, A.; Kayaci, N.; Kanbur, B.B.; Demir, H. Experimental Investigation of Mean Radiant Temperature Trends for a Ground Source Heat Pump-Integrated Radiant Wall and Ceiling Heating System. *Buildings* **2023**, *13*, 2420. [CrossRef]
11. Bouacida, T.; Bentoumi, L.; Bessaïh, R. Experimental study of a low-cost ceiling cooling system in the north Algerian climate. *Energy Build.* **2023**, *293*, 113196. [CrossRef]
12. Causone, F.; Corgnati, S.P.; Filippi, M.; Olesen, B.W. Experimental evaluation of heat transfer coefficients between radiant ceiling and room. *Energy Build.* **2009**, *41*, 622–628. [CrossRef]
13. Rahimi, M.; Sabernaeemi, A. Experimental study of radiation and free convection in an enclosure with a radiant ceiling heating system. *Energy Build.* **2010**, *42*, 2077–2082. [CrossRef]
14. Cholewa, T.; Rosiński, M.; Spik, Z.; Dudzińska, M.R.; Siuta-Olchaa, A. On the heat transfer coefficients between heated/cooled radiant floor and room. *Energy Build.* **2013**, *66*, 599–606. [CrossRef]
15. Yu, T.; Heiselberg, P.; Lei, B.; Pomianowski, M.; Zhang, C.; Jensen, R. Experimental investigation of cooling performance of a novel HVAC system combining natural ventilation with diffuse ceiling inlet and TABS. *Energy Build.* **2015**, *105*, 165–177. [CrossRef]
16. Koca, A.; Gürsel, C. Experimental investigation on the heat transfer coefficients of radiant heating systems: Wall, ceiling and wall-ceiling integration. *Energy Build.* **2017**, *148*, 311–326. [CrossRef]
17. Koca, A.; Acikgoz, O.; Çebi, A.; Çetin, G.; Dalkilic, A.S.; Wongwises, S. An experimental investigation devoted to determine heat transfer characteristics in a radiant ceiling heating system. *Heat Mass. Transf.* **2017**, *54*, 363–375. [CrossRef]
18. Cholewa, T.; Anasiewicz, R.; Siuta-Olcha, A.; Skwarczynski, M.A. On the heat transfer coefficients between heated/cooled radiant ceiling and room. *Appl. Therm. Eng.* **2017**, *117*, 76–84. [CrossRef]
19. Szpytma, M.; Rybka, A. Ecological ideas in Polish architecture—environmental impact. *J. Civ. Eng. Environ. Arch.* **2016**, *XXXIII*, 321–328. [CrossRef]
20. Michalak, P. Selected Aspects of Indoor Climate in a Passive Office Building with a Thermally Activated Building System: A Case Study from Poland. *Energies* **2021**, *14*, 860. [CrossRef]
21. *IEC 60751:2022*; Industrial Platinum Resistance Thermometers and Platinum Temperature Sensors. International Electrotechnical Commission: Geneva, Switzerland, 2022.
22. *ISO 9060:2018*; Solar Energy—Specification and Classification of Instruments for Measuring Hemispherical Solar and Direct Solar Radiation. International Organization for Standardization: Geneva, Switzerland, 2018.
23. *IEC 61724-1:2021*; Photovoltaic system performance—Part 1: Monitoring. International Organization for Standardization: Geneva, Switzerland, 2022.
24. Diaz, F.N.; Lebrun, J.; André, P. Experimental study and modelling of cooling ceiling systems using steady-state analysis. *Int. J. Refrig.* **2010**, *33*, 793–805. [CrossRef]
25. Atef, A.; Noureddine, Z.; Soufiane, F. SPUCAL_mrt as a New Model for Estimating the Mean Radiant Temperature in Arid Lands. *Energy Procedia* **2015**, *74*, 273–280. [CrossRef]
26. Evren, M.F.; Özsunar, A.; Kılkış, B. Experimental investigation of energy-optimum radiant-convective heat transfer split for hybrid heating systems. *Energy Build.* **2016**, *127*, 66–74. [CrossRef]
27. Lauster, M.; Teichmann, J.; Fuchs, M.; Streblow, R.; Mueller, D. Low order thermal network models for dynamic simulations of buildings on city district scale. *Build. Environ.* **2014**, *73*, 223–231. [CrossRef]
28. Cui, Y.; Xie, J.; Liu, J.; Xue, P. Experimental and Theoretical Study on the Heat Transfer Coefficients of Building External Surfaces in the Tropical Island Region. *Appl. Sci.* **2019**, *9*, 1063. [CrossRef]

29. *EN ISO 6946:2017*; Building Components and Building Elements. Thermal Resistance and Thermal Transmittance. Calculation Methods. International Organization for Standardization: Geneva, Switzerland, 2017.
30. Shinoda, J.; Kazanci, O.B.; Tanabe, S.; Olesen, B.W. A Review of the Surface Heat Transfer Coefficients of Radiant Heating and Cooling Systems. *Build. Environ.* **2019**, *159*, 106156. [CrossRef]
31. Awbi, H.B.; Hatton, A. Natural convection from heated room surfaces. *Energy Build.* **1999**, *30*, 233–244. [CrossRef]
32. ASHRAE. *Handbook HVAC Fundamentals*; ASHRAE: Peachtree Corners, GA, USA, 2009.
33. ASHRAE. *2012 ASHRAE Handbook—Heating, Ventilating, and Air Conditioning: Systems and Equipment*; ASHRAE: Peachtree Corners, GA, USA, 2012.
34. Min, T.C.; Schutrum, L.F.; Parmelee, G.V. Natural convection and radiation in a panel heated room. *ASHRAE Trans.* **1956**, *62*, 337–358.
35. Wallentén, P. Convective heat transfer coefficients in a full-scale room with and without furniture. *Build. Environ.* **2001**, *36*, 743–751. [CrossRef]
36. Miriel, J.; Serres, L.; Trombe, A. Radiant ceiling panel heating-cooling systems: Experimental and simulated study of the performances, thermal comfort and energy consumptions. *Appl. Therm. Eng.* **2002**, *22*, 1861–1873. [CrossRef]
37. Helm, I.; Jalukse, L.; Leito, I. Measurement Uncertainty Estimation in Amperometric Sensors: A Tutorial Review. *Sensors* **2010**, *10*, 4430–4455. [CrossRef]
38. Alamdari, F.; Hammond, G.P. Improved data correlations for buoyancy-driven convection in rooms. *Build. Serv. Eng. Res. Technol.* **1983**, *4*, 106–112. [CrossRef]
39. Lewandowski, W.M. Natural convection heat transfer from plates of finite dimensions. *Int. J. Heat Mass Transf.* **1991**, *34*, 875–885. [CrossRef]
40. Le Dreau, J.; Heiselberg, P.; Jensen, R.L. *Experimental Data From a Full-Scale Facility Investigating Radiant and Convective Terminals: Uncertainty and Sensitivity Analysis, Description of the Experimental Data*; DCE Technical reports No. 168; Department of Civil Engineering, Aalborg University: Aalborg, Denmark, 2014; Available online: https://vbn.aau.dk/en/publications/experimental-data-from-a-full-scale-facility-investigating-radian (accessed on 10 January 2025).

energies

MDPI

Article

Performance Analysis of Solar-Integrated Vapour Compression Air Conditioning System for Multi-Story Residential Buildings in Hot Climates: Energy, Exergy, Economic, and Environmental Insights

Hussein A. Al Khiro * and Rabah Boukhanouf

Faculty of Engineering, University of Nottingham, Nottingham NG7 2RD, UK; lazrb@exmail.nottingham.ac.uk
* Correspondence: ezxhk8@exmail.nottingham.ac.uk

Abstract: Decarbonisation in hot climates demands innovative cooling solutions that minimise environmental impact through renewable energy integration and advanced system optimisation. This study investigates the energetic and economic feasibility of a thermo-mechanical vapour compression (TMVC) cooling system that integrates a conventional vapour compression cycle with an ejector and a thermally driven second-stage compressor powered by solar-heated water from evacuated flat-plate collectors. The system is designed to reduce mechanical compressor work and enhance cooling performance in hot climates. A comprehensive 4E (energy, exergy, economic, and environmental) analysis is conducted for a multi-story residential building in Baghdad, Iraq, with a total floor area of approximately 8000 m^2 and a peak cooling demand of 521.75 kW. Numerical simulations were conducted to evaluate various configurations of solar collector areas, thermal storage tank volumes, and collector mass flow rate, aiming to identify the most energy-efficient combinations. These optimal configurations were then assessed from economic and environmental perspectives. Among them, the system featuring a 600 m^2 collector area and a 34 m^3 storage tank was selected as the optimal case based on its superior electricity savings and energy performance. Specifically, this configuration achieved a 28.28% improvement in the coefficient of performance, a 22.05% reduction in energy consumption, and an average of 15.3 h of daily solar-assisted operation compared to a baseline vapour compression system. These findings highlight the potential of the TMVC system to significantly reduce energy usage and environmental impact, thereby supporting the deployment of sustainable cooling technologies in hot climate regions.

Keywords: vapour compression cycle; hot climate; constant volume thermal compression; solar cooling; residential building; Iraq

1. Introduction

Building cooling systems are essential for modern comfort, yet conventional vapour compression cycles pose environmental and energy challenges [1]. These systems rely heavily on electricity, contributing to greenhouse gas emissions and climate change [2]. With rising global temperatures and energy demands, sustainable alternatives such as solar-powered cooling offer a possible solution by reducing fossil fuel dependence, carbon footprints, and energy costs [3,4].

In Iraq, air conditioning accounts for 60% of residential electricity use during peak summer months, contributing 30% of the country's annual CO_2 emissions [5], underscoring the need for efficient cooling solutions. The abundance of solar resources in Iraq highlights the potential of solar cooling systems. The purpose of this study is to evaluate the performance, feasibility, and sustainability of a TMVC cooling system for multi-story residential buildings in hot climates, using comprehensive energy, exergy, economic, and environmental (4E) analysis.

Ismaen et al. (2023) [6] found that a hybrid solar district cooling system in Qatar reduced CO_2 emissions by 104.33% and saved $17,704 annually. Salameh et al. (2022) [7] analysed an evacuated tubes solar-absorption system in the UAE, achieving a COP of 0.793 and a 43.2% cost reduction over its lifecycle. Albatayneh et al. (2021) [8] evaluated the economic feasibility of solar cooling for a 7500 m^2 building in Amman, Jordan. The PV-powered basic vapour compression (BVC) system, with a lower LCOE ($0.05/kWh), outperformed the solar thermal system, achieving a net present value of $7.46 M over 20 years with reduced maintenance costs. Herrando et al. (2019) [9] analysed a solar combined cooling, heating, and power (S-CCHP) system for a university campus in Bari, Italy. The system reduced CO_2 emissions by 911 tons annually, cutting electricity-related emissions by 68%, despite a 16.7-year payback period. Franchini et al. (2018) [10] assessed solar district cooling in Riyadh, Saudi Arabia. Two-stage absorption chillers with parabolic trough collectors (PTC) achieved COPs of 1.3–1.4, saving 70% energy and reducing CO_2 emissions by 1400 tons annually. Mortadi and El Fadar (2022) [11] reviewed solar cooling for a 600 m^2 office across various climates. Photovoltaic thermal (PVT) systems achieved the highest solar coefficient of performance (36–52%) and the lowest cooling costs ($0.059–0.26/kWhc), while PV-BVC systems reduced energy consumption by 74%. The choice of solar collector significantly impacts system efficiency and cost. Mortadi and El Fadar [12] compared solar absorption (SABC) and adsorption (SADC) cooling using flat plate (FPC), evacuated tube (ETC), compound parabolic (CPC), parabolic trough (PTC), and PVT collectors. PVT had the lowest levelised cost of cooling (LCOC) ($0.11–0.3/kWh in arid climates) and shortest payback periods (11.25–25.6 years). ETC had a higher LCOC ($0.15–0.38/kWh) but the lowest emissions (5.86–5.99 tCO_2).

Bellos and Tzivanidis (2023) [13] investigated evacuated flat plate collectors (EFPC) for cooling applications, achieving 40% thermal efficiency at 150 °C, with an exergy efficiency of 13% and energy cost of $0.033/kWh.

While sun-rich regions with high cooling demand can utilise hybrid technologies to mitigate solar intermittency and power cooling sustainably, high upfront costs, complexity, and maintenance are among the challenges for practical implementation [14,15].

This study addresses these limitations by proposing a TMVC cooling system, which integrates an ejector and a solar-activated thermal compressor into a conventional vapour compression cycle. The system uses an evacuated flat plate collector as the thermal source and is dynamically simulated using real hourly weather data for Baghdad, Iraq.

In contrast to conventional technologies, the TMVC system aims to achieve the following:

- Shift part of the compression process to thermal input, reducing mechanical compressor load;
- Enhance overall system COP under variable solar radiation;
- Offer a scalable solution for multi-story residential buildings in hot climate zones.

By conducting various combinations of collector mass flow rate, collecting area, and storage tank volume, the system configurations are examined and compared from energetic and exegetic perspectives. In the first stage of evaluation, the systems are optimised based on energy performance, and the energetically optimal cases are subsequently assessed in terms of both financial and environmental impacts. This innovative methodology leads to the identification of properly designed and suitable systems. More specifically, the observed energy savings, improvements in COP, and the duration of daily solar energy utilisation provide new insights into the feasibility and sustainability of hybrid solar cooling systems tailored to hot climate conditions.

2. Description of the Cooling System

The proposed cooling system consists of three main components: EFPCs, a sensible heat storage tank, and a TMVC system. The TMVC integrates a conventional vapour compression cycle with a liquid ejector replacing the expansion valve, and a solar-powered secondary thermal compression stage operating at constant volume. Pressurised water liquid up to 170 °C circulates through the EFPCs, delivering heat to the storage tank. Hot water enters the tank's upper left, stratifies into thermal zones, and is drawn from the upper right to supply the TMVC's thermal compressor. After heating the superheated refrigerant, the cooled water returns to the tank's lower right. The TMVC cycle is illustrated in Figure 1. Similar to the single-stage conventional vapour compression system, the superheated refrigerant vapour enters the mechanical compressor at point (1), where its pressure and temperature undergo an isentropic compression process. Upon exiting the compressor, the refrigerant enters the thermal compressor (the second vapour compression stage) at point (2), which undergoes further pressure and temperature increase through a constant volume compression process. The thermal compressor consists of a thermal heat source (solar energy), a pressure vessel, a heat exchanger, and a three-way valve. The temperature-controlled three-way valve is installed in the refrigerant line between the mechanical and thermal compressors. This valve directs refrigerant vapour flow through the heat source heat exchanger during periods of high solar insolation or bypasses it otherwise.

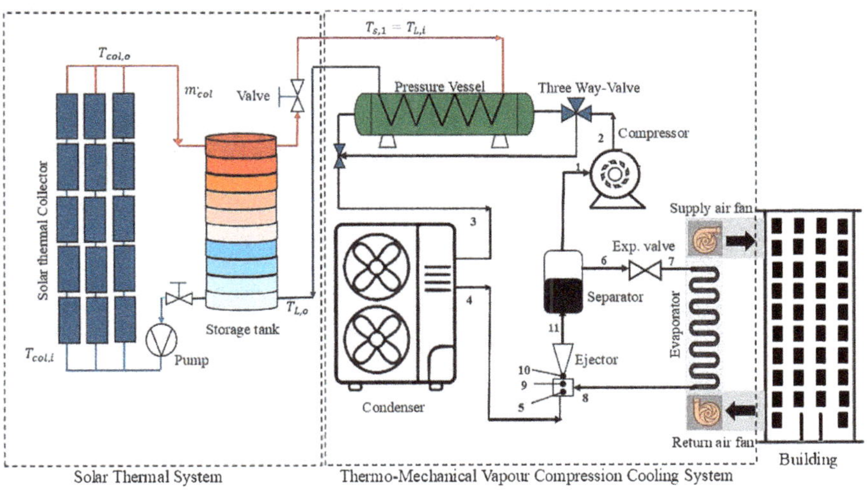

Figure 1. Schematic diagram of the TMVC system.

The primary refrigerant flow (motive flow) discharged from the condenser at point (4) enters the ejector where it undergoes isentropic expansion through a convergent-divergent nozzle and exists at point (5). A secondary flow is entrained into the suction chamber of the ejector (point 8, 9) and mixes with the primary flow in the constant area of the ejector (point 10) before exiting the ejector diffuser as a mixture of liquid and gas at point (11). The refrigerant mixture is separated into vapour and liquid states in the separator, where the refrigerant is directed to the mechanical compressor suction to repeat the cycle, and the liquid leaves at point (6) and is expanded through an expansion valve and enters the evaporator (point 7) to produce a cooling effect. The EFPCs, storage tank volume, and flow rates were optimised via dynamic simulations and energy/exergy analysis. This configuration maximises solar utilisation, enabling full solar operation without mechanical compressor input. Efficient heat transfer between the collector and the TMVC reduces compressor workload, enhances thermal compression efficiency, and saves on energy consumption. The hybrid system's design aligns solar resource availability with building cooling demands in hot climates.

3. Cooling Load Assessment

3.1. Building Specification

Multi-story residential buildings dominate Iraq's housing investment sector, driven by government initiatives to expand the affordable housing supply. The Iraqi National Investment Commission has allocated funding for the construction of over 400,000 housing units in the 2024 government budget [16]. An example of this type of housing unit is adopted as a case study for this paper, as illustrated in Figure 2a model. The building has a ten floors, with a total floor area of 8000 m^2. Each floor contains five apartments of approximately 139 m^2 floor area and a window-to-wall average ratio of 35%. Figure 2b shows the standard floor layout, while Figure 2c presents the monthly outdoor climate conditions (temperature and solar radiation) for Baghdad, Iraq.

The peak cooling load of the building was evaluated using EnergyPlus® 9.5.0 (https://energyplus.net accessed on 30 June 2024) and DesignBuilder® 7.2.0.032 (https://designbuilder.co.uk accessed on 30 June 2024), software tools used for detailed building simulation and analysis. EnergyPlus is a simulation engine developed by the U.S. Department of Energy for modelling building energy performance [17]. DesignBuilder provides a user-friendly interface for EnergyPlus and enables users to model building layouts and assess thermal performance, comfort, lighting, and HVAC system efficiency, and specify the construction materials properties and thermal characteristics as shown in Table 1 [18,19].

Table 1. Building Module Construction Details.

Building Element	Construction Material	U-Value W/m^{2}k
External wall	25 mm cement and sand render + 200 mm hollow concrete block + 10 mm cement and sand render + 25 mm gypsum plastering	1.884
Internal partition	20 mm gypsum plastering + 160 mm brick + 20 mm gypsum plastering	1.718
Flat roof	200 mm concrete, reinforced (2% steel bars) + 20 mm gypsum plastering + 200 mm air gap + 12.7 mm gypsum board	1.726
Internal floor	10 mm ceramic/porcelain + 50 mm cement plastering and sand aggregate + soil	2.881
External ground floor (first floor)	1.5 m concrete, reinforced (with 2% steel) + soil	
Top floor roof	40 mm aerated concrete slab +7.5 mm roofing mastic asphalt + 10 mm soil + 200 mm concrete, reinforced (2% steel bars) + 20 mm gypsum plastering + 200 mm air gap + 12.7 mm gypsum board	1.071
External doors	3 mm steel + 10 mm air gap + 3 mm steel	3.124
Internal doors	35 mm painted oak	2.832
Windows and glass doors	6 mm generic clear glass + 20 mm air gap + 6 mm generic clear glass and polyvinylchloride (PVC) frame	2.699

The peak cooling loads generally occur during the summer months when environmental temperatures reach their highest. In this work, 17 July was selected as the design day based on historical climate data [20]. Furthermore, the occupancy profiles were established based on the behaviour of a typical Iraqi family during the summer holiday. The data presented in Table 2 and Figure 3 are adopted from an early study conducted in Iraq [19]. In addition, these data are supported by common cultural practices, traditional daily routines, and family structures that are widely shared across Iraqi cities. Iraqi households typically experience high daytime occupancy during the summer due to school holidays, family gatherings, and indoor lifestyle preferences driven by extreme outdoor temperatures. These behavioural patterns strongly influence the operation of lighting, cooling appliances, and other household equipment, making them a valid basis for defining occupancy schedules across the country.

Table 2. Thermal properties of air conditioned flat.

Zone	Average Room Area (m^2)	Occupancy Density ($Person/m^2$)	Cooling Set Point/Set Back Temperature
Living Room	36.0	0.142	23/25
Bed 1	19.4	0.1	23/25
Bed 2	19.6	0.111	23/25
Bed 3	17.1	0.1	23/25
Kitchen	11.6	0.2	23/25

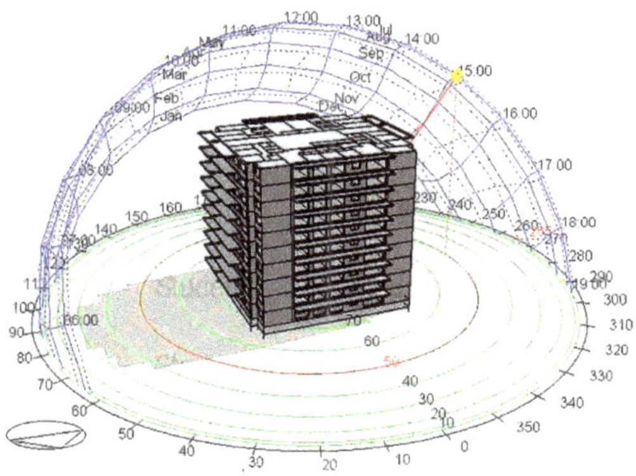

(a)

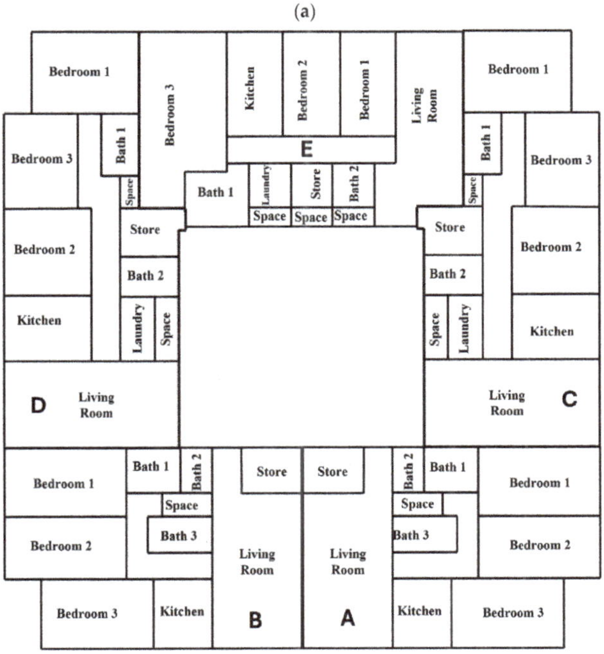

(b)

Figure 2. *Cont.*

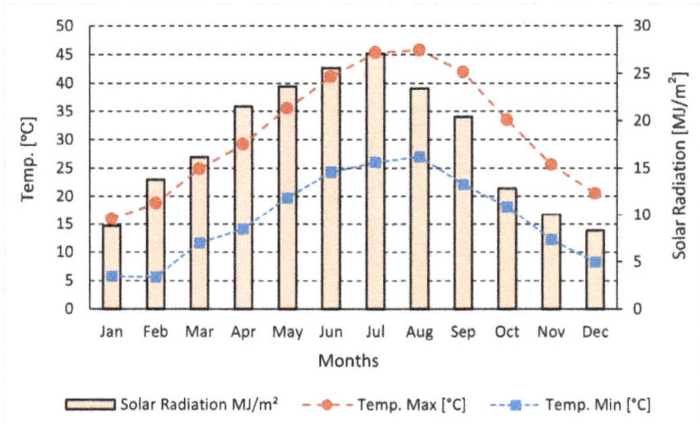

(c)

Figure 2. (**a**) Graphical model of a building; (**b**) floor layout; and (**c**) monthly max and min temperature profile and solar radiation.

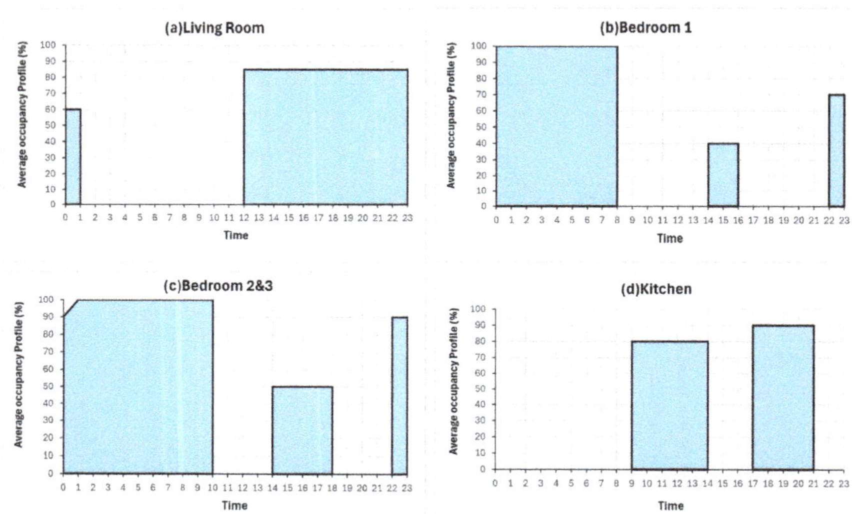

Figure 3. Average occupancy availability (%) for each air-conditioned room.

3.2. Building Cooling Load Analysis

The building cooling load arises from the heat gains through exterior surfaces due to solar radiation and temperature differences, sensible and latent heat gain associated with air ventilation, infiltration, and internal heat generation from occupant activities, lighting systems, and equipment operation.

The cooling load variation throughout the selected design day is illustrated in Figure 4. After the overnight cooling of the building, the cooling load rises again during the day as solar gains through exterior windows, internal heat gains from occupants and equipment increase. The cooling load reaches its daytime peak at about 16:00 and then decreases after sunset as the effect of solar radiation disappears. However, it is worth to note that the ambient temperature during the night remains high and coupled with the released heat absorbed by the building fabric due to thermal mass, a second cooling load peak of 521.75 kW occurs at about 11:00 pm with a design factor of cooling system is 1.2.

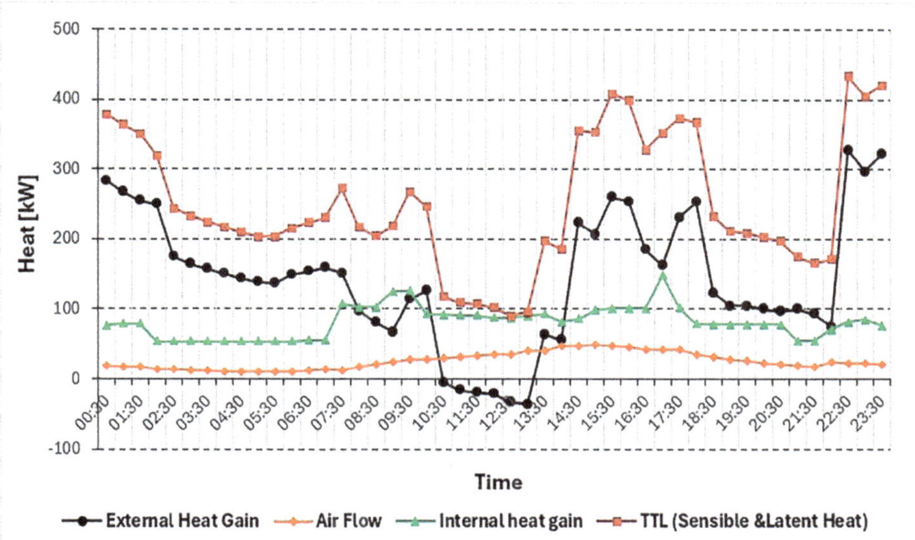

Figure 4. Cooling load analysis on 17 July.

The building's basic characteristics critically influence its energy performance and operational costs. As shown in Table 3, the high window-to-wall ratio (34% of heat gain) and external wall conductivity (19%) create substantial cooling loads, directly affecting the required capacity and operating costs of HVAC equipment. Similarly, internal heat sources (e.g., appliances at 14%) further increase energy demand. The remaining heat gain is shared roughly equally between infiltration, occupants-related, and lighting, each contributing less than 10%. These factors collectively dictate the cost-effectiveness and energy efficiency of HVAC system upgrades.

Table 3. Daily Heat Gain Components.

Heat Gain Components	Daily Gain (kWh)	Percentage (%)
Windows	2102.972	34%
Walls	1173.554	19%
Miscellaneous	841.98	14%
External infiltration	637.1803	10%
Occupancy	547.9913	9%
General lighting	524.9445	9%
Roofs	323.4117	5%

4. Solar Thermal Collector Performance

This approach of using monthly average days provides an effective strategy for assessing system performance throughout the summer period while reducing the consumption of computational resource demands.

4.1. Solar Radiation

The solar irradiance incident on a tilted surface of a solar collector for a location in Baghdad, Iraq, is determined from the following [21]:

$$I_t = I_b R_b + I_d\left(\frac{1+cos\beta}{2}\right) + I\rho_g\left(\frac{1-cos\beta}{2}\right) \quad (1)$$

where I_b is the direct (beam) solar irradiance incident on the horizontal surface, R_b is the ratio of the total irradiance falling on the tilted surface to that on a horizontal surface, accounting for the solar beam angle of incidence, I_d is the diffused irradiance, I is the total hourly irradiance on the horizontal surface, ρ_g is the surface albedo, taken as 0.2 [21], and β is the angle between the horizontal plane and the tilted surface of the collector. The optimum value of β for the summer months is given in Table 4 [22].

Table 4. Optimum value of tilt angle β for Iraq [22].

Month	Optimum Title Angle, β
April	19.9°
May	5.7°
June	0.4°
July	1.8°
August	12.3°
September	28.8°
October	44.4°

The daily solar irradiance falling on a tilted solar collector surface and ambient temperature profiles from April to October are illustrated in Figure 5a,b.

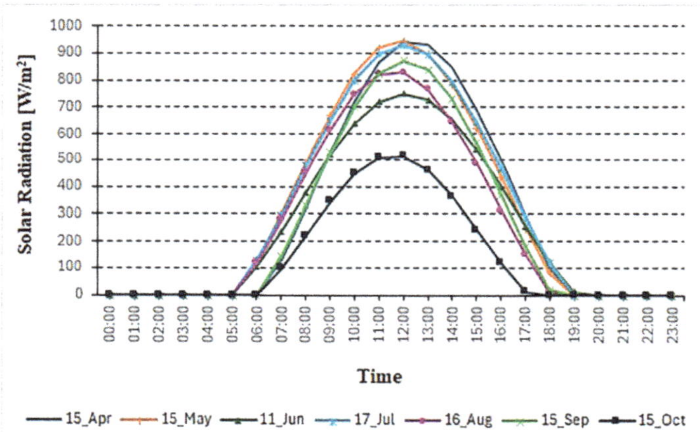

(a)

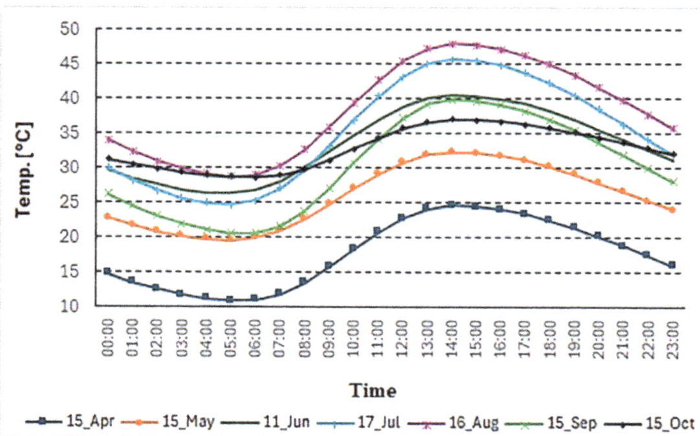

(b)

Figure 5. (**a**) Solar irradiance on a tilted collector surface; (**b**) ambient temperature profile.

4.2. Solar Thermal Collector Efficiency

For this study, EFPC has been selected for analysis as it can maintain high efficiency at high temperatures. The instantaneous thermal efficiency curve of EFPC is determined by a quadratic equation at each incidence angle (θ) as follows [23–25]:

$$\eta(\theta) = 0.729 \cdot K(\theta) - 0.5561 \cdot \frac{T_{col,i} - T_a}{I_t} - 0.0061 \cdot \frac{(Tcol,_i - T_a)^2}{I_t} \tag{2}$$

where $T_{col,i}$ is the solar collector inlet temperature, T_a is the ambient temperature, and the incidence angle modifier, K(θ), is expressed as follows:

$$K_{\theta b} = 1 - b_o\left(\left(\frac{1}{\cos\theta} - 1\right)\right)^c \tag{3}$$

where b_o is the incidence angle modifier coefficient with a value of 0.11, and exponent, c, is an absorber-specific parameter with a value of 1.12 for EFPC [26].

The net thermal energy gain from the solar collector is calculated according to the energy balance in the fluid volume, as follows:

$$Q_u = \dot{m}_{col} \cdot C_p \cdot (T_{col,o} - T_{col,i}) \tag{4}$$

where $\dot{m}_{col}$ is the mass flow rate of the heat transfer fluid, C_p is the specific heat capacity, and $T_{col,i}$ and $T_{col,o}$ are the fluid inlet and outlet fluid temperatures, respectively.

Another useful parameter used in this design is the solar collector fluid mass flow rate per unit of the collector area, S_m, which is expressed as follows [21,27]:

$$S_m = \frac{\dot{m}_{col}}{A_c} \tag{5}$$

In this study S_m is set within the range of 0.01 to 0.04 to optimise heat absorption and transfer efficiency.

5. Hot Water Storage Tank

In this analysis, a stratified thermal energy storage (TES) system was considered to maximise solar energy harvesting and minimise its intermittency; the TES volume is evaluated using a multi-node approach. The tank volume is divided into (N) equally sized horizontal layers, representing well-mixed isothermal zones $(T_{s,i})$, as shown in Figure 6. It is essential to state that the bottom node temperature $(T_{s,N})$ is equal to the solar collector inlet flow $T_{col,i}$, while the top node temperature $(T_{s,1})$ is equal to the load inlet temperature, $T_{Load,i}$. The charging of the thermal store proceeds as water from the collector enters the tank at a fixed inlet position (in this study, at the top of the tank, "physical inlet port") at a temperature $(T_{col,o})$; this approach (multi-nodes) assumes that the incoming water flows perfectly to the node (the virtual inlet port) that is better matched to its density. In other words, the fluid tends to move within the tank toward the layer with a temperature closest to the incoming flow from the collector. Similarly, the inflowing water stream flows from the load that enters the tank at a designated inlet located at the bottom, and subsequently goes towards the horizontal layer (node) that exhibits the closest density match. Furthermore, the model assumes fluid streams are fully mixed before leaving each node.

The heat addition to and subtraction from the tank is controlled by a collector (heat source) control function, (F_i^c) as follows [28]:

$$F_i^c = \left\{ \begin{array}{l} 1 \ \ if\ i = 1\ and\ T_{col,o} > T_{s,1} \\ 1 \ \ if\ T_{s,i-1} \geq T_{col,o} > T_{s,i} \\ 0 \ \ if\ i = 0\ or\ if\ i = N+1 \\ 0 \ \ otherwise \end{array} \right\} \tag{6}$$

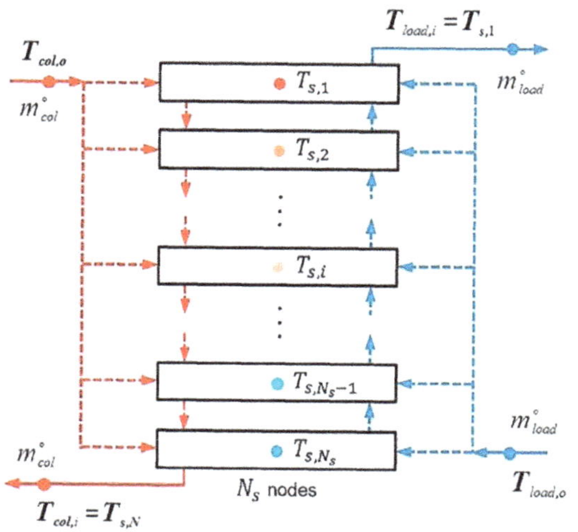

Figure 6. Internal flow associated with node i, adapted with permission from [28], Elsvier, 2018.

The fluid returning from the load (pressure vessel) can be controlled in a similar method with a load return control function F_i^L [21] with the only difference being that the configuration of the physical inlet and outlet ports are at the bottom and the top of the tank, respectively [29], as follows:

$$F_i^L = \left\{ \begin{array}{l} 1 \ \ if\ i = N\ and\ T_{L,o} < T_{s,N} \\ 1 \ \ if\ T_{s,i-1} \geq T_{L,o} > T_{s,i} \\ 0 \ \ if\ i = 0\ or\ if\ i = N+1 \\ 0 \ \ otherwise \end{array} \right\} \tag{7}$$

Thus, the mixed flow rate $\left(m_{mix,i}^{\cdot}\right)$ that represents the net flow into node i from node i−1 is expressed by the following [21]:

$$m_{mix,i}^{\cdot} = \left\{ \begin{array}{ll} 0 & if\ i = 1 \\ \dot{m}_{col} \sum_{j=1}^{i-1} F_j^C - \dot{m}_{Load} \sum_{j=i+1}^{N} F_j^L & \end{array} \right\} \tag{8}$$

In operation, the transfer of heat from the solar collector to the TES (i.e., $\dot{m}_{col} > 0$) occurs when solar radiation is available. Similarly, the discharge of the TES ($\dot{m}_{Load} > 0$) proceeds when the top fluid layer of TES, $T_{s,1}$, is greater than the temperature of the superheated refrigerant discharged from the pressure, T_3'.

Applying energy and mass conservation governing relationships, the temperature of each fluid node of the stratified thermal storage tank can be expressed mathematically as follows [21]:

$$M_{s,i} \cdot \frac{dT_{s,i}}{dt} = \left(\frac{UA_{s,i}}{C_p}\right)_i \cdot (T_a - T_{s,i}) + F_i^C m_{col}^{\cdot} (T_{col,o} - T_{s,i}) + F_i^L m_{load}^{\cdot} (T_{L,o} - T_{s,i}) + \left\{ \begin{array}{ll} m_{mix,i}^{\cdot} (T_{s,i-1} - T_{s,i}) & if\ m_{mix,i}^{\cdot} > 0 \\ \dot{m}_{mix,i+1} (T_{s,i} - T_{s,i+1}) & if\ \ m_{mix,i+1}^{\cdot} < 0 \end{array} \right\} \tag{9}$$

where $M_{s,i}$ is the heat transfer fluid mass of node, i, C_p is the specific heat of the fluid at $T_{s,i}$ and t is the time interval, U is the heat transfer coefficient of the TES and is taken for a well-insulated tank as 0.5 W/m^{2}K. $A_{s,i}$ are the outer area of each node with the top and bottom nodes area as $A_{s,i} = \frac{\pi \cdot d_s^2}{4} + \frac{\pi \cdot d_s \cdot h_s}{No_i}$ and the intermediate layers area being $A_{s,i} = \frac{\pi \cdot d_s \cdot h_s}{No_i}$.

6. Thermo-Mechanical Vapour Compression Cooling Interface

The thermodynamic analysis of the TMVC air conditioning system has been thoroughly presented, and its thermal performance has been evaluated [2,30]. The TMVC system interfaces with TES through a pressure vessel containing a coil heat exchanger immersed in the superheated refrigerant. Heat transfer occurs as the hot fluid from the TES flows through the coil heat exchanger, transferring thermal energy to the superheated refrigerant enclosed within the vessel.

6.1. Energy Performance

The daily useful energy supply from the solar collector, cooling loads, compressor work for the basic vapour compression cycle, and compressor work of the TMVC counterpart are presented as follows [31].

The daily mean thermal efficiency of the solar collector field is defined as the ratio of the net useful energy supplied to the total solar incident and is given by the following:

$$\eta_{th,D} = \frac{\int_{day} Q_{ue} \cdot dt}{\int_{day} Q_s \cdot dt} \tag{10}$$

Similarly, the daily COP of the basic vapour compression cycle and the TMVC system are given by the ratio of the total cooling load supplied to the work consumed by the respective mechanical compressor, as follows:

$$COP_{D,BVC} = \frac{\int_{day} Q_{ev} \cdot dt}{\int_{day} W_{comp,BVC} \cdot dt} \tag{11}$$

$$COP_{D,TMVC} = \frac{\int_{day} Q_{ev} \cdot dt}{\int_{day} W_{comp,TMVC} \cdot dt} \tag{12}$$

Therefore, the daily saving of energy consumption is given as the difference between the basic vapour compression and the TMVC work consumption as follows:

$$D_{ES} = \frac{\int_{day} (W_{comp,BVC} - W_{comp,TMVC}) dt}{\int_{day} W_{comp,BVC} \cdot dt} \tag{13}$$

6.2. Exergy Analysis

Exergy analysis is a more robust tool as it can identify inefficiencies, locate irreversibilities, and assess the effectiveness of energy conversion processes. This allows for better decision-making in system design, improving efficiency, sustainability, and cost-effectiveness [32].

In this study, the exergy flow of the cooling load is given by the following equation [33]:

$$E_{evp} = Q_{evp} \cdot \left(1 - \frac{T_{amb}}{T_{evp}}\right) \tag{14}$$

where T_{amb} is the ambient temperature and T_{evp} is the evaporator temperature.

The useful exergy output from the solar thermal collector is given by [34] as follows:

$$E_{Qu} = Q_u - \dot{m}_{col} \cdot C_p \cdot T_o \cdot ln\left[\frac{T_{col,o}}{T_{col,i}}\right] \quad (15)$$

The daily exergy efficiency of the thermal collector and air conditioning system is expressed as follows [31]:

$$\eta_{D,ex,col} = \frac{\int_{day} E_{Qu} \cdot dt}{\int_{day} E_s \cdot dt} \quad (16)$$

$$\eta_{D,ex,sys} = \frac{\int_{day} E_{evp} \cdot dt}{D_{W,TMVC} + \int_{day} E_s \cdot dt} \quad (17)$$

where E_s is the exergy flow of the sun and adopted from Petela [35] as follows:

$$E_s = Q_s \cdot \left[1 - \frac{4}{3} \cdot \left(\frac{T_{amb}}{T_{sun}}\right) + \frac{1}{3} \cdot \left(\frac{T_{amb}}{T_{sun}}\right)^4\right] \quad (18)$$

With the apparent sun temperature, T_{sun} is taken to be 4350 K (75% of the sun's apparent black body temperature of 5800 K) [36].

6.3. Economic and Environment Analysis

This study evaluates the economic viability of a solar-assisted air conditioning system over its operational lifespan using the levelised cost of cooling (*LCOC*) and simple payback period (*SPBP*). The *LCOC* incorporates capital, maintenance, and operational costs while accounting for system efficiency and environmental impact. This is expressed as follows [11]:

$$LCOC = \frac{NPC}{CLC} \quad (19)$$

where *CLC* is the annual cooling energy supply (kWh) and NPC is the net present cost of the cooling system, expressed by the following:

$$NPC = CC \cdot \frac{DR(1 + DR)^m}{(1 + DR)^m - 1} + EC * EP + C_{m\&o} - EPCS \quad (20)$$

Here, $C_{m\&o}$ is the annual operation and maintenance cost ($/kWh$_c$), *EP* is the electricity tariff ($/kWh), and *EC* is the total electricity consumption of the air conditioning system (kWh) in the summer season. The capital cost of the air conditioning system (solar collector field, storage tank, air conditioner, and associated parts), *CC*, can be evaluated as follows:

$$CC = K_C \cdot A_c + K_V \cdot V + K_{ck} \cdot Q_e + Z_{con} \quad (21)$$

where K_c, K_v, K_{ck}, and Z_{con} are specific coefficients given in Table 5.

DR is the real interest rate, adjusted for inflation, representing the actual return on investment in terms of purchasing power over time, as described by the Fisher equation for real interest rate as follows:

$$DR = \left[\frac{(1 + IR)}{(1 + FR)} - 1\right] \quad (22)$$

where *IR* is the nominal interest rate and *FR* is the inflation rate.

EPCS represents the total environmental penalty cost savings achieved over the system's lifetime through CO_2 emissions reduction, expressed as follows [37]:

$$EPCS = \frac{ER_{CO2} \cdot C_{CO2}}{IR - FR}\left[1 - \left(\frac{1+RF}{1+IR}\right)^n\right] \tag{23}$$

Here, ER_{CO2} represents the annual CO_2 emissions reduction achieved by the solar-assisted air conditioning system.

The economic and environmental parameters used in the analysis are given in Table 5.

Table 5. Economic and Environmental Parameters.

Parameter	Value
Interest rate, IR	7.5%
Inflation rate, FR	3%
CO_2 reduction factor, RF	3%
BVC-specific cost, K_{ck}	324 \$/kW
EFPC specific cost, K_C	450 \$/m^2
Storage-specific cost, K_V	1000 \$/m^3
Condenser cost, Z_{con}	$\left(516.621 \cdot A_{diff,cond}\right) + 268.45$ [38]
Electricity cost, EP	0.15 \$/kWh
Operation and maintenance, $Cm\&o$	3% of capital cost
Annual operation time, SOH	5040 (h)
CO_2 emission factor for electricity, f	0.721 kg CO_2/kWh
Cost of unit CO_2 emission, C_{CO2}	9 \$/tCO_2
m, project lifetime	20 years

The simple payback period (SPBP) assumes that the cash inflow remains constant over the lifetime of the project and is given by the following [39]:

$$SPBP = \frac{CC}{CF_{net}} \tag{24}$$

7. Research Method

7.1. Model Development

The simulation model uses a parametric analysis to evaluate the effects of collector area (ranging from 200 m^2 to 600 m^2, in 50 m^2 increments) and storage tank volume on the system's energy and exergy performance. For each collector area, the storage tank volume varies from 4 m^3 to 40 m^3 in 2 m^3 increments, and the collector mass flow rate ranged from $0.01 < S_{m}. < 0.04$ The selected range of solar collector areas is based on the building's roof space limitation, which accommodates the solar collector field, storage tank, and chiller cooling system. A MATLAB® (version R2023b) model was developed to evaluate the system's performance indices.

A sensitivity analysis has been performed to determine the appropriate model parameters. The dynamic model employed a short time step of 2 min and a 10-node storage tank. In addition to ensure computational convergence of the model, the design equations were solved using real weather data over a continuous period of three days. The simulation was initialised with the assumption that the initial temperatures of all subsystem components were equal to the ambient temperature.

For each collector area, the storage tank volume and collector mass flow rate that maximise the daily TMVC COP, energy savings, and system exergy efficiency are selected as the optimal configurations. As a result, eleven cases are identified as the most suitable solutions. These optimal configurations are then subjected to financial evaluation in the subsequent stage. In this study, the levelised cost of cooling for each case is compared to the

BVC, along with the simple payback period (SPBP) associated with the savings achieved by adding thermal compression equipment to the BVC air-conditioning system.

Table 6 details the system operation condition and Figure 7 presents a chart that illustrates the study method.

Table 6. System parameters.

List of Parameters	Value
Maximum storage tank temperature	170 °C
Superheated temperature	5 °C
Subcooled temperature	5 °C
Evaporator temperature	5 °C
Pressure vessel efficiency	0.8
Compressor mechanical efficiency	0.8
Storage tank heat transfer coefficient	$0.5\ W \cdot m^{-2} \cdot K^{-1}$
Solar thermal system working fluid	Water
Refrigerant working fluid	R1234yf
Solar collector type	EFPC
Solar collector Area	100–600 m^2
Storage tank volume	4–40 m^3
Specific collector mass flow rate (*Sm*)	0.01–0.04 $Kg \cdot s^{-1} \cdot m^{-2}$
Load mass flow rate	0.5 × *Sm*

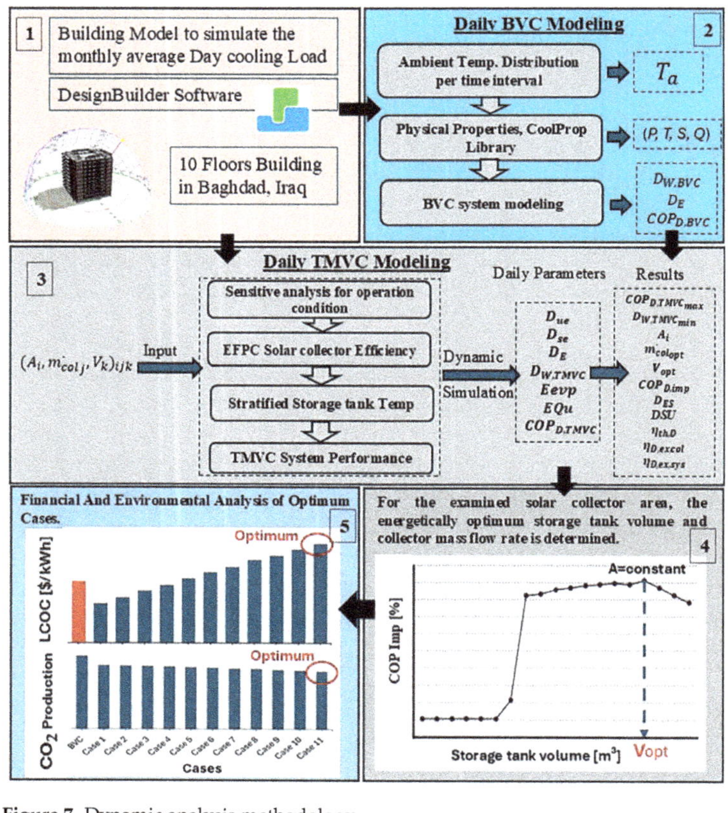

Figure 7. Dynamic analysis methodology.

7.2. Model Validation

To validate the mathematical model, the performance of the solar-assisted air conditioning system was compared with experimental data from Okabi [40]. The experiment involved a 1.69 m^2 evacuated tube solar collector and a 0.193 m^3 water storage tank, with the system operating at a cooling capacity of 4.4 kW. The main parameters of the system, including compressor power consumption, condenser heat rejection, heat input to thermal storage, and storage tank water temperature, were compared with the model's predictions over the experimental period, as shown in Figure 8. In this study, the relative error (RE) and mean relative error (MRE) are used as evaluation metrics for the mathematical model, as follows [41]:

$$RE = \left| \frac{y_{exp} - y_{sim}}{y_{exp}} \right| * 100\% \tag{25}$$

$$MRE = \frac{1}{n} \sum_{i=1}^{n} \left| \frac{y_{exp} - y_{sim}}{y_{exp}} \right| * 100\% \tag{26}$$

Here, y_{exp} refers to the experimental data from the reference [39], while y_{sim} denotes the simulation results.

The results demonstrate a good agreement between this study model's results and the published experimental data, with a maximum relative error of less than 11%.

Extending the operation hours of the solar-assisted air conditioning system after sunset hours would be a desirable design objective. Therefore, the thermal storage tank computer model was validated against Cadau et al. [42] in both charging and discharging modes. As shown in Figure 9a, the charging mode used a 12-node model, where the tank fluid, initially at ambient temperature, was heated by injecting hot water at the top. The results showed strong agreement with the referenced simulation study and maintained acceptable performance compared to experimental findings.

The TES tank was validated in discharge mode using data from Cadau et al. [42]. An 8-node model was used, where the initially hot tank fluid was cooled by injecting cold water at the base. As shown in Figure 9b, the present study and referenced simulation study followed a similar temperature profile trend, though some deviation was observed between the model predictions and experimental data.

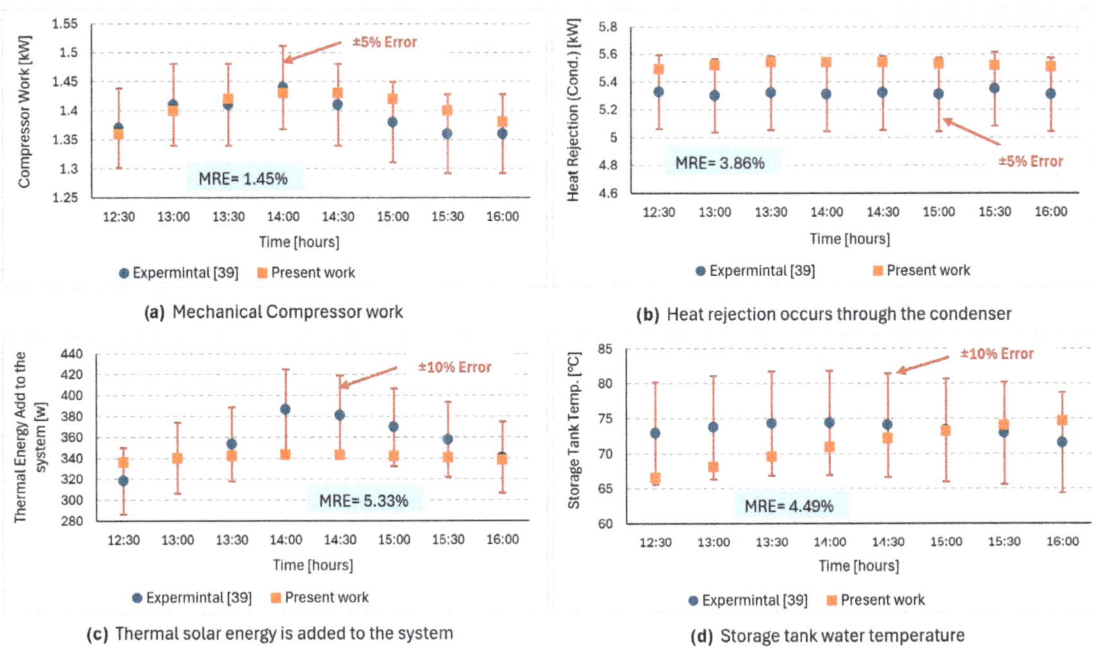

Figure 8. Computer model validation.

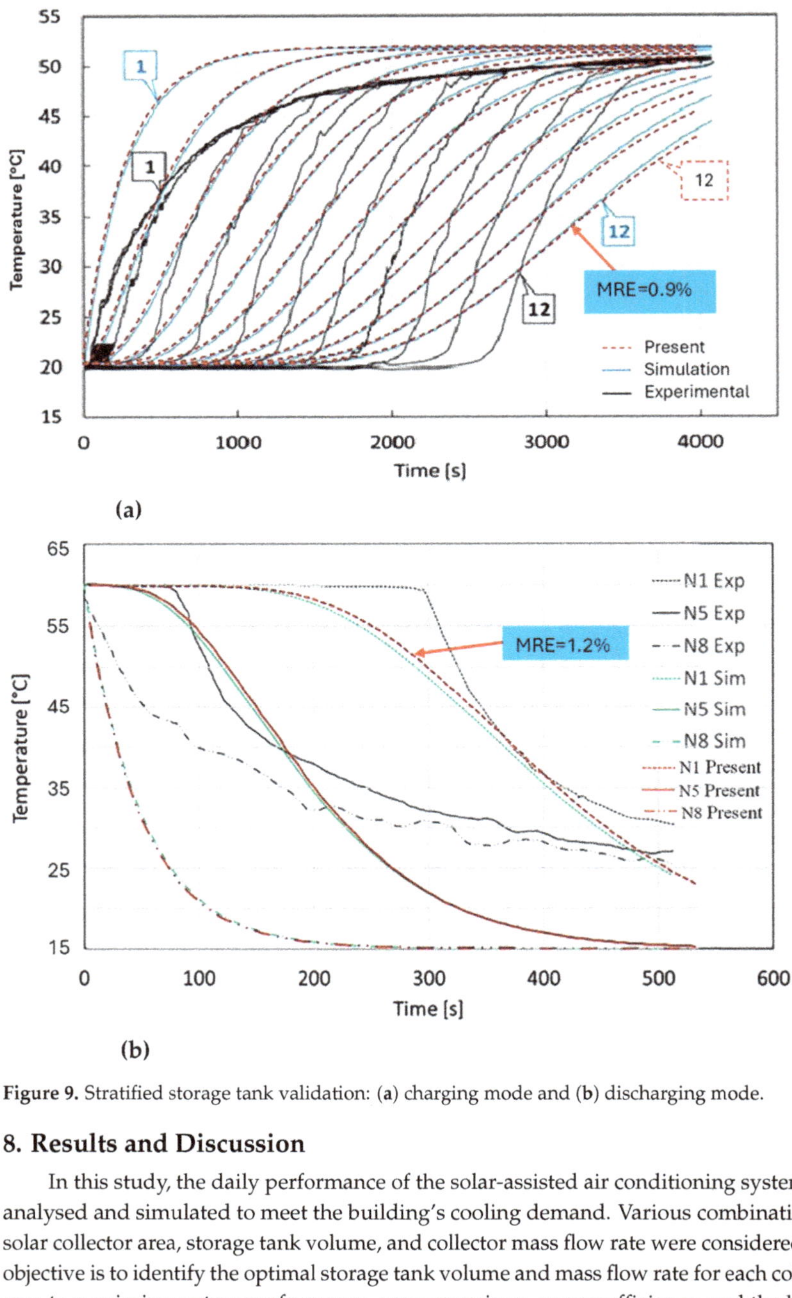

Figure 9. Stratified storage tank validation: (**a**) charging mode and (**b**) discharging mode.

8. Results and Discussion

In this study, the daily performance of the solar-assisted air conditioning system was analysed and simulated to meet the building's cooling demand. Various combinations of solar collector area, storage tank volume, and collector mass flow rate were considered. The objective is to identify the optimal storage tank volume and mass flow rate for each collector area to maximise system performance, energy savings, exergy efficiency, and the hourly utilisation of solar energy throughout the day. The results from this dynamic analysis were then used to compare the optimum configurations. Furthermore, the economic and environmental feasibility of each optimal design, including the associated CO_2 emission reductions, was evaluated.

8.1. Effect of the Collector Mass Flow Rate

The mass flow rate of the collector is a critical factor in determining the energy performance of the TMVC system. It influences both the optimal storage tank volume that maximises improvements in the coefficient of performance (COP) and energy savings compared to the basic vapour compression (BVC) system, as well as the threshold storage tank volume required to initiate the utilisation of solar energy for each collector field area.

As shown in Table 7, as the collector mass flow rate increases from ($0.01 \times Ac$) to ($0.04 \times Ac$) to ensures efficient heat absorption and transfer, both the threshold and the mathematical model optimum storage tank volume show a clear upward trend, indicating that higher mass flow rates require larger storage capacities to maintain system efficiency. An increase in the mass flow rate results in more heat being transferred from the collector to the storage tank per unit of time. To effectively store this additional heat without causing temperature fluctuations, a larger tank volume is necessary to balance the energy input and output. This ensures better thermal stratification, allowing the system to maintain the required temperature gradients to achieve higher COP and energy savings.

Table 7. Effect of collector mass flow rate on TMVC performance and tank optimisation.

	$\dot{m}_{col}$ = 0.01 × Ac [kg/s]			$\dot{m}_{col}$ = 0.02 × Ac [kg/s]			$\dot{m}_{col}$ = 0.03 × Ac [kg/s]			$\dot{m}_{col}$ = 0.04 × Ac [kg/s]		
Ac [m^2]	V_st (thr) [m^3]	V_st (Opt) [m^3]	COP_imp (max) [%]	V_st (thr) [m^3]	V_st (Opt) [m^3]	COP_imp (max) [%]	V_st (thr) [m^3]	V_st (Opt) [m^3]	COP_imp (max) [%]	V_st (thr) [m^3]	V_st (Opt) [m^3]	COP_imp (max) [%]
100	4	4	13.54	4	6	14.43	4	6	13.74	6	6	13.69
150	4	6	15.46	6	6	15.35	6	8	15.28	8	8	14.32
200	4	8	16.94	6	10	16.83	8	10	16.16	10	12	15.97
250	4	10	17.78	8	12	17.96	10	12	17.7	14	14	17.31
300	6	14	19.32	8	16	19.41	12	16	19.5	16	16	18.61
350	6	16	20.87	10	18	21.23	14	20	20.76	18	20	20.38
400	6	20	21.95	12	22	22.54	16	22	22.37	20	24	21.52
450	8	22	23.83	12	24	24.48	18	26	23.94	24	26	23.9
500	8	24	25.27	14	28	25.16	20	28	25.6	26	28	24.52
550	10	28	26.43	16	30	27.27	22	32	26.79	28	32	26.57
600	12	30	27.49	16	34	28.28	24	34	27.93	32	36	27.45

8.2. System Optimisation

According to Figure 10a–c, each collector area has an optimal storage tank volume that maximises the daily energy performance of the TMVC system. These figures illustrate the effect of collector area and storage tank volume, at a collector mass flow rate of ($0.02 \times Ac$), on the COP, COP improvement, and energy savings of the TMVC system compared to the BVC system.

These figures show consistent trends, as for each collector area, there is a threshold storage tank volume at which the TMVC system starts utilising solar energy for thermal compression, leading to improved COP, and energy savings. This improvement continues until it reaches an optimum storage tank volume, providing maximum COP and energy savings. Beyond this point, performance declines either because the storage tank cannot supply sufficient heat for the thermal compressor or provides heat at a lower-than-optimal rate. For smaller collector areas (100–300 m^2), COP improvement and energy savings begin at a small storage tank threshold, typically below 6 m^3, and reach their peak at an optimum storage tank volume of around 4–16 m^3. Beyond this point, COP decreases as the effect of thermal compression fades, eventually stabilising at approximately 12.13% COP improvement and 10.8% energy savings, driven primarily by the ejector's performance.

Conversely, for larger collector areas (400–600 m^2), both the COP improvement and energy savings increase as the storage tank volume increases. The highest improvements, peaking at 28% in COP and 22% in energy savings, are seen with a 34 m^3 storage tank for a

600 m^2 collector. These larger areas require a larger threshold storage tank size because smaller tanks cause the water temperature to rise above 170 °C, leading to boiling.

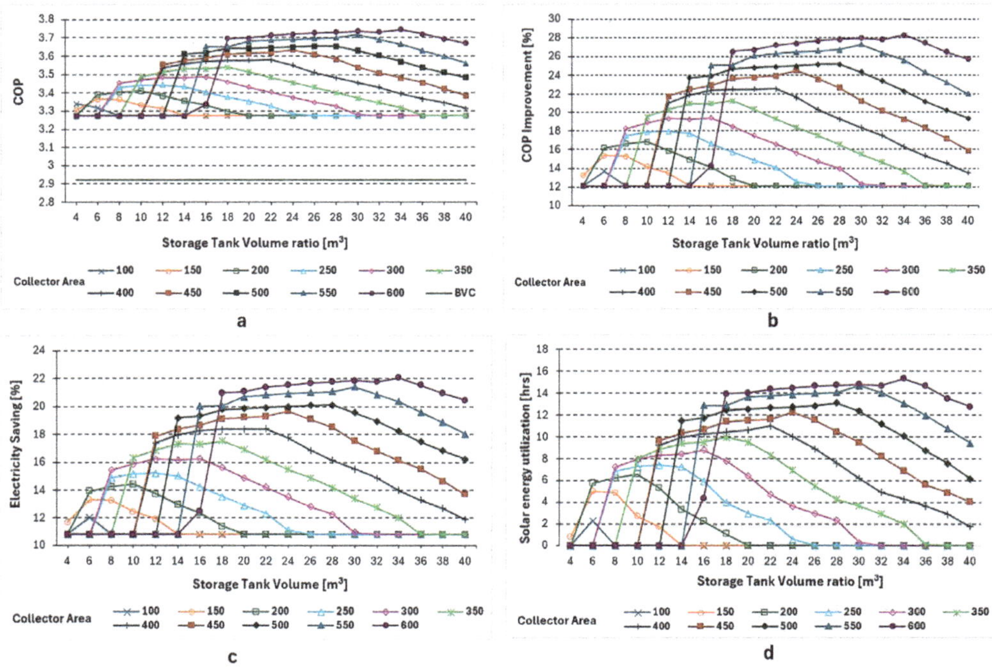

Figure 10. (**a**) Daily TMVC system COP. (**b**) Daily COP improvement. (**c**) Daily electricity saving. (**d**) Utilisation of solar energy daily.

One of the key performance indicators for the solar-assisted air conditioning system is the number of hours it can utilise solar thermal energy daily across the examined configurations. As illustrated in Figure 10d, with a collector area of 400 m^2 and a storage tank volume exceeding 14 m^3, the system can operate on solar thermal energy for more than 10 h per day. The reliance on solar energy increases significantly with larger collector areas. For instance, a configuration featuring a 600 m^2 collector and a storage volume of 34 m^3 enables solar energy utilisation for over 15 h daily. This demonstrates that when the collector area is increased, in conjunction with an adequately sized storage tank, the daily operational hours of solar-driven thermal compression increase, effectively supplying the heat required for the thermal compressor.

Figure 11 illustrates the overall exergy efficiency of the system, highlighting the effects of collector area and storage tank volume. A clear trend is observed where exergy efficiency decreases as the collector area increases. In contrast, exergy efficiency stabilises and exhibits minimal variation with increases in storage tank volume, particularly beyond a certain threshold.

The decline in exergy efficiency with increasing collector area is attributed to the increasing exergy destruction within the system, which occurs from irreversibilities such as temperature gradients between the heat source (solar collector) and the heat sink (environment). These irreversibilities become more pronounced as the collector area increases, leading to higher thermal losses and reduced overall exergy efficiency.

Additionally, when the storage tank fails to provide the required heat to the thermal compressor, the contribution of the solar thermal system diminishes. In such cases, the system's exergy efficiency reverts to a baseline level comparable to a vapour compression system with an ejector, as the solar thermal system's effect fades under less favourable conditions.

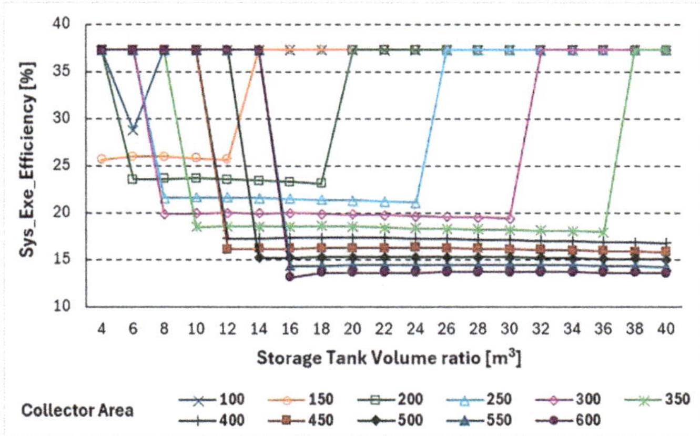

Figure 11. Daily exergy system efficiency.

Figure 12a illustrates the daily thermal efficiency of the solar collector field. The results indicate that increasing the collector area while maintaining a lower storage tank volume leads to a decrease in collector thermal efficiency. This combination results in elevated mean temperatures within the storage tank layers, which, in turn, raise the inlet temperature of the solar collector. A higher inlet temperature negatively impacts the thermal performance of the collector by increasing thermal losses due to the larger temperature difference between the collector surface and the surrounding environment. Consequently, this reduces the overall thermal efficiency of the collector.

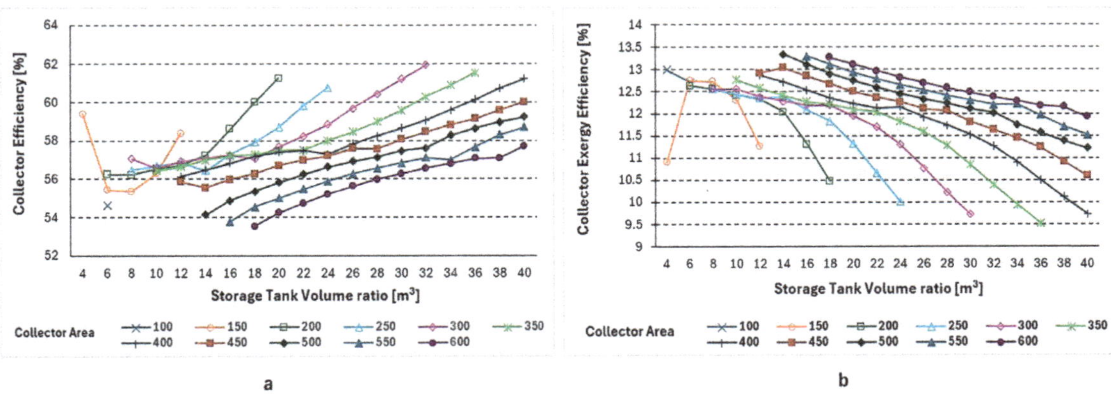

Figure 12. Daily solar thermal collector: (**a**) efficiency, and (**b**) exergy efficiency.

Furthermore, for each collector area, the efficiency curve follows a characteristic trend. It begins at a threshold storage tank volume, where the collector operates with minimal efficiency. As the storage tank volume increases, the efficiency improves, benefiting from a more balanced heat storage and supply. However, as the storage tank volume becomes excessively large, the system's thermal energy potential diminishes, and it can no longer maintain the necessary heat to supply the thermal compressor effectively. This leads to the solar thermal system eventually ceasing operation.

For example, at a collector area of 600 m^2 and a storage tank volume of 18 m^3, the thermal efficiency is approximately 53.54%. However, with the same collector area and a larger storage tank volume of 40 m^3, the efficiency improves significantly to 57.71%. This highlights the importance of balancing the collector area and storage tank volume to optimise thermal efficiency and minimise thermal losses.

Figure 12b shows the variation in collector exergy efficiency with respect to collector area and storage tank volume. It is observed that as the collector area increases, the collector exergy efficiency generally improves, particularly for smaller storage tank volumes, indicating that larger collectors utilise solar energy more effectively. Conversely, for a fixed collector area, the efficiency tends to decrease with increasing storage tank volume. This decline can be attributed to higher thermal losses or reduced efficiency in heat utilisation associated with larger tank capacities. The highest efficiencies are achieved with smaller tank volumes and larger collector areas, with a peak value of 13.3% observed for a collector area of 500 m^2 and a tank volume of 14 m^3. This analysis highlights the importance of optimising the balance between the collector area and storage tank volume to achieve maximum exergy efficiency. Figure 13 summarises the optimal cases, along with their daily energy and exergy results.

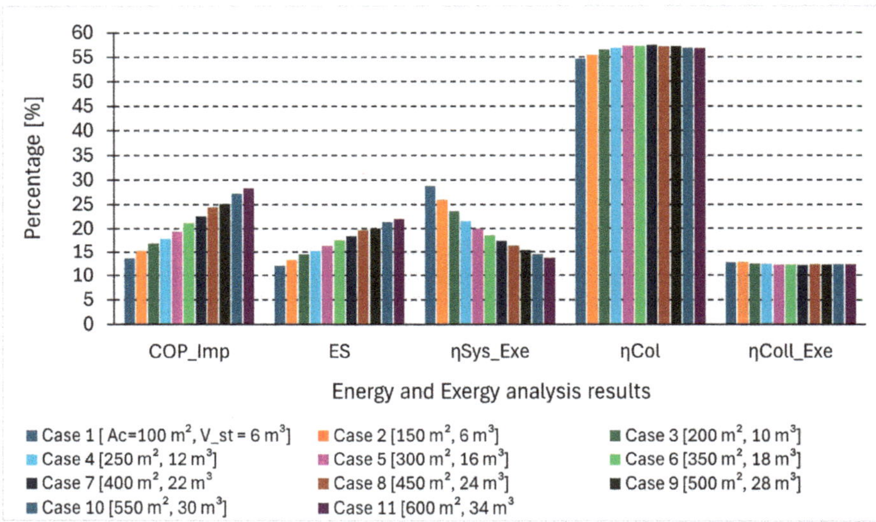

Figure 13. Optimal cases energy and exergy analysis results.

8.3. Dynamic Behaviour of the Optimum Cases

Figure 14 illustrates the mean distributed temperature inside the storage tank, providing insights into the behaviour of the TMVC system throughout the day. The temperature begins to rise around 7 a.m. as solar radiation becomes available, peaking at 3 p.m. During this period, the heat input from the solar source (charging) exceeds the heat output to the load (discharging), leading to an increase in temperature. Afterward, the temperature decreases as discharging surpasses charging, eventually reaching a steady state.

For Cases 5, 7, 9, and 11, the temperature curves exhibit smooth behaviour, indicating regular and successive charging and discharging cycles. This suggests that the heat acquired from the solar collector is sufficient to consistently supply heat from the storage tank to the load. Conversely, Case 3 exhibits fluctuating temperature profiles due to a lag between the charging and discharging processes. This lag indicates that the solar collector's heat gain is initially insufficient to simultaneously increase the tank temperature and meet the load demand, causing fluctuations.

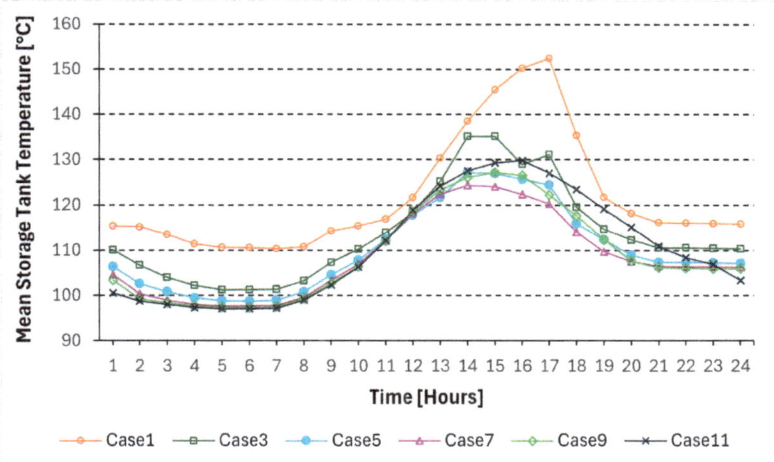

Figure 14. Mean temperature distribution inside the storage tank on 17 July.

In case 1, while the mean temperature is higher, the smaller storage volume limits the total thermal energy that can be stored. This restriction prevents the system from sustaining a steady and sufficient heat supply to the TMVC system over time, particularly during high-demand periods or transient conditions. As a result, the temperatures in Cases 1 and 2 are higher than in the other cases, as the thermal compression process relies on adequate storage tank temperatures. These higher temperatures are accumulated over time due to delayed and irregular charging and discharging cycles.

Figure 15 shows the hourly performance of the TMVC system varies across cases (Cases 1, 3, 5, 7, 9, and 11) and consistently outperforms the BVC in energy saving. During early hours (0–6 a.m.), all the TMVC cases show a lower compressor work average between (40–60 kW) compared to the BVC (50–70 kW), with Cases 9 and 11 performing slightly better due to larger storage volumes. From 7–11 h, Cases 7, 9, and 11 continue to demonstrate reduced work compared to other TMVC cases, reflecting improved thermal integration.

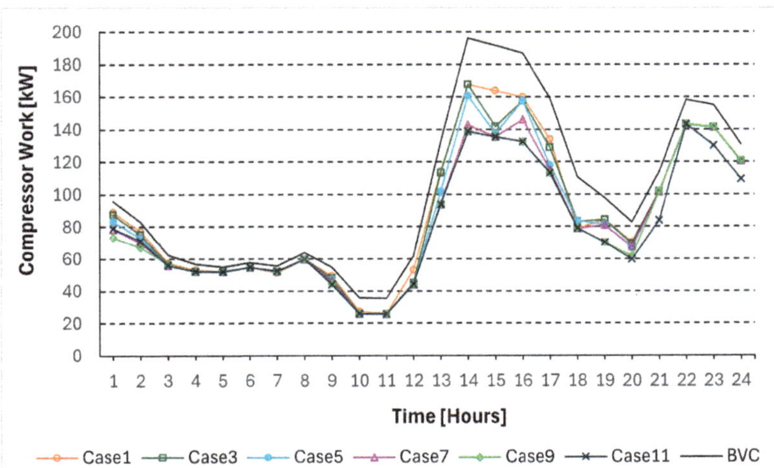

Figure 15. Electricity Consumption Comparison: BVC vs. TMVC on 17 July.

During peak hours (12–14), all the systems experience increased compressor work. However, TMVC cases, particularly Cases 9 and 11, maintain lower demands (140–160 kW) compared to the BVC (160–200 kW) and outperform Cases 1 and 3, which approach the BVC. In the afternoon (15–19), Cases 9 and 11 sustain moderate work levels (100–120 kW), while other TMVC cases and the BVC require more energy (130–160 kW). By evening (20–24), all TMVC cases reduce their work, with Cases 9 and 11 again showing the lowest values (60–100 kW) compared to other cases (~70–110 kW) and the BVC (70–130 kW). Overall, Cases 9 and 11 consistently achieve the best performance, emphasising the benefits of optimised storage and thermal management.

As illustrated in Figure 16, the hourly COP analysis shows that the TMVC system consistently outperforms the BVC throughout the day. TMVC cases, particularly Case 11, maintain higher COP values due to greater heat gain during the charging mode and better temperature distribution within the storage tank, with values ranging from 4.0 to 4.7, compared to the BVC (3.7–4.3) during early hours (1–6). In the afternoon (13–18), TMVC cases sustain a COP of 3.3–3.5, while the BVC drops below 2.5. By evening (19–24), TMVC cases, especially Case 11, recover with COP values rising to 3.7–4.2, surpassing the BVC (2.6–3.5). Overall, the TMVC system demonstrates improved energy efficiency, with Case 11 performing the best during high-load periods.

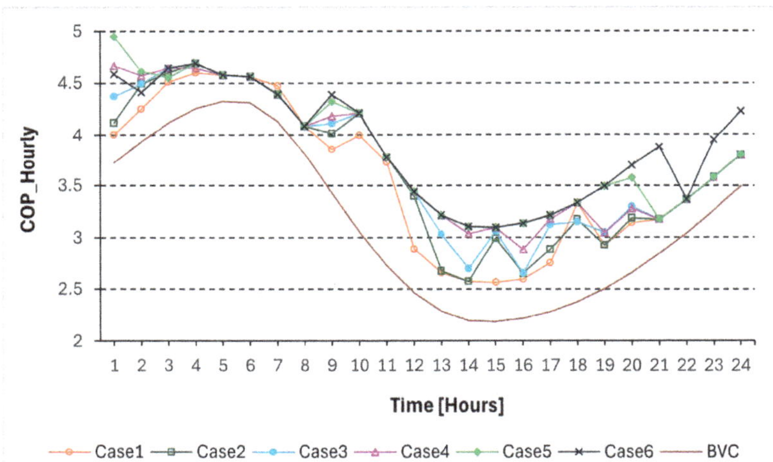

Figure 16. Hourly distribution of the COP on 17 July.

Figure 17 illustrates the hourly thermal efficiency of the solar collector. All the optimal cases exhibit a similar trend: efficiency increases after sunrise as solar radiation becomes available, peaks around noon, and then gradually declines toward sunset. However, Case 11 shows a slight deviation to the left after noon. This deviation occurs due to the increasing temperature distribution, which raises the inlet water temperature to the collector, thereby reducing the collector's efficiency.

Figure 18 shows the monthly average daily electricity consumption for all the months, comparing the BVC with the TMVC optimal case. Electricity consumption is highest in July and August due to higher mean ambient temperatures, which result in a lower COP. The BVC consistently demonstrates the highest compressor work, reflecting greater daily energy consumption compared to the TMVC cases. The integration of a thermal compressor in the TMVC cases demonstrates improved energy efficiency, particularly during high-load months.

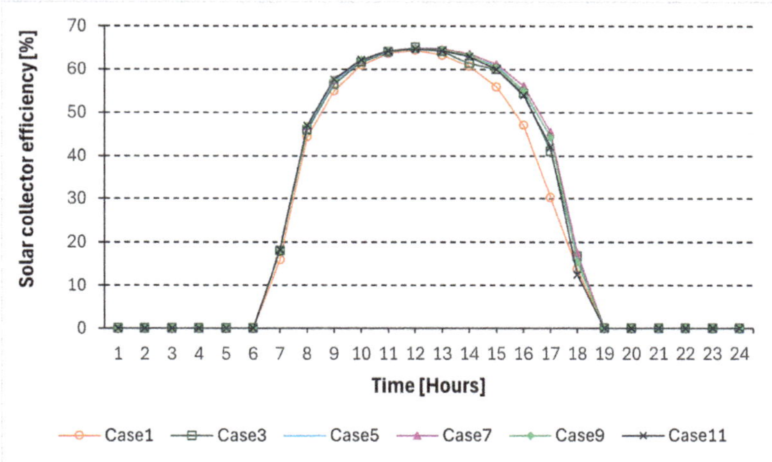

Figure 17. Hourly solar thermal collector efficiency on 17 July.

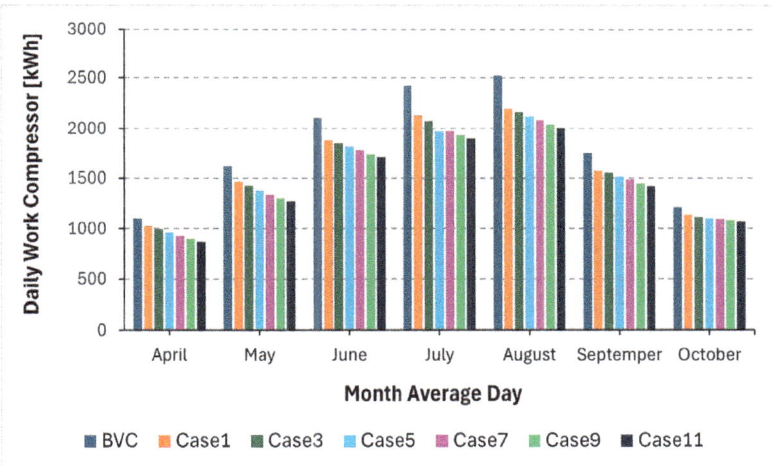

Figure 18. Monthly average daily electricity consumption during the summer season.

8.4. Economic Analysis

An economic analysis was conducted for the optimal cases, comparing them to the basic vapour compression cycle (BVC) using the levelised cost of cooling (LCOC), including the total environmental penalty cost savings accrued over the system's lifetime. This financial evaluation considers all summer months (April to October) to determine the electricity savings achieved through the implementation of the TMVC system.

One of the primary challenges impacting the economic feasibility of renewable energy projects in Iraq, particularly those targeting reductions in electricity consumption, is the government's subsidy for residential electricity prices, which can be as low as \$0.015 per kWh. This substantial subsidy makes it difficult for competing projects to achieve economic viability. To address this, the present study assumes an average electricity price of \$0.15 per kWh for analysis.

In order to reduce the capital cost and achieve acceptable economic results, a sensitivity analysis was conducted to evaluate the impact of reducing the storage tank volume per cubic meter on the TMVC system's COP. The storage tank is the most expensive component of the system, making it a key focus for cost optimisation. The results, presented in Figure 19, identify the optimum storage tank size for each case and count the percentage change in COP when the storage tank volume is reduced to an acceptable level that maintains the internal temperature within acceptable limits.

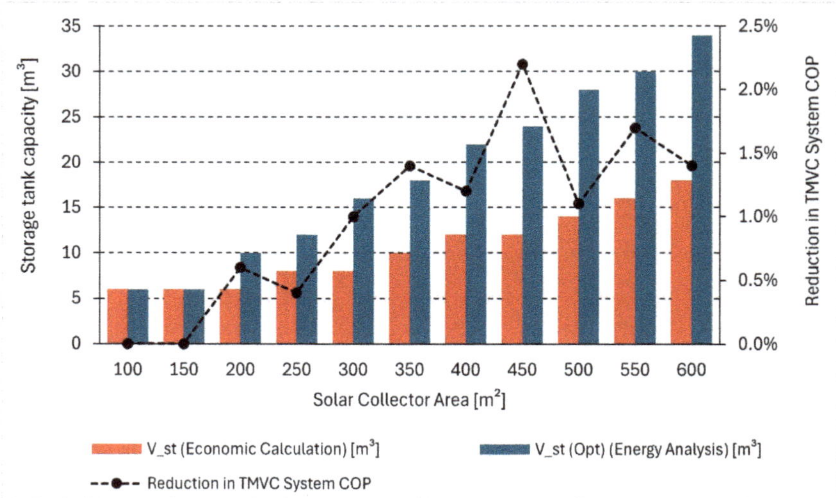

Figure 19. Impact of Storage Tank Volume on TMVC COP.

Figure 20 illustrates the levelised cost of cooling (LCOC) for various configurations of the TMVC system, compared to the baseline vapour compression cycle (BVC) as a reference. As the configurations progress from Case 1 to Case 11, the LCOC generally increases, indicating a rise in the cost of cooling. In configurations with smaller collector areas and storage tank volumes (Cases 1 to 3), the TMVC system achieves a noticeable cost reduction compared to the BVC. Notably, Case 4 achieves an LCOC of 0.053 $/kWh, closely matching the cost of the BVC. Beyond this point, the LCOC continues to rise, with Case 11 exhibiting the highest cost at $0.063/kWh, representing a 16% increase over the baseline.

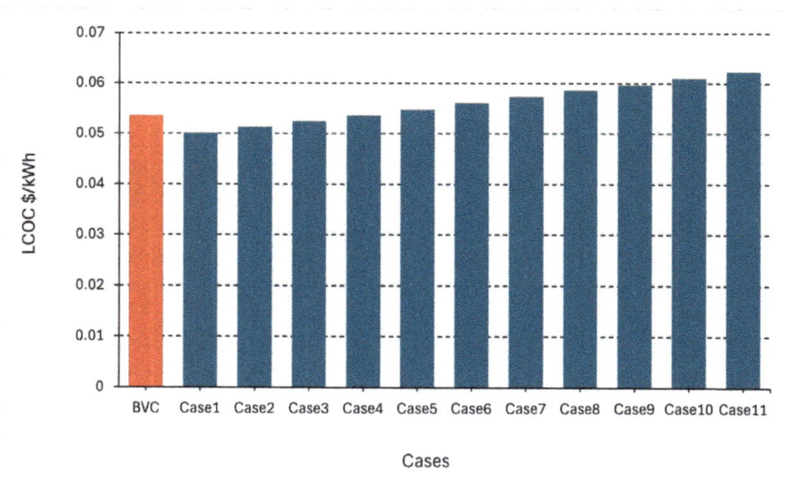

Figure 20. LCOC of the optimum TMVC cases compared to BVC.

Figure 21 illustrates the simple payback period (SPBP) for the various TMVC system configurations. A clear trend is observed: as the collector area and storage tank volume increase across the cases, the SPBP correspondingly rises due to higher capital investment.

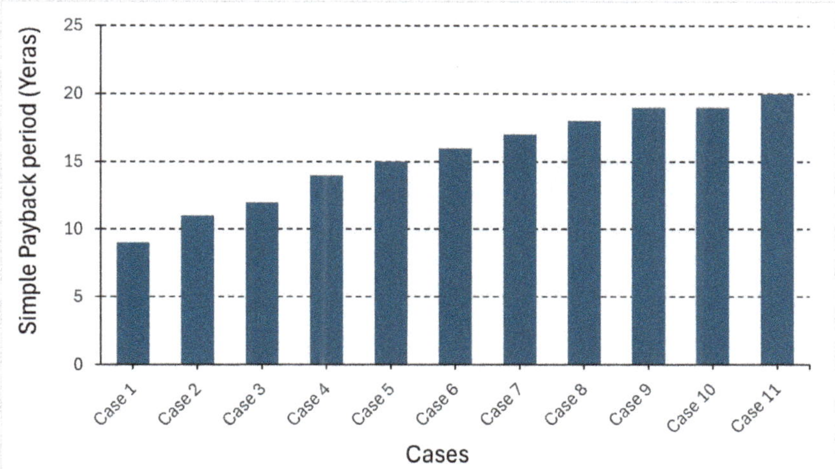

Figure 21. SPBP of the optimum TMVC cases.

Case 1 offers the shortest payback period of 9 years, attributed to its relatively low system cost, while Case 11 exhibits the longest payback period of 20 years despite achieving the highest energy savings and environmental benefits. This highlights the economic-performance trade-off, where configurations with greater sustainability gains (e.g., Case 11) require a longer investment recovery period, whereas lower-cost systems (e.g., Case 1) yield faster returns but more modest energy and emissions reductions.

8.5. Environmental Analysis

The emissions comparison analysed the CO_2 generated from electricity consumption required to operate the BVC and TMVC systems during the summer season, focusing on the reduction achieved by each optimal case. As illustrated in Figure 22, the TMVC system consistently results in lower CO_2 emissions compared to the BVC system. Among the cases, Case 11 stands out as the optimal configuration for emissions reduction, producing 294 tons of CO_2 over the summer, achieving a 21% reduction relative to the BVC system, highlighting its potential for environmental benefits.

8.6. Comprehensive Evaluation Index

In this study, a comprehensive evaluation index method was implemented to rank 11 design cases of a TMVC system based on multiple performance indicators implemented as shown in Figure 23, The approach is adapted from Liu et al., (2022) [43], who proposed a hybrid AHP–entropy method for smart grid evaluation. To simplify and tailor the method for TMVC systems, a two-stage index structure is constructed. The first-level indicators include economy, reliability, environmental impact, and interaction, while the second-level indicators consist of COP improvement, energy saving, solar energy utilization hours, levelised cost of cooling (LCOC), simple payback period (SPBP), CO_2 produced, and required land area for solar equipment installation.

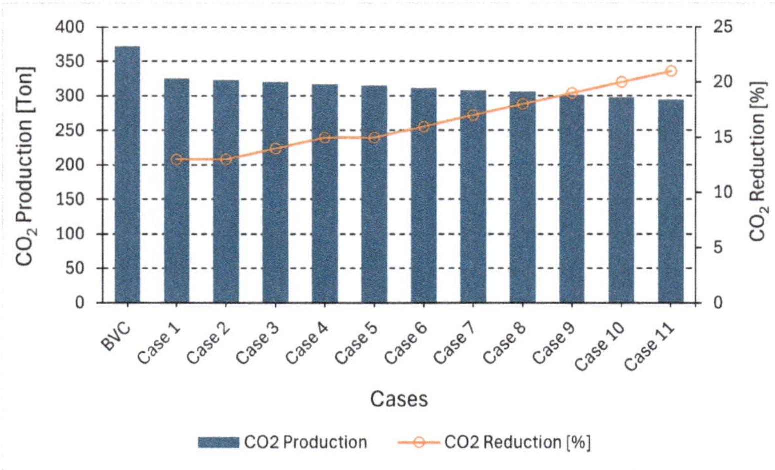

Figure 22. CO_2 emissions and reduction comparison between BVC and TMVC cases.

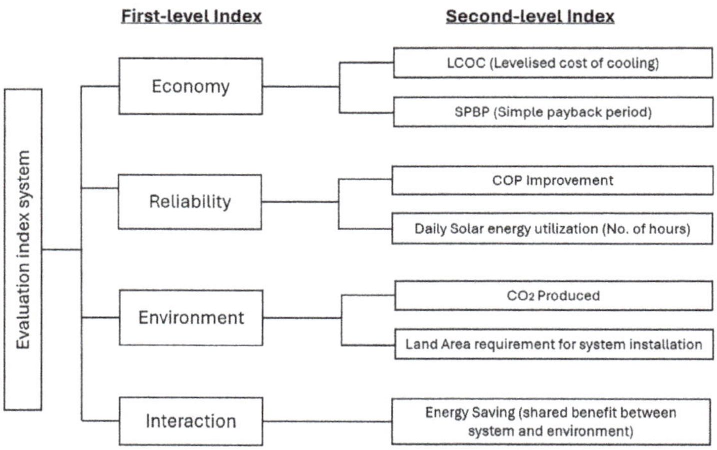

Figure 23. Evaluation index of TMVC system.

The evaluation framework integrates min–max normalisation and the analytic hierarchy process (AHP) to ensure both comparability and rational weighting of diverse criteria.

To ensure comparability across indicators, different units, and scales, min–max normalisation is applied. For benefit indicators like COP improvement, energy savings, and daily solar hours utilisation (*DSU*), where higher values are preferable, normalisation is performed using the following:

$$X' = \frac{X_j - X_{min}}{X_{max} - X_{min}} \tag{27}$$

For cost indicators (e.g., LCOC, SPBP, CO_2 emissions, and land area), where lower values are preferable, normalisation is inverted as follows:

$$X' = \frac{X_{max} - X_j}{X_{max} - X_{min}} \tag{28}$$

This process transforms all values into a [0, 1] range, where 1 denotes the best performance.

The weighting of indicators is determined using the analytic hierarchy process (AHP), a structured decision-making technique that converts qualitative judgments into quantitative weights. Pairwise comparisons are performed between each pair of indicators to construct a judgment matrix. Construct the judgment matrix w_i, and its expression is denoted as follows:

$$w = \begin{bmatrix} & COP_{imp} & ES & DSU & LCOC & SPBP & CO_2 & A_{land} \\ COP_{imp} & 1 & 0.75 & 1 & 1 & 1.5 & 0.75 & 3 \\ ES & 1.333 & 1 & 1.333 & 1.333 & 2 & 1 & 4 \\ DSU & 1 & 0.75 & 1 & 1 & 1.5 & 0.75 & 3 \\ LCOC & 1 & 0.75 & 1 & 1 & 1.5 & 0.75 & 3 \\ SPBP & 0.666 & 0.5 & 0.666 & 0.666 & 1 & 0.5 & 2 \\ CO_2 & 1.333 & 1 & 1.333 & 1.333 & 2 & 1 & 4 \\ A_{land} & 0.333 & 0.25 & 0.333 & 0.333 & 0.5 & 0.25 & 1 \end{bmatrix}$$

Each column of the matrix was normalised by dividing each entry by the sum of its column. The weight vector for each indicator was then derived by taking the average of the normalised rows. The resulting weight of COP improvement, ES, DSU, LCOC, SPBP, CO_2 production, and required land area for solar equipment installation are 0.15, 0.2, 0.15, 0.15, 0.1, 0.2, and 0.05, respectively. These weights align with Iraq's national priorities, which promote sustainable investment and environmental protection. The relatively low weight assigned to the payback period reflects Iraq's capacity to support long-term infrastructure development.

Using these AHP-derived weights w_i, the final comprehensive evaluation score for each TMVC system configuration is computed as a weighted sum of normalised indicator values, as follows:

$$S_i = \sum_1^7 w_i \cdot X_{ji} \tag{29}$$

The final results, as shown in Figure 24, revealed that Case 11 achieved the highest composite score (0.7), indicating the most balanced performance across technical, economic, and environmental criteria. This methodology provides a robust, transparent, and rational basis for multi-criteria decision-making in sustainable cooling system design.

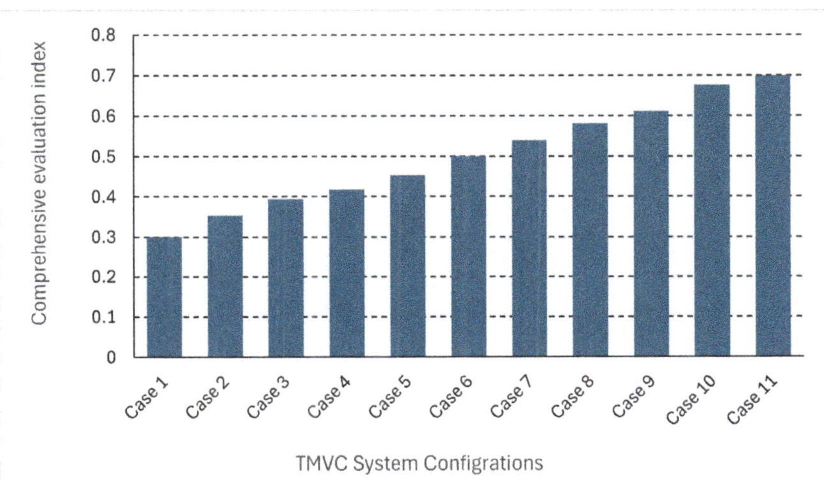

Figure 24. Comprehensive evaluation index for 11 configuration cases.

8.7. Comparison of Economic Index TMVC with Other Systems

According to reference [11], which presents an economic analysis of various solar-assisted cooling systems, including solar thermal absorption (SABC), solar thermal adsorption (SADC), PV-assisted vapour compression (PV-BVC), PVT-assisted absorption (PVT-ABC), and PVT-assisted adsorption (PVT-ADC). The levelised cost of cooling (LCOC) was used as a key indicator to assess their performance across different global cities. In this study, the LCOC of the TMVC case is compared with the average LCOC of each of these solar-assisted systems. As illustrated in Figure 25, TMVC remains economically competitive among other solar cooling technologies and offers a practical solution to reduce electricity consumption in hot climate regions without replacing the existing cooling system, requiring only the integration of solar thermal components.

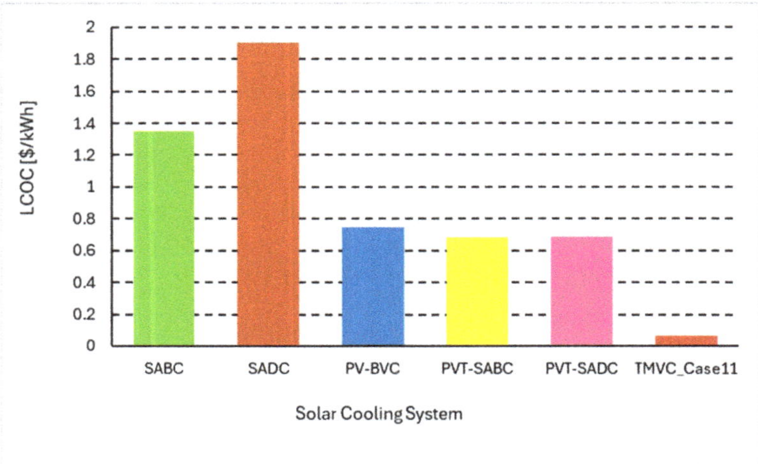

Figure 25. Comparison of LCOC between TMVC and other cooling solar cooling systems.

9. Conclusions

This study evaluated the performance of a solar-assisted thermo-mechanical vapour compression (TMVC) cooling system for multi-story residential buildings in hot climate regions. A comprehensive 4E (energy, exergy, economic, environmental) analysis was conducted using a hybrid simulation approach, where building performance parameters were obtained through DesignBuilder, and system-level simulations and optimisation were performed using MATLAB® R2023b, incorporating real hourly climate data for Baghdad, Iraq.

Eleven system configurations were examined by varying the solar collector area, thermal storage tank volume, and collector mass flow rate. The results showed that increasing the solar field and storage capacity generally enhanced energy performance but also increased system costs. Among the analysed configurations, Case 11 featuring a 600 m^2 solar collector and 34 m^3 storage tank with a collector mass flow rate of 0.02 kg/s was identified as the optimal solution based on a comprehensive evaluation index. It achieved a 28.28% increase in COP, a 22.05% reduction in energy consumption, a 21% reduction in CO_2 emissions, and 15.3 h of average daily solar-assisted operation during summer conditions; however, the daily exergy efficiency drops to below 15% due to irreversibilities such as temperature gradients between the solar collector and the environment, making it a less favourable performance index for the TMVC system. Economically, this case resulted in a simple payback period (SPBP) of 20 years and a levelised cost of cooling (LCOC) of \$0.066/kWh, which, despite being higher than the baseline system by 16%, aligns with the long-term sustainability targets and infrastructure investment priorities outlined in Iraq's national housing and energy policies.

The key advantages of the TMVC system over the conventional vapour compression cycle include shifting part of the compression process to solar thermal input, thereby reducing the mechanical compressor workload. This leads to lower energy consumption and reduces environmental impact, supporting the adoption of sustainable cooling technologies. Additionally, the system offers a scalable solution suitable for multi-story residential buildings or district cooling applications in hot climate zones. Further experimental work is required to evaluate the system's real-world performance and operational reliability.

Author Contributions: Conceptualization, H.A.A.K. and R.B.; methodology, H.A.A.K. and R.B.; software, H.A.A.K.; validation, H.A.A.K.; formal analysis, H.A.A.K.; data curation, H.A.A.K.; writing—original draft preparation, H.A.A.K.; writing—review and editing, H.A.A.K. and R.B.; visualization, H.A.A.K.; supervision, R.B. All authors have read and agreed to the published version of the manuscript.

Funding: This research received no external funding.

Data Availability Statement: Data available upon request.

Acknowledgments: The authors would like to acknowledge "The Higher Committee for Education Development in Iraq" for providing the financial support through a student scholarship.

Conflicts of Interest: The authors declare no conflicts of interest.

Nomenclature

Symbol/Abbreviation	Description
A	Solar collector area (m^2)
CL	Annual cooling energy supplied (kWh)
Cm&o	Annual operation and maintenance cost ($/kWc)
CC	Capital cost of the air conditioning system ($)
COP	Coefficient of performance
COPimp	Improvement in COP (%)
Cond	Condenser
Comp	Compressor
D	Daily
DR	Real interest rate (adjusted for inflation)
DSU	Daily solar energy utilisation in hours
EP	Electricity tariff ($/kWh)
ES	Energy savings (%)
Eth	Thermal exergy (pressure vessel)
Evp	Evaporator
Ex	Exergy flow
f	CO_2 emission factor for electricity (kg CO_2/kWh)
I	Solar irradiance [W/m^2]
LCOC	Levelised cost of cooling ($/kWh)
ηcol	Thermal efficiency of solar collector (%)
$\eta col,exe$	Exergy efficiency of solar collector (%)
$\eta sys,exe$	System exergy efficiency (%)
Opt	Optimum
Qcond	Condenser heat rejection (kW)
Qth	Heat input to thermal storage (kW)
Qu	Heat gain through solar collector (kW)
Sm	Collector mass flow rate per unit area ($kg/s{\cdot}m^2$)

SOH	Annual solar operation hours (h/year)
Tcol,i	Inlet temperature to solar collector (°C)
Tevp	Evaporator temperature (°C)
Tamb	Ambient temperature (°C)
Tsun	Apparent sun temperature (K)
thr	Threshold
U	Overall heat transfer coefficient [W/m^2 k]
Vst	Storage tank volume (m^3)
$\dot{m}$	Mass flow rate (kg/s)
ρg	Ground reflectance (albedo)
TMVC	Thermo-mechanical vapour compression
BVC	Basic vapour compression
EFPC	Evacuated flat plate collector
TES	Thermal energy storage
HVAC	Heating, ventilation, and air conditioning
4E	Energy, exergy, economic, and environmental

References

1. Alsouda, F.; Bennett, N.S.; Saha, S.C.; Salehi, F.; Islam, M.S. Vapor Compression Cycle: A State-of-the-Art Review on Cycle Improvements, Water and Other Natural Refrigerants. *Clean Technol.* **2023**, *5*, 584–608. [CrossRef]
2. Al Khiro, H.A.; Boukhanouf, R. Energy and Exergy Performance Analysis of Solar-Assisted Thermo-Mechanical Vapor Compression Cooling System. *Sustainability* **2024**, *16*, 8625. [CrossRef]
3. Rashid, F.L.; Eleiwi, M.A.; Mohammed, H.I.; Ameen, A.; Ahmad, S. A Review of Using Solar Energy for Cooling Systems: Applications, Challenges, and Effects. *Energies* **2023**, *16*, 8075. [CrossRef]
4. Alazazmeh, A.J.; Mokheimer, E.M. Review of solar cooling technologies. *J. Appl. Mech. Eng.* **2015**, *4*, 180–194. [CrossRef]
5. Kostadin, F. *The Future of Cooling: Opportunities for Energy Efficient Air Conditioning*; International Energy Agency: Paris, France, 2018.
6. Ismaen, R.; Kucukvar, M.; El Mekkawy, T.Y.; Elomri, A. Optimization and enviro-economic assessment of solar-cooling systems towards sustainable development: A case study of Qatar. *J. Clean. Prod.* **2023**, *419*, 138253. [CrossRef]
7. Salameh, T.; Alkhalidi, A.; Rabaia, M.K.H.; Al Swailmeen, Y.; Alroujmah, W.; Ibrahim, M.; Abdelkareem, M.A. Optimization and life cycle analysis of solar-powered absorption chiller designed for a small house in the United Arab Emirates using evacuated tube technology. *Renew. Energy* **2022**, *198*, 200–212. [CrossRef]
8. Albatayneh, A.; Jaradat, M.; Al-Omary, M.; Zaquot, M. Evaluation of Coupling PV and Air Conditioning vs. Solar Cooling Systems—Case Study from Jordan. *Appl. Sci.* **2021**, *11*, 511. [CrossRef]
9. Herrando, M.; Pantaleo, A.M.; Wang, K.; Markides, C.N. Solar combined cooling, heating and power systems based on hybrid PVT, PV or solar-thermal collectors for building applications. *Renew. Energy* **2019**, *143*, 637–647. [CrossRef]
10. Franchini, G.; Brumana, G.; Perdichizzi, A. Performance prediction of a solar district cooling system in Riyadh, Saudi Arabia—A case study. *Energy Convers. Manag.* **2018**, *166*, 372–384. [CrossRef]
11. Mortadi, M.; El Fadar, A. Performance, economic and environmental assessment of solar cooling systems under various climates. *Energy Convers. Manag.* **2022**, *252*, 114993. [CrossRef]
12. Mortadi, M.; El Fadar, A. Cost-effective and environmentally friendly solar collector for thermally driven cooling systems. *Appl. Therm. Eng.* **2022**, *217*, 119234. [CrossRef]
13. Bellos, E.; Tzivanidis, C. A detailed investigation of an evacuated flat plate solar collector. *Appl. Therm. Eng.* **2023**, *234*, 121334. [CrossRef]
14. Al-Yasiri, Q.; Szabó, M.; Szabo, M. Solar absorption cooling systems versus traditional air-conditioning in hot climate. *Res. Dev. Mech. Eng. Lett. Szent István Univ.* **2016**, *14*, 9–16. Available online: https://www.researchgate.net/publication/327781210 (accessed on 2 January 2025).
15. Palomba, V.; Wittstadt, U.; Bonanno, A.; Tanne, M.; Harborth, N.; Vasta, S. Components and design guidelines for solar cooling systems: The experience of ZEOSOL. *Renew. Energy* **2019**, *141*, 678–692. [CrossRef]
16. Republic of Iraq Presidency of Council of Ministers National Investment Commission. Available online: www.nici.gov.iq (accessed on 14 January 2025).
17. U.S. Department of Energy. *Getting Start*; EnergyPlus*TM* Version 22.2.0; U.S. Department of Energy: Washington, DC, USA, 2022.
18. Ministry of Construction, Housing, Municipalities, and Public Works, Iraq. Available online: https://iccts.moch.gov.iq/ (accessed on 2 January 2025).

19. Mustafa, M.; Ali, S.; Snape, J.R.; Vand, B. Investigations towards lower cooling load in a typical residential building in Kurdistan (Iraq). *Energy Rep.* **2020**, *6*, 571–580. [CrossRef]
20. Ministry of Agriculture, Iraq. Available online: https://www.agromet.gov.iq/ (accessed on 2 January 2025).
21. Duffie, J.A.; Beckman, W.A.; Worek, W.M. *Solar Engineering of Thermal Processes*; John Wiley & Sons, Inc.: Hoboken, NJ, USA, 2013; p. 928.
22. Ibrahim, Z.; Aljanabi, M. Influence of Tilt Angle on PV Output for Solar Energy Optimization in Iraq. *Salud Cienc. Tecnol.-Ser. Conferencias* **2024**, *3*, 871. [CrossRef]
23. TVP Solar. Available online: https://www.tvpsolar.com (accessed on 26 March 2023).
24. The Solar Keymark, CEN Keymark Scheme, Database. Available online: https://solarkeymark.eu/database/ (accessed on 20 April 2024).
25. Solar Keymark. *Solar Keymark, Test Report, 2025*; Test License no. 011-7S1890 S; Solar Keymark: Stuttgart, Germany, 2025; Available online: https://www.duurzaamloket.nl/DBF/PDF_Downloads/DS_495.pdf (accessed on 21 May 2025).
26. Tesfamichael, T.; Wackelgard, E. Angular solar absorptance and incident angle modifier of selective absorbers for solar thermal collectors. *Sol. Energy* **2000**, *68*, 335–341. Available online: www.elsevier.com/locate/solener (accessed on 14 June 2023). [CrossRef]
27. Sabiha, M.A.; Saidur, R.; Mekhilef, S.; Mahian, O. Progress and latest developments of evacuated tube solar collectors. *Renew. Sustain. Energy Rev.* **2015**, *51*, 1038–1054. [CrossRef]
28. Saloux, E.; Candanedo, J. Modelling stratified thermal energy storage tanks using an advanced flowrate distribution of the received flow. *Appl. Energy* **2019**, *241*, 34–45. [CrossRef]
29. Saloux, E.; Candanedo, J.A. Control-oriented modelling of stratified storage tanks: An enhanced approach. In Proceedings of the eSim 2018, the 10th Conference of IBPSA-Canada, Montréal, QC, Canada, 9–10 May 2018; pp. 193–201.
30. Al Khiro, H.A.; Boukhanouf, R. Analytical and computer modelling of a thermo-mechanical vapour compression system for space air conditioning in buildings. *Energy Convers. Manag.* **2025**, *323*, 119252. [CrossRef]
31. Bellos, E.; Tzivanidis, C.; Symeou, C.; Antonopoulos, K.A. Energetic, exergetic and financial evaluation of a solar driven absorption chiller—A dynamic approach. *Energy Convers. Manag.* **2017**, *137*, 34–48. [CrossRef]
32. Sangi, R.; Müller, D. Implementation of a solution to the problem of reference environment in the exergy evaluation of building energy systems. *Energy* **2018**, *149*, 830–836. [CrossRef]
33. Evola, G.; Costanzo, V.; Marletta, L. Exergy Analysis of Energy Systems in Buildings. *Buildings* **2018**, *8*, 180. [CrossRef]
34. Ge, Z.; Wang, H.; Wang, H.; Zhang, S.; Guan, X. Exergy Analysis of Flat Plate Solar Collectors. *Entropy* **2014**, *16*, 2549–2567. [CrossRef]
35. Petela, R. Exergy of undiluted thermal radiation. *Sol. Energy* **2003**, *74*, 469–488. [CrossRef]
36. Kalogirou, S.A. Solar thermal collectors and applications. *Prog. Energy Combust. Sci.* **2004**, *30*, 231–295. [CrossRef]
37. Rong, Y.; Zhi, X.; Wang, K.; Zhou, X.; Cheng, X.; Qiu, L.; Chi, X. Thermoeconomic analysis on a cascade energy utilization system for compression heat in air separation units. *Energy Convers. Manag.* **2020**, *213*, 112820. [CrossRef]
38. Jain, V.; Sachdeva, G.; Kachhwaha, S.S. Energy, exergy, economic and environmental (4E) analyses based comparative performance study and optimization of vapor compression-absorption integrated refrigeration system. *Energy* **2015**, *91*, 816–832. [CrossRef]
39. Yilmaz, C. Thermodynamic and economic investigation of geothermal powered absorption cooling system for buildings. *Geothermics* **2017**, *70*, 239–248. [CrossRef]
40. Al-Okbi, A.K.; Vankov, Y.V.; Ziganshin, S.G.; Ali, A.H.H. Investigating the Performance of Solar Thermal Assisted Air Conditioning System Under the Summer Season of Baghdad, Iraq. In Proceedings of the 2024 6th International Youth Conference on Radio Electronics, Electrical and Power Engineering (REEPE), Cairo, Egypt, 29 February 2024; Institute of Electrical and Electronics Engineers Inc.: Piscataway, NJ, USA, 2024; pp. 1–7.
41. Zhang, C.; Hou, B.; Li, M.; Dang, C.; Tong, H.; Li, X.; Han, Z. Refrigerant charge estimation method based on data-physic hybrid-driven model for the fault diagnosis of transcritical CO2 heat pump system. *Energy* **2024**, *309*, 133144. [CrossRef]
42. Cadau, N.; De Lorenzi, A.; Gambarotta, A.; Morini, M.; Rossi, M. Development and Analysis of a Multi-Node Dynamic Model for the Simulation of Stratified Thermal Energy Storage. *Energies* **2019**, *12*, 4275. [CrossRef]
43. Liu, Z.; Xie, Q.; Dai, L.; Wang, H.; Deng, L.; Wang, C.; Zhang, Y.; Zhou, X.; Yang, C.; Xiang, C.; et al. Research on comprehensive evaluation method of distribution network based on AHP-entropy weighting method. *Front. Energy Res.* **2022**, *10*, 975462. [CrossRef]

energies

MDPI

Article

Balancing the Interests of Various Community Groups in Local Government Policy on the Energy Performance of Buildings

Girts Karnitis [1], Maris Pukis [2], Janis Bicevskis [1], Edgars Diebelis [1], Stanislavs Gendelis [3], Edvins Karnitis [1,*] and Ugis Sarma [1]

[1] Department of Computer Science, Faculty of Science and Technology, University of Latvia, 1586 Riga, Latvia; girts.karnitis@lu.lv (G.K.); janis.bicevskis@lu.lv (J.B.); edgars.diebelis@lu.lv (E.D.); ugis.sarma@lu.lv (U.S.)

[2] Scientific Institute of Economics and Management, Faculty of Economics and Social Sciences, University of Latvia, 1586 Riga, Latvia; maris.pukis@lu.lv

[3] Institute of Numerical Modelling, Faculty of Science and Technology, University of Latvia, 1586 Riga, Latvia; stanislavs.gendelis@lu.lv

* Correspondence: edvins.karnitis@lu.lv; Tel.: +371-9120475

Abstract: EU legislation provides the implementation of most building energy performance measures at a subnational level. This obligation is causing a lot of completely new dilemmas that are challenging for local governments (LGs), requiring a radical re-evaluation of the prioritization of LGs' traditional tasks and the ranking of new responsibilities. The attitude of local population and businesses towards the solutions to dilemmas, which are set by LGs decisions, vary widely. Separate groups actively lobby for their mutually contradictory interests, questioning decisions and fighting against them during the decision-drafting and -making process, significantly hindering the work of LGs and prolonging decision-making. The authors' suggested solution to the problem is to make municipal decisions based on verifiable data and facts, thus preventing the manifestations of populism and demagogy, and reducing the possibilities for interest group advocacy. To obtain objective information for balanced decision-making about the benefits and costs of heating system retrofitting projects without carrying out the labor-intensive, time-consuming, and costly design of various options, an express methodology and an easy-to-use tool for project feasibility studies have been developed. The methodology utilizes a limited number of open indicators to streamline the evaluation process, and does not require specific knowledge in thermal physics, economics, or construction.

Keywords: Green Deal policy; the energy performance of buildings; local governments; interest groups; heating simulation

1. Introduction

The promotion of building energy performance, like other Green Deal (GD) initiatives, faces the challenge of competing interests. Although citizens across EU member states expressed strong support for global green policies—including those aimed at improving building energy efficiency—during the 2024 European Parliament elections [1], the priorities of countries, municipalities, industries, households, and other stakeholders often diverge and conflict.

"Local and regional governments are vital for the success and realization of green policies across Europe" [2]. Amendments to EU directives under the Fit for 55 (FF55) legislative package [3–5] have assigned key energy efficiency responsibilities to subnational governments. The European Charter of Local Self-Government [6] has standardized the systems of local governance across Europe and defined their relationships with national governments and citizens. As a result, differences in how local governments (LGs) approach building energy performance within GD initiatives are less influenced by institutional structures and more by contextual factors such as energy supply, climate, historical construction practices, and, importantly, the habits and often contradictory attitudes of local communities.

In the area of building energy performance, the FF55 directives have imposed entirely new and unfamiliar obligations on municipalities. While most energy efficiency measures must be implemented at the subnational level, the EU does not provide sufficient funding to cover the full cost of these projects. Instead, entrepreneurs and households are expected to bear much of the financial burden. As with the GD as a whole, building energy performance programs "can only work if they allow local businesses and civil society to lead the way" [7]. The role of LGs as intermediaries is therefore essential [8] in persuading building owners to invest in retrofitting projects that may have long payback periods.

The initial plans of the GD have been significantly disrupted by the Russian invasion of Ukraine, prompting a reassessment of strategic priorities across Europe. The EU as a whole and many countries have shifted their focus toward enhancing national defense capabilities. This general trend includes increasingly new settings and measures [9]. EU citizens support both implementing common defense and security policies and reinforcing EU capacity to produce military equipment. Ukraine's experience illustrates that, in the event of military conflict, municipalities may become direct targets of missile and drone attacks—posing serious challenges for civil protection systems tasked with maintaining safety and basic services, even amid damaged energy infrastructure.

In the Baltic Sea region, the prevailing approach is to hope for the best but prepare for the worst. In Latvia, civil protection has become an autonomous responsibility of municipalities as part of the national security system. LGs are now expected to provide comprehensive support for both national defense and civilian resilience. This includes (but is not limited to) preparing information systems for residents, establishing civil protection units, maintaining bomb shelters, and organizing the means and resources for the controlled evacuation or accommodation of residents and refugees in the event of war or military threat.

The new, high-stakes obligations—arising both from the FF55 settings on building energy efficiency and the urgent realities of national security—necessitate a re-evaluation of how LGs prioritize their traditional responsibilities, such as education, healthcare, social services, territorial planning, business development, etc. At the same time, LGs must re-rank and integrate emerging responsibilities into their strategic agendas.

The ongoing geopolitical tensions have contributed to global polarization [10], which, in turn, has led to increasing societal fragmentation at the national level and growing social stratification within local communities. This environment has heightened contradictions and intolerance between different social groups [11].

Despite these challenges, local communities want improvement in the quality of life and alignment with shared societal ideals, and progress towards economic and energy sustainability in the area, including a reduction in the burden of heat costs on household budgets (in 2024, 9.2% of the EU27 population reported struggling to keep their homes warm [12]).

However, residents' preferences vary significantly. In organized civil society, interest groups—including business organizations and climate activists—actively lobby public authorities to shape socioeconomic development, legislation, and other issues at all levels of governance. Even passive citizens influence decision-making, as building energy performance policies are often debated in public discourse and social communication.

Given this complex internal and external environment, LGs must now more than ever ensure their decisions align with EU and national strategies while also considering the diverse interests of local communities and business stakeholders. The decision-making process needs to be both faster and more deliberate. Only carefully considered, balanced, and data- and fact-driven decisions should be adopted. Such an approach helps limit the ability of interest groups to unduly influence policy in their favor, ensuring a fairer balance among the various interests represented within the population.

The influence of interest groups on forming climate policy has been studied extensively, particularly in the context of national lobbying efforts and policy positioning [13–17]. These also reflects the opposition towards renewable energy issues from local communities [18–23]. However, research on how local interests affect climate and environmental policies is fragmented across themes, such as whether public participation leads to the more ambitious, transformative local governance of climate policy [24–27] and various another green issues [28–31]. It should be noted that there is also a contradictory position regarding many other LG policy issues (e.g., [32–34]). However, the authors have found no study examining the influence of interest representation on LGs' autonomous decisions in GD related issues.

A more effective approach is to study current and potential interactions between municipalities and interest groups within a specific national context. Latvia, with its moderate level of local government decentralization compared to other EU27 countries [35], presents a suitable environment for examining autonomous decision-making processes at the municipal level.

2. Materials and Methods

LGs act in the interest of their residents by fulfilling both delegated responsibilities (as agents) and autonomous functions (as owners). In the areas of delegated authority, LGs have limited flexibility, as they are bound by EU regulations, transposed directives, and national policy documents (Figure 1) [6]. For example, municipalities typically support GD initiatives funded by the EU or national governments, as these projects often boost local employment and welfare in the short term. However, when additional local resources are required, LGs tend to conduct more comprehensive evaluations, which may include consultations with interest groups such as business associations, residents' councils, and NGOs.

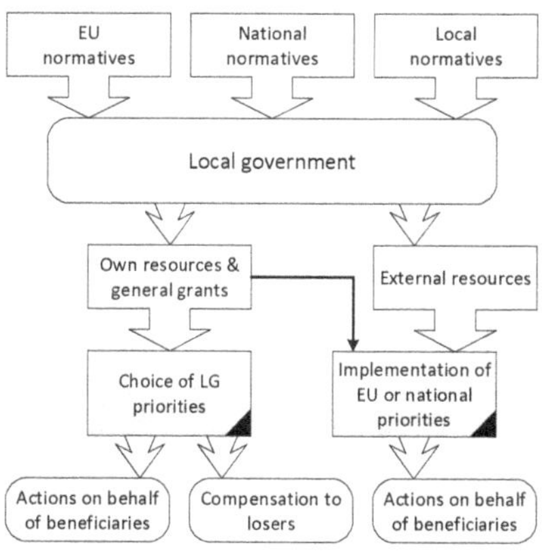

Figure 1. Interests, resources, and the choice of LG priorities. Developed by the authors.

In the areas of autonomous competence, local governments (LGs) also apply regulations adopted at the municipal level. Local priorities are shaped by a combination of EU, national, and local interests, many of which are in conflict. LGs typically analyze policy options by weighing the potential benefits for supporting groups against the possible disadvantages for opposing ones. Increasingly, municipalities are expected to implement actions that benefit certain stakeholders while also offering proportional compensation or mitigation to those negatively affected.

The perspectives of the active members of organized civil society are considered through structured dialogues with various interest groups. When balancing competing preferences, LGs seek to clarify key interests, assess their relevance to building energy performance measures, and evaluate expected outcomes against public expectations. The positions of less active or disengaged citizens are also significant; through public discourse—especially on social media—they can voice strong opposition to initiatives they feel do not reflect their needs or values. These collective assessments inform the development of municipal policy and action plans.

To better understand the types of interests that must be balanced in building energy performance decisions, the authors analyzed publicly available records from discussions on national drafts of the Climate Law [36] and the Transport Energy Law [37], both of which transpose relevant EU directives. The reviews and opinions submitted during these discussions—by ministries, public agencies, business associations, trade unions, municipal associations, and individual activists (e.g., entrepreneurs and environmental advocates)—generally reflect the stance of organized civil society on GD initiatives in the geopolitical context of 2024 (Figure 2).

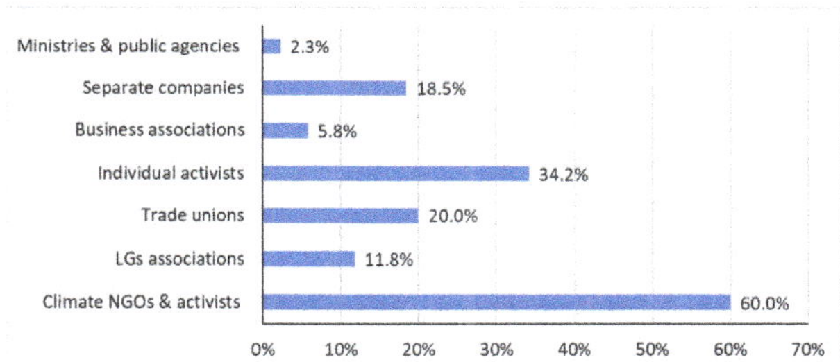

Figure 2. Percentage of opinions based on GD ideology. Source: State Chancellery.

Interest groups participating in national policy debates primarily aim to align GD-related issues with their economic, security, and social objectives. Values-based or ideological motivations are evident primarily among climate activists and related organizations. It is reasonable to assume that similar dynamics are at play at the local level. This is underscored by the rhetoric of many political parties ahead of the 2025 local elections, where the green agenda is frequently criticized as disproportionate, unrealistic, and overly costly.

When implementing building energy performance tasks, LGs often face complex dilemmas in drafting rational and equitable decisions. In a broader sense, rational decisions may be guided by both values and material or other interests. In addition to evaluating the diverse benefits for specific stakeholder groups, LGs can also employ sociological tools—such as surveys or referendums—as direct democracy methods to gauge public sentiment. The higher the degree of pluralism within a community, the more diverse the values, which must be considered.

The dilemmas that may arise across more than one hundred thousand European municipalities [35] vary greatly in content and context. Conflicts can emerge from nearly any of the 20 recommended GD action lines [8], each of which interest groups attempt to influence, some advocating for more radical approaches, others opposing the initiatives altogether. Examples of such dilemmas include (but are not limited to) the following:

- Limited municipal budgets are already stretched thin by mandatory functions such as education, social programs, and other legal obligations. Both new demands—enhancing resilience to security threats and improving building energy efficiency—will inevitably compete for the same financial resources.
- Renovation costs for energy-poor households in apartment buildings (typically around 10% of households) cannot be covered without informing and involving other households. Targeted funding from EU programs and/or from national funds will be used to fight energy poverty, while other households will be pressed to take out long-term bank loans. LGs should offer financial instruments that internalize energy cost savings for loan repayments [2].
- The EU and national financial resources are insufficient to fully eliminate household energy poverty. Redirecting municipal funds toward urgent renovations for the most vulnerable could delay the implementation of other development programs, thus impacting broader socioeconomic progress within the municipality.
- Each renovated building, as well as individuals or local energy communities who seek to optimize their own centralized heat consumption, lessens the load on the district heating (DH) network. However, since network heat losses remain constant, reduced consumption increases the unit cost for other network users.
- Building energy performance is increasingly associated with limiting biomass combustion for heating in favor of emission-free technologies. Renewable woody biomass has been and remains economically beneficial both in individual buildings and in DH systems (woody biomass was the primary resource for 63% of the centrally produced heat in Latvia in 2023), reducing heating costs.
- Linking building energy performance upgrades with the development of electric mobility infrastructure—such as the installation of charging points—poses a challenge for the effective allocation of retrofitting budgets.

Dilemmas such as these, brought about by stringent building energy performance requirements, fall outside the traditional scope of municipal governance. These are not the kinds of decisions LGs have faced in the past. Consequently, new frameworks, approaches, and methods are essential to navigate the evolving landscape of responsibilities.

Elected local politicians, as individuals, participate in collective decision-making within LGs, often acting—consciously or not—according to the principles of rational choice theory (e.g., [38]). This theory suggests that if each actor behaves rationally based on their own understanding, collective decision-making can result in balanced outcomes. These outcomes aim to maximize benefits for supporting groups while minimizing harm to opposing ones, achieving the greatest possible advantage within existing constraints. Although this approach has been criticized for its oversimplification [39], it remains a useful framework for explaining causal relationships in many decision-making scenarios.

Naturally, each decision-maker's choices are influenced by their own subjective interests. In this context, local government members are elected officials, many of whom seek re-election. As the green transformation shifts from a political slogan to a central element of EU and national policy, it increasingly faces skepticism from segments of the electorate who view it as costly and unnecessarily disruptive to their daily lives. According to a 2024 survey [2], 67% of voters indicated that the regulatory framework surrounding the green transition will influence their choices in upcoming municipal and national elections. This voter sentiment inevitably impacts the positions and decisions of LG officials.

The persistent tensions among political, economic, and social interest groups, which are intensified by the current geopolitical climate, make balanced decision-making more critical than ever. Any shift favoring one group over another may lead to long-term consequences, including instability within the municipality. To formulate rational policies, calculations must be made to determine how to achieve the best possible outcomes for the community, while also acknowledging the personal and political interests of decision-makers.

Rational actors make decisions based on the information and calculations available to them [39]. However, public opinion and group stances are shaped not only by objective data but also by other influential sources, such as media messaging, political advocacy, and propaganda, as well as by the general level of information literacy.

The availability of high-quality information is the first and most critical requirement for rational decision-making: "To make decisions, expert stakeholders need to incorporate both research-based and economic information for effective decision-making" [22]. A lack of information is the greatest obstacle to rational choice. In the case of building energy performance, to find optimal solutions in the complex combination of interests of various groups, a quantitative assessment of the retrofitting projects' benefits is necessary for the following: (1) decision-drafting by LG's administrative staff, (2) informed decision-making by elected local politicians, (3) evidence-based dialogue with interest groups, and (4) persuading residents and businesses to invest in building renovation.

Numerous methodologies and tools have been proposed for evaluating retrofitting scenarios. The renovation of individual buildings is the most studied issue. These methodologies are based on various approaches, predominantly but not exclusively addressing economic (e.g., [40]), sustainable (e.g., [41]), architectural (e.g., [42]), and environmental (e.g., [43]) aspects and benefits. Research in this area includes both theoretical and experience-based studies (e.g., [44]).

Methodologies have also been developed for the large-scale retrofitting of building blocks [45] and for buildings with centralized or local energy sources [46,47]. Along with the calculators from pipe manufacturers [48], the integration of the heating system's reconstruction with the transition to the 4G district heating (DH) system [49] and the projected impact of global warming on heat consumption [50] has also been studied. An urban model based on energy prosumption within building blocks has been described [51].

However, the proposed methodologies are poorly usable for pre-design modelling and for evaluating the specific benefits of projects from the dual perspective of the following: (1) the LGs' interests in the sustainable socioeconomic development of their territories, and (2) the interests of the residents and entrepreneurs in reducing heating costs.

To address this gap, an express methodology and a user-friendly tool have been developed to ensure that objective, accessible information about heating system retrofitting projects is available to all stakeholders. This tool provides the following benefits: (1) enables rapid and, at the same time, sufficiently accurate and objective analysis at the pre-design stage of the potential benefits and costs of the various heating system renovation projects' variants in a given area, (2) compares project variants according to their efficiency, (3) uses a limited number of open indicators to speed up the data gathering process, and (4) does not require specialized knowledge in thermal physics, economics, IT, and/or construction, making it practical for use by LG staff and elected officials alike.

3. Results

The obligation to identify optimal solutions within a complex landscape of competing interests, and the need to persuade residents and businesses to invest in building renovations highlights the critical importance for local governments (LGs) to assess the efficiency of diverse heating system retrofitting projects and their alternatives already at the feasibility study stage. Given the significant energy efficiency potential of integrated urban heating systems, the developed methodology and tool were designed not only for evaluating individual building energy performance projects, but also for complex and scalable solutions, such as the retrofitting of district and neighborhood-based heating systems.

3.1. Methodology

The developed methodology enables the flexible, rapid, and sufficiently accurate and objective simulation of potential outcomes and benefits from various reconstruction projects and their variants at the pre-design stage [52]. This tool is designed as an innovation sandbox, which is intended for the simulation, evaluation, and comparison of various renovation/modernization project versions of the overall heating system (including heated buildings, district heating network, and heat sources) for the composition of the application/project that meets the specific funding or project tender conditions to maximize the following key aspects of its efficiency:

- Achievable savings in heat consumption and primary energy resources;
- The reduction in dominant CO_2 emissions;
- Required investments;
- Changes in heating tariffs and costs.

The methodology includes entering and processing key thermal, constructive, structural, and financial data related to the specific elements of the project components. By modifying the values of the indicators associated with these elements, users can generate multiple versions of the reconstruction project. This allows for comparative analysis and identification of the most efficient and cost-effective solutions.

3.2. Defining Key Performance Indicators

The methodology's algorithm calculates the heat consumption savings ΔQ directly, focusing only on aspects influenced by the retrofitting process while ignoring those that remain unaffected [52]. This algorithm was selected due to its efficiency. When developing a functional model of a heating system for retrofitting, a critical prerequisite for the tool's broad and effective use was the reduction in the number of indicators used to characterize the system elements; this was achieved through the definition of key performance indicators (KPIs). This was carried out in two stages.

Aspects that remain constant and could be excluded from the calculations were identified in the first stage:

- The geographical orientation of the building, i.e., also the solar gains;
- The functionality of the building, i.e., also the internal heat gains (equipment and facilities, building occupants, etc.) and hot water consumption;
- The structural dimensions of the building, i.e., the dimensions of the windows, roof, exterior doors, etc.;
- The internal heating pipe network within the building;
- The topography of the DH pipe network;
- The efficiency of the specific primary energy resource utilization;
- The fixed costs of operating the heat sources.

Before classifying these aspects as constants, their impact on the system's heat balance was rigorously assessed. The exclusion of internal and solar heat gains from the building's heat balance was particularly significant, given that these gains can account for 20–50% of total heat consumption, as demonstrated by energy certificate data from the State Construction Control Bureau.

Due to the inaccuracies of current methods in fully calculating these gains, we progressed beyond thermal transmittance calculations and conducted empirical tests on the specific heat capacity of various building materials. This included assessing changes in thermal mass following wall insulation [53]. The test results confirmed that the influence of insulation material on a building's overall thermal mass did not exceed 1%, which justified treating both internal and solar gains as constants for our purposes.

In the second stage, certain simplifications were applied to facilitate calculations while maintaining an acceptable level of accuracy. The methodology for the selection of less important entities included the per-element modelling of heat losses and subsequent expert assessment of the entities' fixed values. Only the KPIs remained necessary as independent variables for their use in calculations of the elements' models while heat loss ΔQ was the dependent variable of the models in all cases. The following key assumptions and generalizations were applied; those for building elements are shown in Figure 3.

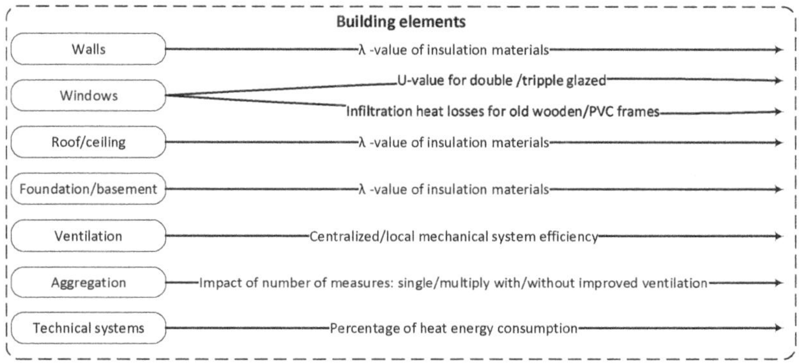

Figure 3. Fixed indicators for the calculation of building elements. Developed by the authors.

The thermal conductivity (lambda value), expressed in W/(m∗K), of the widely used insulating materials varies only slightly, allowing for a fixed value of 0.04 W/(m∗K) to be assumed. For example, mineral wool typically ranges between 0.034–0.042 W/(m∗K), expanded polystyrene (EPS) falls within 0.032–0.038 W/(m∗K), and extruded polystyrene (XPS) varies between 0.030–0.038 W/(m∗K). This approximation is supported by data from material manufacturers, standard values in building energy efficiency guidelines, and research overview articles [54–56]. Additionally, various correction factors, such as the influence of temperature and moisture content, marginally increase the lambda values [57]. Similarly, thermal bridges—such as mounting brackets or the installation details of window frames — also can be considered as an increase in the effective lambda value for calculations [58]. The insulation thickness is the only independent variable in the model.

The windows thermal transmittance (U-value), expressed in W/(m^2∗K), depends mainly on the glazing type. A modern double-glazed window typically exhibits a U-value in the range of 1.3–1.7 W/(m^2∗K), while a triple-glazed window exhibits a U-value as low as 0.6–0.9 W/(m^2∗K). This approach aligns with standard practices outlined in EN ISO 10077−1 and research papers [59–61]. For modelling purposes, fixed representative U-values of 1.6 W/(m^2∗K) and 0.8 W/(m^2∗K) accordingly were used, based on the prevalent window types (which remain the single independent variable), which also considers the effects of installing a thermal bridge [58].

Replacing old, non-airtight windows with modern ones significantly reduces convective heat losses. Older, poorly sealed, and often mechanically deformed windows contribute to higher air infiltration rates, increasing heat losses due to uncontrolled ventilation. Studies [62–64] indicate that replacing outdated windows with tight-sealing and double or triple glazing can reduce air leakage by up to 20%, leading to a notable decrease in the overall convective heat losses. To quantify the reduction in air leakage, blower door tests are commonly employed [65]. For modelling, infiltration heat losses were reduced by 20% in cases involving the replacement of old wooden windows, and by 10% when replacing existing PVC windows.

Replacing a natural ventilation system with a mechanical one with heat recovery can significantly reduce convective heat losses by ΔQvent. Depending on the type of heat recovery system used (an independent variable), ventilation-related heat losses can be reduced by 80% in the case of a central air handling unit [66,67]. The installation of decentralized mechanical systems can be incorporated into heat balance modes with an effective heat recovery rate of 50% for long operation cycles [68]. This improvement is highly effective in colder climates, where uncontrolled ventilation leads to significant energy losses.

Interactions between multiple renovation measures must also be considered. The reduction in heat demand resulting from the renovation of building envelope structures and the installation of a mechanical ventilation system can be assessed separately. However, when multiple energy efficiency measures are implemented simultaneously, the total reduction in heat consumption is not an arithmetic sum of the individual savings due to their interdependencies (a *non-additive effect*) [69].

The mathematical modelling of various building types, incorporating multiple energy efficiency measures in different combinations, enables the estimation of an empirical impact reduction factor (fr). This factor accounts for the interdependence between measures and depends on both the number and type of improvements applied, as follows:

- When a single measure is implemented, fr = 1;
- When multiple building envelope components are renovated without improvements to the ventilation system, fr = 0.85 (range 0.79–0.92);
- When multiple building envelope components are renovated, including a mechanical ventilation system, fr = 0.75 (range 0.70–0.81).

Although the actual value of fr may vary depending on the building type, climate, existing conditions, and specific combinations of the measures, these generalized factors serve as useful modelling guidelines.

Modernization of the building's technical systems (smart sensors for data acquisition on the temperature, humidity, air pressure, CO_2 and VOC concentrations, as well as equipment for the remote control of heating and ventilation in each specific room) was evaluated critically by examining the recommendations of Latvian and foreign specialists (e.g., [70]). A maximum of 10% of the post-renovation heat energy consumption was included in the calculations as a heat savings ΔQtech value from the modernization carried out.

Simulating DH networks is overly complicated and time-consuming. The number of parameters of different natures should be used to accurately define DH networks and perform the modelling of processes by using algorithms commonly used in the design of heat networks [71,72]:

- The length and internal (nominal) diameter of the pipes of each DH network section;
- Pipelines' thermal insulation thickness and thermal conductivity;
- Temperatures of the heat carrier in the supply and return pipes and the ambient temperature;
- The heat load and heat energy consumption of all heat energy users connected to the DH network;
- Local and linear hydraulic resistances, optimal flow rate of the heat carrier, and the required pressure drop at the farthest consumer.

A reduction in heat consumption results in a decrease in the heat mass transfer and flow rate of the heat carrier through the DH pipelines, which affects hydraulic processes, but has a negligible effect on thermal conductivity and heat loss. Assuming that only pre-insulated pipes are used in the DH networks, it is possible to create a simplified calculation model for each specific section of the DH network. This was used to perform an approximate but sufficiently accurate assessment of the impact of the heat energy demand reduction on DH network sections as a result of implementing measures to increase the energy efficiency of buildings.

To simplify the DH network modelling algorithm, two complex indexes were developed for each pipe size used in the network. Dimensions of the pipes are standardized, and the thermal modes of the DH networks are similar in the country ($\Delta T \approx 40$ °C); therefore, the values of both indexes could be generalized nationwide. The nominal pipe diameter was used as the determining KPI (independent variable) in the simplified model.

Specific heat loss from the pipeline (W/m) was designed to simulate the amount of heat loss at each section of the DH network. In general, this index depends on the structural and thermal characteristics of the DH pipes, as well as the temperatures of the heat carrier and the environment. For a high-precision analytical calculation of heat loss, the formulas included heat transfer through the steel pipe, insulation layer, and casing pipe.

For practical calculations, depending on the required degree of accuracy, the calculation formula can be simplified by omitting the parameters that have a smaller impact on the results [73]. The influence of the heat transfer coefficients from the outer surface of the pipe and especially from the heat carrier to the inner surface of the pipe is negligible compared to the influence of the thermal insulation layer of the pipeline. Therefore, the calculation of the heat loss index was based on technical data from the product catalogue of pre-insulated pipeline manufacturers [74,75] and the assumptions about the average practical performance of the DH network operating mode [76,77].

Maximum heat load (MW) was used to evaluate the threshold at which a reduction in heat demand justified replacing a specific DH network section with a smaller-diameter pipe. This is the only effective means of reducing heat loss in the affected section.

While the selection of the pipeline diameter usually requires complex hydraulic calculations, the simplified assessment method relies on average values for temperature differentials and flow velocity, as recommended in DH design guidelines [75–77]. To account for uncertainties, these values are conservatively set at 80% of their theoretical maximums.

The thermal efficiency of heat sources (HS) was assumed to be in line with today's standards. The HS should be properly maintained and operated, and then the efficiency of using a specific primary energy resource can be equalized. The primary energy resource used, or a proportional combination of different resources became the KPI of the HS in the context of the variable costs. The amount of heat energy produced by HS and consequently CO_2 emissions is decreasing due to the renovation of buildings and the reconstruction of the DH system. Another *green* option is the use of primary energy resources with lower emissions. The methodology envisaged the use of both options. A change in primary energy resources entails replacing HS equipment and requires corresponding investments.

The identified KPIs for all heating system elements are summarized in Figure 4. All of them are available in existing documents—in the building's energy certificate and attached documents, and in documents registering the operation of DH networks and heat sources. The municipal-level indicators used in the methodology are available in normative documents or published by the heat provider—average and minimum temperatures during the heating period, as well as constructive and operational data of the DH system. The methodology algorithm, including models of the elements, is detailed in [52] and does not require any specialized or proprietary data, making it accessible and broadly applicable.

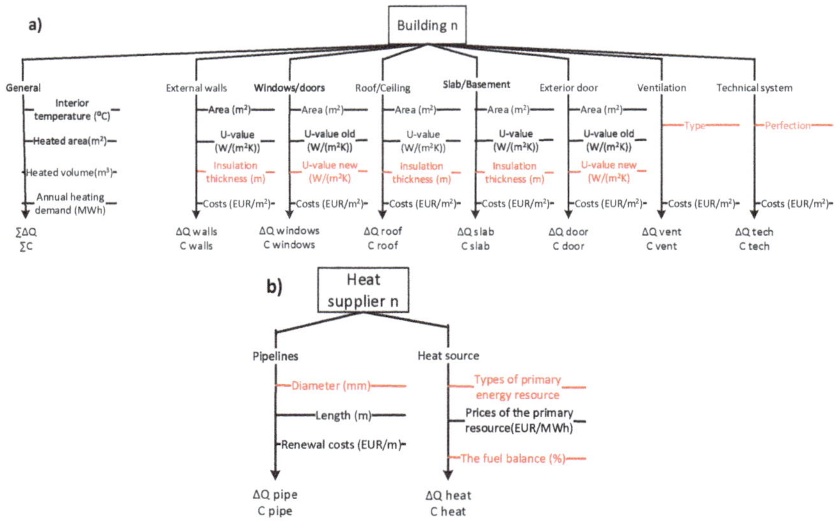

Figure 4. KPIs of the elements of the building (**a**) and heat supplier (**b**). ΔQ—heat loss change, c—costs; the fixed indicators are marked in black; the red ones are independent variables and can be changed while searching for the optimal project version. Developed by the authors.

3.3. Usability of the Tool

The system was designed as an online platform (cloud-based service) and supports three user types: system administrator, consumer administrators, and end users (Figure 5). A single system administrator (DG) manages the universal system-level data applicable to all users—such as standard pipe diameters and the thermal transmittance of glass units. The system administrator is also responsible for creating new consumer profiles and assigning consumer administrator (A) rights.

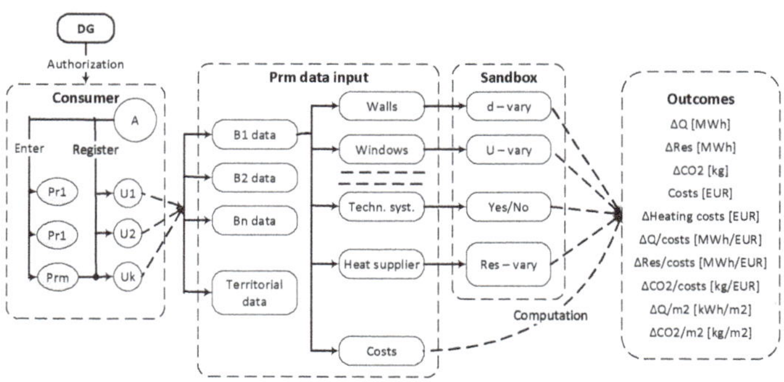

Figure 5. The tool: a structural diagram. Developed by the authors.

Consumer administrators manage thermal efficiency projects (Prm) and register individual users (Uk), granting them access to the platform for executing heating system projects. These projects may include components such as buildings (Bn), heat suppliers, and inlet pipes. After data entry, users can begin developing project versions within the innovation sandbox and identify the optimal configuration.

The innovation sandbox functionality is illustrated using the partial result sets for renovation projects targeting apartment buildings from Series No. 316 (Figure 6a) and Series No. 602 (Figure 6b), prepared at the request of the Ministry of Economy. The red data points and trendlines represent the achievable performance thresholds for building renovation.

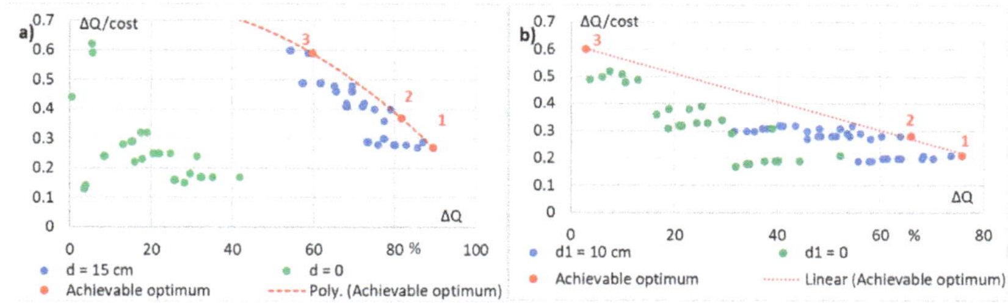

Figure 6. Versions of the heating system reconstruction projects: series No. 316 (**a**), series No. 602 (**b**). Developed by the authors.

The Series No. 316 buildings, constructed from silicate bricks in the 1960s and 1970s, were found to meet structural safety requirements but exhibited poor thermal efficiency. For the specifically analyzed case, most windows had already been replaced with double-glazed units, reducing the specific heat consumption to 126 kWh/m^2.

The Series No. 602 buildings, constructed with large concrete panels in the late 1970s, were also considered structurally sound. Approximately 44% of the external wall surface was insulated with 10 cm insulation, and over 80% of the windows had been replaced with double-glazed units, bringing the current specific heat consumption to 107 kWh/m^2.

In both cases, the scope of the presented renovation versions consisted of possible combinations of the following: (1) one wall insulation variant (d = 15 cm (W15)), (2) one basement coating variant with a 10 cm thick insulation layer (B10), (3) one 20 cm roof insulation variant (R20), (4) replacement of the unchanged windows with double-glazing (W1.6) or all windows with triple-glazed (W0.8) models, and (5) the installation of either a central (VentC) or local (VentL) mechanical ventilation system (Figure 6). Of course, by using several insulation layers, installation of the technical systems, and replacement of the inlet pipes, a broader range of renovation versions could be achieved.

Figure 6 shows the limit, as $f\{\Delta Q; \Delta Q/cost\}$, that can be achieved by implementing the renovation measures of the concrete building. The choice of the optimal version was determined by the settings of the relevant project (Table 1). The optimal compositions of renovation measures for the most typical project settings were shown to achieve the following: (point 1) maximum heat savings (ΔQ), (point 2) heat savings above the specified threshold at maximum achievable project efficiency ($\Delta Q > \Delta Q_{min}$), and (point 3) maximum project efficiency (ΔQ/cost).

Table 1. Compositions of the achievable optimal versions. Developed by the authors.

Point (Figure 6)	Series No. 316		Series No. 602	
	Project Task	Composition	Project Task	Composition
1	ΔQ → max	W15 + B10 + R20 + + W0.8 + VentC	ΔQ → max	W15 + B10 + R20 + W0.8 + VentC
2	ΔQ > 80%	W15 + B10 + R20 + + W0.8 + VentL	ΔQ > 60%	W15 + B10 + R20 + W0.8 + VentL
3	ΔQ/cost → max	W15 + B10 + W1.6	ΔQ/cost → max	B10

4. Discussion

The third global wave of democracy, a 70-year period of relatively stable sustainable human development and globalization, has ensured unprecedentedly rapid growth in the quality of life of all humanity. The swift victory over the profoundly serious COVID-19 pandemic very well illustrated the possibilities provided by global cooperation and solidarity. Unfortunately, it also marked the end of the period of prosperity.

Currently, it has already been replaced by the following: (1) autocratic tendencies in many countries instead of democracy, (2) growing turbulence and its transition to direct military conflicts in many regions of the world instead of respectful relations between countries, and (3) destroyed supply and trade chains and created national isolationism instead of the global division of labor and cooperation. World powers are returning to the principles of 18th century power politics. National governments and diplomatic services face difficult and challenging tasks ahead. The peaceful life of a diplomat has been replaced by quick, responsible decision making that ask for high-level professionals.

These strategic shifts inevitably generate social tensions, as different societal groups respond differently to new political and economic directions. These conflicts often extend to the municipal level, where local interest groups vie to protect their specific agendas. Local positions, like "wind power generators are definitely needed, but just not in my backyard" [78], are immensely popular.

The NATO setting on allocating 5% of GDP to defense means a reduction in LGs' resources too, significantly affecting the ability to provide already accustomed services to residents (social programs, education, and other mandatory functions that must be performed in the quality prescribed by normative acts); the question arises on priorities. There is a part of the local community who is confident that Russia will not attack a NATO Member State. As such, civil protection does not seem so important to them.

In the current geopolitical situation, it will be difficult to implement the full scope of the ambitious GD plans. Unfortunately, the EC has not made decisions on reducing and/or extending specific programs, creating friction among separate stakeholder groups. For example, local woody biomass as a primary energy resource plays a huge role in heating buildings in Latvia in accordance with the Kyoto Protocol [79]. The restructuring of the energy sector in EU countries, which began in 2022, led to a rapid increase in heating costs, which immediately affected energy-poor households (Figure 7). However, in Latvia, these increases were more moderate due to extensive biomass use. The orientation to electricity in the short term is associated with a considerable risk of repeated significant increases in heating costs. The recent massive blackout that affected the Iberian Peninsula on 28 April 2025, as well as a series of blackouts in the Americas, show that relying solely on electricity as the only source of heating is not safe. Nevertheless, high-income households often advocate for this shift.

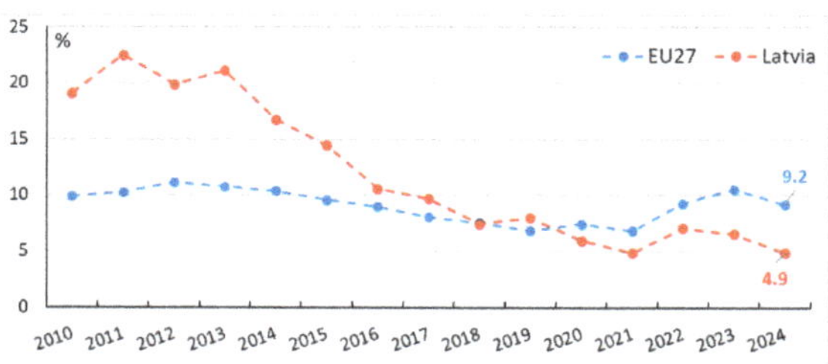

Figure 7. The percentage of the population unable to keep their home adequately warm by poverty status. Source: Eurostat [12].

These examples highlight the need for data- and fact-driven, carefully thought-out, well-balanced, rational municipal decision-making, not just for effective regulation, but also for promoting social stability in increasingly strained environments. Although local issues often diverge from international agendas, to enhance building energy performance, LGs must apply diplomatic skills to align EU and national legislation with local realities.

The issue at hand involves reconciling the priorities of local communities at the municipal level with global goals. The elected decision-makers in the municipality are the closest authority to the public: they are best informed about the relations between local interest groups, and therefore they are primarily responsible for implementing the EC principle "nobody will be left behind" in the local territory. The success of LGs depends on their ability to address arising dilemmas by balancing expectations across diverse interest groups.

Every LG decision creates both winners and losers. Providing compensation for those negatively affected by it can also be considered an ethical principle. For example, according to the Kaldor–Hicks compensation principle, in addition to direct compensation to those who lose, theoretical compensation could also be provided by winners to losers in certain scenarios [80–82]. Thus, it can be recommended that the increase in DH network tariffs, which occurs when some consumers are reducing heat consumption in buildings, should be compensated for all network consumers from the achieved benefits, thus not only eliminating the formation of opposition among residents against individual energy efficiency solutions, but also encouraging other consumers to seek solutions that are beneficial to them.

The proposed tool is specially designed for simple and fast, but at the same time, sufficiently accurate evaluation of the efficiency of specific building heating system repair project options. Computational testing of the methodology confirms that calculation deviations using the proposed simplified methodology for the renovation projects of buildings to be renovated typically remain within 10%, with 60–70% of deviations below 5% (Figure 8). Variations in computed heat loss values for pipes are similarly minor, not exceeding 7–8%. This level of accuracy is entirely acceptable for feasibility studies, an opinion confirmed by field specialists reviewing the prototype.

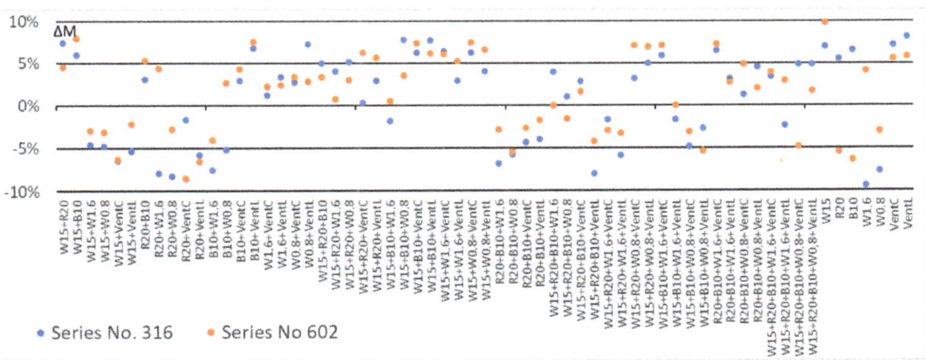

Figure 8. Computational testing of the methodology. ΔM—relative deviation of the simplified models from the full-scale calculation. Developed by the authors.

Figure 6 illustrates the outcomes to be obtained and the options for choice according to the project rules set. Wall insulation was the decisive process for Series No. 316; without it (d = 0), the achieved heat reduction ΔQ did not exceed 40%, and the efficiency (ΔQ/cost) remained low, except in cases involving basement insulation (B10). Optimal results required wall insulation (W15). In contrast, the Series No. 602 building did not exhibit a dominant effect from wall insulation, with a lower achievable heat reduction ΔQ percentage and overall lower efficiency of the versions due to an already existing partial wall insulation. These findings indicated that renovating series No. 316 buildings yielded greater benefits with lower investment. These buildings should be prioritized in the municipality's renovation programs, albeit with case-by-case verification.

5. Conclusions

Improving the energy efficiency of buildings is one of the GD's key programs, to which the attitude of various groups of residents and businesses is far from unambiguous, and in which the role of the municipality is the most challenging. LGs meet a lot of dilemmas including (but not limited to) the following:

- Ongoing uncertainty in various aspects of the EU green policy due to growing military threats, which gives local interest groups wide opportunities to interpret the situation in their own interests;
- The conflicting opinions of various interest groups, which are short- and medium-term beneficiaries or losers from the implementation of the EU recommendations;
- Diplomacy, needed for the possible rapprochement of these opinions, for balancing decisions to respect all opinions (of course, partially) and avoiding risks arising from an unequal approach and a unilateral choice in the decisions made;
- Prioritizing and concentrating municipal resources, when EU building energy efficiency policy is competing with traditional and local societal challenges in areas such as education, health, and social care, etc., where group interests have become balanced over time;
- A shortage of resources to compensate community groups adversely affected by retrofitting projects for the urban heating system;
- Convincing residents and businesses as building owners to make long-term investments in building energy efficiency projects under conditions of high uncertainty.

Any uncertainty in relation to external conditions, especially in the regulatory environment, is a direct basis for various community groups to actively lobby for their subjective interests. The ongoing adaptation of the regulatory environment in accordance with the rapidly changing geopolitical and tense regional situation is the function of the national government, which contacts the EC if necessary. This will significantly reduce the opportunities for various interest groups to use differently interpretable situations in their own interests.

A second source of uncertainty is associated with the lack of sufficiently high-quality data for objective LG decisions on the implementation of urban heating system retrofitting projects. The absence of data and/or calculation inaccuracies are sufficient to cause the estimated project benefits and costs to deviate from the true values, which is an obstacle to the adoption of optimal project options. Only data- and facts-driven decisions can reduce the opportunities for interest groups to question them and even fight against them during the decision-drafting and -making process.

LG administrative employees are preparing decisions on heating system retrofitting projects, and elected LG decision-making body members are adopting them. They are all usually not experts in thermal physics, construction, and IT, and cannot professionally evaluate the projects. A methodology and a user-friendly tool have been developed to support them in objective decisions on the renovation of a single building or the reconstruction of the DH system.

The developed methodology enables the following: (1) manages all components of the overall urban heating system, (2) is designed to meet the requirements of relevant projects and available funding options, (3) allows for the combination of multiple individual projects, (4) provides objective and sufficiently accurate results for the initial simulation and evaluation of project variants, (5) does not require specific knowledge in thermal physics, economics, or construction, ensuring user-friendliness, and (6) utilizes a limited number of indicators to streamline the simulation process. This tool provides insights into (1) achievable heat consumption and primary energy savings, (2) the reduction in dominant CO_2 emissions, (3) changes in heating tariffs and costs, and (4) required investments.

Field experts of the Latvian Association of Local and Regional Governments and municipalities have evaluated this tool as useful for municipalities to streamline the sustainable planning and management of heating system projects in their territory, facilitating the prioritization and balancing of decisions and actions.

It should be mentioned that the methodology was developed in accordance with the regulatory environment and heat supply practice of Latvia. To use this methodology and tool in other countries, it will be necessary to further develop the methodology in accordance with the regulatory environment of these countries.

These are our recommendations:

- Given that public sentiment is most accurately understood at the municipal level, LGs should not only be consulted but also actively be involved in national-level decision-making.
- LGs should strengthen partnerships with private-sector stakeholders through effective guidance, collaborative planning, and the coordination of decisions aimed at improving building energy performance.

Author Contributions: Conceptualization, M.P.; methodology, M.P. and E.K.; software, E.D.; validation, M.P. and J.B.; formal analysis, S.G.; investigation, U.S.; resources, G.K.; data curation, E.D.; writing—original draft preparation, M.P. and E.K.; writing—review and editing, E.K.; visualization, J.B.; project administration, G.K.; funding acquisition, E.K. All authors have read and agreed to the published version of the manuscript.

Funding: This research was funded by the Latvian Council of Science, Project lzp-2021/1-0108 (University of Latvia project Nr. Z-LZP123-ZR-N-231) "Sustainable management of the urban heating system under EU Fit for 55 package: research and development of the methodology and tool". Information on the ongoing project is available online https://www.lu.lv/zinatne/projekti/nacionalas-programmas-un-projekti/flpp-2021-gada-konkurss/#c123732 (in Latvian) accessed on 5 May 2025.

Data Availability Statement: The original contributions presented in the study are included in the article, further inquiries can be directed to the corresponding author.

Conflicts of Interest: The authors declare no conflicts of interest.

References

1. UNFCCC. Paris Agreement. 2015. Available online: https://unfccc.int/sites/default/files/english_paris_agreement.pdf (accessed on 30 April 2025).
2. CEMR. Local Green Transition. 2024. Available online: https://ccre-cemr.org/wp-content/uploads/2024/10/CEMR-Local-Green-Transition-2024.pdf (accessed on 30 April 2025).
3. EU (2023/1791). Directive of 13 September 2023 on Energy Efficiency and Amending Regulation (EU) 2023/955. Available online: https://eur-lex.europa.eu/eli/dir/2023/1791/oj/eng (accessed on 30 April 2025).
4. EU (2024/1275). Directive of 24 April 2024 on the Energy Performance of Buildings. Available online: https://eur-lex.europa.eu/eli/dir/2024/1275/oj/eng (accessed on 30 April 2025).
5. EU (2023/2413). Directive of 18 October 2023 Amending Directive (EU) 2018/2001, Regulation (EU) 2018/1999 and Directive 98/70/EC as Regards the Promotion of Energy from Renewable Sources, and Repealing Council Directive (EU) 2015/652. Available online: https://eur-lex.europa.eu/eli/dir/2023/2413/oj/eng (accessed on 30 April 2025).
6. Council of Europe. European Charter of Local Self Government, Treaties No.122; Strasbourg, France, 1985. Available online: https://www.coe.int/en/web/impact-convention-human-rights/european-charter-of-local-self-government#/ (accessed on 30 April 2025).
7. EC. Local Green Deals; A Blueprint for Action. 2023. Available online: https://www.intelligentcitieschallenge.eu/sites/default/files/2023-03/2023-Local%20Green%20Deals-update-final.pdf (accessed on 30 April 2025).

8. Pukis, M.; Bicevskis, J.; Gendelis, S.; Karnitis, E.; Karnitis, G.; Eihmanis, A.; Sarma, U. Role of Local Governments in Green Deal Multilevel Governance: The Energy Context. *Energies* **2023**, *16*, 4759. [CrossRef]
9. EC. A New Era for European Defence and Security, 2024. Available online: https://commission.europa.eu/priorities-2024-2029/security-and-defence_en (accessed on 15 May 2025).
10. Bremmer, I. Welcome to a World Defined by Polarization, Instability, and Disruption. Carnegie Corporation of New York. 2025. Available online: https://www.carnegie.org/our-work/article/welcome-to-a-world-defined-by-polarization-instability-and-disruption/ (accessed on 30 April 2025).
11. Brotz, H.M. Social Stratification and the Political Order. *Am. J. Sociol.* **1959**, *64*, 571–578. [CrossRef]
12. Eurostat. Inability to Keep Home Adequately Warm. 2025. Available online: https://ec.europa.eu/eurostat/databrowser/view/ilc_mdes01/default/table?lang=en (accessed on 30 April 2025).
13. Truijens, D.; Hanegraaff, M. It ain't over 'til it's over: Interest-group influence in policy implementation. *Political Stud. Rev.* **2024**, *22*, 387–401. [CrossRef]
14. Hagen, A.; Altamirano-Cabrera, J.C.; Weikard, H.P. National political pressure groups and the stability of international environmental agreements. *Int. Env. Agreem.* **2021**, *21*, 405–425. [CrossRef]
15. Anger, N.; Asane-Otoo, E.; Böhringer, C.; Oberndorfer, U. Public interest versus interest groups: A political economy analysis of allowance allocation under the EU emissions trading scheme. *Int. Environ. Agreem. Politics Law Econ.* **2016**, *16*, 621–638. [CrossRef]
16. Marchiori, C.; Dietz, S.; Tavoni, A. Domestic politics and the formation of international environmental agreements. *J. Environ. Econ. Manag.* **2017**, *81*, 115–131. [CrossRef]
17. Marris, E. Why young climate activists have captured the world's attention. *Nature* **2019**, *573*, 471–472. [CrossRef]
18. Rahmad, Y.; Hedenus, F.; Jewell, J.; Vinichenko, V. Spatial heterogeneity in deployment and upscaling of wind power in Swedish municipalities. *Renew. Sustain. Energy Transit.* **2025**, *7*, 100104. [CrossRef]
19. Scheifele, F.; Popp, D. Not in my backyard? The local impact of wind and solar parks in Brazil. *Energy Econ.* **2025**, *29*, 108481. [CrossRef]
20. Bally, F.; Sebi, C. Shifting public perception: A longitudinal analysis of national and local media narratives on nuclear and wind energy in France. *Technol. Forecast. Soc. Change* **2025**, *215*, 124111. [CrossRef]
21. Lindvall, D.; Sörqvist, P.; Lindeberg, S.; Barthel, S. The polarization of energy preferences—A study on social acceptance of wind and nuclear power in Sweden. *Energy Policy* **2025**, *198*, 114492. [CrossRef]
22. Carattini, S.; Figge, B.; Gordan, A.; Löschel, A. Municipal building codes and the adoption of solar photovoltaics. *J. Environ. Econ. Manag.* **2024**, *124*, 102937. [CrossRef]
23. Nunes, A.M.M.; Júnior, E.P.S.; de Araújo, J.M.; Melo, A.K.A.; Rolim, M.J.C.P.; Simioni, F.J.; Carvalho, M.; Junior, L.M.C. Impact assessment of public policies in the municipalities covered by the Brazilian Incentive program for alternative electricity sources (PROINFA). *Renew. Energy* **2024**, *235*, 121342. [CrossRef]
24. Wagner, P.M.; Ocelík, P.; Gronow, A.; Ylä-Anttila, T.; Schmidt, L.; Delicado, A. Network ties, institutional roles and advocacy tactics: Exploring explanations for perceptions of influence in climate change policy networks. *Soc. Netw.* **2023**, *75*, 78–87. [CrossRef]
25. Cattino, M.; Reckien, D. Does public participation lead to more ambitious and transformative local climate change planning? *Curr. Opin. Environ. Sustain.* **2021**, *52*, 100–110. [CrossRef]
26. Bick, N. Citizen involvement in local sustainability policymaking: An in-depth analysis of staff activities and motivations. *Sustain. Sci.* **2024**, *19*, 1865–1880. [CrossRef]
27. Pennacchioni, G. Harnessing Collective Intentionality for Climate Action: An Institutional Perspective on Sustainability. *Topoi* **2024**, *44*, 197–208. [CrossRef]
28. Cass, E.; Harris, C.N.; Shao, W.; Yeates, E.; Moradkhani, H.; Lyons, J. Stakeholder compound flood hazard communication and decision making in Mobile, AL. *Int. J. Disaster Risk Reduct.* **2025**, *122*, 105469. [CrossRef]
29. Takahashi, T.; Hori, Y.; Otsuka, I.; Shibata, S.; Tsuge, T. Innovativeness of Japanese forest owners and municipalities regarding the valori-sation of forest ecosystem services: Quantitative evaluation of mutual influences. *For. Policy Econ.* **2024**, *166*, 103269. [CrossRef]
30. Tilman, A.R.; Haight, R.G. Public policy for management of forest pests within an ownership mosaic. *Ecol. Econ.* **2025**, *234*, 108602. [CrossRef]
31. Moberg, K.R. Limits to local democracy in practice? The case of governing sustainable land use in Norwegian municipalities. *Land Use Policy* **2025**, *152*, 107505. [CrossRef]
32. Fredriksson, A.; Soes, M.S.M. Quantifying political effects in the spatial allocation of public services. *Socio Econ. Plan. Sci.* **2025**, *99*, 102180. [CrossRef]
33. Sebo, M.; Gradus, R.; Budding, T. The impact of independent local parties on spending: Evidence from Dutch municipalities. *Eur. J. Political Econ.* **2024**, *13*, 102603. [CrossRef]

34. Laliotis, I.; Mourelatos, E.; Lohtander, J. Religiosity, attitudes toward science, and public health: Evidence from Finland. *Econ. Hum. Biol.* **2025**, *56*, 101460. [CrossRef]
35. Peteri, G. Local Finances and the Green Transition Managing Emergencies and Boosting Local Investments for a Sustainable Recovery in CEMR Member Countries. 2022, CEMR. Available online: https://www.kdz.eu/system/files/downloads/2023-04/CCRE-Local%20finance%20UK%20v2-1.pdf (accessed on 30 April 2025).
36. State Chancellery. Draft Legislation. The Draft of Climate Law, 21-TA-62 2024. Available online: https://tapportals.mk.gov.lv/legal_acts/7987de45-93fd-45e3-ac4c-948251c622d9 (accessed on 30 April 2025). (In Latvian)
37. State Chancellery. Draft Legislation. The Draft of Transport Energy Law 23-TA-1451 2024. Available online: https://tapportals.mk.gov.lv/legal_acts/042cde65-37a0-4e35-a005-109648ea5037 (accessed on 30 April 2025). (In Latvian)
38. Boudon, R. Beyond Rational Choice Theory. *Annu. Rev. Sociol.* **2003**, *29*, 1–21. [CrossRef]
39. Herfeld, C. Revisiting the criticisms of rational choice theories. *Philos. Compass* **2021**, *17*, e12774. [CrossRef]
40. Huang, J.; Wang, S.; Teng, F.; Feng, W. Thermal performance optimization of envelope in the energy-saving renovation of existing residential buildings. *Energy Build.* **2021**, *247*, 111103. [CrossRef]
41. Pombo, O.; Rivela, B.; Neila, J. The challenge of sustainable building renovation: Assessment of current criteria and future outlook. *J. Clean. Prod.* **2016**, *123*, 88–100. [CrossRef]
42. Jiang, S.; Wang, M.; Ma, L. Gaps and requirements for applying automatic architectural design to building renovation. *Autom. Constr.* **2023**, *147*, 104742. [CrossRef]
43. Huedo, P.; Lopez-Mesa, B.; Mulet, E. Development of an Assessment Tool for Building Envelope Retrofit Based on Environmental Indicator. In *The Sustainable Renovation of Buildings and Neighbourhoods*; Mercader-Moyano, P., Ed.; Bentham Books: Sharjah, United Arab Emirates, 2018; pp. 81–102. [CrossRef]
44. Liu, T.; Ma, G.; Wang, D.; Pan, X. Intelligent green retrofitting of existing buildings based on case-based reasoning and random forest. *Autom. Constr.* **2024**, *162*, 105377. [CrossRef]
45. Husiev, O.; Campos-Celador, A.; Alvarez-Sanz, M.; Teres-Zubiaga, J. Why district renovation is not leading the race? Critical assessment of building renovation potential under different intervention levels. *Energy Build.* **2023**, *295*, 113288. [CrossRef]
46. Terés-Zubiaga, J.; Bolliger, R.; Almeida, M.G.; Barbosa, R.; Rose, J.; Thomsen, K.E.; Montero, E.; Briones-Llorente, R. Cost-effective building renovation at district level combining energy efficiency & renewables—Methodology assessment proposed in IEA EBC Annex 75 and a demonstration case study. *Energy Build.* **2020**, *224*, 110280. [CrossRef]
47. Weinberger, G.; Amiri, S.; Moshfegh, B. Investigating techno-economic effects and environmental impacts of energy renovation of residential building clusters on a district heating system. *Energy Build.* **2021**, *251*, 111327. [CrossRef]
48. Kingspan Group. LOGSTOR Calculator. 2022. Available online: https://www.logstor.com/en/services/digital-tools/logstor-calculator/ (accessed on 30 April 2025).
49. Wahi, P.; Konstantinou, T.; Tenpierik, M.J.; Visscher, H.J. Lower-Temperature-Ready Renovation: An Approach to Identify the Extent of Renovation Interventions for Lower-Temperature District Heating in Existing Dutch Homes. *Buildings* **2023**, *13*, 2524. [CrossRef]
50. Ziemele, J.; Gendelis, S.; Dace, E. Impact of global warming and building renovation on the heat demand and district heating capacity: Case of the city of Riga. *Energy* **2023**, *276*, 127567. [CrossRef]
51. Bruck, A.; Ruano, S.D.; Auer, H. Values and implications of building envelope retrofitting for residential Positive Energy Districts. *Energy Build.* **2022**, *275*, 112493. [CrossRef]
52. Karnitis, G.; Gendelis, S.; Pukis, M.; Sarma, U.; Diebelis, E.; Karnitis, E.; Bicevskis, J. Retrofitting urban heating systems under the EU Fit for 55 package: Methodology for feasibility studies of projects. *Latv. J. Phys. Tech. Sci.* **2024**, *61*, 25–40. [CrossRef]
53. Gendelis, S. Applications of the Temperature Step Method for Determining the Specific Heat Capacity of Building Materials. In *Nano, Bio, Green and Space: Technologies for a Sustainable Future, Proceedings of the 23rd International Multidisciplinary Scientific GeoConference SGEM 2023, Albena, Bulgaria, 3–9 July 2023*; Trofymchuk, O., Rivza, B., Eds.; STEF92 Technology: Stolichna, Bulgaria, 2023; Volume 23. [CrossRef]
54. *ISO 10456:2007*; Building Materials and Products—Hygrothermal Properties—Tabulated Design Values and Procedures for Determining Declared and Design Thermal Values. ISO: Geneva, Switzerland, 2007.
55. Sooriyalakshmi, N.; Helena, H.J. A brief overview on thermal conductivity of insulating materials. *Technol. Innov. Eng. Res.* **2022**, *6*, 78–90. [CrossRef]
56. Ali, A.; Issa, A.; Elshaer, A. A Comprehensive Review and Recent Trends in Thermal Insulation Materials for Energy Conservation in Buildings. *Sustainability* **2024**, *16*, 8782. [CrossRef]
57. Le, D.H.A.; Pásztory, Z. An overview of factors influencing thermal conductivity of building insulation materials. *J. Build. Eng.* **2021**, *44*, 102604. [CrossRef]
58. Šadauskienė, J.; Ramanauskas, J.; Krawczyk, D.A.; Klumbytė, E.; Fokaides, P.A. Investigation of Thermal Bridges of a New High-Performance Window Installation Using 2-D and 3-D Methodology. *Buildings* **2022**, *12*, 572. [CrossRef]

59. *ISO 10077-1:2017*; Thermal Performance of Windows, Doors and Shutters—Calculation of Thermal Transmittance—Part 1: General. ISO: Geneva, Switzerland, 2017.
60. Rana, A.; Alam, M.S.; Charles, K.; Perera, P.; Hewage, K.; Sadiq, R. Thermal Performance of Double and Triple Glazed Windows; Experimental Results from Lab and In-Situ Measurements. In Proceedings of the 1st International Conference on New Horizons in Green Civil Engineering (NHICE-01), Victoria, BC, Canada, 25–27 April 2018. Available online: https://www.researchgate.net/publication/326316386_Thermal_performance_of_double_and_triple_glazed_windows_Experimental_results_from_lab_and_in-situ_measurements (accessed on 30 April 2025).
61. Huang, Y.; El Mankibi, M.; Cantin, R. Thermal performance characterization of supply-air double windows: A new guarded hot box protocol and numerical modelization. *Energy Build.* **2023**, *287*, 112993. [CrossRef]
62. Kalamees, T. Air tightness and air leakages of new lightweight single-family detached houses in Estonia. *Build. Environ.* **2007**, *42*, 2369–2377. [CrossRef]
63. Chan, W.R.; Nazaroff, W.W.; Price, P.N.; Sohn, M.D.; Gadgil, A.J. Analyzing a database of residential air leakage in the United States. *Atmos. Environ.* **2005**, *39*, 3445–3455. [CrossRef]
64. Alfano, F.; Dell'Isola, M.; Ficco, G.; Tassini, F. Experimental analysis of air tightness in Mediterranean buildings using the fan pressurization method. *Build. Environ.* **2012**, *53*, 16–25. [CrossRef]
65. *ISO 9972-2015*; Thermal Performance of Buildings—Determination of Air Permeability of Buildings—Fan Pressurization Method. 3rd ed. ISO: Geneva, Switzerland, 2015.
66. Michalak, P. Annual Energy Performance of an Air Handling Unit with a Cross-Flow Heat Exchanger. *Energies* **2021**, *14*, 1519. [CrossRef]
67. Zender-Świercz, E.A. Review of Heat Recovery in Ventilation. *Energies* **2021**, *14*, 1759. [CrossRef]
68. Pekdogan, T.; Tokuç, A.; Ezan, M.A.; Başaran, T. Experimental investigation of a decentralized heat recovery ventilation system. *J. Build. Eng.* **2021**, *35*, 102009. [CrossRef]
69. Shan, R.; Lai, W.; Tang, H.; Leng, X.; Gu, W. Residential Building Renovation Considering Energy, Carbon Emissions, and Cost: An Approach Integrating Machine Learning and Evolutionary Generation. *Appl. Sci.* **2025**, *15*, 1830. [CrossRef]
70. Vandenbogaerde, L.; Verbeke, S.; Audenaert, A. Optimizing building energy consumption in office buildings: A review of building automation and control systems and factors influencing energy savings. *J. Build. Eng.* **2023**, *76*, 107233. [CrossRef]
71. del Hoyo Arce, I.; López, S.H.; López Perez, S.; Rämä, M.; Klobut, K.; Febres, J.A. Models for fast modelling of district heating and cooling networks. *Renew. Sustain. Energy Rev.* **2018**, *82*, 1863–1873. [CrossRef]
72. Guelpa, E.; Capone, M.; Sciacovelli, A.; Vasset, N.; Baviere, R.; Verda, V. Reduction of supply temperature in existing district heating: A review of strategies and implementations. *Energy* **2023**, *262*, 125363. [CrossRef]
73. Wieland, A.; Dollhopf, S.; Weidlich, I.; Pourbozorgi Langroudi, P. Heat Loss Determination of District Heating Pipelines. A Comparison of Numerical and Analytical Methods. *Environ. Clim. Technol.* **2024**, *28*, 927–939. [CrossRef]
74. Kingspan Group. LOGSTOR. District heating products. Available online: https://www.logstor.com/en/products/ (accessed on 30 April 2025).
75. *EN 13941*; Design and Installation of Thermal Insulated Bonded Single and Twin Pipe Systems for Directly Buried Hot Water Networks. iTeh, Inc.: Newark, DE, USA, 2009. Available online: https://standards.iteh.ai/catalog/standards/cen/157e2da8-8a70-489e-983f-ea77a0b4f967/en-13941-1-2019?srsltid=AfmBOorJziL4GhI2SYHdjf0TFPNL5PChkG1zJILiHq5Iwbh_Wc5YQEfm (accessed on 30 April 2025).
76. Krawczyk, D.A.; Teleszewski, T.J. Reduction of Heat Losses in a Pre-Insulated Network Located in Central Poland by Lowering the Operating Temperature of the Water and the Use of Egg-shaped Thermal Insulation: A Case Study. *Energies* **2019**, *12*, 2104. [CrossRef]
77. Averfalk, H.; Werner, S. Economic benefits of fourth generation district heating. *Energy* **2020**, *193*, 116727. [CrossRef]
78. Tilburg University. Wind Turbines: Not in Your Backyard? *Tilburg University Magazine*, 13 January 2025. Available online: https://www.tilburguniversity.edu/magazine/overview/wind-turbines-not-your-backyard (accessed on 30 April 2025).
79. UNFCC. Kyoto Protocol to the United Nations Framework Convention on Climate Change. 1998. Available online: https://unfccc.int/resource/docs/convkp/kpeng.pdf (accessed on 30 April 2025).
80. Mukoyama, T. In defence of the Kaldor-Hicks criterion. *Econ. Lett.* **2023**, *224*, 111031. [CrossRef]
81. Wight, J.B. The Ethics behind Efficiency. *J. Econ. Educ.* **2017**, *48*, 15–26. [CrossRef]
82. Bostani, M.; Malekpoor, A. Critical Analysis of Kaldor-Hicks Efficiency Criterion, with Respect to Moral Values, Social Policy Making and Incoherence. *Adv. Environ. Biol.* **2012**, *6*, 2032–2038.

energies

MDPI

Article

An Integrated Building Energy Model in MATLAB

Marco Simonazzi, Nicola Delmonte, Paolo Cova and Roberto Menozzi *

Department of Engineering and Architecture, University of Parma, 43124 Parma, Italy; marco.simonazzi@unipr.it (M.S.); nicola.delmonte@unipr.it (N.D.); paolo.cova@unipr.it (P.C.)
* Correspondence: roberto.menozzi@unipr.it

Abstract: This paper discusses the development of an Integrated Building Energy Model (IBEM) in MATLAB (R2024b) for a university campus building. In the general context of the development of integrated energy district models to guide the evolution and planning of smart energy grids for increased efficiency, resilience, and sustainability, this work describes in detail the development and use of an IBEM for a university campus building featuring a heat pump-based heating/cooling system and PV generation. The IBEM seamlessly integrates thermal and electrical aspects into a complete physical description of the energy performance of a smart building, thus distinguishing itself from co-simulation approaches in which different specialized tools are applied to the two aspects and connected at the level of data exchange. Also, the model, thanks to its physical, white-box nature, can be instanced repeatedly within the comprehensive electrical micro-grid model in which it belongs, with a straightforward change of case-specific parameter settings. The model incorporates a heat pump-based heating/cooling system and photovoltaic generation. The model's components, including load modeling, heating/cooling system simulation, and heat pump implementation are described in detail. Simulation results illustrate the building's detailed power consumption and thermal behavior throughout a sample year. Since the building model (along with the whole campus micro-grid model) is implemented in the MATLAB Simulink environment, it is fully portable and exploitable within a large, world-wide user community, including researchers, utility companies, and educational institutions. This aspect is particularly relevant considering that most studies in the literature employ co-simulation environments involving multiple simulation software, which increases the framework's complexity and presents challenges in models' synchronization and validation.

Keywords: energy system modeling; building energy modeling; renewable energy; heating/cooling systems; smart grid

1. Introduction

The integration of buildings as active components of smart electric grids—particularly in the micro-grid context—is a process in rapid acceleration for environmental as well as economic reasons [1–3]. The penetration of Distributed Energy Resources (DERs)—in this context, chiefly photovoltaic (PV) power generation—coupled with Battery Energy Storage Systems (BESSs), and the electrification of heating via heat pumps, are rapidly changing the role of buildings from pure and relatively simple electric loads into more complicated entities with the possibility of energy self-sufficiency (at least for limited stretches of time) and active contributions to grid management with injections of excess power production and sharing of energy storage capabilities [2–6]. In the evolution of urban environments along the Smart City path, smart energy grids and micro-grids (MGs) are and increasingly will be essential components, and buildings will be key players in the process [7,8].

The growing complexity of the energy identity and role of buildings calls for a new level of attention to the modeling of their energy footprints, both passive (consumption) and active (generation) [9,10]. Historically, building models have evolved in the direction of increasing environmental and sustainability awareness (from the *Intelligent Building* to the *Smart Building*, to the *Green Building*, and finally to the *Zero Energy Building*), as well as in that of enhanced inward and outward functionalities and services (the *Grid-interactive Efficient Building*) [11].

On top of that, the trend toward complete electrification of building heating/cooling systems requires that electrical and thermal energy models are integrated in a unified comprehensive approach [12], traditionally focusing each on its specific domain and using different tools and modeling approaches.

The general context in which this work belongs is that of the development of integrated energy district models to guide the evolution and planning of smart energy grids for increased efficiency, resilience, and sustainability. A remarkable example is given by [13], which takes into consideration the energy demand of a whole neighborhood, with the main objective of developing and deploying a monitoring plan to be coupled with a model for the simulation of energy performance. A detailed breakdown of the energy paths and the good match between measured and simulated data were shown. Generally speaking, district-scale and urban-scale energy models have been the subject of extensive research activity at least since the early 2000s: see for example [14] for a comprehensive review touching the aspects of climate modeling, building energy demand, energy infrastructure modeling, building thermal performance simulation, and transportation modeling. Our recent activity in particular has resulted in the creation of a complete electrical model of the University of Parma South Campus (UPSC) [15,16] to be ultimately coupled with previously developed models of the thermal energy grid [17,18].

Several papers and literature reviews have been published in the past few years on topics connected with smart building energy performance modeling and Building Energy Management System development (BEMS), a few representative examples of which are reviewed hereafter.

In [19] the focus is on building *thermal* simulation and optimization of Heating, Ventilation Air Conditioning System (HVAC) operation. HVAC optimization and thermal simulation—the latter carried out using a lumped element thermal model based on the equivalent electric circuit approach—are performed by two separate software tools.

The aspect of *electrical* energy consumption on the other hand is tackled by Moya et al. [20], as applied to a smart building with PV generation, electric energy storage, and Electric Vehicle (EV) facilities, with the goal of minimizing the energy supplied by the power grid and, consequently, the energy cost.

Other studies have considered both aspects, i.e., *thermal and electrical*, in their building energy models. In [21], for instance, the BEMS features two power loops, the thermal one and the electrical one, separate except in that they are both connected to a Combined Heat and Power (CHP) fuel cell, the goal being minimization of energy consumption and building automation. A co-simulation approach, i.e., the use of two independent but coupled software tools, is also presented in [22]: here the tools are the EnergyPlus® engine for building-level energy modeling and a Modelica library for the electrical distribution system. This approach makes it possible to exploit the specific strength of each tool, thus offering accurate system modeling on both accounts, but requires taking care of tool coupling and data exchange, here leveraging the Functional Mock-up Interface (FMI) approach. Model validation was successful, albeit limited to a very simple testbed. The relevant literature on the co-simulation of buildings and smart energy systems in general is reviewed with a taxonomic approach in [23].

In this context, this work describes in detail the development and use of an Integrated Building Energy Model (IBEM) for a university campus building featuring a heat pump-based heating/cooling system, PV generation, and BESS. The IBEM combines the dynamic thermal model with the electric grid model, providing a flexible tool for analyzing and designing smart energy buildings. The main features that characterize this work with respect to the scenario outlined above are the following:

- The model seamlessly integrates thermal and electrical aspects into a complete, physical description of the energy performance of a smart building;
- The building model is inserted into a comprehensive electrical model of a micro-grid (namely, that of the University of Parma South Campus); given its standard smart building features of grid connection, PV rooftop generation, heat pump-based conditioning system, blueprint-based thermal exchange parameters, and generic load consumption description, the model can be instanced repeatedly within the micro-grid model with case-specific parameter settings;
- Unlike other available models based on a data-driven approach, ours is based on physical/analytical descriptions of the components, which makes it easily adaptable and scalable and provides it with predictive capabilities in the planning phase;
- the whole model (IBEM and micro-grid) is implemented in the MATLAB Simulink environment, thus being fully portable and exploitable within the very wide community of MATLAB users, including researchers, utility companies, educational institutions (e.g., the University of Parma provides free access to MATLAB to all of its students via a Campus Agreement License); this aspect is particularly relevant considering that most studies in the literature employ co-simulation environments involving multiple simulation software, which increases the framework's complexity [22] and presents challenges in models' synchronization and validation [23].

The main goal of the present work is therefore the development of a MATLAB Simulink IBEM model based on a physical description of the relevant components, including PV generation, heat pump-based conditioning system, and thermal and electric loads, to be seamlessly integrated into our campus microgrid model; since it is based on an actual campus building, the IBEM can be experimentally validated and be adapted to describe new smart/green buildings thus helping the future development of the campus microgrid.

The structure of the paper is the following: Section 2 deals with the modeling approach and briefly describes the campus MG model in which the IBEM is inserted; Section 3 describes the IBEM in detail, while examples of simulation results are illustrated in Section 4; finally, Section 5 draws conclusions and outlines future developments.

2. Modeling Approach and Campus Micro-Grid Model

The UPSC MG model [15,16] was built in MATLAB Simulink using the Simscape Electrical Specialized Power Systems library to study and guide campus evolution in the direction of a smart energy district. For the sake of reducing the computational overhead of the calculation of economic and environmental sustainability figures over long periods of time, we adopted a constant-frequency discrete-time three-phase phasor-domain simulation [24]. The UPSC grid model, connected to a voltage source representing the national utility grid at the Point of Common Coupling (PCC), features a transformation cabinet at each node, transferring power from medium-voltage to low-voltage utilities, physical descriptions of the cables with per unit length values of resistance, inductance, and capacitance, and specific in-house-developed blocks modeling PV generation facilities (with Maximum Power Point Tracking), BESSs, electric vehicle charging stations, and a variety of loads including classrooms, scientific laboratories, offices, sport facilities, canteens and cafeterias; building and street outdoor lighting is also modeled. Full details and a schematic diagram of the UPSC MG can be found in [16].

3. Integrated Building Energy Model

In this section we provide a detailed description of the VisLab building, which is one of the most recently built facilities in the UPSC. The building hosts a spinoff company working in the field of autonomous driving and computer vision, and features offices, laboratories (generic loads), and a server room. Unlike the other campus buildings, it is equipped with its own heat pump heating/cooling system, which makes it independent of the central campus heating/cooling system. In addition, the building features a 27 kW_p PV rooftop plant.

Figure 1 shows a schematic block diagram of the IBEM of the VisLab building, as implemented in MATLAB Simulink. The three-phase plus neutral AC lines of the campus electric grid are connected to the heat pump-based heating/cooling system, the loads (generic electric loads, the server room, and outdoor lighting), and the PV plant.

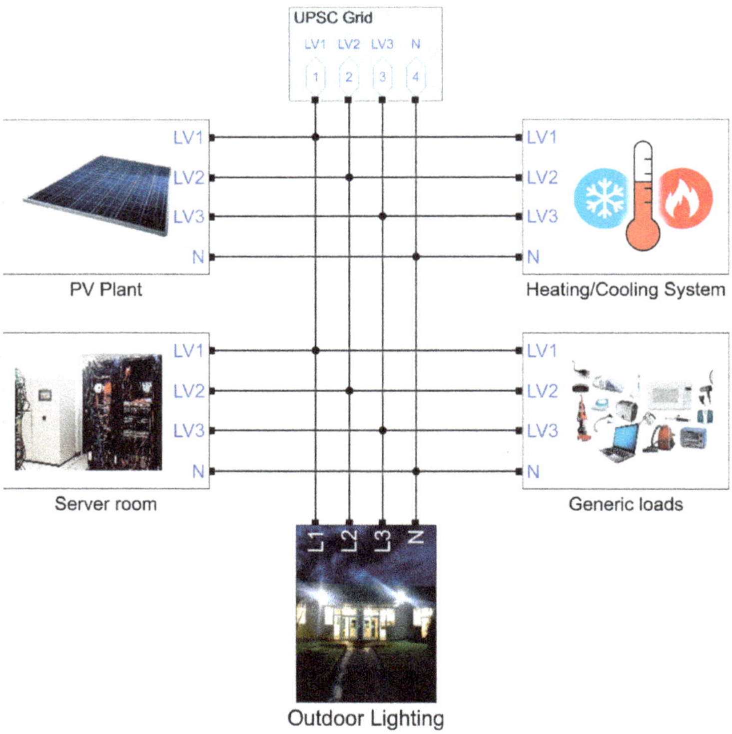

Figure 1. Building implementation in Simulink.

3.1. Load Modeling

Loads are modeled considering weekly power consumption profiles. Due to the limited deployment of the planned smart metering network we had to depend on data from legacy meters that record monthly consumption for selected buildings.

To address this limitation, we choose to consider typical weekly consumption profiles for offices and research laboratories obtained from measurement campaigns performed on a few selected UPSC buildings during different seasonal periods (April, July, and December) with 10 s resolution. These load profiles were then scaled based on the annual consumption trend (derived from the monthly data recorder on the VisLab building) to obtain a realistic overall load profile.

Figure 2 shows normalized weekly power profiles recorded from representative office and research laboratory facilities in the UPSC framework. These profiles are extended and integrated with monthly consumption trends to obtain the annual consumption profile illustrated in Figure 3.

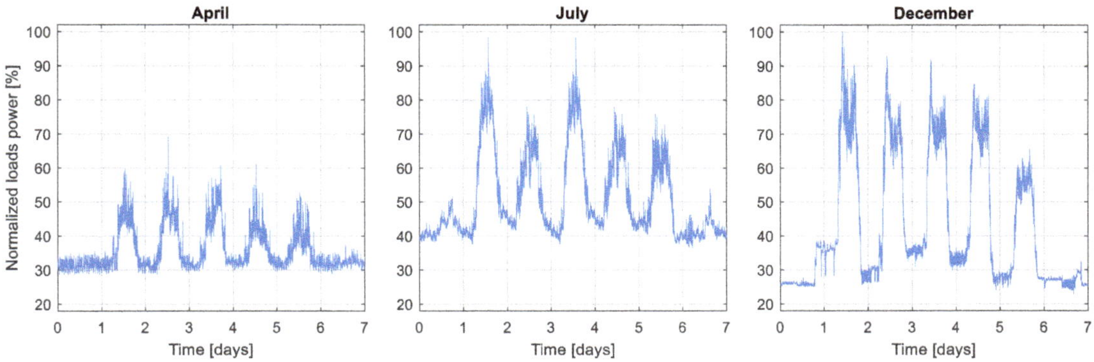

Figure 2. Normalized weekly power patterns recorded from representative office and research laboratory facilities in (**a**) a typical week in April (midseason), (**b**) a typical week in July (summer), and (**c**) a typical week in December (winter).

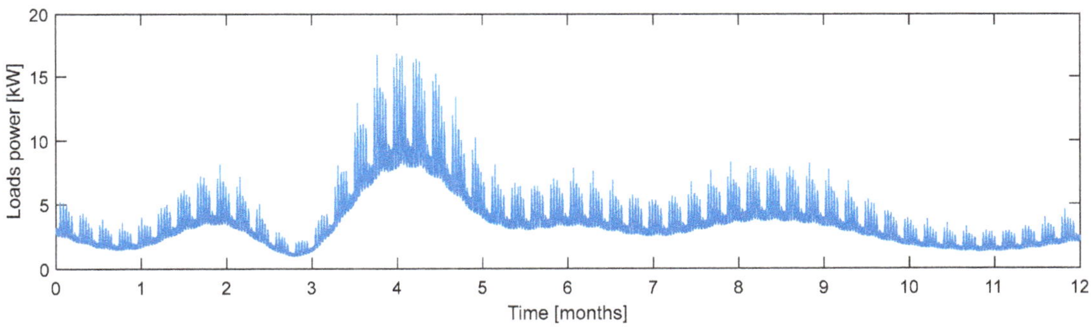

Figure 3. Annual consumption profile of the VisLab building obtained by extending and integrating the normalized weekly profiles with monthly consumption trends.

Additional details about the modeling of loads and outdoor lighting power consumption can be found in [16].

3.2. Building Heating/Cooling System Modeling

The integration of thermal and electrical energy aspects into a single model is going to receive more and more attention in the literature due to the increasing diffusion of heat pump systems, often fed by rooftop PV [25,26]. This subsection shows an example of a combined electrical/thermal model.

In order to reduce the model's complexity, we combined all the rooms into a single building *Air Thermal Mass*. Similarly, the roof, walls, and windows are each represented by a single thermal mass. Figure 4 shows the Simulink implementation, where the thermal masses describing the roof, walls, and windows are connected on one side to the indoor air thermal mass and on the other side to the external atmosphere. The heat conduction and convection coefficients serve as input parameters regulating the heat flow on either side. The outdoor air temperature comes from a regional dataset of measured climate data.

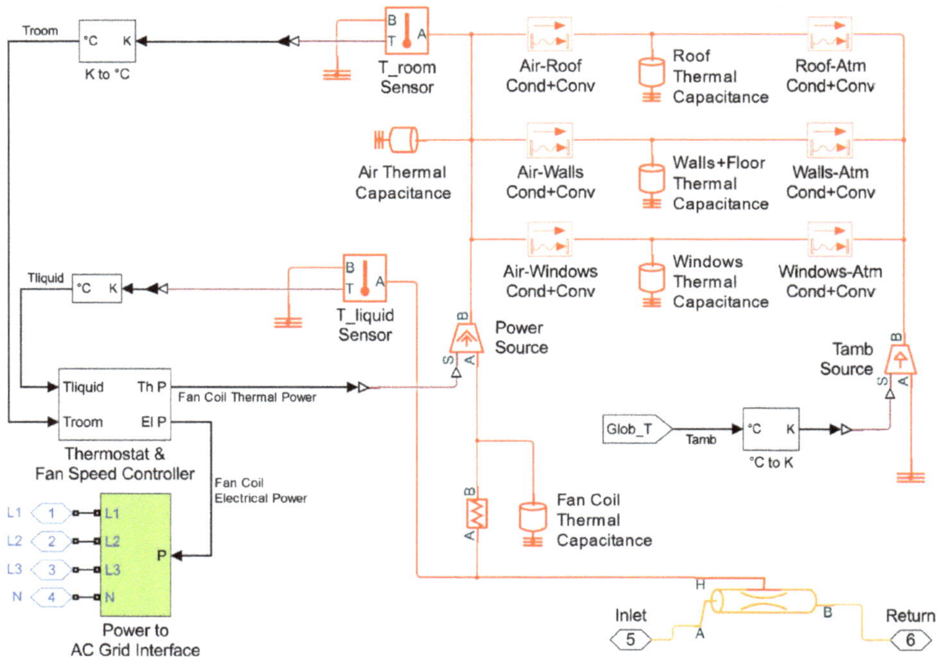

Figure 4. Thermal model of the VisLab building.

The conductive and convective heat transfers are modeled by means of the library elements *Conductive Heat Transfer* and *Convective Heat Transfer* implementing, respectively, the Fourier and Newton laws in the MATLAB Simscape environment.

In Table 1 we summarize the main parameters of the thermal network representing the building. They are derived from the building architectural project according to the UNI Italian standards UNI 10077-1 [27] (regarding the transmittance of window components), UNI 10351 [28] (regarding the thermo-physical properties of construction materials), and UNI 10355 [29] (regarding the thermal resistance of the hollow core concrete slab area).

Table 1. Main parameters of the thermal network representing the building.

Parameter	Roof	Walls and Floor	Windows	Internal Volume
Heat transfer coefficient [$W\cdot m^{-2}\cdot K^{-1}$]	12	24	25	-
Thermal conductivity [$W\cdot m^{-1}\cdot K^{-1}$]	0.038	0.038	0.78	-
Area [m^2]	770	800	60	-
Thickness [m]	0.2	0.2	0.01	-
Mass of the air [kg]	4925	307,200	1620	9475
Specific heat [$J\cdot K^{-1}\cdot kg^{-1}$]	835	835	840	1005

The heating or cooling action performed by the fan coil units is modeled by means of a controlled thermal *Power Source* that transfers heat from the convector coil to the indoor air mass according to the control signal *Fan Coil Thermal Power*. The convector coil is a pipe wherein flows the thermal fluid coming from the heat pump, with a thermal mass representing its thermal capacitance (bottom right of Figure 4).

The *Fan Coil Thermal Power* is computed by the *Thermostat and Fan Speed Controller* subsystem, the implementation of which is shown in Figure 5. The power value is obtained from the nominal heating (*HeaterPow*) or cooling (*CoolerPow*) capabilities of the fan coil, according to the season of operation—whether it is summer for cooling or winter for heating. This value is then reduced by applying two factors. The first one is the cooling/heating thermal efficiency, the second one is the normalized fan speed.

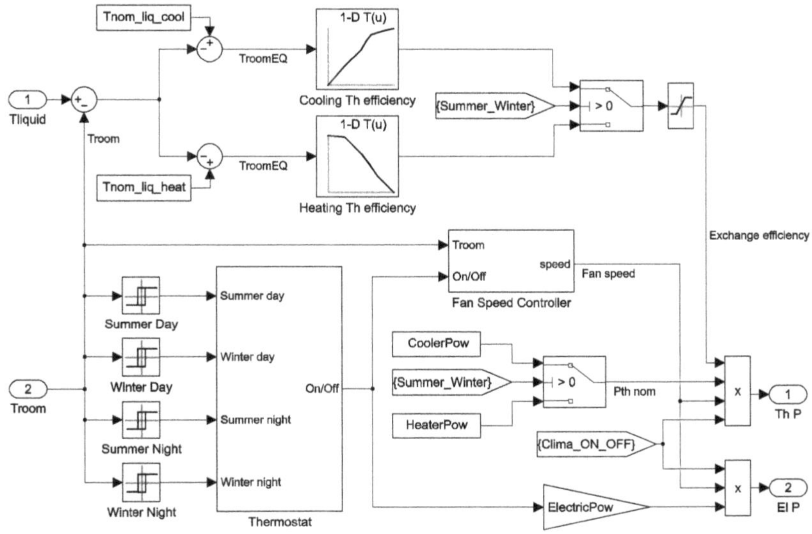

Figure 5. Thermostat and Fan Speed Controller subsystem implementation in Simulink model.

During midseasons, the fan coil stays off. However, in summer and winter, the fan is activated by a hysteresis thermostat (see Figure 5) that has the four different temperature set points shown in Table 2, established on the basis of user comfort. These set points depend on the season and working hours. The system is designed to operate in the *normal* mode during working days and hours, while also offering a *quiet* mode. The *quiet* mode serves as a compromise between energy savings and the need to maintain the temperature within acceptable bounds.

Table 2. Normal and quiet modes' temperature hysteresis thresholds applied in the Thermostat and Fan Speed Controller subsystem.

		Season	
		Summer	**Winter**
Mode	**Normal**	22 ÷ 23 °C	20 ÷ 21 °C
	Quiet	26 ÷ 28 °C	13 ÷ 14 °C

When the fan coil is active, its speed depends on the difference between the room temperature and the thermostat set-point, as detailed in Table 3 (in *quiet* mode the speed is L1).

Table 3. Fan speed as a function of the difference between the room temperature and the temperature set point of the thermostat controller.

$\Delta T = T_{room} - T_{set}$	Fan Speed Level
$\Delta T \leq 0.5$ °C	L1 (30% of max speed)
0.5 °C < $\Delta T \leq 1.5$ °C	L2 (70% of max speed)
$\Delta T > 1.5$ °C	L3 (max speed)

The fan state (on/off, speed) is combined with the heat exchange efficiencies shown in Figure 6 to yield the *Fan Coil Thermal Power*. The equivalent room temperature on the horizontal axes of the charts in Figure 6 is not the actual room temperature but an equivalent value ($Troom_{EQ}$ in Figure 5) that accounts for the variations of both room and fluid temperatures. As shown in the top left corner of Figure 5, in order to obtain the equivalent room temperature, we compute the difference between the actual liquid temperature and the reference value chosen by the fan coil manufacturer when measuring the heat exchange efficiency curves. This approach accounts for the varying behavior due to changes in liquid temperature. The computed equivalent room temperature value is finally fed as input to the efficiency curves of the fan coil, shown in Figure 6. This efficiency represents the heating/cooling capability of the fan coil based on the temperature of the environment in which it operates and is defined to be 1 at nominal room temperature, namely 20 °C in heating mode and 27 °C in cooling mode. The resulting behavior in the heating case in Figure 6 (top) shows that efficiency decreases as the actual room temperature increases and/or as the fluid temperature decreases, while the opposite happens in the cooling case.

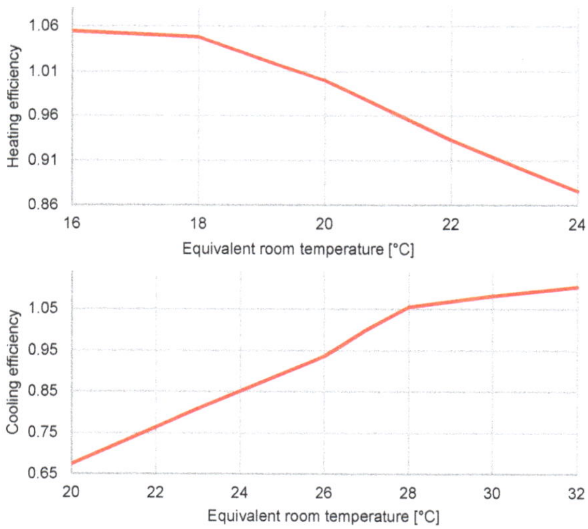

Figure 6. Fan coil heat exchange efficiency curves as a function of the equivalent room air temperature for heating (nominal temperature: 20 °C) (**top**), and cooling (nominal temperature: 27 °C) (**bottom**). The efficiency is defined to be 1 at the nominal temperature. Data from the manufacturer data sheet.

The algorithm governing the operation of the fan coil unit model (*Thermostat and Fan Speed Controller*, Figure 4) is summarized by the following set of equations:

$$P_{th} = a \cdot c_S \cdot P_{th_{nom}} \cdot f\left(T_{room_{eq}}\right) \quad (1)$$

$$T_{room_{eq}} = T_{room} \cdot \left(T_{liquid} \cdot T_{liquid_{ref}} \right) \quad (2)$$

$$P_{el} = b \cdot c_S \cdot P_{el_{nom}} \quad (3)$$

$$a = \begin{cases} 1, & s = \text{L3} \\ 0.7, & s = \text{L2} \\ 0.3, & s = \text{L1} \\ 0.05, & s = \text{L0} \end{cases} \quad b = \begin{cases} 1, & s = \text{L3} \\ 0.7, & s = \text{L2} \\ 0.3, & s = \text{L1} \\ 0, & s = \text{L0} \end{cases} \quad (4)$$

with

P_{th}	computed thermal power in watts provided by the fan coil to the indoor air mass.
a	fan thermal exchange capability (non-zero even when off, due to coil-to-air heat exchange).
c_S	binary variable indicating the activation state of the conditioning system (when zero, it means that the recirculating liquid is also stopped).
$P_{th_{nom}}$	nominal thermal power in watts of a fan coil unit (different when heating or cooling).
$f(\bullet)$	non-linear efficiency/room temperature function of a fan coil unit (see Figure 6).
$T_{room_{eq}}$	computed equivalent room temperature in degrees Celsius.
T_{room}	temperature of the air inside the building in degrees Celsius.
T_{liquid}	temperature of the liquid inside the coil in degrees Celsius.
$T_{liquid_{ref}}$	reference temperature of the liquid inside the coil (50 °C when heating, 10 °C when cooling).
P_{el}	computed amount of electrical power absorbed by the fan coil unit in watts.
b	like a, but applied to the electrical power absorbed by the unit.
$P_{el_{nom}}$	nominal electrical power rating (in watts) of a unit.
s	fan speed setting (Table 3, L0 means that the fan is off).

The electrical power consumed by the fan coil is computed according to the speed of the fan and is absorbed from the campus grid by means of the *Power to AC Grid Interface* block (Figure 4).

We coupled the building subsystem model (Figure 4) with the heat pump unit subsystem model (Figure 7), which features the following:

- A pair of pipes implementing a lumped model of the thermal liquid circuit.
- A water tank, which is the thermal storage unit of the system.
- Two recirculation pumps.
- A heat exchanger, whereby the thermal power generated by the heat pump is transferred to the thermal liquid.
- A controlled thermal power source connected to the heat exchanger, representing the thermal pump heating action.
- A temperature source for outdoor temperature reference.

The model implemented in Figure 7 consists of two thermal liquid circuits, each with its own *Circulating Pump*. *Circulating Pump 1* pumps water from the tank through a heat exchanger where the water is heated up or cooled down by the heat pump (*Power Source*), before flowing back into the tank. The heat exchanger is also coupled with the ambient temperature (*Tamb Source*) to emulate the system thermal losses. The second circuit, driven by *Circulating Pump 2*, pumps water from the tank through the pipeline that supplies the fan coil unit. The pumps are modeled by means of the *Fixed Displacement Pump* block from the Simscape library, supplied by an *Angular Velocity Source* and set at the desired rotating speed. The amount of thermal power provided to the water by the heat pump is computed by the *Act. Curves* block (Figure 8) and it is proportional to the difference between the water temperature set-point and the actual value of the temperature of the liquid in the tank. The control logic uses different temperature set-point ranges depending on the time of day and on the working days calendar, as shown in Table 4.

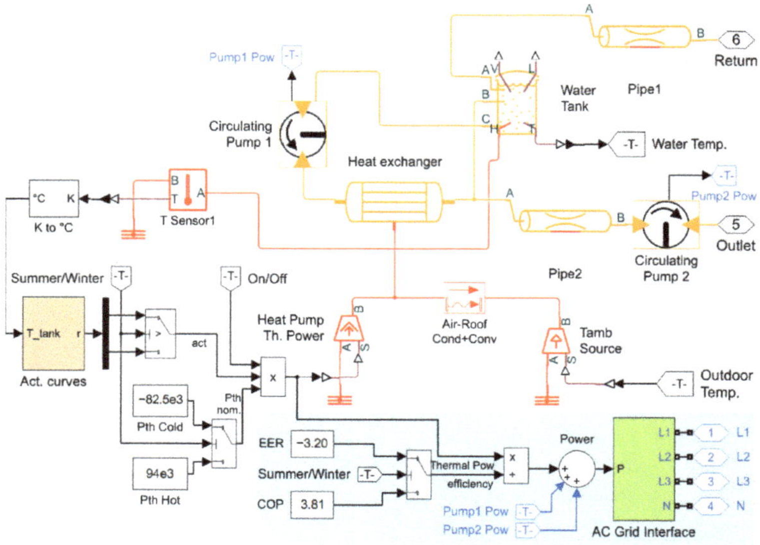

Figure 7. Model of the heat pump unit with the water tank, the heat exchanger and the circulating pumps. Physical ports 5 and 6 correspond to the same ports in Figure 4: the liquid circulates from the heat pump outlet to the fan coil inlet, then it returns into the water tank.

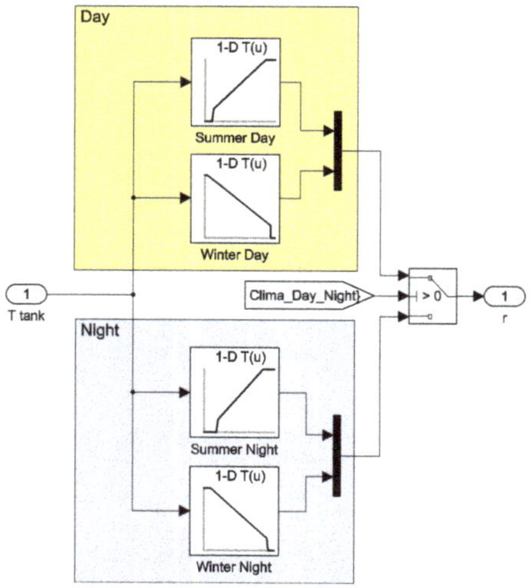

Figure 8. Details of the implementation of the Act. Curves block (Figure 7).

Table 4. Water temperature range thresholds employed in the control of the heat pump unit.

		Season	
		Summer	**Winter**
Mode	**Normal**	10 ÷ 18 °C	40 ÷ 50 °C
	Quiet	16 ÷ 20 °C	38 ÷ 42 °C

The electrical consumption of the heat pump is computed by applying the Energy Efficiency Ratio (EER) and Coefficient of Performance (COP) to the value of generated thermal power, according to the operating mode of the system (cooling or heating). The electrical power value is finally absorbed from the campus grid (*AC Grid Interface* block in Figure 7).

4. Simulation Results

The time dependence of the electrical power consumption of the heating/cooling system displayed in Figure 9 for a sample week in January shows the daily early morning peaks due to the heating pump restoring the liquid to *Normal* conditions after the nighttime rest, and the intra-day oscillations due to the on-off and step-speed regulation of the fan coil units. The total electrical energy consumption for the air conditioning is about 11 MWh during the first part of the year (heating mode), 5 MWh during the summer period (cooling mode), and 7 MWh during the final part of the year (heating mode), with a global annual consumption of about 23 MWh. Figure 10a shows the details of the power consumption of the conditioning system of the building during an entire sample year, while Figure 10b shows how the temperature of the vector liquid and the amount of thermal power provided by the heat pump to the liquid vary during different periods of the year.

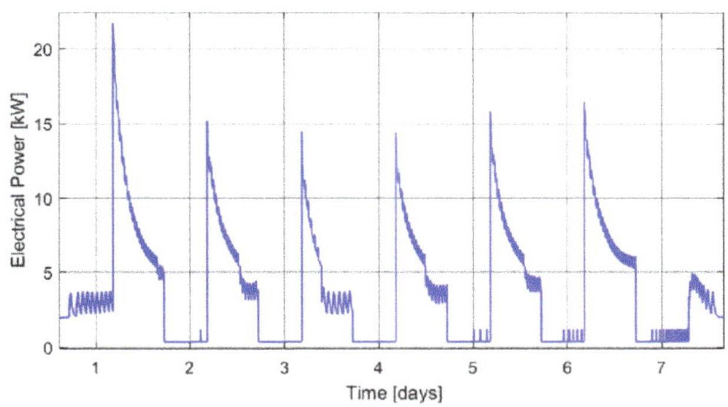

Figure 9. Power consumption of the air conditioning system of the VisLab building for a week in January.

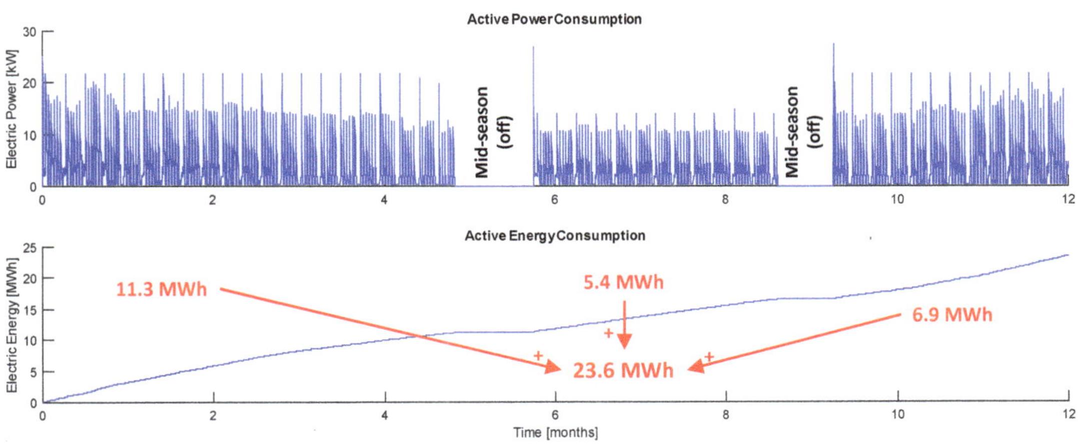

(**a**)

Figure 10. *Cont.*

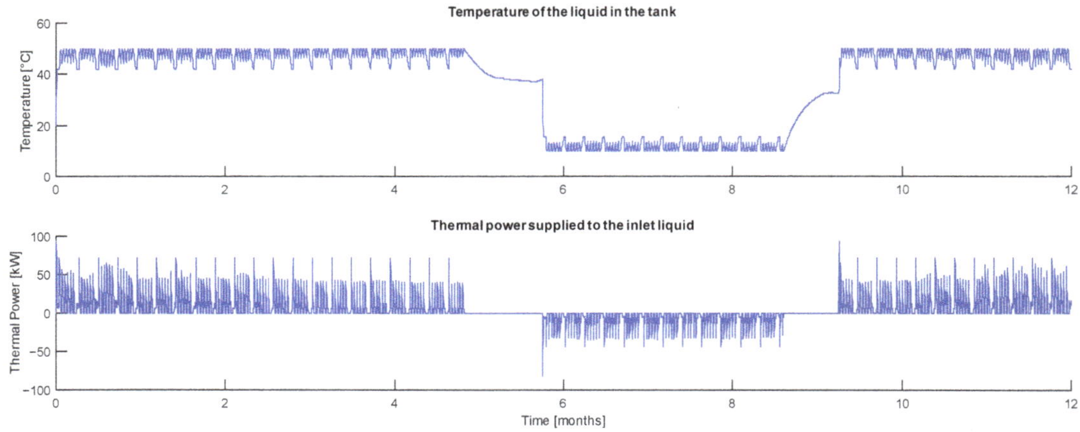

(b)

Figure 10. Example of simulation showing (**a**) the electrical consumption of the heating/cooling system during an entire year and (**b**) the temperature of the vector liquid and the amount of thermal power provided by the heat pump to the liquid during different periods of the year.

The monthly electrical energy budget for the simulated building is presented in Figure 11. In Figure 11a, we compare the consumption of the air conditioning system (blue circles), the electrical loads (green circles), and the energy production from the PV system (orange squares). It is clear that the photovoltaic production is insufficient to meet the total load demand. However, on average, PV production can satisfy the energy demand of the heat pump air conditioning system over the entire year. In fact, the total photovoltaic production amounts to 28.5 MWh, while the consumption by the air conditioning system is 23.6 MWh.

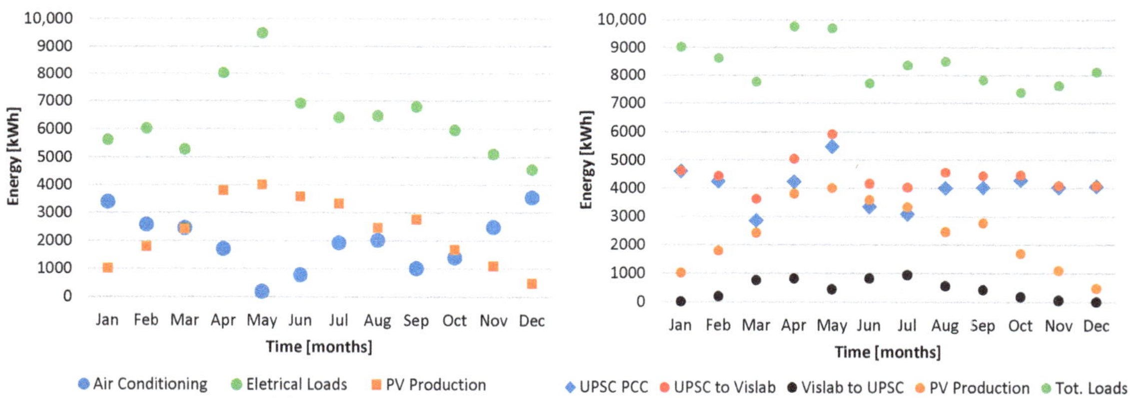

(a) (b)

Figure 11. Electrical energy budget for the simulated building: (**a**) comparison between air conditioning system consumption (*blue*), electrical loads (*green*) and PV energy production (*orange*); (**b**) detailed balance between produced PV energy (*orange*), total loads consumption including air conditioning (*green*) and energy exchange with the UPSC grid (*blue*); the latter is further split between the energy absorbed from the UPSC grid (*red*) and that injected into the UPSC grid (*black*).

In Table 5 we show an example of sensitivity analysis where we evaluate how sensitive the electrical power output of the model (E_{el}) is to variations in key parameters of the building thermal network, namely the heat transfer coefficients, the thermal conductivities and the COP/EER coefficients. Starting from the blueprint specifications for the VisLab building, we varied the parameters by ±10%.

Table 5. Sensitivity of the heating/cooling model to variations in the thermal network parameters.

Heat Transfer Coefficient	Thermal Conductivity	COP	EER	Electrical Energy (E_{el})	ΔE_{el} [%]
Table 1	Table 1	3.81	3.20	23.65 MWh/year	
+10%	Table 1	3.81	3.20	24.38 MWh/year	+3.1%
Table 1	+10%	3.81	3.20	24.12 MWh/year	+2.0%
+10%	+10%	3.81	3.20	24.89 MWh/year	+5.2%
Table 1	Table 1	+10%	+10%	21.83 MWh/year	−7.68%
+10%	Table 1	+10%	+10%	22.50 MWh/year	−4.83%
Table 1	+10%	+10%	+10%	22.26 MWh/year	−5.86%
+10%	+10%	+10%	+10%	22.97 MWh/year	−2.86%
Table 1	Table 1	−10%	−10%	25.87 MWh/year	+9.38%
+10%	Table 1	−10%	−10%	26.67 MWh/year	+12.78%
Table 1	+10%	−10%	−10%	26.38 MWh/year	+11.56%
+10%	+10%	−10%	−10%	27.23 MWh/year	+15.13%

In Figure 11b, we delve into a more detailed balance of the energy dynamics. Here, the focus is on the produced PV energy (orange circles), the total consumption of all loads including the air conditioning (green circles), and the net energy flowing into the PPC from the UPSC grid into the building (blue diamonds); the latter is further broken down into two components: the energy absorbed from the UPSC grid (red circles) and that injected into the UPSC grid (black circles). This detailed breakdown helps us to understand the interaction between the building's energy consumption, its internal energy production, and its reliance on the UPSC grid. Figure 12 provides a comprehensive annual overview of the electrical breakdown. The PV generation presents a load-matching index of 28.4%, covering the whole air conditioning system energy demand, which represents 23.5% of the total electrical loads. Finally, Figure 13 shows the estimated CO_2 emissions based on the monthly consumption of energy absorbed from the UPSC grid. We considered two scenarios: without PV generation by the VisLab building (Figure 13, orange circles) and with PV generation (Figure 13, blue circles). The emission factor $\left[\frac{gco_2}{kWh}\right]$ is calculated using data from the geographical region where the UPSC is located [30] and adjusted according to the amount of renewable energy self-produced within the UPSC. The estimate shows that, on an annual basis, the presence of internal generation from renewable sources can reduce the building's energy carbon footprint by approximately 47%.

Figures 14 and 15 present comparisons between simulation results and real-world data. Currently, we only have access to monthly data from legacy metering devices, lacking granular field data. Figure 14 compares the simulated PV energy production with actual production on both a monthly and annual basis. Figure 15, on the other hand, contrasts the measured and simulated net electrical energy exchange between the Vislab building and the UPSC grid. In both cases, we observe a good match between the cumulative annual energy shares. Model error metrics corresponding with the data in Figures 14 and 15 (month-by-month relative errors and overall year-round RMSE) are reported in Table 6. It is important to note that the climatic and environmental data (namely, solar irradiance, ambient temperature, wind direction, and speed) used as input for the model are not derived from on-site measurements, but from averaged climatic databases corresponding to the geographical area in which the UPSC is located [31].

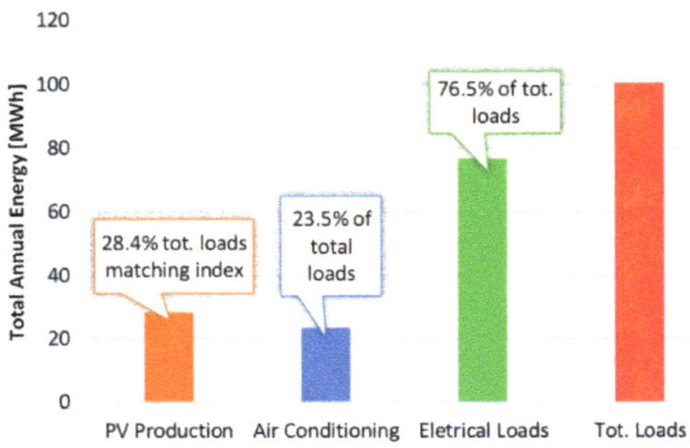

Figure 12. Total annual electrical energy breakdown. The PV shows a load-matching index of about 28.4%.

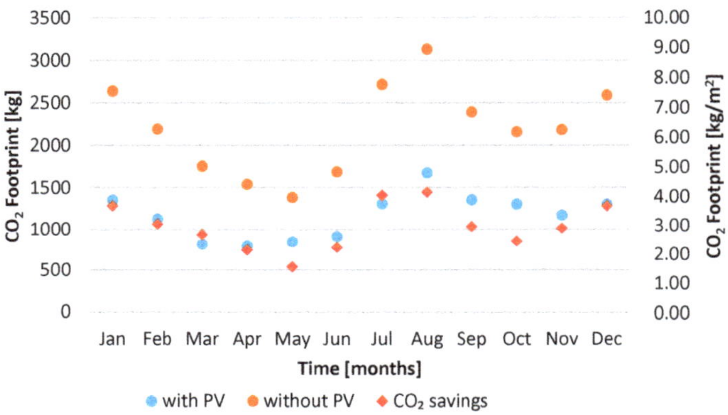

Figure 13. Estimated monthly CO_2 emitted by the VisLab building, considering two different scenarios: with (*blue*) and without (*orange*) PV rooftop generation. The right axis shows the unit area CO_2 emissions.

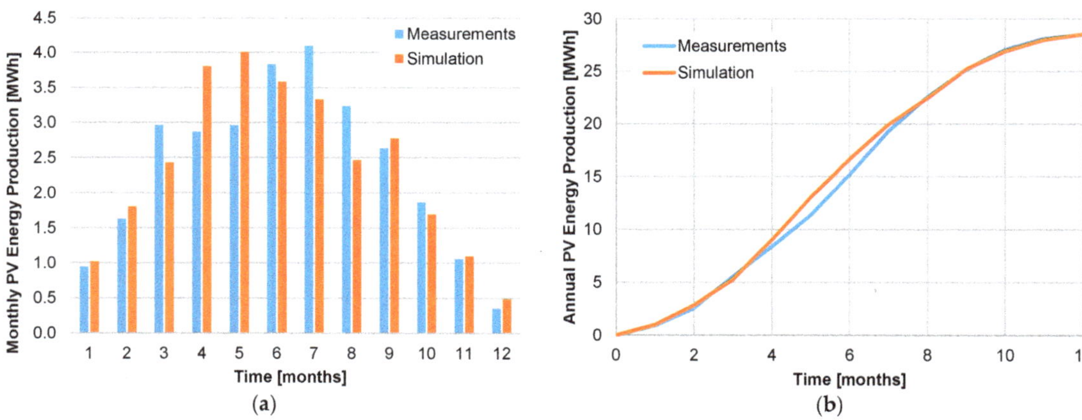

Figure 14. Comparison of monthly (**a**) and annual (**b**) PV energy production results with on-field-measured data.

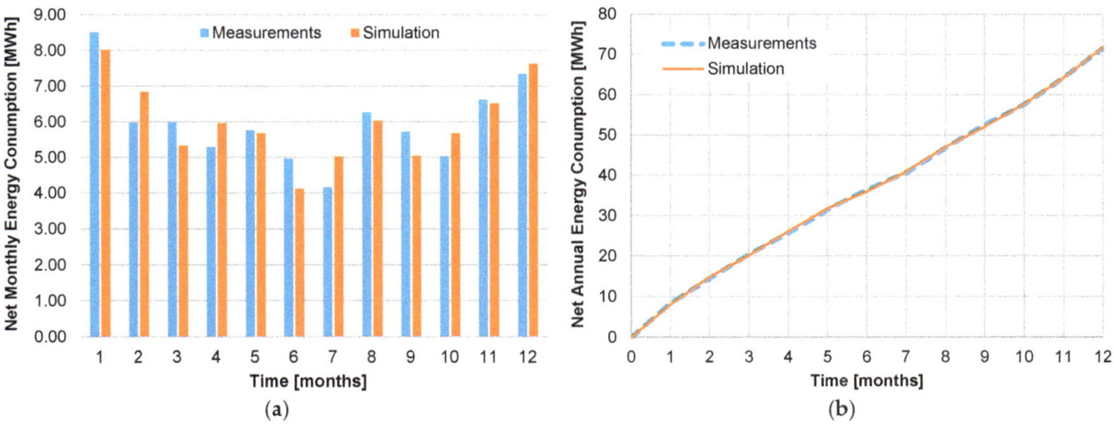

Figure 15. Comparison of measured and simulated monthly (**a**) and annual (**b**) net electrical energy exchange with the UPSC grid.

Table 6. Model error metrics for monthly PV energy production and net building electrical energy consumption.

Month	Error	
	PV Energy (Figure 14)	**Energy Consumption (Figure 15)**
1	8.2%	5.8%
2	10%	14%
3	18%	11%
4	32%	13%
5	35%	1.3%
6	6.6%	17%
7	19%	21%
8	24%	3.8%
9	5.3%	12%
10	9.0%	13%
11	3.8%	1.6%
12	34%	3.7%
RMSE	547 kWh	603 kWh

The methodology we adopted allows for easy adaptation of the building model to various specific cases. This is due to its standardized smart building features, including grid connectivity, rooftop photovoltaic generation, a heat pump-based climate control system, blueprint-derived thermal network, and a generalized load consumption profile, all of which can be tailored through simple adjustments to case-specific parameters. This means that once the case study is defined, the model can be fully customized by adjusting the numerous available parameters. For example, PV generation can be configured based on specific technology and local climatic and weather data; inverter efficiency curves can also be included, and so on. On the other hand, the building model is fully parameterized both in terms of electrical loads and thermal network (e.g., building thermal exchange coefficients, heating unit thermal efficacy, heat pump COP and EER, etc.). Furthermore, by integrating climate-responsive parameters and load behavior, the model can be recalibrated to accommodate different environmental conditions and energy demands.

Moreover, the proposed model is well-suited for exploring new energy scenarios at both building and district levels, taking into account the gradual introduction and planning of new components (e.g., RES, BESS, etc.). For instance, in [32] the authors demonstrate how the model can be used to optimize the planning of maintenance interventions on PV systems in order to identify the right balance between costs and benefits, while in [16] we study the introduction of PV and BESS, starting from a legacy grid scenario. These applications highlight the versatility of the simulation framework in supporting energy planning, grid integration, and policy development.

A few limitations of our approach—at least as far as the present stage of the research is concerned—are finally worth pointing out here.

- The use of the constant-frequency discrete-time three-phase phasor-domain approach allowed us to keep the computational overhead within bounds compatible with the calculation of economic and environmental sustainability figures over long periods of time. On the other hand, this simplification prevents the electrical campus model from accounting for AC frequency variation due to changes in power consumption or generation and other non-steady-state phenomena. This is clearly a limitation as far as the simulation of the interaction between the building and the campus micro-grid is concerned.
- Another significant limitation at the present stage of this activity is the lack of a pervasive metering network able to provide the model with building-specific power data taken at short time intervals. The deployment of metering units has just recently started and it is expected that consistent data collection will start being available in the coming months. This will provide us with the necessary information for evaluating the model's accuracy and, if necessary, improving it.
- It is also worth mentioning that we did not set out to develop a Building Energy Management System, so no optimization algorithm is presently included for energy efficiency or cost minimization.

5. Conclusions

In this work, we presented an Integrated Building Energy Modeling (IBEM) approach, developed in the MATLAB environment, to simulate a building that is a representative example of the current trends towards sustainability (increasing electrification and localized energy production by rooftop PV). The model seamlessly integrates dynamic thermal and electrical behaviors by including the heating/cooling system model, photovoltaic generation, and electrical loads into a complete, physical description of the energy performance of a smart building, and is part of the comprehensive MATLAB Simulink electrical model of the University of Parma South Campus micro-grid.

The key results of this work can therefore be summarized as follows:

- We have developed a MATLAB Simulink IBEM model based on a physical description of all the relevant components, and seamlessly integrated it into our campus micro-grid model;
- The physical, white-box approach we followed makes it straightforward to apply the building model to different specific instances, given its standard smart building features of grid connection, PV rooftop generation, heat pump-based conditioning system, blueprint-based thermal exchange parameters, and generic load consumption description, with a simple change of case-specific parameter settings;
- The fact that the whole model (IBEM and micro-grid) is implemented in the MATLAB Simulink environment makes it fully portable and exploitable within the very

wide community of MATLAB users, including researchers, utility companies, and educational institutions.

We used the model to obtain a number of simulations describing the detailed energy performance of the building over a whole year, showing its usefulness in the building design and energy assessment phases. The results confirm that the model effectively meets the initial objectives of performing detailed scenario simulations on a monthly and annual timescale providing data about energy behavior, enabling empirical comparisons, and demonstrating strong potential for real-world deployment. Although complete experimental validation is at the present stage hindered by limited availability of field metering data, the comparison between the available experimental data and simulations is encouraging.

Thanks to the adopted approach, while the model is developed and validated within the context of a specific building and climate, its core principles and architecture offer a high degree of adaptability. The modular nature the framework—encompassing energy generation, storage, distribution, and loads—allows for customization to suit various building types. Thus, with appropriate adjustments, it holds significant potential for broader application across diverse contexts and scenarios.

We believe, therefore, the model to represent a useful and effective tool to guide the design of smart/green buildings and plan their construction and integration in campus grids. Practical uses of the model include the design of building energy infrastructure, planning of its evolution and upgrades based on evolving economic and regulatory trends, and the possible contributions of smart/green buildings to surrounding grids. Furthermore, the use of the MATLAB environment can make it a widely available and effective educational tool.

- Future developments of this activity will follow these directions, in chronological order:
- The IBEM will be enhanced by the introduction of a BESS;
- The model validation will increasingly rely on field data coming from a metering network currently under deployment;
- Algorithms will be introduced to maximize energy efficiency and minimize costs and carbon emissions.

Author Contributions: Conceptualization, M.S., N.D., P.C. and R.M.; investigation, M.S.; methodology, M.S.; writing—original draft, M.S.; writing—review and editing, N.D., P.C. and R.M.; supervision, R.M. All authors have read and agreed to the published version of the manuscript.

Funding: Project funded under the National Recovery and Resilience Plan (NRRP), Mission 4 Component 2 Investment 1.5-Call for tender No. 3277 of 30 December 2021 of the Italian Ministry of University and Research, funded by the European Union–NextGenerationEU. Project code: ECS00000033, Concession Decree No. 1052 of 23 June 2022, adopted by the Italian Ministry of University and Research, CUP D93C22000460001, project title: Ecosystem for Sustainable Transition in Emilia-Romagna.

Data Availability Statement: The original contributions presented in this study are included in the article. Further inquiries can be directed to the corresponding author.

Conflicts of Interest: The authors declare no conflicts of interest.

Abbreviations

The following abbreviations are used in this manuscript:

DER	Distributed Energy Resources
PV	Photovoltaic
BESS	Battery Energy Storage System

MG	Micro-Grid
UPSC	University of Parma South Campus
BEMS	Building Energy Management System
HVAC	Heating, Ventilation Air Conditioning System
EV	Electric Vehicle
CHP	Combined Heat and Power
FMI	Functional Mock-up Interface
IBEM	Integrated Building Energy Model
PCC	Point of Common Coupling
EER	Energy Efficiency Ratio
COP	Coefficient of Performance

References

1. Cao, J.; Spulbar, C.; Eti, S.; Horobet, A.; Yüksel, S.; Dinçer, H. Innovative Approaches to Green Digital Twin Technologies of Sustainable Smart Cities Using a Novel Hybrid Decision-Making System. *J. Innov. Knowl.* **2025**, *10*, 100651. [CrossRef]
2. Wang, Y.; Wang, Y.; Ni, J.; Zhang, H. Integration of Smart Buildings with High Penetration of Storage Systems in Isolated 100% Renewable Microgrids. *J. Energy Storage* **2025**, *105*, 114633. [CrossRef]
3. Kılkış, B.; Çağlar, M.; Şengül, M. Energy Benefits of Heat Pipe Technology for Achieving 100% Renewable Heating and Cooling for Fifth-Generation, Low-Temperature District Heating Systems. *Energies* **2021**, *14*, 5398. [CrossRef]
4. Herrando, M.; Ramos, A. Photovoltaic-Thermal (PV-T) Systems for Combined Cooling, Heating and Power in Buildings: A Review. *Energies* **2022**, *15*, 3021. [CrossRef]
5. Zhang, S.; Ocłoń, P.; Klemeš, J.J.; Michorczyk, P.; Pielichowska, K.; Pielichowski, K. Renewable Energy Systems for Building Heating, Cooling and Electricity Production with Thermal Energy Storage. *Renew. Sustain. Energy Rev.* **2022**, *165*, 112560. [CrossRef]
6. Stamatellos, G.; Zogou, O.; Stamatelos, A. Interaction of a House's Rooftop PV System with an Electric Vehicle's Battery Storage and Air Source Heat Pump. *Solar* **2022**, *2*, 186–214. [CrossRef]
7. Rojek, I.; Mikołajewski, D.; Galas, K.; Piszcz, A. Advanced Deep Learning Algorithms for Energy Optimization of Smart Cities. *Energies* **2025**, *18*, 407. [CrossRef]
8. Muse, L.P.; Routray, S.; Oleinikova, I. Smart Grids for Smart Cities. *IEEE Smart Grid Bulletin* **2022**.
9. Brown, A.; Foley, A.; Laverty, D.; McLoone, S.; Keatley, P. Heating and Cooling Networks: A Comprehensive Review of Modelling Approaches to Map Future Directions. *Energy* **2022**, *261*, 125060. [CrossRef]
10. Olympios, A.V.; Kourougianni, F.; Arsalis, A.; Papanastasiou, P.; Pantaleo, A.M.; Markides, C.N.; Georghiou, G.E. A Holistic Framework for the Optimal Design and Operation of Electricity, Heating, Cooling and Hydrogen Technologies in Buildings. *Appl. Energy* **2024**, *370*, 123612. [CrossRef]
11. Bayasgalan, A.; Park, Y.S.; Koh, S.B.; Son, S.-Y. Comprehensive Review of Building Energy Management Models: Grid-Interactive Efficient Building Perspective. *Energies* **2024**, *17*, 4794. [CrossRef]
12. Hoseinpoori, P.; Olympios, A.V.; Markides, C.N.; Woods, J.; Shah, N. A Whole-System Approach for Quantifying the Value of Smart Electrification for Decarbonising Heating in Buildings. *Energy Convers. Manag.* **2022**, *268*, 115952. [CrossRef]
13. Causone, F.; Scoccia, R.; Pelle, M.; Colombo, P.; Motta, M.; Ferroni, S. Neighborhood Energy Modeling and Monitoring: A Case Study. *Energies* **2021**, *14*, 3716. [CrossRef]
14. Sola, A.; Corchero, C.; Salom, J.; Sanmarti, M. Simulation Tools to Build Urban-Scale Energy Models: A Review. *Energies* **2018**, *11*, 3269. [CrossRef]
15. Simonazzi, M.; Delmonte, N.; Cova, P.; Ferrari, G.; Zanichelli, F.; Menozzi, R. Modeling of a University Campus Micro-Grid for Optimal Planning of Renewable Generation and Storage Deployment. In Proceedings of the 2021 IEEE International Smart Cities Conference (ISC2), Manchester, UK, 7–10 September 2021; IEEE: Piscataway, NJ, USA, 2021; pp. 1–7.
16. Simonazzi, M.; Delmonte, N.; Cova, P.; Menozzi, R. Models for MATLAB Simulation of a University Campus Micro-Grid. *Energies* **2023**, *16*, 5884. [CrossRef]
17. Gambarotta, A.; Morini, M.; Rossi, M.; Stonfer, M. A Library for the Simulation of Smart Energy Systems: The Case of the Campus of the University of Parma. *Energy Procedia* **2017**, *105*, 1776–1781. [CrossRef]
18. De Lorenzi, A.; Gambarotta, A.; Morini, M.; Rossi, M.; Saletti, C. Setup and Testing of Smart Controllers for Small-Scale District Heating Networks: An Integrated Framework. *Energy* **2020**, *205*, 118054. [CrossRef]
19. Bianco, G.; Bracco, S.; Delfino, F.; Gambelli, L.; Robba, M.; Rossi, M. A Building Energy Management System Based on an Equivalent Electric Circuit Model. *Energies* **2020**, *13*, 1689. [CrossRef]

20. Moya, F.; Torres-Moreno, J.; Álvarez, J. Optimal Model for Energy Management Strategy in Smart Building with Energy Storage Systems and Electric Vehicles. *Energies* **2020**, *13*, 3605. [CrossRef]
21. Khan, M.H.; Asar, A.U.; Ullah, N.; Albogamy, F.R.; Rafique, M.K. Modeling and Optimization of Smart Building Energy Management System Considering Both Electrical and Thermal Load. *Energies* **2022**, *15*, 574. [CrossRef]
22. Frank, S.; Ball, B.; Gerber, D.L.; Cu, K.; Othee, A.; Shackelford, J.; Ghatpande, O.; Brown, R.; Cale, J. Advances in the Co-Simulation of Detailed Electrical and Whole-Building Energy Performance. *Energies* **2023**, *16*, 6284. [CrossRef]
23. Alfalouji, Q.; Schranz, T.; Falay, B.; Wilfling, S.; Exenberger, J.; Mattausch, T.; Gomes, C.; Schweiger, G. Co-Simulation for Buildings and Smart Energy Systems—A Taxonomic Review. *Simul. Model. Pr. Theory* **2023**, *126*, 102770. [CrossRef]
24. Introducing the Phasor Simulation Method. Available online: https://it.mathworks.com/help/physmod/sps/powersys/ug/introducing-the-phasor-simulation-method.html (accessed on 1 August 2022).
25. Song, Y.; Peskova, M.; Rolando, D.; Zucker, G.; Madani, H. Estimating Electric Power Consumption of In-Situ Residential Heat Pump Systems: A Data-Driven Approach. *Appl. Energy* **2023**, *352*, 121971. [CrossRef]
26. Akbarzadeh, S.; Sefidgar, Z.; Sadegh Valipour, M.; Elmegaard, B.; Arabkoohsar, A. A Comprehensive Review of Research and Applied Studies on Bifunctional Heat Pumps Supplying Heating and Cooling. *Appl. Therm. Eng.* **2024**, *257*, 124280. [CrossRef]
27. *UNI 10077-1*; Thermal Performance of Windows, Doors and Shutters—Calculation of Thermal Transmittance. UNI (Italian National Standards Body): Milan, Italy, 2018.
28. *UNI 10351*; Building Materials—Thermo-Hygrometric Proprieties—Procedure for Determining the Design Values. UNI (Italian National Standards Body): Milan, Italy, 2021.
29. *UNI 10355*; Chemical Analysis of Ferrous Materials—Inductively Coupled Plasma Optical Emission Spectrometric Analysis of Unalloyed and Low Alloyed Steels—Determination of Si, Mn, P, Cu, Ni, Cr, Mo and Sn, Following Dissolution with Nitric and Sulphuric Acids [Routine Method]. UNI (Italian National Standards Body): Milan, Italy, 2013.
30. The Global Electricity Data Platform. Available online: https://app.electricitymaps.com/zone/IT-NO/72h/hourly (accessed on 14 February 2025).
31. ARPAE Emilia Romagna Dext3r. Available online: https://simc.arpae.it/dext3r/ (accessed on 18 June 2024).
32. Simonazzi, M.; Chiorboli, G.; Cova, P.; Menozzi, R.; Santoro, D.; Sapienza, S.; Sciancalepore, C.; Sozzi, G.; Delmonte, N. Smart Soiling Sensor for PV Modules. *Microelectron. Reliab.* **2020**, *114*, 113789. [CrossRef]

energies

MDPI

Brief Report

Conversion to Fourth-Generation District Heating (4GDH): Heat Accumulation Within Building Envelopes

Stanislav Chicherin [1,2]

[1] Thermo and Fluid Dynamics (FLOW), Faculty of Engineering, Vrije Universiteit Brussel (VUB), Pleinlaan 2, 1050 Brussels, Belgium; stanislav.chicherin@vub.be

[2] Brussels Institute for Thermal-Fluid Systems and Clean Energy (BRITE), Vrije Universiteit Brussel (VUB) and Université Libre de Bruxelles (ULB), 1050 Brussels, Belgium

Abstract: This study investigates improving district heating (DH) systems by analyzing the effects of low-temperature operation on network efficiency, heat losses, and indoor temperature stability. A mathematical model is developed to simulate building heat performance under different supply temperatures, substation connection types, and envelope materials. The methodology involves detailed hourly heat load simulations and optimization techniques to assess the impact of temperature flexibility and heat accumulation within buildings. The results reveal that a 10 °C reduction in supply temperature leads to a heat loss decrease of up to 20%, significantly improving system efficiency. Moreover, buildings with higher thermal inertia and indirect substation connections exhibit better resilience to short-term temperature fluctuations, ensuring more stable indoor conditions. The analysis also demonstrates that optimizing temperature control can reduce operational costs by 19%, primarily by minimizing excessive heat supply and utilizing stored thermal energy effectively. Despite slight temperature fluctuations in extreme conditions, the system maintains indoor comfort levels within acceptable limits. This study concludes that transitioning to a lower-temperature DH system is feasible without compromising reliability, provided heat accumulation effects and supply flexibility are carefully managed. These findings offer a replicable approach for improving DH efficiency in networks with diverse building configurations.

Keywords: energy storage; thermal inertia; transient; 4GDH; fourth-generation district heating

1. Introduction

1.1. Motivation and the Research Gap

The escalating global energy demand, pressing sustainability goals, and the urgent need for climate change mitigation underscore the importance of energy efficiency across all sectors. As the world's population grows and economies develop, the strain on finite energy resources intensifies, leading to environmental degradation, geopolitical instability, and economic vulnerabilities. Improving energy efficiency—achieving more output with less energy input—offers a crucial pathway for decoupling economic growth from increased energy consumption and its associated negative impacts. Reducing the overall energy demand can alleviate the pressure on energy production infrastructure, conserve natural resources, decrease greenhouse gas emissions, and enhance energy security. This makes energy efficiency a cornerstone of any strategy for achieving a sustainable and resilient energy future.

The building sector is a particularly significant area for energy efficiency improvements. Globally, buildings account for a substantial portion of total energy consumption and associated carbon emissions. Heating, ventilation, and air conditioning (HVAC) and domestic hot water (DHW) systems represent major energy end-uses within buildings. District heating (DH) systems play a vital role in supplying thermal energy to urban areas, offering potential advantages in terms of fuel flexibility, economies of scale, and reduced local emissions compared to individual building-level heating solutions. However, inefficiencies within DH networks, such as heat losses during distribution and suboptimal operational strategies, can significantly diminish their environmental and economic benefits. Therefore, enhancing the energy performance of buildings connected to DH systems and optimizing the operation of the DH networks themselves is crucial for realizing the full potential of district heating in a sustainable energy landscape.

Despite the recognized importance of energy efficiency in DH systems and connected buildings, a notable gap exists in the comprehensive understanding and effective implementation of strategies that holistically integrate building thermal characteristics with DH network operation. While considerable research has focused on optimizing individual components of the system—such as improving insulation materials, enhancing boiler efficiency, or developing advanced control algorithms for network flow—less attention has been paid to the dynamic interplay between the thermal behavior of diverse building types and the operational parameters of the DH network, particularly under varying conditions and in the context of advanced operational strategies like low-temperature district heating (LTDH). The existing literature often treats buildings as uniform loads or focuses on specific building typologies in isolation, neglecting the heterogeneity of the building stock connected to a typical DH network and the implications of this diversity for overall system efficiency and stability [1,2]. Furthermore, the potential for utilizing the thermal inertia of building envelopes as an inherent form of distributed energy storage within the DH system remains largely underexplored in conjunction with flexible network operation. More details are listed in Section 1.2.

This study addresses this gap by investigating the impact of building thermal performance characteristics, specifically focusing on the heat capacity and heat loss rates of different building typologies connected to a DH network. By analyzing the thermal response of various building types to fluctuations in DH supply temperature and external weather conditions, we seek to quantify the potential for leveraging building thermal inertia to enhance the efficiency and flexibility of DH system operation. Specifically, this research focuses on evaluating the benefits of LTDH in conjunction with the inherent heat accumulation capacity of building envelopes, aiming to demonstrate how a more integrated approach, considering both the DH network and the connected buildings as a coupled thermal system, can lead to significant reductions in heat losses, improved network stability, and enhanced overall energy efficiency. The analysis presented in the subsequent sections utilizes real-world case studies and simulation data to provide concrete insights into the potential of this integrated approach.

1.2. Previous Works

Meesenburg et al. [3] compare several low-temperature options, considering an SH share and involving a heat pump in a generation. They conclude that the feasibility of a configuration depends on the plot ratio of the supplied area and the proportion between capital costs in a DH plant and the additional investments in local facilities. Through simulation, it was observed that the developed control mechanism successfully stabilized the system's temperature, keeping it consistently within a range of 2 Kelvin around the pre-defined value (like the temperature of a room). Buffa et al. [4] simulate the coordinated balancing effects of several local units. This idea is more beneficial than the free-floating temperature approach in unidirectional and bidirectional DH systems.

Low-temperature DH networks can be implemented without the obligate integration of heat pump technology [5].

On the other hand, the essential element of any DH system is an energy transfer station—a substation. As in [6], this study evaluates various substation models to determine their suitability for characterizing network flexibility within DH systems. In Vandermeulen et al.'s papers [6], temperature flexibility is achieved by temporarily increasing the supply temperature. An accurate model of a DH system behavior is essential to evaluate the benefits obtained. Based on such a model, Jebamalai et al. [7] conclude which level of heat storage is best for hourly usage and which for seasonal usage. The options are accumulating heat into building envelopes, utilizing either centralized storage or substation thermal energy accumulators. However, Jebamalai et al.'s [7] focus was not on the flexibility itself but on the detail of the influence of these combinations mentioned above.

Heat demand profiles show that storage systems have smoother consumption and lower peaks than instantaneous DHW substations [8,9]. Kristensen et al. [10] use a Bayesian model to study their influence, link building, and archetype levels, factoring in building diversity. Superposing multiple curves of DHW consumption of instantaneous systems also results in more evenly distributed heat demand profiles with realistic behavior [8,11]. Kristensen et al. [10] leverage the previously defined archetype segmentation to calibrate uncertain input parameters in physics-based building energy models.

Other scientists have faced the same obstacles since the historical supply temperature. For example, according to the operational data, the DH system in the Skultuna area, Sweden, can achieve temperatures up to 110 °C. Saletti et al. [12] successfully cover another focus of their research—reducing heat losses. That makes our studies toward low-temperature DH closer and simpler to compare.

1.3. Use Case and Practical Applications

A literature review indicates that the feasibility of a concept can be assessed by comparing annual heat and electricity generation, taking into account the network section's return temperature, as demonstrated in [13]. The DH service users might also sense a positive effect, although indirectly, as the potential for heat price reduction through operator gains results in a benefit shared by all district heating consumers. Like us, Barone et al. [14] chose the week from 1–7 January 2020, to thoroughly study time histories of supply and return temperatures for four sample substations in Naples, Italy.

This work introduces a novel approach by analyzing the transition from low-temperature to standard (150/70) operation during increased heat demand periods, such as winter's onset. Unlike Hammer et al. [15], who suggest shutting down the DH network during low-demand periods with high heat losses and relying on decentralized thermal storage, our method considers pre-charging building envelopes before full-load operation. This pre-charging strategy results in a significantly reduced indoor temperature drop compared to a standard scenario.

The impact of building types and substation connections on energy performance is another area that requires further investigation. Although previous studies categorize buildings based on their construction year, substation connections, and envelope types, a deeper understanding of how these factors influence energy efficiency and heating demand over extended periods is essential. This is particularly important in large-scale urban settings, where building diversity can significantly affect system performance. Moreover, while this study acknowledges the challenges posed by older building stock, more data on the energy performance of these buildings, especially in comparison to newer, more energy-efficient structures, would be valuable. Understanding how DH systems can be upgraded to accommodate older buildings is crucial for developing strategies to reduce energy consumption in urban infrastructures.

1.4. Objectives, Novelty, and the Outline

The contributions of this study lie in its methodology, which provides insights into the feasibility of transitioning district heating systems toward low-temperature concepts. It demonstrates the potential of low-temperature and flexible temperature operation for reducing energy consumption and operational costs in DH systems, particularly by incorporating heat accumulation in building envelopes. This study also offers a detailed case study of Omsk, providing valuable data on how different building types and substation connections affect heating demand and system performance. This work serves as a model for assessing other district heating systems, offering a basis for further research and optimization in similar climates and urban settings. Additionally, this study emphasizes the importance of system flexibility and efficient temperature management, which could lead to significant energy savings and improved system stability in the future.

The mathematical model developed in this study introduces several innovative aspects that differentiate it from existing models used in DH system analysis. Unlike conventional models that often rely on static or annual average values, this model employs dynamic optimization using mixed-integer linear programming with an hourly resolution. This level of granularity allows for a more precise assessment of heat demand fluctuations and the potential for temperature flexibility. Additionally, the model integrates heat accumulation within building envelopes, a factor often neglected in previous studies, to assess its impact on supply temperature regulation and overall system efficiency.

One key innovation is incorporating flexible temperature control, considering immediate and delayed responses to outdoor temperature variations. This feature enables a better evaluation of how supply temperature reductions influence indoor thermal stability, energy consumption, and system-wide heat losses. The model also accounts for real operational constraints, including regulating valve dynamics and the influence of substation connection types on secondary loop temperature variations. Furthermore, it provides an in-depth analysis of how different envelope materials contribute to heat retention and dissipation, offering valuable insights into optimizing DH network performance in diverse building environments.

The introduction sets the context by outlining this study's objectives. Following this, the methodology section details the approach, including analyzing different building types, substation connections, envelope materials, and the operational data used to assess the heating demand. The case study describes particular buildings connected to a DH system in Omsk. The results and discussion section presents the findings from the simulations, focusing on heat demand variations, energy consumption, and the impact of different system configurations. This section also compares the results with other studies and discusses the potential benefits of low-temperature operations in DH systems. This paper concludes with a summary of the key findings, contributions to the field, and recommendations for future research, particularly in relation to integrating low-temperature heating and optimizing DH systems in similar climates.

2. Materials and Methods

This study employs a structured methodology to analyze the heating performance of different building types within the DH system. The approach integrates data collection, modeling, and simulation to assess the impact of LTDH operation on energy efficiency and heat loss reduction. The methodology consists of the following five components:

1. Selection of case study and building types;
2. Data collection and heat demand analysis;
3. Mathematical modeling and simulation;
4. Assessment of low-temperature operation and system flexibility;
5. Validation and comparative analysis.

To capture the diversity of buildings connected to the system, representative building cases were selected based on three primary characteristics: substation connection type (either direct or indirect connection to the DH network), building type (office buildings and residential buildings), envelope material (brick, prefabricated panels, or foam concrete wall blocks). This categorization results in nine unique building scenarios, comprehensively comparing different heating configurations and their energy performance.

This study analyzes heating demand based on real operational data collected between 11 November and 17 November, a transition period between moderate and cold weather. The primary focus is SH demand, with data from previous research and official records on building energy consumption. The analysis considers outdoor temperature profiles (to capture seasonal variations affecting heat demand), heat accumulation ability (evaluated based on building materials and construction details, supported by the previous literature), and supply and return temperature trends (observed to understand system behavior during cold periods).

These parameters help determine different DH configurations' energy efficiency and potential transition toward LTDH operation.

This study employs a mathematical model to simulate heat transfer and energy demand under different operational scenarios. The model incorporates building envelope characteristics (thermal conductivity, glazing ratio, and specific heat loss coefficients for each building type) and heat transfer equations to estimate heat accumulation, losses, and energy consumption over time. The mathematical model was compared with previous studies that used annual-resolution data, ensuring a more dynamic and realistic assessment.

To evaluate the feasibility of LTDH, different temperature scenarios were tested: conventional high-temperature DH operation (supply/return temperatures of 95/70 °C or higher), LTDH (reducing the supply temperature to 50–60 °C while maintaining efficient heat delivery), flexible temperature operation (dynamic supply temperature adjustments based on outdoor conditions and heat accumulation properties).

Indoor temperature profiles, heat loss reduction, and energy savings were analyzed for different cases. This study also investigated the impact of flexible temperature operation on compensation times and system stability.

The results were validated against reference buildings from similar studies, ensuring the model's accuracy in estimating heat demand and losses. The findings were further compared with case studies from other DH networks, such as those in Estonia and Sweden, to highlight similarities and differences in system performance under varying climatic conditions.

Like Turski et al. [16], this approach utilizes the specific heat of water to accumulate energy by artificially raising the supply flow temperature. The difference is the model we apply. The model was adopted as per the Russian scientist Koryagin M.V. (unpublished):

$$\delta t_{in} = \mu \cdot \frac{Q_{\max}}{F_0} \cdot \left(\frac{\Omega_{\max} - \Omega_{\min}}{Y_0} + \frac{\eta_{om}}{\overline{\alpha}} \right) \cdot \xi, \tag{1}$$

$$\Delta t_{in}^{-} = \mu \cdot \frac{Q_{\max}}{F_0} \cdot \left(\frac{\eta_{om}}{\overline{\alpha}} - \frac{\Omega_{\min}}{Y_0} + \frac{F_0 m}{q_0} \right) \cdot \xi, \tag{2}$$

$$\Delta t_{in}^{+} = \delta t_{in} - \Delta t_{in}^{-}, \tag{3}$$

where μ is a factor to compensate for error due to replacing a vector with a scalar;

Q_{max} is the building heat demand [W];

F_0 is the area of the envelopes' surface [m^2];

Y_0 is the overall heat transfer coefficient [W/(m^2·°C)];

$\frac{\eta_{om}}{\alpha}$ is the factor of combined convection and thermal radiation heat transfer;

ξ is a factor that characterizes the ability of furniture to absorb heat;

Ω is a factor indicating that solar and internal heat gains are non-steady-state;

q_0 represents building heat losses [W/°C].

The discharging time is equal to the time, which is enough for the indoor temperature drop ν_{in}(z), adopted from the ideas of Russian scientist Koryagin M.V. (unpublished):

$$\nu_{in}(z) = \frac{\nu'_{01}}{1-\beta \cdot m} \cdot e^{-z \cdot m} + \left(\nu'_{01} - \frac{\nu'_{01}}{1-\beta \cdot m}\right) \cdot e^{-z/\beta}, \tag{4}$$

If charging is a fast process, which may take place when there is negligible heat capacity of an SH system available, i.e., if a substation is connected directly (with no heat exchanger and no hydraulic separation of the primary and secondary circuits),

$$\nu_{in}(z) = \nu_{01}{}' \cdot e^{-z/\beta}, \tag{5}$$

and when the forecasted outdoor temperature t_{out} drops below the current temperature $t_{out.c}$,

$$t_{out} = t_{out.c} + \Sigma Q_{ihg}/\Sigma Q_{sp.hl} = t_{out.c} + \nu_t, \tag{6}$$

where ΣQ_{ihg} is internal heat gains [W];

$\Sigma Q_{sp.hl}$ is specific heat losses [W].

The building's heat accumulation capacity allows for substantial compensation periods, enabling the balancing of heat source output. Thus, z and β values can be considered to analyze the time and thermal performance of building envelopes to withstand temperature drops to the lowest values of indoor temperature $t_{in.l}$ (Equations (7) and (8), respectively):

$$z = \beta \cdot \ln \frac{k_t \cdot (t_{in} - t_{out} - \sum Q_{ihg}/\sum Q_{sp.hl})}{t_{in.l} - t_{out} - \sum Q_{ihg}/\sum Q_{sp.hl}}, \tag{7}$$

where k_t is a factor indicating the number of floors, glazing ratio, type of SH system, etc.;

t_{in} is the design indoor temperature [°C];

β [h] is

$$\beta = \frac{k_t \sum \delta_i c_i \rho_i F_i / 2}{3.6\left[\sum k_j F_j + Lc\rho\right]}, \tag{8}$$

where δ_i is the thickness of the i-th insulation layer [m];

ρ_i is the density of the i-th insulation material [kg/m^3];

c_i is the specific heat capacity of the i-th insulation material [W/kg°C];

F_i is the surface area of the i-th insulation material [m^2];

k_j is the heat transfer coefficient [W/m^2°C];

F_j is the surface area of the building envelope [m^2];

L is the infiltration rate [m^3/h];

ρ is the density of infiltrated air [kg/m^3];

c is the specific heat capacity of infiltrated air [W/kg°C].

The cost savings are assessed with the assumptions of the potential of low-temperature operation with no indoor temperature drop, which reduces heat losses during fall and spring, and a heat price of 30 EUR/MWh.

The linear heat loss density for each buried pipe, W/m, is given by

$$q_s^{und} = \frac{\pi(\tau_s^{design} - t_{soil}^{design})}{\frac{\ln\frac{d_{i.s}^{und}+2\delta}{d_{i.s}^{und}}}{2\pi\lambda} + \frac{\ln\frac{4h}{d_{i.s}^{und}+2\delta}}{2\pi\lambda_{soil}}}, \quad (9)$$

$$q_r^{und} = \frac{\pi(\tau_r^{design} - t_{soil}^{design})}{\frac{\ln\frac{d_{i.r}^{und}+2\delta}{d_{i.r}^{und}}}{2\pi\lambda} + \frac{\ln\frac{4h}{d_{i.r}^{und}+2\delta}}{2\pi\lambda_{soil}}}, \quad (10)$$

where τ_s^{design} and τ_r^{design} represent the design feed and return line temperatures, respectively [°C];

t_{soil}^{design} is the design soil temperature [°C];

$d_{i.s}^{und}$ and $d_{i.r}^{und}$ are the i-th network section's feed and return diameter, respectively [m];

δ is the insulation thickness [m];

λ is the thermal conductivity of the insulation material, W/(m°C);

h is the pipe depth, m;

λ_{soil} is the heat conductivity coefficient of the soil at the actual average monthly temperature, W/(m°C).

For the thermal conductivity λ, we adopted the value from Dalla Rosa et al.'s paper [17]. In contrast, Hammer et al. [15] used 0.03 W/(m°C).

Due to the absence of operational data, we applied the soil's mean heat conductivity coefficient at the measured temperature. Dalla Rosa et al. [18] employed 1.6 W/(m°C).

Unlike this study, Meesenburg et al. [3] estimated energy loss empirically, dividing the total annual heat demand by the estimated trench length. That calculation incorporated annual specific heat demand, the plot ratio, and the characteristic width. Arabkoohsar et al. [5] assessed energy losses as a derivative of dimensionless parameters based on line temperatures and diameters. Cai et al. [19] calculated temperature drops along pipes using soil temperature and heat transfer coefficients, but not heat losses directly. However, like Ref. [3], they adjusted heat losses based on supply and return temperatures.

Energy losses for the aboveground pipes, W/m, are given by

$$q_s^{above} = \frac{\pi(\tau_s - t_{out})}{\frac{\ln\frac{d_{i.s}^{above}+2\delta}{d_{i.s}^{above}}}{2\pi\lambda} + \frac{1}{2\pi\alpha\left(d_{i.s}^{above}+2\delta\right)}}, \quad (11)$$

$$q_r^{above} = \frac{\pi(\tau_r - t_{out})}{\frac{\ln\frac{d_{i.r}^{above}+2\delta}{d_{i.r}^{above}}}{2\pi\lambda} + \frac{1}{2\pi\alpha\left(d_{i.r}^{above}+2\delta\right)}}, \quad (12)$$

where α is the heat transfer coefficient at the ground surface, including convection and radiation ranging from 11.6 (if the wind is negligible) to 29 W/(m^2°C) (the maximum value according to the national design guideline):

$$\alpha = 11.6 + 7\sqrt{w}, \quad (13)$$

where w is the velocity of wind [m/s].

The simulation environment used in this research is based on ZuluThermo© (Saint-Petersburg, Russia, Politerm, LLC) and Microsoft Excel, where all calculations and scenario analyses were implemented using built-in mathematical functions and formulae. This study leverages Excel's computational capabilities to model the heat demand, supply temperature variations, and thermal inertia of buildings within the DH network of Omsk. The mathematical model incorporates heat transfer equations, energy balance formulations, and optimization conditions, ensuring the simulated results align with real-world operational data.

The equations provided in this study are embedded in the Excel environment, allowing for iterative computations and scenario testing under different supply temperature settings. ZuluThermo© is utilized for assessing the temperature and flow rate adjustments, enabling the analysis of heat accumulation effects and temperature compensation times across various building types and substation configurations. This approach ensures transparency and flexibility, making it possible to fine-tune the input parameters and observe the resulting variations in energy efficiency, heat losses, and indoor temperature stability.

Additionally, MS Excel facilitates statistical evaluations by processing large datasets of temperature profiles and demand curves. The model simulates how different envelope materials, building heights, and substation connection types influence the DH system's thermal performance by integrating data tables and conditional logic functions. The ability to visualize trends through Excel's charting tools provides an intuitive way to interpret how supply temperature reductions impact overall network efficiency and operational costs.

3. Case Study

The city of Omsk has had DH since the late 1930s. The number of consumers is approximately 10,000.

This study considered two types of substation connection (direct or indirect), two consumer types (office and residential buildings, e.g., Figure 1), and three envelope materials, i.e., nine combinations in total.

Figure 1. Old multi-story residential building.

For comparison, in [10], consumers were initially grouped into 11 categories, drawing partly from the classification system devised by the Danish Building Research Institute as part of the EU-funded IEE projects TABULA and EPISCOPE. These projects focused on defining residential building archetypes across 20 European countries. Unlike Kristensen et al. [10], not only the construction year of the buildings was considered for the segmentation.

In this study, building load and demand refer exclusively to consumers' SH needs, determined based on operational data collected from November 11th to November 17th (Figure 2). This period was chosen as it represents a typical transition phase between moderate and cold weather conditions (Figure 3).

Figure 2. Outdoor temperature profile for Omsk, 2020.

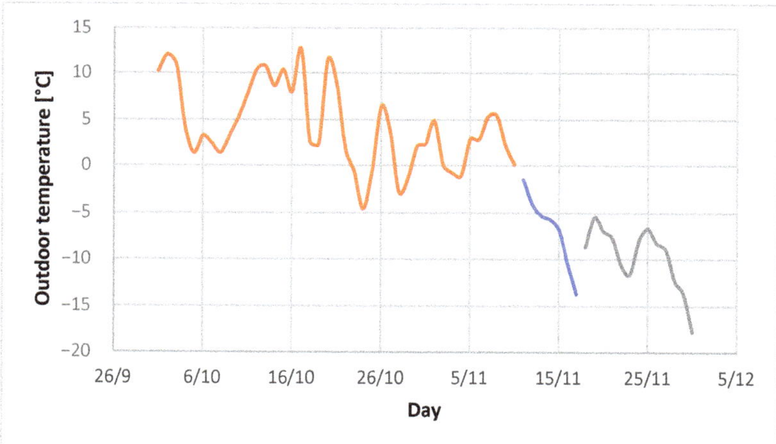

Figure 3. Periods of moderate and low temperatures during Fall 2020. Orange—moderate outdoor temperatures. Blue—the first appearance of 2 days with consecutive daily average outdoor temperatures below 0 °C during the SH season. Grey—consistent negative temperatures (5 or more consecutive days).

This heat accumulation ability was evaluated based on the factors and typical construction details available in the previous authors' papers [20,21] and corroborated by the comparison of assessed energy consumption for reference buildings from each consumer type, substation connection, and construction period (e.g., 2005–2010, Figure 4) available within the papers from Na et al. [22] and Gan et al. [23].

Figure 4. Modern high-rise residential building (2007).

Although primary supply and return temperatures have tended to decrease in recent years, because of the considerable share of old buildings for which the high temperature of water entering an SH system is still of high importance, the temperature regime within the system remains high, up to 111/70 °C during the coldest days in winter. Absolutely the same trend was reported by Volkova et al. [13], although they detected maximum values of 120/70 °C. At the same time, we have found out that in spring and autumn, the DH system is already operating at approximately 70 °C in the feed pipe [24]. This study goes beyond mere data analysis, serving as a case-study-driven demonstration of a methodology that can be applied to assess other DH systems. Moreover, it provides insights into whether these systems are prepared to transition toward low-temperature concepts. Nonetheless, to involve renewables in a generation, better feedback might be obtained for the operating conditions of 50–60 °C, which are close to 70 °C in fall and spring but can only be achieved utilizing temperature flexibility and heat accumulation.

Both design scenarios were modeled using hourly profiles in MS Excel with the specialized software ZuluThermo© (Version 10.0.0.8075u). In [25], the authors optimized similar things through mixed-integer linear programming, but yearly resolutions were applied. Table 1 summarizes the inputs used in this paper.

We also performed a statistical study of the neighborhood, linking building heat performance based on the building construction year and the glazing ratios (Figure 5) based on the randomized demand profiles.

The same results of the statistical survey are presented by Andric et al. [26]. For detailed information on how the number of floors is considered for calculating heat demands, please check the authors' recent paper [27].

The design heat demand of the considered buildings ranges from 0.4 to 1.1 MW per building. All nine buildings are the same distance from the DH plant; six are picked for a thorough look. All the assessments have been performed considering the return temperature of 40–45 °C for the return line after the properly tuned regulating valve during a warm day, in which the outdoor temperature is above 0 °C, and the fact that the substation typically decreases the supply temperature from 60 to 50 °C during these conditions despite the 95/70 design temperature regime. For comparison, Arabkoohsar et al. [5] study a DH system where the design outdoor temperature is −25 °C and a heat pump boosts the supply temperature from 40 to 50 °C.

Table 1. Design properties affecting heat demand of the buildings in Omsk obtained for the case study.

Building	Construction Year (Period)	Number of Floors	Type of Building	Type of Substation Connection	Case
		Envelope type: brick			
a	2007	14	Residential	Indirect	#2
b	2000s	5	Office	Direct	
c	1953	3	Residential	Direct	#5
		Envelope type: foam concrete wall blocks			
d	2020	9	Office	Indirect	#4
e	1990s	9	Residential	Direct	#3
f	2000s	9	Office	Direct	
		Envelope type: prefabricated panel			
g	1960s	14	Residential	Indirect	#6
h	1960s	5	Office	Direct	
j	1970s	5	Residential	Direct	#1

Figure 5. New high-rise office building (2020).

4. Results and Discussion

Based on Table 1, the considerations of the building energy performance are listed in Table 2.

Considering both the type of insulation and the topology of the DH system, applying Equations (9)–(13), we found that the reduction in heat losses for the case study compared to the baseline scenario is up to 20% with a supply temperature drop of 10 °C (detailed below). That is quite a good achievement since around 15% of the heat produced is typically lost [28]. For comparison, heat losses in the Lahekalda network, Estonia, account for 236.1 MWh (6%), with the possibility of further reduction to 205.2 MWh (4%) [13].

Table 2. C_{env}, $Q_{sp.hl}$, and β-values for the considered cases. Adopted as per the Russian scientist Koryagin M.V. (unpublished).

Case #	C_{env} [10^{-2}] [kJ/°C]	$Q_{sp.hl}$ [W/°C]	β [h]
#1	102.6	53.5	53
#2	123.6	29.6	116
#3	113.9	39.1	80.9
#4	99.7	31.8	87
#5	129	52.4	68.4
#6	73.6	29.3	69.7

Figure 6 presents the evolution of indoor temperature for the reference-case scenarios #1–6 and for excessive heat from the DH plant provided in a potential case of combined low- and flexible-temperature operation.

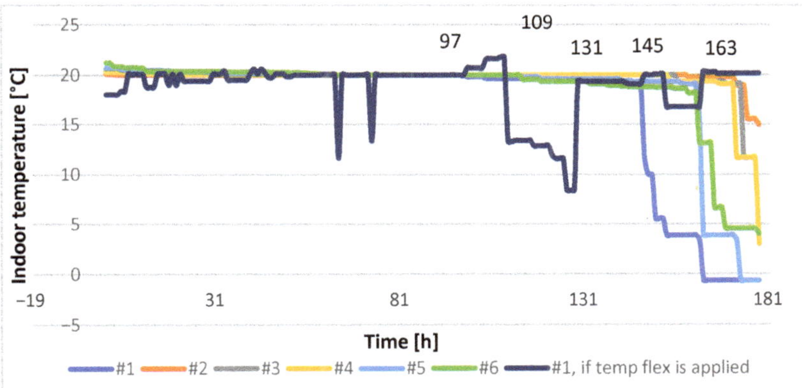

Figure 6. Indoor temperature variation for the studied period from 11 November to 17 November (0..181 h). #1: residential panel-built building (direct connection), #2: residential brick-built building (indirect connection), #3: residential concrete-block-built building, #4: office concrete-block-built building, #5: residential brick-built building (direct connection), #6: residential panel-built building (indirect connection).

In this figure, the indoor temperature of the farthest nodes from the substation is close to 5 °C almost immediately after the outdoor temperature drop of 140–141 h. In contrast, the temperatures of the nearly located buildings (e.g., #2, #3, and #4) are still fine, mainly affected by the type of substation connection and envelope material. However, the pertinent point here, in Figure 6, is an overheating effect when the supply temperature is manually set higher than necessary (previously obtained when the heat demand was still moderate—97..109 h); although flexible temperature operation is outside the scope of this research, it is here to highlight the relevance of the present stage of research. To achieve higher temperatures on such an occasion, a training period was necessary; the compensation time was initially 47 h (94..131 h), but now, it is limited to 18 h (145..163 h). Turski et al. [16] determined compensation times, combined with the time resulting from the heat accumulation ability of the DH network, and they were almost the same: 24 and 48 h.

The heat transfer and energy flux [W/m] results are not depicted but show a similar trend to costs and losses—almost a direct correlation with supply temperature. The seasonal network heat losses decreased from 14.1% for the low-temperature option. They reached a minimum of 11.3%, with the associated savings of EUR 20.2 million, saving excess heat during 60–70 °C operation, including heat accumulation.

Figure 7 summarizes the results of a sample week (1–7 January).

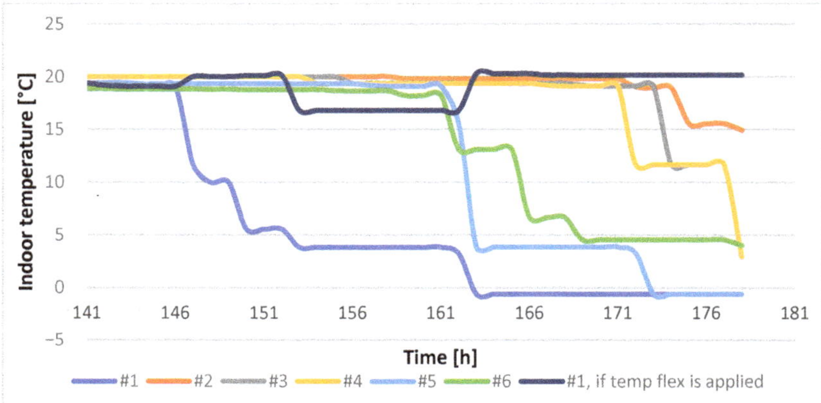

Figure 7. Indoor temperature profiles with the last hours (141..181 h) highlighted. The temperature drop from −8 to −20 is assumed to happen between 142 and 144 h. #1: residential panel-built building (direct connection), #2: residential brick-built building (indirect connection), #3: residential concrete-block-built building, #4: office concrete-block-built building, #5: residential brick-built building (direct connection), #6: residential panel-built building (indirect connection).

From Figure 7, we conclude that indoor temperatures mostly range between 4 and 15 °C (0 °C represents the minimum threshold temperature obtained during the 163rd hour); for others, it was still between 13 and 20 °C, with two exclusions only.

For the simulation data of buildings #2, #3, and #4, the acceptable indoor temperature considering only the SH system pump electricity consumption lasts as long as 25–27 h. Here, the reason is that the volume of hot water circulating in the secondary loop is 25%. Heat losses account for about the same 5% of the supplied thermal energy, as Buffa et al. [4] report, and still, a drop in temperature in the SH system and, consequently, the indoor temperature to 0 °C is inevitable. In #2, heat storage is already operated with short cycle times to buffer peak heat demands. For #3, residual heat demands occur less frequently and are less prominent due to the thermal performance of envelopes and less heat capacity ($Q_{sp.hl}$ is only 39.1 W/°C). These combinations of material/height/substation types are the best for constructing new office and residential buildings. The most interesting case is #4, where C_{env} accounts for $99.7 \cdot 10^{-2}$ kJ/°C, although the glazing ratio is as much as 40%. The situation has also improved with the type of building. An office building with no DHW consumption shows the most stable heat consumption profile. That makes using heat storage much less frequent and leads to larger cycle times. Wirtz et al. [29] detail the same correlation between heat consumption and storage use and conclude that cold storage is operated with the shortest cycle times over the year.

Basically, profiles on an hourly time interval show a much-reduced peak temperature drop. For a modern building and the default-mode heat production, the indoor temperature is reduced only up to 53% (11 °C) due to the higher heat capacity and/or an indirect connection to a substation. The reduction is more visible for buildings #1, #5, and #6, accounting for 0, 20, and 25% of the nominal value at 16 and 23 h intervals, respectively. We also limit indoor temperature drop to 17 °C (#1, if temp flex is applied). For comparison, Turski et al. [16] found that it was promising to increase heat production by 9.6 MW with a compensation time of 19.8 h. Similarly, a decrease in the energy delivery by 4.8 MW with a compensation time of 43.8 h is possible. According to their scenario, the indoor temperature is reduced by 5 K. Braas et al. [8] achieve peak load reduction by 53% at a 3 min time interval.

Based on the data obtained, the conventional approach was statistically assumed to be better for an average monthly outdoor temperature of −8 °C and higher (before the temperature drop during 145–146 h). The trend obtained for the LTDH, highlighted by the regression fit lines added to the graph, is drastically decreased compared to the reference scenario. Moreover, the new supply temperature is kept steadier, particularly when the outdoor temperature is relatively low. That complies well with Saletti et al.'s [12] findings.

Despite low fluctuations, main discharge, and late discharge periods, the model works well for both modes. The problem is that for the rebound and early discharge phases, even a small difference (up to 1 °C) in the primary supply temperature may result in significant daily variations. However, average errors may be negligible [6]. Despite being next to their threshold boundary, both low-temperature and reference scenarios indicated that the indoor temperature had deviated from its design value, as shown for test building #1 (refer to Figures 6 and 7). According to the DH expert, a possible solution is the proper function of a substation control system to prevent short fluctuations.

The control logic formulated in the previous work [30] did not account for the low-temperature concept or the simultaneous operation of other technologies, such as TES or heat accumulation. The substation design temperature was set at 110 °C, with a thermostat adjusted to a DOT of −20 °C, covering 97% of outdoor conditions [30]. Additionally, it was recommended to set the supply temperature to 50 °C during fall and spring when the average five-day outdoor temperature is 0 °C or higher. Even −8 °C is acceptable as a threshold value, as supported by Figure 3, but valve dynamics are much more important. They should never be ignored when considering flexible operations.

When heat accumulation within building envelopes facilitates the transition to LTDH, the supply temperature drops below 60 °C, reducing the average temperature difference between the distribution network and the surrounding soil by 38%. This, in turn, lowers network heat losses. However, this approach is only feasible if outdoor temperatures below −15 °C are rare or do not persist for long periods in spring or fall. Over the past decade, even in winter, temperatures below −20 °C have never lasted for five consecutive days [24], supporting the viability of this concept. For comparison, Saletti et al. [12] reduced the supply temperature to below 80 °C, achieving a 20% reduction in the temperature difference between the distribution network and the soil, leading to lower heat losses. Additionally, their findings showed a 16% reduction in peak loads and a 23% decrease in mass flow rates, contributing to an apparent drop in pumping power. However, to simplify the analysis, the flow rate at the substation is still assumed to remain fixed, as in practice, the regulating devices and valves almost achieve it.

The key finding is that incorporating low-temperature operation with centralized storage reduces O&M costs by 19% compared to a scenario without heat accumulation, specifically at operating temperatures of 50–60 °C. The maximum storage capacity allows for a 16 h delay in transitioning to normal operation (as observed in building #1) when all studied buildings contribute to limiting abrupt flow rate increases, provided the minimum indoor temperature remains above 0 °C to prevent damage to the space heating system. However, such extreme conditions are rarely encountered in practice and serve only as an upper threshold, as supply temperature adjustments typically take up to five hours. Moreover, weather forecasts are generally accurate, enabling proactive measures to be implemented several hours before an outdoor temperature drop. These insights apply similarly to other areas within the DH system. For instance, for the city scale (approximately 3000 MW substation heat demand), the maximum network cost reduction is about 5–6% with an acceptable 10 h delay since most of the residential buildings are directly connected, and there are up to 30% of houses in Omsk older than those constructed in the 1970s. However, most of them are made of brick rather than panel-built and are more like building #5 from the heat accumulation point of view. Nevertheless, that requires a meticulous study and represents the future area of research.

The building-level storage further provides a higher maximum network cost reduction of 6.57%. Still, it is combined with a TES, whose capacity is 1000 m^3 and which can store the hot water with negligible heat losses for at least 24 h [7]. Jebamalai et al. [7] also conclude that optimum storage capacity is possible for all cases and depends on storage distribution.

The mass flow rate to the Skultuna area, Sweden, ref. [12] is reduced by 23%. There are other examples where almost similar results were derived when the supply temperature is controlled optimally, taking heat accumulation into account. The supply temperature is also more constant [12].

Fito et al. [25] promote applying an energy-based, demand-oriented algorithm, which recommends rejecting waste heat at 35 °C and combining it with a heat pump and a 40 MWh TES. This design ensures the potential to cover 49% of heat demand with no additional fuel consumption. According to the conclusion presented in [13], a decrease in return temperature by up to 5 °C results in an increase in power and heat production of 400 and 1015 MWh annually, respectively, which are apparently more prominent than we have. Hammer et al. [15] suggest fully charging another artificial energy accumulator to let adjoining supply lines idle and limit the hot water flow rate, which results in a reduced heat loss, and therefore, the simplified calculation shows less energy loss, namely 45.3 kW (heat loss of 82 MWh divided by operation time of 1809 h). On the other hand, both the TES-based and the DH-plant-focused energy-based optimizations do not agree on the same DH system design. Moreover, we suggest changes in the control system only: supplying heat, for example, at 50–60 °C and using the potential of building envelope storage, with no heat pump or TES.

Figure 8 is more about the future application of this research and represents the potential benefits of low-temperature flexible operation if β- and z-values are involved in the supply temperature control.

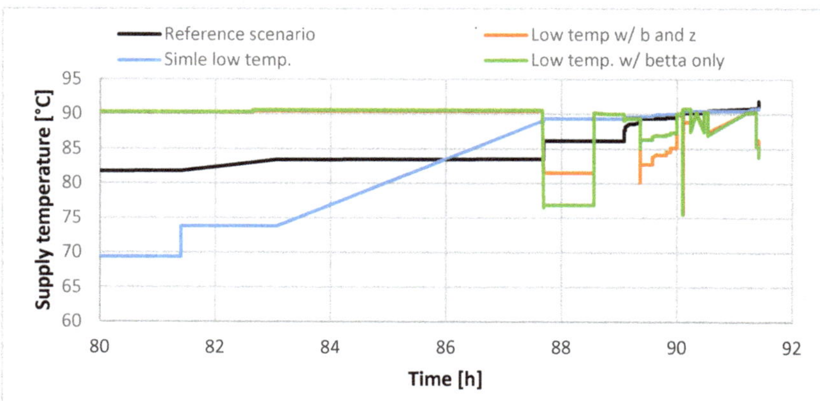

Figure 8. The pattern of the supply temperature during 80–92 h according to the low-temperature regime, never (blue curve), fully (orange one), or partially (green), taking thermal inertia into account. The reference scenario (black) represents ordinary operation according to the 150/70 temperature curve.

Figure 8 also indicates that this 80–92 h temp increase was correct and enough not to increase the indoor temperature above 20 °C, although 98–109 h did.

Here, supply temperatures mostly range between 75 and 90 °C (68 °C represents the minimum threshold temperature potentially obtained), whereas reference ones are between 82 and 92 °C. Barone et al. [14] report the same supply temperatures ranging between 90 and 88 °C, where 88 °C represents the minimum threshold temperature obtained at 05:00, while return ones are between 87.5 and 79 °C. Like Saletti et al. [12], we expect the optimal mass flow rate to experience fewer fluctuations during the simulation period, although during the previous management conditions, the operation of the pump changed and varied more sharply.

5. Conclusions

In summary, the supply temperature patterns of six typical buildings in Omsk, Russia, were analyzed using the reference-group-based approach. As DH systems transition to 4GDH, there is significant potential for innovative DH designs that address future distribution network requirements, including efficiency and cost-effectiveness. Building similarities were assessed using pointwise and distributional distance metrics based on indoor temperature data. While the reference-group methodology has proven to be an effective and efficient solution, it can be further enhanced by integrating it into a combined low- and temperature-flexible operation strategy. An analysis based on the stability proportion criterion was conducted to recommend optimal substation valve adjustments and the best material, height, and substation type combinations for office and residential building construction.

By integrating real operational data, mathematical modeling, and optimization techniques, we assess the system's ability to transition toward LTDH while maintaining efficiency and reliability. The research highlights how supply temperature reductions, when managed effectively, can significantly lower heat losses—up to 20% in some cases—without compromising indoor comfort levels. The findings confirm that flexible temperature operation and heat accumulation strategies can enhance overall system efficiency, reduce operational costs, and prepare the network to integrate renewable energy sources.

One of the key contributions of this research is demonstrating that even in a DH network dominated by older buildings, where high supply temperatures have traditionally been necessary, there is potential for gradual adaptation to lower temperatures. This study provides empirical evidence that, under certain conditions, the supply temperature can be reduced to 50–60 °C without severe disruptions. However, the results highlight challenges, such as improved substation control strategies for mitigating temperature fluctuations and ensuring a smooth transition. Heat accumulation within buildings, particularly in materials with higher thermal inertia, is important for successful LTDH implementation.

Beyond these findings, this study underscores the need for further exploration in several key areas. Future research should focus on refining the control logic of substations, incorporating predictive weather-based adjustments to optimize heat supply dynamically. Additionally, a deeper investigation into the integration of TES at both the building and network levels could further enhance the flexibility and efficiency of DH systems. Another promising avenue is examining how LTDH can be combined with decentralized renewable energy sources and heat pumps, creating a more resilient and sustainable urban heating infrastructure.

Ultimately, this research contributes to the broader discussion on modernizing DH networks, offering valuable insights into the feasibility and challenges of transitioning to LTDH. As cities worldwide seek to improve energy efficiency and reduce carbon footprints, the lessons learned from this case study in Omsk can serve as a foundation for further advancements in DH system optimization and sustainability.

Funding: This project received funding from VLAIO in Belgium, ICON project OPTIMESH (VLAFLX7, https://researchportal.vub.be/en/projects/icon-project-optimesh & FLUX50 ICON Project Collaboration Agreement—HBC.2021.0395. Accessed on 1 March 2025).

Institutional Review Board Statement: Not applicable.

Informed Consent Statement: Not applicable.

Data Availability Statement: The data presented in this study are available on request from the corresponding author due to privacy reasons.

Conflicts of Interest: The author declares no conflicts of interest.

References

1. Farouq, S.; Byttner, S.; Bouguelia, M.-R.; Nord, N.; Gadd, H. Large-scale monitoring of operationally diverse district heating substations: A reference-group based approach. *Eng. Appl. Artif. Intell.* **2020**, *90*, 103492. [CrossRef]
2. Chicherin, S.; Starikov, A.; Zhuikov, A. Justifying network reconstruction when switching to low temperature district heating. *Energy* **2022**, *248*, 123618. [CrossRef]
3. Meesenburg, W.; Ommen, T.; Thorsen, J.E.; Elmegaard, B. Economic feasibility of ultra-low temperature district heating systems in newly built areas supplied by renewable energy. *Energy* **2020**, *191*, 116496. [CrossRef]
4. Buffa, S.; Cozzini, M.; D'antoni, M.; Baratieri, M.; Fedrizzi, R. 5th generation district heating and cooling systems: A review of existing cases in Europe. *Renew. Sustain. Energy Rev.* **2019**, *104*, 504–522. [CrossRef]
5. Arabkoohsar, A.; Alsagri, A.S. A new generation of district heating system with neighborhood-scale heat pumps and advanced pipes, a solution for future renewable-based energy systems. *Energy* **2020**, *193*, 116781. [CrossRef]
6. Vandermeulen, A.; Van Oevelen, T.; van der Heijde, B.; Helsen, L. A simulation-based evaluation of substation models for network flexibility characterisation in district heating networks. *Energy* **2020**, *201*, 117650. [CrossRef]
7. Jebamalai, J.M.; Marlein, K.; Laverge, J. Influence of centralized and distributed thermal energy storage on district heating network design. *Energy* **2020**, *202*, 117689. [CrossRef]
8. Braas, H.; Jordan, U.; Best, I.; Orozaliev, J.; Vajen, K. District heating load profiles for domestic hot water preparation with realistic simultaneity using DHWcalc and TRNSYS. *Energy* **2020**, *201*, 117552. [CrossRef]
9. Chicherin, S. A method for assessing heat losses in developing countries with a focus on operational data of a district heating (DH) system. *Sustain. Energy Grids Netw.* **2022**, *30*, 100616. [CrossRef]
10. Kristensen, M.H.; Hedegaard, R.E.; Petersen, S. Long-term forecasting of hourly district heating loads in urban areas using hierarchical archetype modeling. *Energy* **2020**, *201*, 117687. [CrossRef]
11. Chicherin, S.; Zhuikov, A.; Kolosov, M.; Junussova, L.; Aliyarova, M.; Yelemanova, A. Optimizing building heat consumption: Weekday and weekend profiles. *Energy Rep.* **2021**, *7*, 166–170. [CrossRef]
12. Saletti, C.; Zimmerman, N.; Morini, M.; Kyprianidis, K.; Gambarotta, A. Enabling smart control by optimally managing the State of Charge of district heating networks. *Appl. Energy* **2021**, *283*, 116286. [CrossRef]
13. Volkova, A.; Krupenski, I.; Ledvanov, A.; Hlebnikov, A.; Lepiksaar, K.; Latõšov, E.; Mašatin, V. Energy cascade connection of a low-temperature district heating network to the return line of a high-temperature district heating network. *Energy* **2020**, *198*, 117304. [CrossRef]
14. Barone, G.; Buonomano, A.; Forzano, C.; Palombo, A. A novel dynamic simulation model for the thermo-economic analysis and optimisation of district heating systems. *Energy Convers. Manag.* **2020**, *220*, 113052. [CrossRef]
15. Hammer, A.; Sejkora, C.; Kienberger, T. Increasing district heating networks efficiency by means of temperature-flexible operation. *Sustain. Energy Grids Netw.* **2018**, *16*, 393–404.
16. Turski, M.; Sekret, R. Buildings and a district heating network as thermal energy storages in the district heating system. *Energy Build* **2018**, *179*, 49–56.
17. Chicherin, S.; Zhuikov, A.; Junussova, L.; Yelemanova, A. Multiple-fuel District Heating System of a Transportation Facility: Water Performance-based View. *Transp. Res. Procedia* **2021**, *54*, 31–38.
18. Rosa, A.D.; Li, H.; Svendsen, S. Method for optimal design of pipes for low-energy district heating, with focus on heat losses. *Energy* **2011**, *36*, 2407–2418. [CrossRef]
19. Cai, H.; You, S.; Wang, J.; Bindner, H.W.; Klyapovskiy, S. Technical assessment of electric heat boosters in low-temperature district heating based on combined heat and power analysis. *Energy* **2018**, *150*, 938–949.

20. Zhuikov, A.V.; Kolosov, M.V.; Radzyuk, A.Y.; Chicherin, S.V. Research of energy efficiency of temperature control systems in buildings. *AIP Conf. Proc.* **2021**, *2337*, 030014.
21. Chicherin, S.; Zhuikov, A.; Kolosov, M.; Junussova, L.; Aliyarova, M.; Yelemanova, A. Controlling Temperatures in Low-Temperature District Heating: Adjustment to Meet Fluctuating Heat Load. In *Lecture Notes in Networks and Systems*; Beskopylny, A., Shamtsyan, M., Eds.; Springer International Publishing: Cham, Switzerland, 2022; pp. 287–297.
22. Na, S.; Hong, S.W.; Jung, S.; Lee, J. Performance evaluation of building designs with BIM-based spatial patterns. *Autom. Constr.* **2020**, *118*, 103290. [CrossRef]
23. Gan, V.J.; Deng, M.; Tan, Y.; Chen, W.; Cheng, J.C.P. BIM-based framework to analyze the effect of natural ventilation on thermal comfort and energy performance in buildings. In *Energy Procedia*; Elsevier: Amsterdam, The Netherlands, 2019; Volume 158, pp. 3319–3324.
24. Chicherin, S.; Anvari-Moghaddam, A. Adjusting Heat Demands Using the Operational Data of District Heating Systems. *Energy* **2021**, *235*, 121368. [CrossRef]
25. Fitó, J.; Hodencq, S.; Ramousse, J.; Wurtz, F.; Stutz, B.; Debray, F.; Vincent, B. Energy- and exergy-based optimal designs of a low-temperature industrial waste heat recovery system in district heating. *Energy Convers. Manag.* **2020**, *211*, 112753. [CrossRef]
26. Andrić, I.; Fournier, J.; Lacarrière, B.; Le Corre, O.; Ferrão, P. The impact of global warming and building renovation measures on district heating system techno-economic parameters. *Energy* **2018**, *150*, 926–937. [CrossRef]
27. Junussova, L.; Zhuikov, A.; Matiushenko, A.; Chicherin, S.; Ilicheva, A. Assessing building energy efficiency with the help of specific heat demand characteristics: Boreal regions of Russia case study. In Proceedings of the E3S Web of Conferences, Online, 25 November 2020; Volume 208.
28. Chicherin, S.; Mašatin, V.; Siirde, A.; Volkova, A. Method for Assessing Heat Loss in A District Heating Network with A Focus on the State of Insulation and Actual Demand for Useful Energy. *Energies* **2020**, *13*, 4505. [CrossRef]
29. Wirtz, M.; Kivilip, L.; Remmen, P.; Müller, D. 5th Generation District Heating: A novel design approach based on mathematical optimization. *Appl. Energy* **2020**, *260*, 114158. [CrossRef]
30. Chicherin, S. Methodology for analyzing operation data for optimum district heating (DH) system design: Ten-year data of Omsk, Russia. *Energy* **2020**, *211*, 118603. [CrossRef]

energies

MDPI

Review

A Systematic Review of Sensitivity Analysis in Building Energy Modeling: Key Factors Influencing Building Thermal Energy Performance

Rajendra Roka [1,*], António Figueiredo [1], Ana Vieira [2] and Claudino Cardoso [1]

[1] CERIS—Civil Engineering Research and Innovation for Sustainability, Civil Engineering Department, University of Aveiro, Campus Universitário de Santiago, 3810-193 Aveiro, Portugal; ajfigueiredo@ua.pt (A.F.); claudino@ua.pt (C.C.)

[2] Geotechnics Department, National Laboratory for Civil Engineering, Av. do Brasil 101, 1700-075 Lisboa, Portugal; avieira@lnec.pt

* Correspondence: rajendraroka@ua.pt; Tel.: +351-920-289-000

Abstract: Improving building thermal energy performance is essential to reducing energy consumption, minimizing carbon emissions, and enhancing occupants' thermal comfort. For this purpose, there is an increasing research interest in this field of building energy performance. This review aims to present a precise and systematic overview of the sensitivity analysis in optimizing the thermal energy performance of buildings. The investigation covers various aspects, including sensitivity analysis techniques, key measures and variables, objectives and criteria, software tools, optimization methods, climate zones, building typology, and climate change effects. The findings reveal that sensitivity analysis is a powerful technique for optimizing energy performance and identifying adaptive strategies such as dynamic shading, reflective coatings, and efficient HVAC set points to address climate change. Most of the study also highlights that the temperature set point is the key influential parameter in both heating-dominant and cooling-dominant climate zones. This review offers critical insights on advancing sustainable building design, informing policy, and guiding future research in energy-efficient building solutions.

Keywords: whole building energy simulation; sensitivity analysis; optimization tools; key input parameters

1. Introduction

Building thermal energy modeling (BTEM) has become a crucial tool for designing energy-efficient buildings, optimizing performance for occupants' thermal comfort, and supporting decision-making in the sustainable construction of buildings. Studying the thermal energy performance of buildings is an essential aspect of modern construction and architecture, as it should consider energy efficiency, sustainability, and environmental concerns [1]. Assessing the efficiency of the thermal performance of the building is necessary to reduce energy consumption and carbon emissions without compromising the thermal comfort level [2]. To achieve this, sensitivity analysis of the building energy performance is essential, as it helps to identify the critical parameters that need attention or improvement. The accuracy and reliability of BTEM depend on the various input parameters such as weather conditions, building materials, occupancy schedule, building openings, etc. Sensitivity Analysis (SA) is widely used to identify the most influential parameters affecting building energy performance. One of the definitions of SA is a systematic and methodological approach to studying how variation or changes in a model's input

 https://doi.org/10.3390/en18092375

parameters affect the system's output [3]. It has become a crucial method for assessing the reliability and robustness of real-world systems and models in simulation by quantifying the degree to which the input variability impacts the outputs [4]. Figure 1 demonstrates the flow diagram for sensitivity analysis that could be adopted in building thermal energy performance analysis.

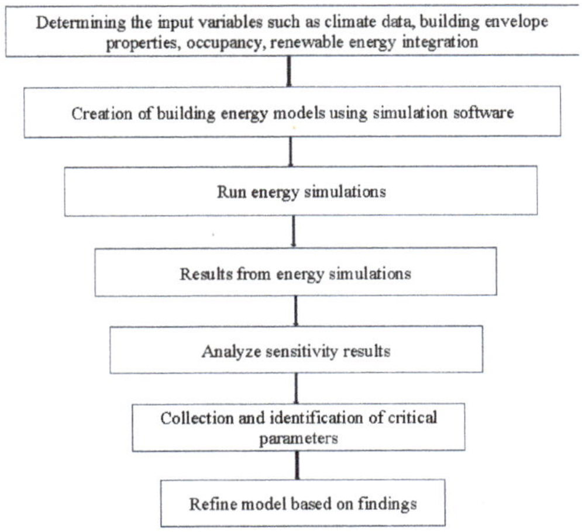

Figure 1. Flow diagram for sensitivity analysis adopted in building energy performance analysis.

It is helpful in various types of applications, such as calibrating energy models [5,6], building design [7], building energy retrofit, and climate change impacts on building energy [8]. Figure 2 illustrates the building energy simulation model, which highlights the creation of the building model, as well as several input parameters, output, and interpretation methods.

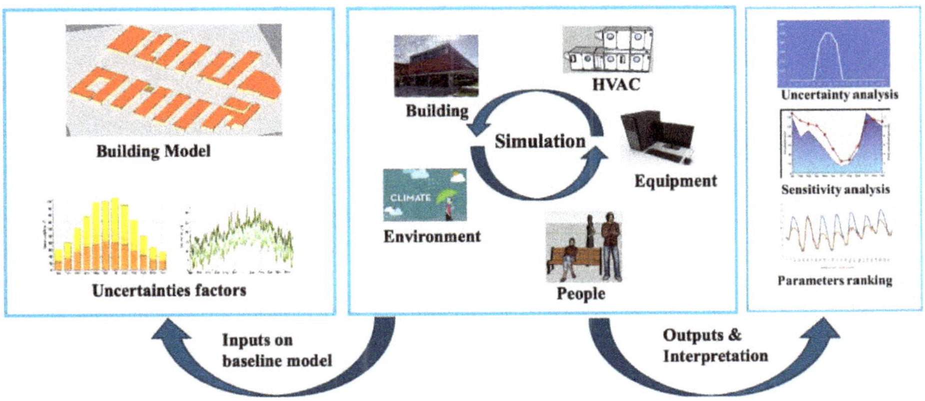

Figure 2. Illustration of a conceptual framework for building energy simulation with uncertainty analysis.

The concept of SA in building thermal energy performance was introduced after energy modeling and simulation tools were developed in the early 1980s. However, its application started prominently after developing sophisticated building energy simulation programs such as Department of Energy-Version 2 (DOE-2) and EnergyPlus (EP). The early simulation of the building energy system by varying building material and geometrical properties was performed by Manke [9] and presented at the American Society of Mechanical Engineers

(ASME) conference in 1996. In addition, one of the early papers that implemented sensitivity analysis specifically in building thermal energy performance and laid the foundation of global sensitivity analysis (GSA) was published by Saltelli [10] in the Technometrics Journal.

Despite several studies and significant achievements in the sensitivity analysis of building thermal energy performance, many areas still need in-depth exploration. The complexity of building systems and their components, evolving technologies, climate change, and their effect on the demand for building energy emphasize the necessity for continued study in this sector. Previous reviews based on the SA of building energy performances remain limited.

Wei [11] published a review article that offers a foundational review that primarily focuses on exploring the methodological framework of SA, highlighting its implementation steps and categorizing various sensitivity analysis methods. Pang et al. [12] performed a similar review, mainly emphasizing input parameter categorization, input-output nexus, sampling methods, and the uncertainties associated with the sampling methods. More recently, Mendes et al. [13] conducted a review expanding the scope by evaluating the advantages and limitations of the SA in assessing the thermal performance of buildings via energy simulations.

Despite these contributions, there remains a critical need for further review due to the rapid evolution of SA methodologies, advancements in analytical techniques, integration of emerging technologies in building energy systems, and the growing importance of climate change considerations in recent studies. The review also explored the most critical input parameters for the building's energy performance. This review endeavors to synthesize and assess the latest developments, methodologies, and applications in this field over the specified period. The primary purpose of this review is to deliver a comprehensive overview of how sensitivity analysis has enhanced and been applied to building energy performance and the corresponding evolution. By exploring the research performed, attempt to recognize trends, highlight innovative approaches, and address the implications of these outcomes for future research and practical applications.

The remainder of this paper is structured as follows: Section 2 provides the details of the literature search methodology. Section 3 overviews the publication trends and impacts of sensitivity analysis methods commonly applied in BTEM. Section 4 reviews the complete methodology of SA techniques, tools, and processes in BTEM, discussing their strengths and limitations. Section 5 critically analyzes the most influential input parameters in BTEM as identified through SA and how these input parameters vary across different climatic regions, building types, and SA methodology. Section 6 explored some of the importance of temperature adaptability due to climate change considerations in recent studies. Finally, Section 7 concludes with key findings and offers recommendations for enhancing sensitivity analysis in BTEM applications. This review aims to provide researchers and practitioners with a comprehensive understanding of SA methodologies, guiding the selection of appropriate techniques and identifying potential areas for improvement to enhance predictive accuracy in building energy simulations.

2. Literature Search Methodology

This systematic review followed a methodology to identify relevant papers from previously published works on the topic of sensitivity analysis of the building's thermal energy performance. Two databases, namely Scopus and Web of Science (WoS) core collection, were selected for the search strategy on 2 September 2024. The search was based on keywords ("Sensitivity analysis" OR "global sensitivity analysis" AND "Building energy simulation OR Building performance simulation") in the title, abstract, and keyword field of both databases. A total of 92 published papers in Scopus and WoS were thoroughly analyzed for review assessment. The whole methodology illustrating the identification, screening, inclusion, and exclusion process is shown in Figure 3.

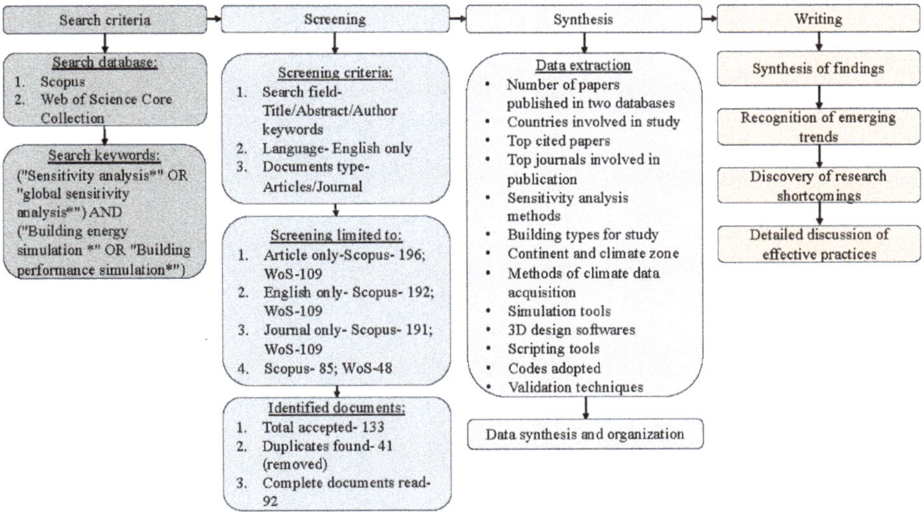

Figure 3. Flow diagram illustrating the literature search process using the keyword (*) "Sensitivity analysis" as the primary search term.

3. Overview of the Publications in Scopus and WoS

Figure 4 illustrates the overview of the number of publications related to sensitivity analysis on building thermal energy performance per year in the Scopus and WoS databases. The curve shows the increasing number of published papers with the keyword "sensitivity analysis" over time. There were very few studies and publications until 2005, and the number of publications increased from 2013 and continued to increase steadily until 2023. However, the research and publications increased rapidly from 2020 to 2023.

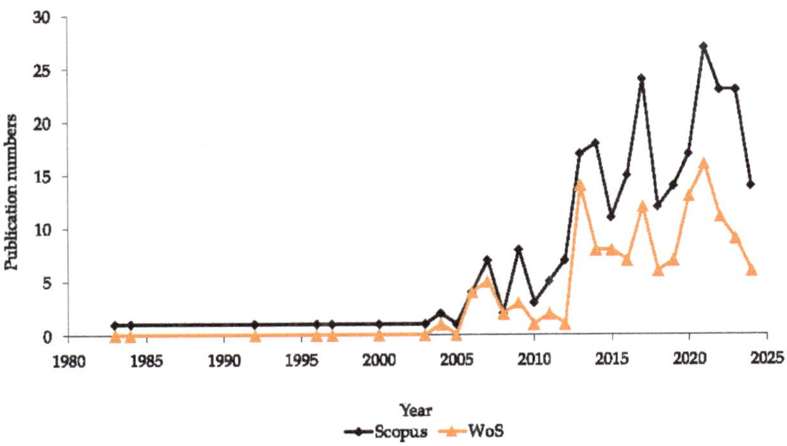

Figure 4. Publications per year related to sensitivity analysis in building energy performance in the Scopus and WoS databases.

During this period, researchers have been highly involved in studying and publishing articles related to sensitivity analysis on building energy performance. The noticeable increase in research publications in BTEM in this period can be attributed to the European

Union's strategic policy framework on climate neutrality by 2050. In addition, significant advancements in building energy simulation tools, such as EnergyPlus updates and the integration of Python APIs, have made simulations more accessible and affordable. Another important aspect is that the COVID-19 pandemic triggered the orientation of many researchers toward simulation-based research activities and increased publications.

Figure 5 depicts the Scopus keyword co-occurrence network in the sensitivity analysis, representing the number of published papers under the keyword sensitivity analysis. The figure shows the strong connection between SA and BTEM, highlighting their essence in optimizing thermal comfort, heating and cooling, and annual thermal loads. This visualization emphasizes how SA helps to improve building energy simulation models, enabling data-driven decision-making for achieving energy-efficient and thermally comfortable buildings.

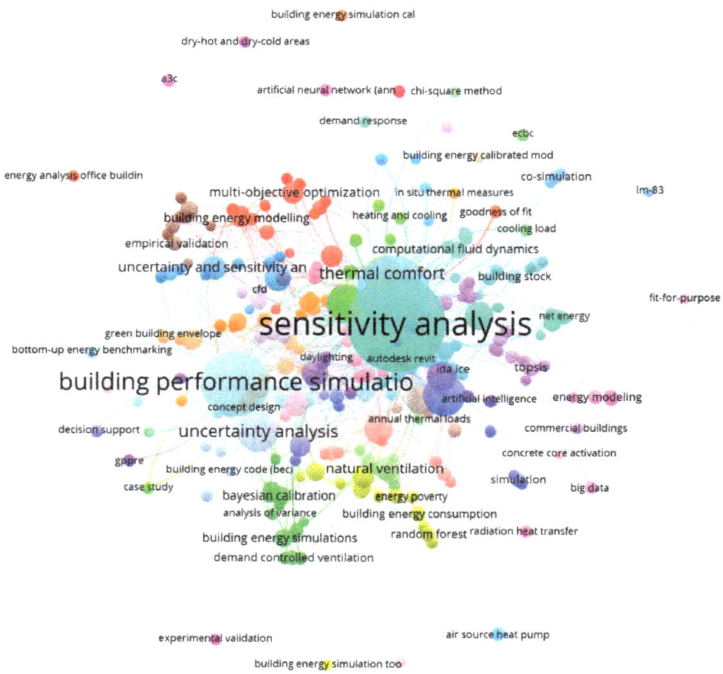

Figure 5. Scientific landscape of research on SA of BTEM, with colors representing thematic clusters of research keywords identified through co-occurrence analysis.

Researchers from many countries are involved in studying building energy performance using sensitivity analysis techniques. Figure 6 presents information about the top 15 countries that contributed the most to the publication related to the building energy and sensitivity analysis, as recorded in the Scopus database. Counting publications is based on the affiliations of first authors listed in the documents and associating them with specific countries or territories. The United States has overtaken all other countries in the publication, whereas many European countries demonstrate their interest in the subject. The USA and the UK are the two top contributors in this study area. At the same time, Asian countries such as China and Hong Kong show a growing publication trend in this research field. In turn, Table 1 illustrates the top 20 studies on the sensitivity analysis framework of building energy performance, ranked by the number of citations in Scopus and WoS from 2020 to 2024, and Table 2 presents the top 10 studies published in the journal, ranked by impact factor over a recent five-year period, according to WoS.

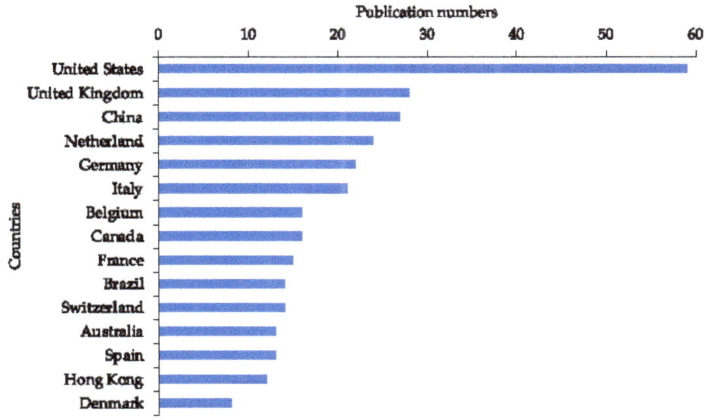

Figure 6. The top 15 countries with the highest contributions to the publications related to building energy and sensitivity analysis, based on data from the Scopus database.

Table 1. Top 20 papers ranked according to the number of citations in Scopus and WoS as of 01.09.2024.

Pos	References	Year of Publication	Number of Citations		Pos	References	Year of Publication	Number of Citations	
			Scopus	WoS				Scopus	WoS
1	[14]	2020	195	171	11	[15]	2021	36	34
2	[16]	2020	91	82	12	[17]	2022	35	29
3	[18]	2021	87	41	13	[19]	2022	34	27
4	[20]	2020	48	43	14	[21]	2020	28	23
5	[22]	2022	47	37	15	[23]	2020	27	23
6	[24]	2021	45	43	16	[25]	2021	26	25
7	[26]	2020	44	35	17	[27]	2023	25	23
8	[28]	2022	40	33	18	[29]	2021	24	19
9	[30]	2021	38	36	19	[31]	2022	21	19
10	[32]	2022	37	34	20	[33]	2021	20	17

4. SA Techniques Used in Building Thermal Energy Performance

Sensitivity analysis helps investigate how variations in input parameters ($x_1, x_2, x_3, \ldots, x_i$) are attributed to the effect in the output (y_j). SA contributes significantly to examining the variability in the output due to the input factors. That means it can identify which input factors have the most significant effect on the output, which input parameters have minimal or negligible impacts, and how the interactions between input variables impact the output (y_j). The motivation for performing a sensitivity analysis could be model evaluation, simplification, refinement, or exploratory modeling. There are three commonly used sensitivity analysis modes to identify and rank the input factors considering their effect: factor prioritization, factor fixing, and factor mapping. Factor prioritization SA application mode identifies the uncertain factor (x_i) that has the most significant impact on the output variability (y_j), and that factor should be prioritized. On the other hand, factor fixing helps identify the input parameters that have negligible influence on the output [34]. Fixing these factors to a nominal value or even eliminating them eases the model's complexity. In addition, factor mapping aims to pinpoint the input parameters that cause the undesirable model behavior [35].

Table 2. The top 10 journals ranked according to impact factor (IF) over the most recent five-year period in WoS.

Nos	References	Journal Name	IF
1	[14]	Renewable and sustainable energy reviews	15.9
2	[26,36,37]	Applied energy	11.2
3	[31]	Automation in construction	10.3
4	[24]	Energy	8.9
5	[38]	Sustainable energy technologies and assessments	8.0
6	[19,28,39–42]	Building and environment	7.4
7	[18,43]	Solar energy	6.7
8	[20,21,23,29,30,44–51]	Energy and buildings	6.7
9	[15,32,33,52–57]	Journal of building engineering	6.4
10	[33,58]	Energy for sustainable development	5.5

4.1. Local Sensitivity Analysis (LSA) vs. Global Sensitivity Analysis (GSA)

Specifically, two SA techniques have been adopted to analyze building energy performance: local and global sensitivity analysis. LSA is a straightforward approach that implies varying only one input parameter at a time, maintaining all other parameters constant. The impact on output due to varying input will be observed, which also helps to isolate the effect of individual parameters [59]. Local sensitivity represents the first-order (or linear) sensitivity coefficients $\delta x_i/\delta y_j$, which considers a linear approximation of the dependence of the output (y_j) on the (x_i) parameter changes [56]. LSA aims to explore how small perturbations in input parameters influence model performance and is performed by varying input parameters around specific reference values. Because of its ease of use and low computational requirements, the LSA technique has been widely used in several studies related to building energy modeling [57].

However, LSA is prone to significant biases if the model is not linear. This is because LSA considers input parameters to be independent, resulting in an underestimation of the importance of interactions among input model parameters [60]. Similarly, LSA typically ignores interactions between parameters and does not account for the distribution of input parameters. Ibraheem et al. [61] conducted a sensitivity test for PV-generated electricity using One-at-a-Time (OAT) analysis. They observed that the depth-to-length ratio of the building is a more sensitive input parameter than the window-to-wall ratio, orientation, and inclination angle. Figure 7 illustrates an example of the sensitivity index for building energy use using LSA. The plot was obtained by changing the parameters' base value by ±5%, ±10%, and ±15% and the effect on the building energy use was plotted. That helps to identify the most influential parameter that affects building energy use.

Global sensitivity analysis (GSA) is a holistic approach used to assess the impact of multiple input parameters on output parameters. It also executes the analysis of the effects of interactions between the input parameters. The study of uncertainties associated with the output of a model can be attributed to various sources of uncertainties in the input of the model [62]. Figure 8 depicts the scatter plot that shows the relationship patterns between the absorption of ceiling, aspect ratio, and window-to-wall ratio and the source energy consumption using GSA techniques. GSA aims to reveal the global effects of each parameter on the output of the model, considering any interactive effects of the input factors.

However, the model requires high computational resources as it considers variations within the entire space of variability of the input parameters. In addition, the quality of the sampling strategy determines the accuracy of GSA, and when high-order indices are significant, it is difficult to interpret the interaction effect. GSA overcomes the possible limitations of LSA, which is restricted to the linear approximation of output dependence on the variability of input factors [64]. GSA performs a comprehensive analysis, which evaluates the impacts of input factors over the entire range, considering nonlinear relationships and interactions between input factors to address the limitation of LSA, which only finds small perturbations around base values. The decision to select LSA or GSA depends on the objective of SA. LSA is preferred when a quick understanding of local model behavior is intended, particularly in a linear model, showing negligible interactions between input parameters. At the same time, GSA is selected with a nonlinear model and desired to understand the interactions between the input parameters [62].

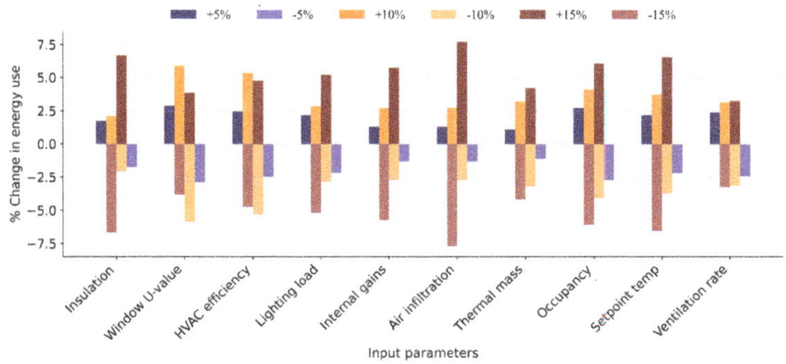

Figure 7. Sensitivity index of the building energy use with different input parameters [63].

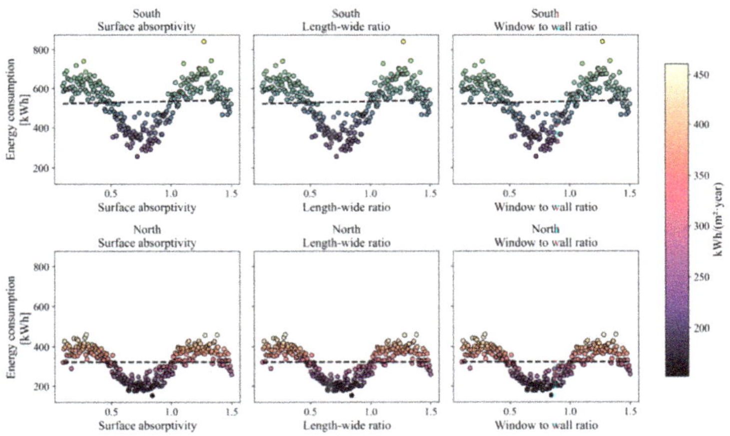

Figure 8. GSA method illustrating the variation in source energy consumption with different input parameters [65].

The GSA technique has been widely used in several studies related to building energy modeling. It has advantages over LSA in dealing with complex, nonlinear systems with interactions and full parameter exploration [64]. Furthermore, the regression-based method (RBM) [66] establishes the use of correlation coefficients to estimate the information between the uncertain factors of input and output parameters. Jans-Singh et al. [67] used the standard regression coefficient method to analyze the energy model of an archetype school building. A sensitivity analysis was performed based on linear regression and the calculation of standard regression coefficients (SRC) to evaluate the impact of reducing infiltration on discomfort time in a building design by a researcher in a review [63]. RBM is a broader method of sensitivity analysis that uses regression models. In contrast, SRC is a specific form of RBM that standardizes the coefficients and makes them comparable.

Besides the above methods, the surrogate model, also called a metamodel, assesses a simple solution for the complex physics-based building model as an alternative option. The surrogate model is useful when the whole building energy model is computationally expensive. It can be combined with the GSA techniques for efficient sensitivity analysis. Several researchers used a surrogate model as a higher-order model for sensitivity analysis of the building energy performance [62,65]. Techniques such as artificial neural networks (ANNs) [68] and genetic algorithms [69] are also used to map input data to output. Figure 9 shows one of the surrogate models, an artificial neural network (ANN), applied to the building energy model, showing the input variables and the output performance parameters. The model comprises seven input parameters affecting energy consumption, thermal comfort, and carbon emissions. ANN provides an alternative to traditional building simulation tools such as EnergyPlus and TRNSYS, using a data-driven approach by learning patterns from historical or simulated data.

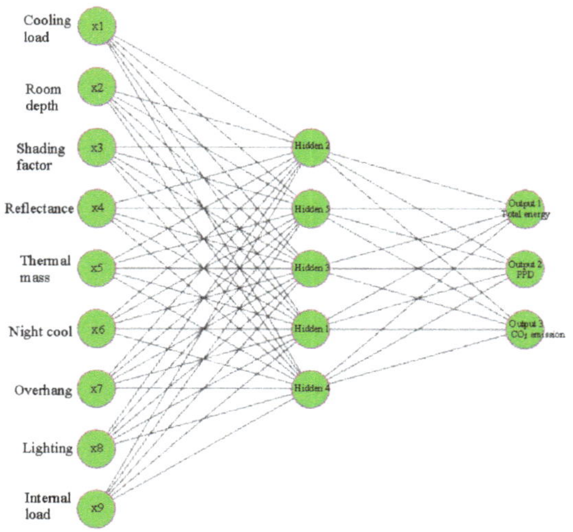

Figure 9. A surrogate model (ANN) for predicting total energy consumption applied to the building energy model, showing the input variables and the output performance parameters [70].

Figure 10 illustrates the review results, which confirm that LSA and GSA are the most widely used techniques for sensitivity analysis. Fifty-eight percent of the studies applied GSA techniques, and 25% used LSA techniques to model building energy performance. GSA is the most popular among the studies, as it considers input parameter interactions and identifies the best scenarios.

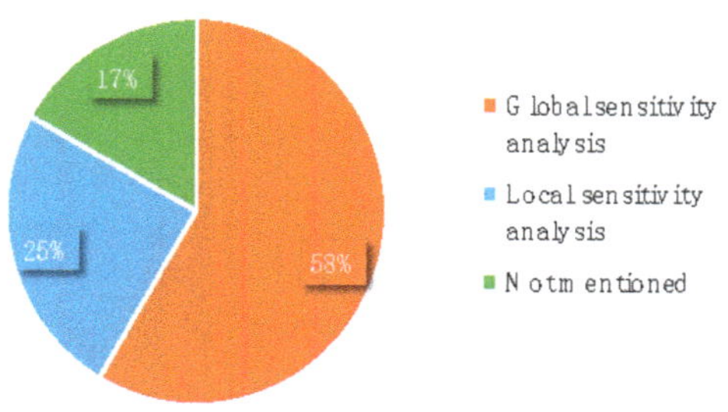

Figure 10. Percentage of local and global sensitivity analysis methods adopted in the review studies.

4.2. Sampling Methods for SA

In the sensitivity analysis of building energy modeling, sampling techniques play a significant role in exploring the input factor space and addressing how variations in these factors impact the model's output and ensure the accurate and efficient SA. Table A1 of this paper presents an overview of commonly used sampling methods, including their descriptions, advantages, and limitations observed in the review studies. Before conducting any sensitivity analysis, a sampling strategy is often required and referred to as a design of experiments.

Generally, sampling can be performed using a random or stratified method. Morris' screening method for GSA is also evident in the review by many researchers [30]. This method addresses the drawbacks of local sensitivity analysis by tabulating partial derivatives within several locations in the range of variations of input variables. The Monte Carlo method is widely used for random sampling by several authors in this review [71,72]. It uses a computational method to estimate complex mathematical behavior to assess the uncertainty and variability in model outcomes. Nevertheless, the Monte Carlo method could leave some spaces in the parameter space and affect clustering in those spaces when the parameters are in large numbers [73].

In addition, Latin hypercube sampling (LHS) is a stratifying technique used by many authors in this review. It is a method that confirms a thorough exploration of the input spaces by dividing the spaces equally, anticipating intervals, and ensuring sampling from each interval. The technique is more effective when the number of samples is much larger than the number of uncertain factors [70,74]. Among the GSA techniques, the Sobol method, a variance-based method of GSA, is prevalent in the literature in this review. This method takes into account complex and nonlinear factor interactions during sensitivity indices calculation [33]. Apart from the Sobol method, the researchers also used other variance-based methods in this review, such as the Fourier amplitude sensitivity test (FAST) [51,75] and extended-FAST [76].

On the other hand, the sample size in SA is an essential factor to be considered to obtain accurate, reliable, and computationally efficient results. An appropriate sample size is required to ensure that the model accurately captures the influence of input parameters and interactions. The choice of sample size for SA is presented in the literature. As a starting point, a rule of thumb can estimate the sample size. Sample size N is at least 10 times the number of input factors (x). However, this is not sufficient for highly nonlinear models. For variance-based methods, Monte Carlo-based sampling can be used with N in the range of 1000 to 10,000 or even more. That depends upon the complexity of the model and input parameters. For Sobol's indices, the total number of model evaluations is determined by $N(x + 2)$, where x is the number of input factors. Asadi et al. [77] used the Monte Carlo sampling techniques to run 70,000 energy models with different input samples to simulate the effects of building shape on energy performance. For Morris screening, a typical sample size N is $r(x + 1)$, where r is the number of trajectories (r = 10 to 50). In LHS, N is commonly used $N \geq 100$ to $N \geq 1000$, depending on the desired accuracy and number of inputs. Zhu et al. [32] generated 2090 samples, which are 190 times the input variables, to estimate the cooling and heating loads of the building using LHS sampling methods. Figure 11 illustrates different sampling techniques for the sensitivity analysis of the total building energy consumption. The median values obtained by various sampling techniques are almost similar; however, the upper and lower quartiles and minimum and maximum values show significant differences.

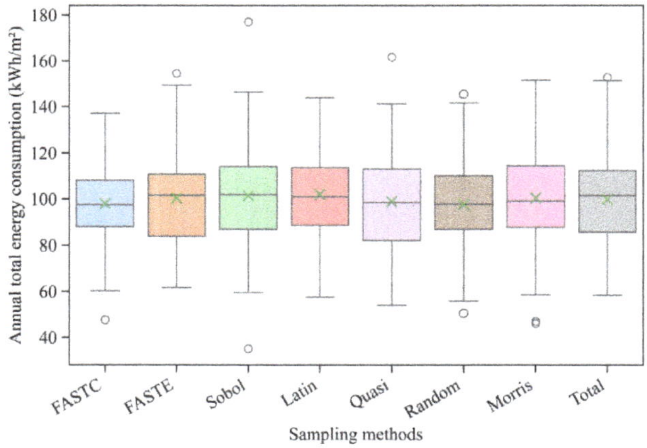

Figure 11. Different sampling methods and simulation results for building energy consumption [16].

4.3. Steps of SA for Building Energy Simulation

Once a clear objective is drawn for the SA in building energy performance, it is necessary to identify the most influential input parameters to optimize building energy efficiency. Then, define the range or distribution of each input factor. Convenient building energy simulation tools such as EnergyPlus, TRNSYS, DesignBuilder, or others can be selected to execute SA. Choosing an appropriate SA method, depending on the complexity of the model, is essential. Then, sample points will be generated using sampling methods as described in the previous section. Finally, the results will be analyzed to quantify the contribution of input parameters to the output variance and visualize the results using different charts or plots.

Visualization is one key component of the research to present and communicate after synthesizing a large amount of simulation-generated data. The guidelines for effective data visualization for research purposes are given by Kelleher and Wagener [78]. The different visualization tools help to illustrate this clearly and understandably. Table A2 of the paper shows the various names of plots to visualize the results from the sensitivity analysis, with descriptions and example plots. The examples of the plots were taken from different papers, as referenced in the table.

4.4. Energy Simulation and Post-Processing Tools in SA

Simulation tools are crucial components of SA nowadays because they allow complex systems to be solved. The interaction of multiple input parameters and nonlinear relationships often made the analytical solutions impractical or impossible. In addition, manual calculation can be very time-consuming and computationally exhaustive. Using standardized simulation software ensures faster, more efficient modeling. The simulation research group at Lawrence Berkeley Laboratory first developed a simulation program called DOE-2, funded by the U.S. Department of Energy during the late 1970s, which was used for detailed building energy simulations. The early simulation program was used for military and space applications [79]. Figure 12 depicts a bar chart related to the simulation tools used in this review's studies.

In 1971, the American Society of Heating, Refrigerating, and Air-Conditioning Engineers (ASHRAE) developed ASHRAE LOADS algorithms, which are a two-step calculation procedure for the dynamic heating and cooling load in a building. Later, Building Loads Analysis and System Thermodynamics (BLAST) was developed by different developers and funded by the Corps of Engineers Construction Engineering Research Laboratory.

More sophisticated simulation software, EnergyPlus (EP), was designed as a successor to DOE-2 and BLAST [80]. EP is a popular and widely used building thermal dynamics and energy simulation tool, and it is more extensively used in studies than other software. EP is a dynamic, whole-building energy simulation tool, highly detailed and open-source, developed by multiple developers and funded by the U.S. Department of Energy. EP can be easily coupled with external scripting tools such as Python to develop a sensitivity analysis framework [81]. TRNSYS (Transient System Simulation Tool), eQuest, DOE-2 (Department of Energy), and IDA ICE (Indoor Climate and Energy) are highly detailed and flexible tools for simulating building energy use. TRNSYS is suited for dynamic building energy modeling and integrating renewable energy system technologies. It can be linked with external sensitivity analysis environments, as it gives easily readable text output files by statistical software, such as MATLAB and Python [82]. In addition, software such as Apache, ANSYS Fluent, a CFD (Computational Fluid Dynamics) simulation tool, and Windows focus on fulfilling the specific aspects of the energy simulation.

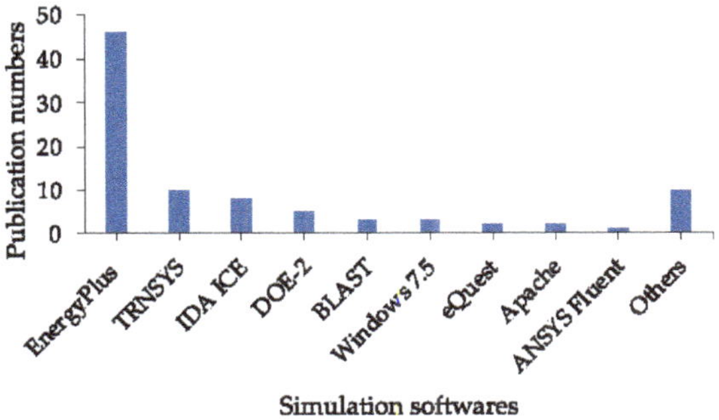

Figure 12. Different simulation software used in the papers selected for review.

Figure 13 illustrates the 3D design software that supports geometry design using other simulation software as a calculation engine. DesignBuilder is the most popular 3D design tool and uses EP as a calculation engine [83]. OpenStudio is a graphical user interface (GUI) for EP designed to work with SketchUp. SketchUp, Grasshopper, Autodesk, and CityGML are other 3D design tools widely used in conjunction with other energy simulation software.

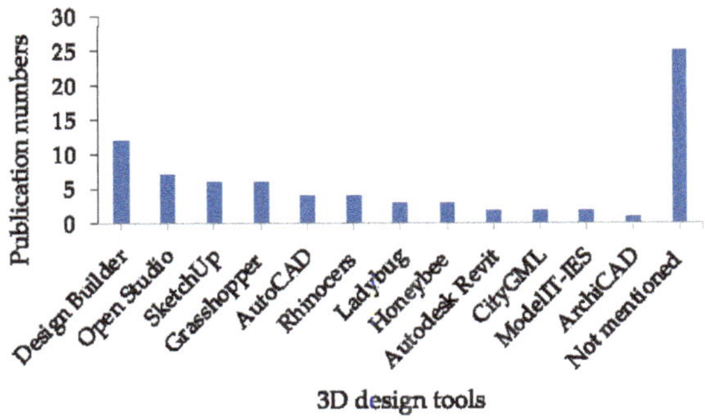

Figure 13. Different 3D design software used in the papers selected for review.

Post-processing tools are crucial for analyzing and visualizing the results from the sensitivity analysis of the building energy performance. Figure 14 shows different programming languages that help to interpret large datasets, generate meaningful insights, and facilitate decision-making by integrating, communicating, and optimizing with simulation software.

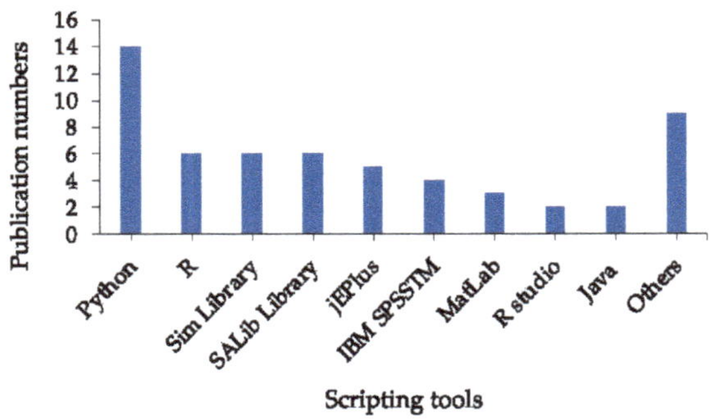

Figure 14. Different scripting tools for sensitivity analysis used in the papers selected for review.

There are standard post-processing tools, as built-in tools within energy simulation software, such as EP output viewer, TRNSYS TESS visualizer, DesignBuilder reporting module, and others; standalone and third-party tools, such as Excel, Python, MATLAB, Paraview, Dymola, and others; and GIS and BIM-based visualization tools [84,85]. Python is the most popular programming language for simulation, and it uses the SALib sensitivity analysis library in Python. A Python feature called an energy management system (EMS) allows EP to integrate and exchange data with many outside tools and libraries. Python implementations of widely used sensitivity analysis techniques, such as Sobol, Morris, and FAST, are helpful in systems modeling. In addition, other scripting tools such as R and R Studio [11], MATLAB [86], Java and MySQL [87], JSON, and jEplus [88] are also used with the integration of simulation software. Figure 15 illustrates the open-source sensitivity analysis software tools available based on programming language and the methods they support.

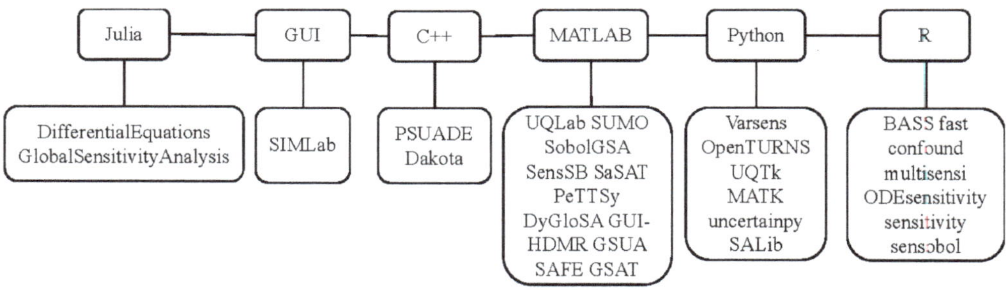

Figure 15. Open-source sensitivity analysis software tools available based on the programming language and the methods they support.

To enhance the credibility of the simulation results from the BTEM using a software tool, model calibration needs to be explicitly addressed in accordance with ASHRAE 14 guidelines [89]. Some industry-standard statistical indicators, such as Coefficient of Variation of Root Mean Square Error (CVRMSE) and Mean Bias Error (MBE), can evaluate model accuracy and measured data for validation purposes. The calibration process helps to reduce the performance gap between the real building behavior and the simulated data. Figueiredo et al. [90] performed a study to compare monitored and simulated data and reduce the performance gap in dynamic building simulation using optimization. Also, a multistage calibration technique for thermal dynamic building simulation using evolutionary algorithms was used to calibrate models in EnergyPlus. The good correlation established between the measured and simulated data gives validity to the simulated results.

4.5. SA and Codes/Standards Adopted

Following the codes in building energy simulations is necessary to meet the specific energy efficiency and performance standards. The codes are detailed, structured guidelines in compliance with energy standards to optimize the building designs for energy efficiency. Figure 16 illustrates the codes and standards that are most frequently used in the articles for the study. Codes often share mandatory compliance requirements in many cases and baseline performance metrics in some cases, against which the proposed design of buildings will be evaluated. Simulation results should exhibit that new designs of buildings meet or comply with these requirements quoted by codes. For instance, ASHRAE developed and formulated the standards and guidelines that are broadly administered and executed in the building energy efficiency sector [91]. ASHRAE periodically publishes and updates standards and guidelines related to HVAC systems.

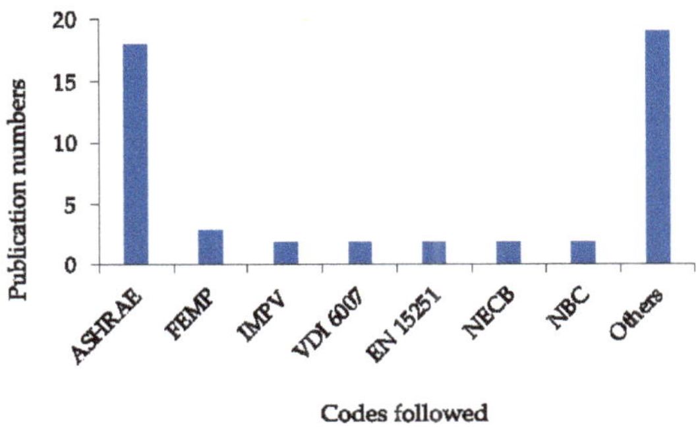

Figure 16. Different building and energy performance codes employed in the reviewed studies.

This review shows that ASHRAE standards are the most popular among designers, researchers, and engineers compared to other codes for building energy efficiency. Among the selected studies, around 36% used the ASHRAE standard, and the rest used other available standards. For instance, Carlucci et al. [29] used a small office model from ASHRAE standard 90.1 [92] and modeled it in EnergyPlus. Furthermore, each country has its standards, such as Danish building regulations and an industry guideline on indoor climate simulations [53], German standards [93], Indian National Building Code (NBC) [58], North American standards for building energy performance (NEBC) [59], Scottish building standards [71], and the Regulation of Energy Systems for Building Climatization (RSECE) in Australia [94].

5. Analysis of Sensitivity Patterns Across Building Typologies, Climate Zones, and SA Methodology to Identify Key Parameters

5.1. Methodology

A three-dimensional classification matrix was developed to identify key input parameters from the SA studies in building thermal energy modeling. Building typologies, climate zones, and SA methods are three key dimensions to analyze.

5.1.1. Building Typologies

Building stocks' heating and cooling energy demand accounts for 40% of the total energy demand [95]. The review identified the various building typologies analyzed for SA studies. The following distribution of studies was identified: residential buildings (30%), institutional buildings (19%), educational buildings (12%), and the remaining categories. The demand for heating and cooling in hospitals, institutional, and commercial buildings is generally high and cannot compromise indoor thermal comfort and air quality. Thus, more studies are needed to reduce the energy demand by optimizing the use of energy resources and building components. Figure 17 illustrates different building typologies analyzed for BTEM in the reviewed studies. Fewer studies have been conducted on commercial, industrial, and hospital buildings than on residential, institutional, and educational buildings. However, these sectors contribute to a higher energy demand rate for heating and cooling than residential buildings. Bugenings et al. [53] studied a novel solution for school renovation by replacing the conventional retrofitting system with a combination of diffuse ceiling ventilation and a double skin façade. The result shows an 11% lower energy demand than the traditional renovation system by achieving equal indoor air quality and thermal comfort. Himmetoğlu et al. [38] studied a hospital building using a multi-objective approach to determine the most suitable green envelope design for building energy demand.

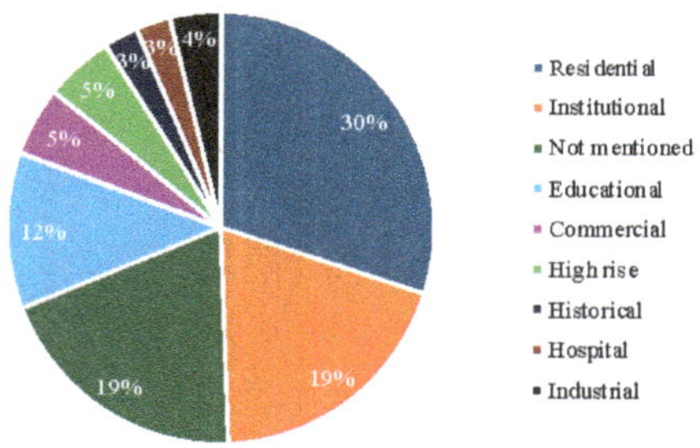

Figure 17. Different building types analyzed for BTEM in the reviewed studies.

5.1.2. Integration of Climate Zones

The energy demand for building heating and cooling may vary according to climate zones to maintain thermal comfort within an indoor environment. For the purpose of BTEM, the ASHRAE Standard 169 [96] offers a globally recognized framework of climate zones built upon long-term meteorological data, including heating degree days (HDD), cooling degree days (CDD), humidity, and precipitation. The standard serves as a foundation for climate zone categorizations into 18 distinct climate zones in building energy simulation and design. Figure 18a depicts the percentage of studies in the seven continents based on selected papers. Case studies in Asia and Europe are more dominant than those in Africa, Australia, and America. Figure 18b illustrates the percentage of studies in all kinds of hot, moderate, and cold climate zones among the selected studies. The figure shows that the studies were conducted in all climate zone types. Specifically, more studies on hot climate zones were conducted than on cold and moderate climate zones.

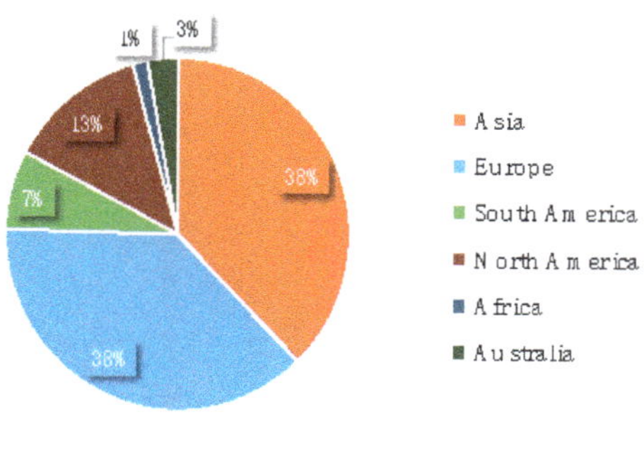

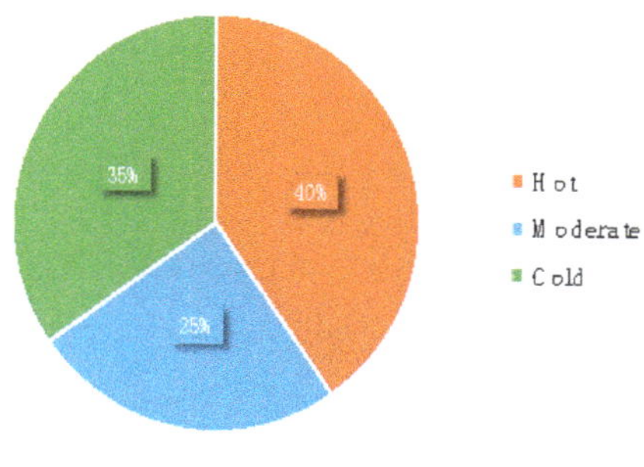

Figure 18. Percentage of studies in the reviewed literature: (**a**) according to continent; (**b**) in different climate zones.

Climate data accuracy is fundamental for predicting a building's energy performance, optimizing energy efficiency, and ensuring indoor thermal comfort. Table 3 provides information about several climate databases and simulated data that researchers use. Climate data, which comprises input variables such as precipitation, temperature, humidity, solar radiation, and wind speed, provides fundamental inputs for building energy simulations of how a building interacts with its environment throughout the year. Figure 19 illustrates that the selected studies used 24% of climate data sourced from local weather stations, 14% from climate databases based on different national standards, and 13% from the climate database of EPW files. Furthermore, incorporating local climate data allows for assessing renewable energy potential, such as solar, wind power, and shallow geothermal energy. Climate data for building energy simulation can be accessed from multiple sources, including local weather stations, installing weather monitoring equipment, and data loggers. Standardized climate datasets such as Typical Meteorological Year (TMY) files from sources such as the National Renewable Energy Laboratory (NREL) and EnergyPlus weather (EPW) files provide reliable reference TMY files for many global locations. Additionally, satellite-derived climate data and commercial third-party weather data services, such as Meteonorm, Meteoblue, or Weather Analytics offer comprehensive historical, typical, and forecasted weather data. For instance, the hourly weather data could be obtained using the commercial software Meteonorm [91].

Table 3. Some examples of climate databases with references used in the reviewed studies.

Nos	Climate Databases and Simulated Data	References
1	Copenhagen IWEC (International Weather for Energy Calculations)	[29]
2	Chinese standard weather data (CSWD)	[32]
3	The climate data are based on the international weather measurements for energy calculations (IWEC2.0) maintained by the National Climatic Data Centre.	[36,51,61]
4	French building energy regulation (RT2012), created from observed data over the period 1994–2008.	[74]
5	The first is the CWEC, which is developed using statistical criteriafrom the Canadian Weather Energy and Engineering Datasets (CWEEDS).	[14]
6	Local to regional database with the experience of 30 years of measurements.	[97]
7	Weather file obtained from the database for the city of São Paulo, from years 1988–2021.	[42]
8	Generated according to "Climate Design Data 2009 ASHRAE Handbook" from a period of 30 years of historical data.	[55]
9	Bangkok weather data	[97]
10	Simulated deterministically using TMY weather data, the Indian Meteorological Department to develop yearly simulation weather files.	[58]
11	A microclimate model ENVI-met generated the input micro-scale weather data.	[56]
12	The information on the weather and the climate data is included in the CDWN weather file.	[98]

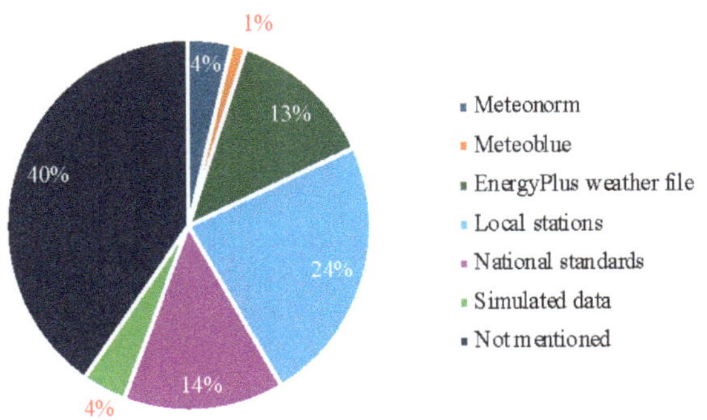

Figure 19. Different methods of climate data acquisition adopted worldwide in the reviewed studies.

5.1.3. SA Methods

Chapter 4 provides a comprehensive survey of SA techniques, highlighting the classifications and steps of SA methods in building thermal energy modeling. Pursuing that discussion, the section outlines the specific techniques employed in the review studies to analyze the influence of input parameters across various climate zones and building typologies.

5.2. Key Influential Factors

SA for building thermal energy performance considers several key input parameters to assess their influence on heating and cooling energy consumption and overall performance. Table 4 shows the standard building parameters considered in the sensitivity analysis. The range of parameters can vary depending on the building's type, location, surrounding climate conditions, and the scope of the study analysis.

Table 4. Overview of standard key input parameters considered in the sensitivity analysis of BTEM.

Input Parameters	Common Input Factors
Building envelope	Wall and roof insulation, window type, and glazing, including its U-value and solar heat gain coefficient (SHGC), and window-to-wall ratio (WWR)
Building orientation	Orientation, shape, and size
Internal loads	Occupancy density, lightening loads, and appliance and equipment loads
HVAC systems	Systems' efficiency, set point temperatures, and ventilation rates
Thermal mass	Building materials
Renewable energy	Photovoltaic panels, solar hot water systems, and shallow geothermal systems
Infiltration	Air leakage rates
Operational schedules	Occupancy schedules and systems schedules

Table 5 reveals the key influential parameters predicted by various studies for building thermal energy performance in different scenarios and considerations. The table comprehensively overviews key influential factors for building energy performance. In this review, eight studies predicted that the most critical parameter for building energy efficiency is the temperature set point [22], which is the highest recurrent parameter mentioned by researchers compared to other parameters. Temperature set points in heating and cooling systems are the target temperature values that the HVAC system aims to maintain the thermal comfort of the occupants inside the building. When the room temperature falls below the heating set point or rises above the cooling set point, the HVAC system activates to bring the indoor temperature back within the desired range.

Four typologies, including residential, institutional, educational, and hospital buildings, were selected to represent a range of occupancy patterns, internal heat gains, and operational equipment schedules. The impact of input parameters varies according to the building's intended use. Occupancy density has a lesser influence on residential buildings. However, it significantly impacts commercial buildings, schools, and office buildings [99]. According to Liu et al. [16], floor area and building coverage ratios are the most influential parameters, and envelope insulation is the least sensitive parameter in hot and humid high-rise residential buildings when assessed using Morris's screening SA method.

Also, shading devices and glazing types are key influential factors for residential buildings to minimize the heating and cooling loads. Set point temperature adjustments significantly impact the energy demand of commercial buildings as temperature fluctuations due to occupancy density require GVAC systems to compensate dynamically [100]. In the office building in mixed humid climates assessed using the variance-based SA method, window-to-wall ratio (WWR), and aspect ratio (ASR) are found to be the most sensitive parameters [65]. Similarly, Alghamdi et al. [17] assessed the BTEM of educational buildings in warm climates using the Monte Carlo technique, and cooling set point temperatures and roof construction were identified as the most sensitive parameters.

Building thermal energy performance is highly dependent on climatic factors, as building heating and cooling demands vary when exposed to different climate conditions. Cold climate zones exhibit high heating demand and low cooling demand. At the same time, hot climate zones exhibit high cooling demand and low heating demand. In a hot climate zone such as Baghdad, the angle of inclination of a roof shows sensitive parameters for the net energy demand [61]. In a cold climate in Quebec, Canada, architectural and electrical parameters are sensitive to the building energy model [59]. Segarra et al. [91] studied energy analysis across three different climate zones: the hot climate zone of Oslo, Spain's moderate climate, and Greece's hot climate. Wind speed and outdoor temperature were identified as the most influential parameters influencing energy demand.

The temperature set point directly influences the HVAC system and the intensity of its operation in both hot and cold climate regions. In addition, the greater the differences in the indoor and outdoor temperatures, the more energy the HVAC system requires to maintain that set point [57]. Maučec et al. [33] predicted that the U-factor of a window, the solar heat gain coefficient (SHGC), and a set point temperature are the dominant factors for the prefabricated timber building in both warm and cold climate areas.

Table 5. Examples of key input factors identified in the reviewed studies that influence BTEM.

Nos	Descriptions	References
1	Glazing thermal properties (particularly SHGC) is an influential input factor in terms of cooling energy efficiency compared to other building envelope materials.	[56]
2	The combination of wall insulation, basement ceiling insulation, and a secondary window application is the most sensitive in building energy efficiency. Changing the base case with the above-mentioned combination helps to reduce the total energy consumption by 8.53%.	[20]
3	The most influential input factor in the energy demand calculation is the temperature set point, the external wall area, and the U-value of the opaque surfaces. The deviation in the energy needs calculation drops from 18% to 10%.	[22]
4	Cooling set point temperatures and roof insulation significantly reduce energy consumption by 43.7% and 41.0%, respectively.	[25]
5	Temperature set point is much more sensitive to the building's energy efficiency. Such as, if the temperature set points increased from 20 °C to 22 °C, for instance, the energy consumption for space heating increases by 11.5%.	[101]
6	The most influential parameters on energy consumption were insulation and cooling set point played a key role with the contribution of 33% and 31%, respectively.	[28]
7	The occupancy density and start/end time of working hours are highly sensitive due to their significant impact on average occupancy profiles.	[98]
8	The implementation of reflective paints on the outer wall would achieve the highest percentages of whole-building energy savings, up to 21%, for cooling demand.	[25]
9	The window-to-wall ratio and HVAC set point are the two most contributing factors for the energy savings of up to 4%.	[63]
10	The apartment's floor area, equipment load, windows-to-floor ratio, mechanical ventilation airflow, and cooling temperature set point are the most critical design parameters for energy-efficient buildings.	[30]
11	Shading and SHGC values are the most effective parameters.	[97]
12	The window-to-wall ratio is the section of passive solar design that is the most influential to energy performance.	[18]
13	The most influential component is the floor area ratio and building coverage ratio for the energy performance of residential communities.	[17]

Table 5. *Cont.*

Nos	Descriptions	References
14	The windows' U-factor, SHGC, and a set point temperature for heating are the most critical factors for heating energy demand in cold climates.	[102]
15	The solar protection strategies are still the highly sensitive strategies for building energy performance in hot climate regions.	[16]
16	The window-to-wall ratio, aspect ratio, glazing type, absorptance of the wall, and shade transmittance are major influencing parameters. However, each parameter has an impact on different proportions depending on the building orientation and performance parameters.	[62]
17	The window's SHGC, wall painted color, wall U-value, and length of roof eaves are the most effective parameters and could reduce energy consumption by up to 19%.	[42]
18	The occupant heating set point, infiltration rates, occupant density, and building thermo-physical properties have a greater impact on energy consumption.	[81]

Moreover, in hot and dry climate zones, the temperature set point is the most influential parameter in multistorey residential buildings. Windows SHGC is another influential parameter that many researchers predicted in the review studies [93]. A high SHGC of windows leads to excessive solar heat gain, which makes cooling systems cope with the cooling demand in hot and humid climates. So, reflective paint on the outer walls of the building contributes up to 21% energy savings in cooling and is very useful, particularly in hot and arid regions where solar radiation is high enough, roof insulation contributes to reducing up to 41% of cooling demand as it receives direct solar radiation [100]. In cold climate regions where the heating demand is dominant, wall insulation helps to reduce heat loss from the building and improves heating efficiency [47]. The other critical parameters are the window-to-wall ratio [31], occupants' density [103], and wall U-value [97], which significantly influence heating energy demand, particularly in colder climates.

6. Temperature Adaptability

The building should cope with the demand for cooling as climate change affects the cooling demand of buildings, especially in hot and arid regions. It is necessary to ensure the occupants' thermal comfort and that the building remains energy-efficient despite rising global temperatures. It is essential to develop climate-responsive strategies to cope with situations such as adaptive insulation, dynamic shading, efficient HVAC temperature set points, and passive solar design. These parameters should be analyzed by considering the projected climate conditions to optimize building energy performance for the future scenario. The implementation of dynamic shading systems, such as external louvers, automated blinds, or electrochromic glazing, can be an impactful strategy in response to real-time solar radiation [104]. Similarly, applying reflective coatings on the roofs and facades of the buildings helps to reduce solar absorption and surface temperature. It reveals that reflective coatings have the potential to reduce solar heat gain by about 40% [105]. Given that, SA helps uncover the most influential factors impacting heating and cooling loads under future climate change scenarios. Cooling set point temperatures become more influential in hot climates due to increased cooling demand [100].

At the same time, window shading devices play a key role in reducing the cooling demand in projected climate conditions [106]. SA also reveals the combined effect of multiple input parameters, considering future temperature increases and extreme weather events. The combined effect of cooling set point and roof insulation will significantly affect building energy performance due to future climate conditions compared to historical ones [100]. SA helps to prioritize adaptive strategies such as reflective paints [18] and glazing SHGC [82] to mitigate overheating risks in climate change scenarios. In addition,

SA gives policymakers the enlightenment to understand which input parameters are more sensitive to climate shifts, which can lead to the preparation of suitable energy codes and regulations in advance. For example, SA indicated that temperature set points and HVAC systems [65] are dominant factors under extreme future climate scenarios. So, the regulations may focus on adaptive measures for these factors. Figure 20 shows the effect of climate sensitivity on building energy consumption in five representative building models. When the percentage of energy consumption change is observed in all models, the energy consumption gradually increases from 2020 to 2100. This is because the projected climate model increases the cooling degree days.

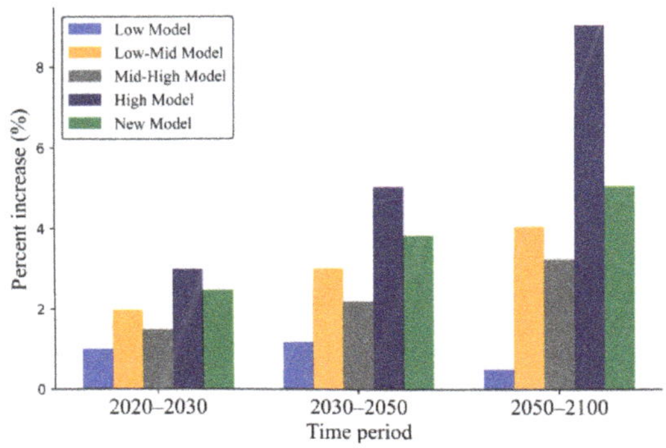

Figure 20. Total percentage energy consumption changes from 2020 to 2100 across different building models [106].

However, the climate change effect assessment heavily depends on the availability and quality of TMY data for specific locations. Several methodologies have been developed for generating TMY datasets with different priorities, such as matching statistical properties, minimizing extreme events, or eliminating anomalous years. There is the possibility of climate data uncertainties, and in many cases, the treatment of these uncertainties remains inadequate, which can lead to significant errors in model predictions [107]. Addressing these limitations needs a shift toward probabilistic, adaptive, and climate-responsive frameworks [108]. Additionally, assessing the impact of extreme weather events and evaluating uncertainty ranges would provide a more robust understanding of input parameter sensitivity under various climatic conditions [39].

7. Conclusions and Future Works

Sensitivity analysis is fundamental for optimizing building thermal energy performance through simulation, reducing energy consumption, and mitigating climate change impacts. This review highlights the importance of conducting this type of analysis with a view to improving energy performance from a sustainability perspective. This systematic review highlights key insights into the methodologies, tools, influential parameters, and adaptive strategies for the effect of climate change, incorporating BTEM and SA. The key insights are:

- Since 2005, there has been a significant rise in research using SA techniques in BTEM.
- The USA is the most involved country in studying BTEM using the SA technique, followed by China and various European countries.
- GSA is the most widely used method, surpassing LSA in analyzing building energy performance.
- The case studies of residential buildings dominate the other types of buildings, followed by institutional and educational buildings.

- Most studies focus on cases in Europe and Asia, particularly in hot climate regions.
- Climate data for BTEM is mainly extracted from local meteorological stations. However, Meteonorm software is a widely used tool, as it provides reliable data from several meteorological sources in a designated format.
- EnergyPlus and DesignBuilder are the most commonly used and popular simulation tools for BTEM.
- Python and its library, called the SALib library, are the most used scripting tools for SA.
- ASHRAE standards are the most frequently referenced codes in the studies.
- Temperature set point is the most influential input parameter, as concluded by researchers in both heating- and cooling-dominant climate zones.
- Adaptive strategies, such as dynamic shading, reflective coatings, and optimized HVAC set points, are crucial in addressing climate change effects.

Considering sustainability, some areas need improvements and focus for future research to optimize thermal energy performance in buildings. More investigations are necessary to analyze how different climate zones impact building thermal energy performance and which input parameters are most influential in each region. The Earth's temperature is continuously rising, significantly affecting building thermal energy demand, necessitating rigorous studies on adaptive strategies to maintain thermal comfort while improving energy efficiency. Future research should focus on integrating machine learning and real-time data analytics to improve SA's accuracy, applicability, and predictive capabilities in dynamic building environments.

Author Contributions: Conceptualization, R.R.; methodology, R.R.; formal analysis, R.R.; investigation, R.R.; writing—original draft preparation, R.R.; writing—review and editing, R.R., A.F. and A.V.; visualization, R.R.; supervision, C.C. All authors have read and agreed to the published version of the manuscript.

Funding: This study was funded by the Portuguese Foundation for Science and Technology (FCT) under the 2022 Call for Ph.D. Studentships – Regular Line in Scientific and Academic Institutions, grant number (2022.10333.BD).

Data Availability Statement: The contributions presented in this study are included in the article. Further inquiries can be directed to the corresponding author.

Acknowledgments: The authors greatly acknowledge the logistical support from CERIS—Civil Engineering Research and Innovation for Sustainability, the Department of Civil Engineering, the University of Aveiro (UA), and the National Laboratory of Civil Engineering (LNEC).

Conflicts of Interest: The authors declare no conflicts of interest.

Appendix A

Table A1. Comparison of different sampling methods used in SA for building thermal energy analysis.

Sampling Types	Method	Description	Advantages	Limitations	References
Screening method	Morris Method	Evaluates the effect of small perturbations in input factors to identify the most impactful factors.	Computationally efficient, suited for preliminary sensitivity analysis.	Generates only qualitative sensitivity rankings instead of precise quantitative measures.	[46,109]
Random sampling	Monte Carlo sampling (MCS)	Sampling from probability distributions assigned to input factors to generate multiple model simulations.	Easy to implement, provides reliable predictions when many samples are used.	Computationally expensive, needing numerous simulations for precise results.	[110]

Table A1. *Cont.*

Sampling Types	Method	Description	Advantages	Limitations	References
Stratified sampling	Latin hypercube sampling (LHS)	Divides the input factor range into equal probability intervals and ensures that each interval is sampled once.	More efficient than MCS, leading to better coverage of input variability.	Computationally demanding, however, reduces variance compared to pure random sampling.	[111]
Quasi-random Sampling	Sobol' sequences	Uses low-discrepancy sequences to assign sample points that are more evenly distributed than solely random methods.	Improves convergence rates compared to MCS, using fewer samples to provide more accurate sensitivity estimates.	Need careful observation to ensure proper distribution of sample points.	[112]
Variance-based method	Sobol' sensitivity analysis	GSA method that decomposes the output variance to estimate contributions from each input and their interactions.	Provides detailed sensitivity indices, recording both first-order and higher-order effects.	Computationally intensive with a large number of simulations required.	[66]
Deterministic sampling	FAST (Fourier amplitude sensitivity test)	Uses Fourier transformations to quantify sensitivity indices based on spectral decomposition of model output variations.	Lower computational cost compared to Sobol' analysis to achieve similar GS insights.	Less user-friendly for interpreting interaction effects compared to variance-based methods.	[113]

Table A2. Some examples of visualization tools for sensitivity analysis results in building energy simulation.

Plot Name	Description	Plots	Taken From
Scatter plots	Identify correlations and trends and conduct a preliminary analysis of input and output relationships.	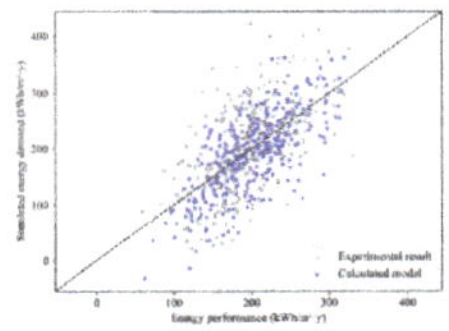	[114]
Colored scatter plots	Visualize combined effects and interactions between parameters.	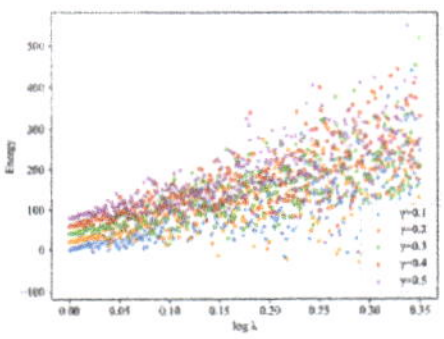	[115]
Bar plot	Presenting sensitivity indices with comparing relative importance of factors.	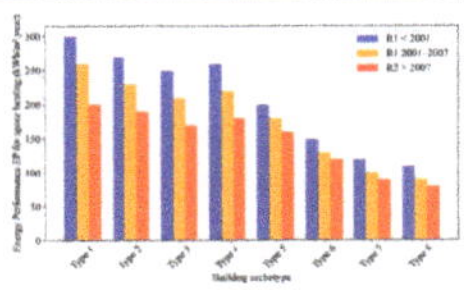	[116]
Box plot	Helps to understand variability and uncertainty.	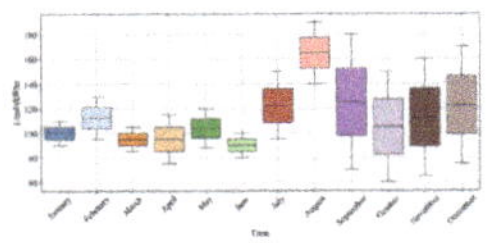	[117]
Convergence plot	Ensures robustness of SA by assessing stability of sensitivity indices with sample size.	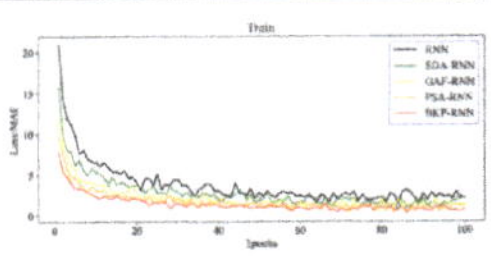	[118]

Table A2. *Cont.*

Plot Name	Description	Plots	Taken From
Radial convergence plot	Presents and compares sensitivity indices in a compact format.	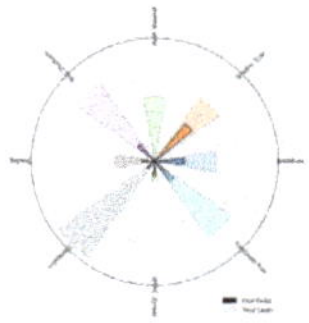	[119]
Circos	Illustrates complex interactions in high-dimensional data.	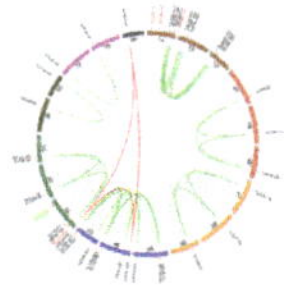	[120]
Pattern plot	Identify patterns by summarizing multi-scenario analysis.	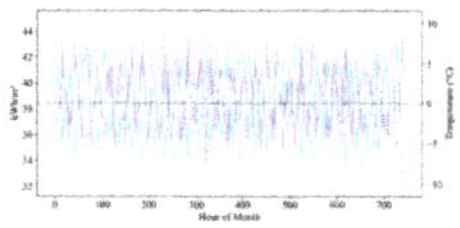	[86]

References

1. Saltelli, A.; Aleksankina, K.; Becker, W.; Fennell, P.; Ferretti, F.; Holst, N.; Li, S.; Wu, Q. Why so many published sensitivity analyses are false: A systematic review of sensitivity analysis practices. *Environ. Model. Softw.* **2019**, *114*, 29–39. [CrossRef]
2. Figueiredo, A.; Silva, T.; Gonçalves, M.; Samagaio, A. Application of Novel Phase Change Material Constructive Solution for Thermal Regulation of Passive Solar Buildings. *Buildings* **2024**, *14*, 493. [CrossRef]
3. Razavi, S.; Jakeman, A.; Saltelli, A.; Prieur, C.; Iooss, B.; Borgonovo, E.; Plischke, E.; Piano, S.L.; Iwanaga, T.; Becker, W.; et al. The Future of Sensitivity Analysis: An essential discipline for systems modeling and policy support. *Environ. Model. Softw.* **2021**, *137*, 104954. [CrossRef]
4. Rabitz, H. Systems Analysis at the Molecular Scale. *Science* **1989**, *246*, 221–226. [CrossRef] [PubMed]
5. Figueiredo, A.; Vicente, R.; Oliveira, R.; Rodrigues, F.; Samagaio, A. Multiscale Modelling Approach Targeting Optimisation of PCM into Constructive Solutions for Overheating Mitigation in Buildings. *Appl. Sci.* **2020**, *10*, 8009. [CrossRef]
6. Ratto, M.; Tarantola, S.; Saltelli, A. Sensitivity Analysis in Model Calibration: GSA-GLUE Approach. *Comput. Phys. Commun.* **2001**, *136*, 212–224. [CrossRef]
7. Hopfe, C.J.; Hensen, J.L.M. Uncertainty analysis in building performance simulation for design support. *Energy Build.* **2011**, *43*, 2798–2805. [CrossRef]
8. Tian, W.; De Wilde, P. Uncertainty and sensitivity analysis of building performance using probabilistic climate projections: A UK case study. *Autom. Constr.* **2011**, *20*, 1096–1109. [CrossRef]
9. Manke, J.M.; Hittle, D.C.; Hancock, C.E. *Calibrating Building Energy Analysis Models Using Short Term Test Data*; American Society of Mechanical Engineers: New York, NY, USA, 1996; Volume 536.
10. Saltelli, A.; Tarantola, S.; Chan, K.P.S. A quantitative model-independent method for global sensitivity analysis of model output. *Technometrics* **1999**, *41*, 39–56. [CrossRef]
11. Wei, T. A review of sensitivity analysis methods in building energy analysis. *Renew. Sustain. Energy Rev.* **2013**, *20*, 411–419.
12. Pang, Z.; O'Neill, Z.; Li, Y.; Niu, F. The role of sensitivity analysis in the building performance analysis: A critical review. *Energy Build.* **2020**, *209*, 109659. [CrossRef]
13. Mendes, V.F.; Cruz, A.S.; Gomes, A.P.; Mendes, J.C. A systematic review of methods for evaluating the thermal performance of buildings through energy simulations. *Renew. Sustain. Energy Rev.* **2024**, *189*, 113875. [CrossRef]
14. Berardi, U.; Jafarpur, P. Assessing the impact of climate change on building heating and cooling energy demand in Canada. *Renew. Sustain. Energy Rev.* **2020**, *121*, 109681. [CrossRef]
15. Bac, U.; Alaloosi, K.A.M.S.; Turhan, C. A comprehensive evaluation of the most suitable HVAC system for an industrial building by using a hybrid building energy simulation and multi criteria decision making framework. *J. Build. Eng.* **2021**, *37*, 102153. [CrossRef]
16. Liu, S.; Kwok, Y.T.; Lau, K.K.L.; Ouyang, W.; Ng, E. Effectiveness of passive design strategies in responding to future climate change for residential buildings in hot and humid Hong Kong. *Energy Build.* **2020**, *228*. [CrossRef]

17. Alghamdi, S.; Tang, W.; Kanjanabootra, S.; Alterman, D. Effect of Architectural Building Design Parameters on Thermal Comfort and Energy Consumption in Higher Education Buildings. *Buildings* **2022**, *12*, 329. [CrossRef]
18. Vukadinović, A.; Radosavljević, J.; Đorđević, A.; Protić, M.; Petrović, N. Multi-objective optimization of energy performance for a detached residential building with a sunspace using the NSGA-II genetic algorithm. *Solar Energy* **2021**, *224*, 1426–1444. [CrossRef]
19. Rupp, R.F.; Parkinson, T.; Kim, J.; Toftum, J.; de Dear, R. The impact of occupant's thermal sensitivity on adaptive thermal comfort model. *Build. Environ.* **2022**, *207*, 108517. [CrossRef]
20. Bravo Dias, J.; Carrilho da Graça, G.; Soares, P.M.M. Comparison of methodologies for generation of future weather data for building thermal energy simulation. *Energy Build.* **2020**, *206*, 109556. [CrossRef]
21. Eriksson, M.; Akander, J.; Moshfegh, B. Development and validation of energy signature method—Case study on a multi-family building in Sweden before and after deep renovation. *Energy Build.* **2020**, *210*, 109756. [CrossRef]
22. Prataviera, E.; Vivian, J.; Lombardo, G.; Zarrella, A. Evaluation of the impact of input uncertainty on urban building energy simulations using uncertainty and sensitivity analysis. *Appl. Energy* **2022**, *311*, 118691. [CrossRef]
23. Gelesz, A.; Catto Lucchino, E.; Goia, F.; Serra, V.; Reith, A. Characteristics that matter in a climate façade: A sensitivity analysis with building energy simulation tools. *Energy Build.* **2020**, *229*, 110467. [CrossRef]
24. Mukhamet, T.; Kobeyev, S.; Nadeem, A.; Memon, S.A. Ranking PCMs for building façade applications using multi-criteria decision-making tools combined with energy simulations. *Energy* **2021**, *215*, 119102. [CrossRef]
25. William, M.A.; Suárez-López, M.J.; Soutullo, S.; Hanafy, A.A. Building envelopes toward energy-efficient buildings: A balanced multi-approach decision making. *Int. J. Energy Res.* **2021**, *45*, 21096–21113. [CrossRef]
26. Westermann, P.; Welzel, M.; Evins, R. Using a deep temporal convolutional network as a building energy surrogate model that spans multiple climate zones. *Appl. Energy* **2020**, *278*, 115563. [CrossRef]
27. Wang, S.; Yi, Y.K.; Liu, N. The ANN Architecture Analysis: A Case Study on Daylight, Visual, and Outdoor Thermal Metrics of Residential Buildings in China. *Buildings* **2023**, *13*, 2795. [CrossRef]
28. Saryazdi, S.m.E.; Etemad, A.; Shafaat, A.; Bahman, A.M. Data-driven performance analysis of a residential building applying artificial neural network (ANN) and multi-objective genetic algorithm (GA). *Build. Environ.* **2022**, *225*, 109633. [CrossRef]
29. Carlucci, S.; Causone, F.; Biandrate, S.; Ferrando, M.; Moazami, A.; Erba, S. On the impact of stochastic modeling of occupant behavior on the energy use of office buildings. *Energy Build.* **2021**, *246*, 111049. [CrossRef]
30. Yu, H.; Wang, M.; Lin, X.; Guo, H.; Liu, H.; Zhao, Y.; Wang, H.; Li, C.; Jing, R. Prioritizing urban planning factors on community energy performance based on GIS-informed building energy modeling. *Energy Build.* **2021**, *249*, 111191. [CrossRef]
31. Singh, M.M.; Deb, C.; Geyer, P. Early-stage design support combining machine learning and building information modelling. *Autom. Constr.* **2022**, *136*, 104147. [CrossRef]
32. Zhu, L.; Zhang, J.; Gao, Y.; Tian, W.; Yan, Z.; Ye, X.; Sun, Y.; Wu, C. Uncertainty and sensitivity analysis of cooling and heating loads for building energy planning. *J. Build. Eng.* **2022**, *45*, 103440. [CrossRef]
33. Maučec, D.; Premrov, M.; Leskovar, V.Ž. Use of sensitivity analysis for a determination of dominant design parameters affecting energy efficiency of timber buildings in different climates. *Energy Sustain. Dev.* **2021**, *63*, 86–102. [CrossRef]
34. Pianosi, F.; Beven, K.; Freer, J.; Hall, J.W.; Rougier, J.; Stephenson, D.B.; Wagener, T. Sensitivity analysis of environmental models: A systematic review with practical workflow. *Environ. Model. Softw.* **2016**, *79*, 214–232. [CrossRef]
35. Edwards, N.R.; Cameron, D.; Rougier, J. Precalibrating an intermediate complexity climate model. *Clim. Dyn.* **2011**, *37*, 1469–1482. [CrossRef]
36. Yue, N.; Caini, M.; Li, L.; Zhao, Y.; Li, Y. A comparison of six metamodeling techniques applied to multi building performance vectors prediction on gymnasiums under multiple climate conditions. *Appl. Energy* **2023**, *332*, 120481. [CrossRef]
37. Abokersh, M.H.; Spiekman, M.; Vijlbrief, O.; van Goch, T.A.J.; Vallès, M.; Boer, D. A real-time diagnostic tool for evaluating the thermal performance of nearly zero energy buildings. *Appl. Energy* **2021**, *281*, 116091. [CrossRef]
38. Himmetoğlu, S.; Delice, Y.; Kızılkaya Aydoğan, E.; Uzal, B. Green building envelope designs in different climate and seismic zones: Multi-objective ANN-based genetic algorithm. *Sustain. Energy Technol. Assess.* **2022**, *53*, 102505. [CrossRef]
39. Shi, D.; Gao, Y.; Zeng, P.; Li, B.; Shen, P.; Zhuang, C. Climate adaptive optimization of green roofs and natural night ventilation for lifespan energy performance improvement in office buildings. *Build. Environ.* **2022**, *223*, 109505. [CrossRef]
40. Salimi, S.; Hammad, A. Sensitivity analysis of probabilistic occupancy prediction model using big data. *Build. Environ.* **2020**, *172*, 106729. [CrossRef]
41. Zhao, C.; Zhang, L.; Zhang, Y. Exploring the effect of longwave radiation exchange on the energy balance of building façades in subtropical regions. *Build. Environ.* **2023**, *233*, 110096. [CrossRef]
42. Olinger, M.S.; Melo, A.P.; Lamberts, R. Developing a surrogate model for naturally ventilated cellular offices in Brazil. *Build. Environ.* **2023**, *233*, 110075. [CrossRef]
43. Amorim, R.P.L.; Melo, A.P.; Mantelli Neto, S.L.; Lamberts, R. Sky emissivity model calibration with data from Brazil and building simulation sensitivity analysis. *Solar Energy* **2023**, *263*, 111963. [CrossRef]

44. Liu, X.; Polsky, Y.; Qian, D.; Mcdonald, J. An Analysis on Cost Reduction Potential of Vertical Bore Ground Heat Exchangers Used for Ground Source Heat Pump Systems. *Proceedings* **2019**, *1*, 1–15.
45. Østergård, T.; Jensen, R.L.; Mikkelsen, F.S. The best way to perform building simulations? One-at-a-time optimization vs. Monte Carlo sampling. *Energy Build.* **2020**, *208*, 109628. [CrossRef]
46. Benz, A.; Taraben, J.; Debus, P.; Habte, B.; Oppermann, L.; Hallermann, N.; Voelker, C.; Rodehorst, V.; Morgenthal, G. Framework for a UAS-based assessment of energy performance of buildings. *Energy Build.* **2021**, *250*, 111266. [CrossRef]
47. Ozbalta, T.G.; Yildiz, Y.; Bayram, I.; Yilmaz, O.C. Energy performance analysis of a historical building using cost-optimal assessment. *Energy Build.* **2021**, *250*, 111301. [CrossRef]
48. Zhong, F.; Chaudhry, H.N.; Calautit, J.K. Effect of roof cooling and air curtain gates on thermal and wind conditions in stadiums for hot climates. *Energies* **2021**, *14*, 3941. [CrossRef]
49. Magni, M.; Ochs, F.; Streicher, W. Comprehensive analysis of the influence of different building modelling approaches on the results and computational time using a cross-compared model as a reference. *Energy Build.* **2022**, *259*, 111859. [CrossRef]
50. Im, P.; Jackson, R.; Bae, Y.; Dong, J.; Cui, B. Probabilistic reliability assessment and case studies for predicted energy savings in residential buildings. *Energy Build.* **2020**, *209*, 109658. [CrossRef]
51. Satola, D.; Houlihan-Wiberg, A.; Gustavsen, A. Global sensitivity analysis and optimisation of design parameters for low GHG emission lifecycle of multifamily buildings in India. *Energy Build.* **2022**, *277*, 112596. [CrossRef]
52. Geraldi, M.S.; Gnecco, V.M.; Barzan Neto, A.; Martins, B.A.d.M.; Ghisi, E.; Fossati, M.; Melo, A.P.; Lamberts, R. Evaluating the impact of the shape of school reference buildings on bottom-up energy benchmarking. *J. Build. Eng.* **2021**, *43*, 103142. [CrossRef]
53. Bugenings, L.A.; Schaffer, M.; Larsen, O.K.; Zhang, C. A novel solution for school renovations: Combining diffuse ceiling ventilation with double skin facade. *J. Build. Eng.* **2022**, *49*, 104026. [CrossRef]
54. Goffart, J.; Woloszyn, M. EASI RBD-FAST: An efficient method of global sensitivity analysis for present and future challenges in building performance simulation. *J. Build. Eng.* **2021**, *43*, 103129. [CrossRef]
55. Nik-Bakht, M.; Panizza, R.O.; Hudon, P.; Chassain, P.Y.; Bashari, M. Economy-energy trade off automation—A decision support system for building design development. *J. Build. Eng.* **2020**, *30*, 101222. [CrossRef]
56. Alyakoob, A.; Hartono, S.; Johnson, T.; Middel, A. Estimating cooling loads of Arizona State University buildings using microclimate data and machine learning. *J. Build. Eng.* **2023**, *64*, 105705. [CrossRef]
57. Zhan, J.; He, W.; Huang, J. Dual-objective building retrofit optimization under competing priorities using Artificial Neural Network. *J. Build. Eng.* **2023**, *70*, 106376. [CrossRef]
58. Chaturvedi, S.; Rajasekar, E. Application of a probabilistic LHS-PAWN approach to assess building cooling energy demand uncertainties. *Build. Simul.* **2022**, *15*, 373–387. [CrossRef]
59. Panizza, R.O.; Nik-Bakht, M. On the invariance of energy influential design parameters in a cold climate–a meta-level sensitivity analysis based on the energy, economy, and building characteristics. *Adv. Build. Energy Res.* **2022**, *16*, 466–488. [CrossRef]
60. Kadir, K.; Mehdi Salehi Dezfouli, M.; Gabrielli, L.; Greta Ruggeri, A.; Scarpa, M. Roadmap to a Sustainable Energy System: Is Uncertainty a Major Barrier to Investments for Building Energy Retrofit Projects in Wide City Compartments? *Energies* **2023**, *16*, 4261. [CrossRef]
61. Ibraheem, Y.; Piroozfar, P.; Farr, E.R.P.; Ravenscroft, N. Energy Production Analysis of Photovoltaic Shading Devices (PVSD) in Integrated Façade Systems (IFS). *Front. Built Environ.* **2020**, *6*, 81. [CrossRef]
62. Saltelli, A.; Annoni, P.; Azzini, I.; Campolongo, F.; Ratto, M.; Tarantola, S. Variance based sensitivity analysis of model output. Design and estimator for the total sensitivity index. *Comput. Phys. Commun.* **2010**, *181*, 259–270. [CrossRef]
63. Elhadad, S.; Orban, Z. A Sensitivity Analysis for Thermal Performance of Building Envelope Design Parameters. *Sustainability* **2021**, *13*, 14018. [CrossRef]
64. Hamm, N.A.S.; Hall, J.W.; Anderson, M.G. Variance-based sensitivity analysis of the probability of hydrologically induced slope instability. *Comput. Geosci.* **2006**, *32*, 803–817. [CrossRef]
65. Singh, R.; Buddhi, D.; Thapa, S.; Prakash, C.; Singh, R.; Sharma, A.; Sheoran, S.; Saxena, K.K. Sensitivity Analysis for Decisive Design Parameters for Energy and Indoor Visual Performances of a Glazed Façade Office Building. *Sustainability* **2022**, *14*, 14163. [CrossRef]
66. Nouri, A.; van Treeck, C.; Frisch, J. Sensitivity Assessment of Building Energy Performance Simulations Using MARS Meta-Modeling in Combination with Sobol' Method. *Energies* **2024**, *17*, 695. [CrossRef]
67. Jans-Singh, M.; Ward, R.; Choudhary, R. Co-simulating a greenhouse in a building to quantify co-benefits of different coupled configurations. *J. Build. Perform. Simul.* **2021**, *14*, 247–276. [CrossRef]
68. Prada, A.; Pernigotto, G.; Baggio, P.; Gasparella, A. Uncertainty propagation of material properties in energy simulation of existing residential buildings: The role of buildings features. *Build. Simul.* **2018**, *11*, 449–464. [CrossRef]
69. Ibraheem, Y.; Piroozfar, P.A.E.; Farr, E.R.P.; Ravenscroft, N. Methodological evaluation of Integrated Façade Systems: Sensitivity analysis of net energy in a base-case model. *Int. J. Build. Pathol. Adapt.* **2020**, *38*, 107–126. [CrossRef]

70. Hosamo, H.; Mazzetto, S. Performance Evaluation of Machine Learning Models for Predicting Energy Consumption and Occupant Dissatisfaction in Buildings. *Buildings* **2025**, *15*, 39. [CrossRef]
71. Hopfe, C.J.; McLeod, R.S. Enhancing resilient community decision-making using building performance simulation. *Build. Environ.* **2021**, *188*, 107398. [CrossRef]
72. Mejia-Solis, E.; Arias, J.; Palm, B. Simple solutions for improving thermal comfort in huts in the highlands of Peru. *Heliyon* **2023**, *9*, e19709. [CrossRef]
73. Cozza, S.; Patel, M.K.; Chambers, J. Uncertainty in potential savings from improving energy label: A Monte Carlo study of the Swiss residential buildings. *Energy Build.* **2022**, *271*, 112333. [CrossRef]
74. Pannier, M.L.; Recht, T.; Robillart, M.; Schalbart, P.; Peuportier, B.; Mora, L. Identifying optimal renovation schedules for building portfolios: Application in a social housing context under multi-year funding constraints. *Energy Build.* **2021**, *250*, 111290. [CrossRef]
75. Alsharif, R.; Arashpour, M.; Golafshani, E.M.; Hosseini, M.R.; Chang, V.; Zhou, J. Machine learning-based analysis of occupant-centric aspects: Critical elements in the energy consumption of residential buildings. *J. Build. Eng.* **2022**, *46*, 103846. [CrossRef]
76. Yang, S.; Tian, W.; Cubi, E.; Meng, Q.; Liu, Y.; Wei, L. Comparison of Sensitivity Analysis Methods in Building Energy Assessment. *Procedia Eng.* **2016**, *146*, 174–181. [CrossRef]
77. Asadi, S.; Amiri, S.S.; Mottahedi, M. On the development of multi-linear regression analysis to assess energy consumption in the early stages of building design. *Energy Build.* **2014**, *85*, 246–255. [CrossRef]
78. Kelleher, C.; Wagener, T. Ten guidelines for effective data visualization in scientific publications. *Environ. Model. Softw.* **2011**, *26*, 822–827. [CrossRef]
79. Zhu, D.; Hong, T.; Yan, D.; Wang, C. A detailed loads comparison of three building energy modeling programs: EnergyPlus, DeST and DOE-2.1E. *Build. Simul.* **2013**, *6*, 323–335. [CrossRef]
80. Crawley, D.B.; Lawrie, L.K.; Winkelmann, F.C.; Buhl, W.F.; Huang, Y.J.; Pedersen, C.O.; Strand, R.K.; Liesen, R.J.; Fisher, D.E.; Witte, M.J.; et al. EnergyPlus: Creating a new-generation building energy simulation program. *Energy Build.* **2001**, *33*, 319–331. [CrossRef]
81. Wijesuriya, S.; Kishore, R.A.; Mitchell, M.; Booten, C. Enhancing EnergyPlus capabilities to model dynamic building envelopes using python plugin. *Energy Build.* **2025**, *339*, 115776. [CrossRef]
82. Meiers, J.; Frey, G. Interfacing TRNSYS with MATLAB for Building Energy System Optimization. *Energies* **2025**, *18*, 255. [CrossRef]
83. Del Ama Gonzalo, F.; Moreno Santamaría, B.; Montero Burgos, M.J. Assessment of Building Energy Simulation Tools to Predict Heating and Cooling Energy Consumption at Early Design Stages. *Sustainability* **2023**, *15*, 1920. [CrossRef]
84. Vera-Piazzini, O.; Scarpa, M.; Peron, F. Building Energy Simulation and Monitoring: A Review of Graphical Data Representation. *Energies* **2023**, *16*, 390. [CrossRef]
85. Villano, F.; Mauro, G.M.; Pedace, A. A Review on Machine/Deep Learning Techniques Applied to Building Energy Simulation, Optimization and Management. *Thermo* **2024**, *4*, 100–139. [CrossRef]
86. Xuanyuan, P.; Zhang, Y.; Yao, J.; Zheng, R. Sensitivity Analysis and Optimization of Energy-Saving Measures for Office Building in Hot Summer and Cold Winter Regions. *Energies* **2024**, *17*, 1675. [CrossRef]
87. Bourdeau, M. Assessment of the Performances of Building Energy Retrofit Using Sensor Networks for the Monitoring of Energy Consumption and Usages. Ph.D. Thesis, Université Gustave Eiffel, Champs-sur-Marne, France, 2022.
88. Delgarm, N.; Sajadi, B.; Azarbad, K.; Delgarm, S. Sensitivity analysis of building energy performance: A simulation-based approach using OFAT and variance-based sensitivity analysis methods. *J. Build. Eng.* **2018**, *15*, 181–193. [CrossRef]
89. Coakley, D.; Raftery, P.; Keane, M. A review of methods to match building energy simulation models to measured data. *Renew. Sustain. Energy Rev.* **2014**, *37*, 123–141. [CrossRef]
90. Figueiredo, A.; Kämpf, J.; Vicente, R.; Oliveira, R.; Silva, T. Comparison between monitored and simulated data using evolutionary algorithms: Reducing the performance gap in dynamic building simulation. *J. Build. Eng.* **2018**, *17*, 96–106. [CrossRef]
91. Segarra, E.L.; Ruiz, G.R.; González, V.G.; Peppas, A.; Bandera, C.F. Impact assessment for building energy models using observed vs. third-party weather data sets. *Sustainability* **2020**, *12*, 6788. [CrossRef]
92. *ANSI/ASHRAE Standard 90.1-2019*; Energy Standard for Buildings Except Low-Rise Residential Buildings. American Society of Heating, Refrigerating and Air-Conditioning Engineers: Atlanta, GA, USA, 2019.
93. Gorzalka, P.; Schmiedt, J.E.; Schorn, C.; Hoffschmidt, B. Automated Generation of an Energy Simulation Model for an Existing Building from UAV Imagery. *Buildings* **2021**, *11*, 380. [CrossRef]
94. Carratt, A.; Kokogiannakis, G.; Daly, D. Development and performance evaluation of a minimum input model calibration methodology for residential buildings. *J. Build. Perform. Simul.* **2023**, *16*, 680–704. [CrossRef]
95. Roka, R.B.; de Figueiredo, A.J.P.; Vieira, A.M.C.P.; Cardoso, J.C. de P. A systematic review on shallow geothermal energy system: A light into six major barriers. *Soils Rocks* **2023**, *46*, e2023007622. [CrossRef]
96. *ANSI/ASHRAE Standard 169-2020*; Climatic Data For Building Design Standards. ASHRAE Standing Standard Project Committee: Atlanta, GA, USA, 2021.

97. Inprom, N.; Jareemit, D. Efficient envelope designs to maximize cooling energy savings in housing complexes in Bangkok neighborhoods. *Nakhara: J. Environ. Des. Plan.* **2021**, *20*, 103.
98. Ren, H.; Wang, S. GPPre: A Python-Based Tool in Grasshopper for Office Building Performance Optimization. *J. Harbin Inst. Technol.* **2021**, *28*, 47–60.
99. Akkose, G.; Meral Akgul, C.; Dino, I.G. Educational building retrofit under climate change and urban heat island effect. *J. Build. Eng.* **2021**, *40*. [CrossRef]
100. Liu, C.; Ma, W.; Hao, J.; Luo, D.; Zuo, J.; Zhang, C. Energy Retrofitting Assessment of Public Building Envelopes in China's Hot Summer and Cold Winter Climate Region. *Buildings* **2022**, *12*, 1866. [CrossRef]
101. Ahn, J.; Haberl, J.S.; And, Ã. Origins of whole-building energy simulations for high-performance commercial buildings: Contributions of the 1968 and 1971 ASHRAE algorithms for weighting factor-based hourly heating and cooling load calculations. *Sci. Technol. Built Environ.* **2025**, *31*, 312–326. [CrossRef]
102. Schünemann, C.; Schiela, D.; Ortlepp, R. Guidelines to calibrate a multi-residential building simulation model addressing overheating evaluation and residents' influence. *Buildings* **2021**, *11*, 242. [CrossRef]
103. Ono, E.; Tekler, Z.D.; Lam, K.P.; Jin, Y.; Yan, D.; Chong, A. Evaluating the sensitivity and robustness of occupancy models for building energy simulation during design. *Build. Environ.* **2024**, *261*, 111739. [CrossRef]
104. Lu, W. Dynamic Shading and Glazing Technologies: Improve Energy, Visual, and Thermal Performance. *Energy Built Environ.* **2024**, *5*, 211–229. [CrossRef]
105. Yuan, J.; Jiao, Z.; Chai, J.; Farnham, C.; Emura, K. Reflective coatings: Enhancing building performance and sustainability. *Nano-Struct. Nano-Objects* **2024**, *39*, 101296. [CrossRef]
106. Zhai, Z.J.; Helman, J.M. Implications of climate changes to building energy and design. *Sustain. Cities Soc.* **2019**, *44*, 511–519. [CrossRef]
107. Ecevit, A.; Akinoglu, B.G.; Aksoy, B. Generation of a typical meteorological year using sunshine duration data. *Energy* **2002**, *27*, 947–954. [CrossRef]
108. Rady, M.; Muhammad, M.K.I.; Shahid, S. Evolving typical meteorological year (TMY) data for building energy simulation: A comprehensive review of methods, challenges, and future directions. *Adv. Build. Energy Res.* **2025**, *19*, 1–31. [CrossRef]
109. Tajuddeen, I.; Rodrigues, E. A Morris sensitivity analysis of an office building's thermal design parameters under climate change in sub-Saharan Africa. *Build. Environ.* **2024**, *262*, 111771. [CrossRef]
110. Tahmasebinia, F.; Jiang, R.; Sepasgozar, S.; Wei, J.; Ding, Y.; Ma, H. Implementation of BIM Energy Analysis and Monte Carlo Simulation for Estimating Building Energy Performance Based on Regression Approach: A Case Study. *Buildings* **2022**, *12*, 449. [CrossRef]
111. Choi, Y.; Song, D.; Yoon, S.; Koo, J. Comparison of Factorial and Latin Hypercube Sampling Designs for Meta-Models of Building Heating and Cooling Loads. *Energies* **2021**, *14*, 512. [CrossRef]
112. Praks, P.; Brkić, D. Approximate Flow Friction Factor: Estimation of the Accuracy Using Sobol's Quasi-Random Sampling. *Axioms* **2022**, *11*, 36. [CrossRef]
113. Chen, C.; Wang, M.Y.; Shen, C.; Huang, Y.; Zhu, M.; Wang, H.; He, L.; Julien, D.B. Sensitivity Analysis of Factors Influencing Rural Housing Energy Consumption in Different Household Patterns in the Zhejiang Province. *Buildings* **2023**, *13*, 463. [CrossRef]
114. Kureshi, R.R.; Mishra, B.K.; Thakker, D.; John, R.; Walker, A.; Simpson, S.; Thakkar, N.; Wante, A.K. Data-Driven Techniques for Low-Cost Sensor Selection and Calibration for the Use Case of Air Quality Monitoring. *Sensors* **2022**, *22*, 1093. [CrossRef]
115. Zhu, S.; Ma, C.; Wu, Z.; Huang, Y.; Liu, X. Exploring the Impact of Urban Morphology on Building Energy Consumption and Outdoor Comfort: A Comparative Study in Hot-Humid Climates. *Buildings* **2024**, *14*, 1381. [CrossRef]
116. Mauro, M.; Mach, A.; Parra, M.; Teamah, H. Post-Occupancy Evaluation of a Passive Multi-Unit Residential Building and a Single-Family Passive House. *Sustainability* **2025**, *17*, 3799. [CrossRef]
117. Xie, Z.; Wang, X.; Zheng, L.; Chang, H.; Wang, F. A Period-Based Neural Network Algorithm for Predicting Building Energy Consumption of District Heating. *Energies* **2022**, *15*, 6338. [CrossRef]
118. Wang, H.; Wen, W.; Zhang, Z.; Gao, N. Construction of Building Energy Consumption Prediction Model Based on Multi-Optimization Model. *Buildings* **2023**, *13*, 1677. [CrossRef]
119. Sobol, I.M. Global sensitivity indices for nonlinear mathematical models and their Monte Carlo estimates. *Math. Comput. Simul.* **2001**, *55*, 271–280. [CrossRef]
120. Sorooshnia, E.; Rahnamayiezekavat, P.; Rashidi, M.; Sadeghi, M.; Samali, B. Passive Intelligent Kinetic External Dynamic Shade Design for Improving Indoor Comfort and Minimizing Energy Consumption. *Buildings* **2023**, *13*, 1090. [CrossRef]

MDPI AG
Grosspeteranlage 5
4052 Basel
Switzerland
Tel.: +41 61 683 77 34

Energies Editorial Office
E-mail: energies@mdpi.com
www.mdpi.com/journal/energies

www.ingramcontent.com/pod-product-compliance
Lightning Source LLC
Chambersburg PA
CBHW040806250926
51850CB00007BA/1097
* 9 7 8 3 7 2 5 8 7 9 3 7 3 *